CONSTRAINTS ON LEISURE

CONSTRAINTS
ON
LEISURE

Edited by

MICHAEL G. WADE, Ph.D.

Professor of Physical Education
Department of Physical Education
Southern Illinois University at Carbondale
Carbondale, Illinois

Foreword by

Michael Ellis, Ph.D.
Professor and Chair
Department of Physical Education
University of Oregon
Eugene, Oregon

CHARLES C THOMAS • PUBLISHER
Springfield • Illinois • U.S.A.

Published and Distributed Throughout the World by

CHARLES C THOMAS • PUBLISHER
2600 South First Street
Springfield, Illinois 62717

© *1985 by* CHARLES C THOMAS • PUBLISHER

ISBN 0-398-05048-1

Library of Congress Catalog Card Number: 84-8645

With THOMAS BOOKS *careful attention is given to all details of manufacturing and
design. It is the Publisher's desire to present books that are satisfactory as to their physical
qualities and artistic possibilities and appropriate for their particular use.* THOMAS
BOOKS *will be true to those laws of quality that assure a good name and good will.*

Printed in the United States of America
SC-R-3

Library of Congress Cataloging in Publication Data

Wade, Michael G.
    Constraints on leisure.

    Bibliography: p.
    1. Leisure—Addresses, essays, lectures.
2. Leisure—Psychological aspects—Addresses, essays,
lectures. 3. Leisure—Social aspects—Addresses, essays,
lectures. 4. Leisure—Economic aspects—Addresses,
essays, lectures. I. Title.
GV174.W33 1984   790'.01'35   84-8645
ISBN 0-398-05048-1

CONTRIBUTORS

LYNN A. BARNETT, Ph.D., Associate Professor, Department of Leisure Studies, University of Illinois at Urbana-Champaign

M. JEANINE BENNETT, Ph.D., Assistant Professor, Department of Physical Education, University of Oregon

GUY R. DIRKIN, M.S., Graduate Student, Department of Leisure Studies, University of Illinois

THOMAS L. GOODALE, Ph.D., Professor, Department of Recreology, University of Ottawa

JOHN H. HOOVER, M.S., Graduate Student, Department of Special Education, Southern Illinois University at Carbondale

BENJAMIN K. HUNNICUTT, Ph.D., Associate Professor, Department of Recreation Education, University of Iowa

SEPPO E. ISO-AHOLA, Ph.D., Professor, Department of Recreation, University of Maryland

MARY JO KANE, M.S., Graduate Student, Department of Leisure Studies, University of Illinois

DOUGLAS A. KLEIBER, Ph.D., Associate Professor, Department of Leisure Studies, University of Illinois

ROGER C. MANNELL, Ph.D., Associate Professor, Department of Recreation and Leisure Studies, University of Waterloo

FRANCIS A. McGUIRE, Ph.D., Assistant Professor, Department of Parks, Recreation and Tourism Management, Clemson University

WILLIAM H. RICKARDS, Ph.D., Assistant Professor, Department of Recreation, Illinois State University

MICHAEL G. WADE, Ph.D., Professor, Department of Physical Education, Southern Illinois University at Carbondale

PETER A. WITT, Ph.D., Associate Vice President for Research, North Texas State University

FOREWORD

This is one of the few modern books on leisure and its related phenomena that starts from the premise that leisure is a desired state of mind that accompanies voluntary behavior. It concerns itself with the fundamental conditions that must exist for a person to feel leisurely and immediately gets down to the business of identifying those conditions that pre-empt leisureliness. This matter is of central concern to all in the various facilitating and caring professions whose task is to improve the likelihood that others will experience the benefits of leisure.

Any latter day consideration of leisure or voluntary behavior must build upon debates that reach back to ancient times on the matter of will. The old, and not so old, philosophers have come back time and again to the notion of man's will. Does free will exist or is it illusory? Is it merely a convenience to assert that the decision to act as observed was under the control of the mind of the actor alone because the time motive governing the behavior is hidden?

The debate has mutated and has emerged in three new forms. One is the genteel debate among ethologists about the possibility of altrustic behavior on the part of animals. The second is the fierce and more encompassing debate raised by sociobiologists arguing that the forces governing behavior cross over from individual to individual and from generation to generation mediated by responsibilities to the gene pool. The third, of course, involves the question raised by leisure scientists as to whether voluntary behavior can exist; in other words, can we act of our own free will.

The third debate is tiresome in its customary forms because it hinges on whether an act can be truly or totally free. This book also avoids that trap. It deals with constraints on leisure, and running tacitly throughout the contributions of the authors is the notion of relative leisureliness. The identification of multiple layers of constraints suggests ways to peel them off and so more nearly approach true leisure.

Relative leisureliness as a concept is more nearly in accord with our subjective experience than the split between leisure and its opposite. The degree of enjoyment, the mediating affect that accompanies experiences, can be communicated to others. "How was the weekend?" is answered with a variety of answers somewhere between affective disaster to the rating "One of my life's peak experiences." Obviously, conditions have to be just right on a multitude of parameters to have a peak experience. They occur rarely and do not last for long. What, then, prevents us from achieving leisure more often? This book starts to address that question.

Leisureliness is a question of degrees of freedom. One must first be freed of results of a clamoring physiology. One's biological substance must be secure. Then one's capacity to manage one's behavior within the required setting must be secure. The initial limitations on technique must have been transcended so that one can play at the edges of one's abilities with the security that there is a known and mastered core that makes an essay into novelty a question of success rather than certain failure. It is only when one is freed to some extent from technique that one can enjoy the activity and can contemplate enjoying extending it.

To find leisure requires the effort to control the constraints and improve the chances. Both the costs and the rewards lie on continua. People in their search for enjoyment maximize their rewards against their costs. This blunt notion now permits us to search for the constraints and the costs of their removal in order to maximize our potential for achieving leisureliness. This book makes an important contribution to this process.

Michael Ellis
Department of Physical Education
University of Oregon

PREFACE

It is important at the outset that I define clearly what I mean by leisure. During my tenure as both a member and director of the Leisure Behavior Research Laboratory at the University of Illinois (1970 to 1981), the main research and intellectual thrust of that laboratory focused primarily on leisure behavior from a lifespan-development perspective. That is to say that research was conducted on a variety of subject populations and leisure issues that spanned development from cradle to grave. During that period of time, there was a move from the simplistic definition of leisure as being nonwork to a more experiential focus, arguing that leisure was the nature of a particular kind of experience rather than a particular kind of activity. Nevertheless, it has always seemed clear to me that the notion of voluntary participation in an activity — whether it be locomotor or strictly experiential — was at least a unique feature that encompassed a definition of leisure. Certainly, it would be difficult to find an activity which might be termed leisure which was not voluntary. The idea of nonvoluntary leisure seems to me a *nonsequitur!* The contributions to this book broadly adhere to the notion that leisure is a voluntary enterprise, whether expressed strictly through observable behavior or in a more experiential or abstract terms.

The *Oxford American Dictionary* defines constraint as "to compel or to oblige," and it further refers to constraint as "compulsion." Thus, a book entitled *Constraints on Leisure* reviews a perspective of those components which tend to truncate our ability to pursue the leisure experience rather than attempt a discussion on the plethora of situations and activities which permit or encourage leisure behavior. The chapters in this book do not begin to cover all the constraining forces on leisure but do at least delineate some important ones. The book is divided into three parts. Part I deals with the psychological constraints which impinge upon leisure. In this section the constraints emanate primarily from individual human behavior and include a chapter which focuses on the developmental disability termed mental retardation. Part II focuses on a socio-economic perspective of leisure constraints, with the Mannell and Iso-Ahola chapter serving as an excellent transition into this section. Part III builds on both the intra- and inter-personal factors that are discussed in Parts I and II, using these as a backdrop for an examination of the potential leisure-oriented constraints across the life-cycle.

This book has taken awhile to complete due in large part to my own transition of moving from one university to another! It has been an interesting project and one in which several colleagues and friends have played a part. My thanks to Joe Bannon, Head of Leisure Studies at the University of Illinois, for his encouragement and guidance in promoting the work of the Leisure Behavior Research Laboratory; to my colleagues at the laboratory, Lynn Barnett and Douglas Kleiber, for their support and enthusiasm; to John Hoover, graduate student extraordinary and friend, whose enthusiasm and cooperation motivated me to complete this project; and thanks also to our excellent typist at SIUC, Debra Schwarm.

CONTENTS

xi

CONSTRAINTS ON LEISURE

Chapter I

INTRODUCTION: ASPECTS OF A BIOLOGY OF LEISURE

MICHAEL G. WADE

Before we can consider constraining influences on the leisure experience, the nature of the intricate relationship between man and his environment deserves attention. We must realize that from the outset any experience or activity exists within a set of constraints that influence our earthbound existance. The late James Gibson, drew our attention to the illogicality of considering human behavior outside of the context of the environment. Gibson (1979) expressed this as "affordance"; he theorized that man and his environment are inseparable, with each life-form located optimally in an environmental context he termed an "econiche." We will discuss the impact of these ideas later, but for now it is sufficient to say that our behavior and anatomical structure is constrained by the environment. The anatomy of homo sapiens and his ability to move and interact is dictated in no small way by environmental characteristics and thus, the most immediate constraints are those placed upon us as a function of the environment. Movement is subject to a gravitational force; we breathe in a nitrogen-oxygen atmosphere that dictates living systems be able to metabolize oxygen; changes in temperature and the chemical makeup of the atmosphere relative to altitude and other variables constrain the nature, level and scope of man's activity. Both the physical and organic structure of homo sapiens has developed across the ages in concert with the environment, with modern man coming to be structured by those constraints. A complete discussion of biological constraints on leisure requires its own book, and we have but one chapter. What follows then is perhaps less than complete, but

3

hopefully captures the essence of what is needed to understand the idea of how biology and man's necessity for interaction with the environment is the original determinant of the nature and scope of leisure behavior.

As noted above, our existence on earth is constrained by environmental chemistry and physics. Our anatomy is a mechanical system designed for movement and direct interaction in a gravity based environment, and as such represents an underlying set of mechanical constraints on our behavior. Just as we vary across an anatomical spectrum, so it follows that the scope and variety of our leisure behavior will vary. Anatomical anomalies possessed by some individuals force them to deal with these and added constraints on their behavior. The mechanical system of levers which comprise the human structure, in cooperation with the muscle system, produces forces of varying intensity and duration, and much of our leisure behavior requires the production of such forces, expressed kinematically as velocity and acceleration. Nearly all sporting activities, for example, require the marshalling of mechanical forces for action, and our ability to perform at all, depends in large part on our system of muscles and joint complexes, acting together in a controlled, purposeful manner.

The skeletal system of muscles and joints form the observable apparatus which enables us to move. But from a broader biological perspective there are more obscure and subtle expressions which both permit and constrain our leisure behavior; in a real sense our physical biology is a fixed entity. Viewed within the context of a dynamic environment, demands are placed on the biological system to conform according to encountered demands. Beyond our fundamental requirements for food, shelter and reproduction, many behaviors may be regarded as playful, thus displaying the general characteristics of leisure-behavior.

The origin of such behavior has a biological basis which both reflects and complements a psychological need. The biology of such behavior appears to be focussed in the arousal mechanisms of the central nervous system (CNS), namely the reticular arousal system (RAS). Trauma to this system produces dramatic effects on the organism's metabolism and there can be significant reductions in levels of alertness. Changes in the arousal level of the organism come about via the interactive effects between the cortex and the RAS. Maintaining arousal of excitation level at an optimal value is a dynamic characteristic of animals and man. This view has been supported by Leuba (1955), Berlyne (1960), and Fiske and Maddi (1961). Ellis (1973) argued cogently in favor of this explanation of play and leisure behavior, and yoked the dynamic aspects of behavioral biology with Berlyne's (1966) ideas on the arousal potential in the organism, (something Berlyne called "epistemic behavior"). The basic idea behind such a proposal is that the organism exhibits stimulus seeking behavior. Novel stimuli proffer a rich source of information which enables the system to maintain an acceptable level of arousal either by reducing stimulus information when it is excessive, or by seeking to create information flow when arousal is sub-optimal. Ellis (1973) commandeered these ideas to promote a theoretical perspective of play and leisure activity. The model suggests a dynamic rise and fall in the level of arousal as the organism interacts with the environment and its variegated stimuli. The ever changing level of arousal potential in the environment produces a dynamic interaction which provides potential for periodic components in behavior produced by such interactive effects. This idea is now explored further.

Activity and Cyclic Phenomena in Leisure Behavior

The subjective feelings of differences in productivity and mood that are experienced at different times during the day, are well documented. An early study by Arai (1912) reported her own performance of mental multiplication problems for twelve hour periods on each of four successive days. A replication of the Arai study by Huxtable, et al., (1946) supported the existence of a within-day effect on problem solving time and a between-day effect associated with increased percentage of error over successive days.

Freeman and Wonderlic (1935) found evidence of unimodal, bimodal and multimodal fluctuations when subjects oscillated their index finger between two stops for a period of twenty minutes (number of oscillations per five seconds over twenty minutes) and also in time with a metronome. Their conclusions were, however, equivocal; not all subjects exhibited a periodicity in their motor performance. The authors concluded that periodicity of this nature was an extremely subtle variable and suggested it played only a minor role in performance or was a reflection of individual differences. Evidence of the relationship between various performance tasks and the time of day has been provided by Colquhoun (1968) on vigilance, Thor (1962) on time estimation, and Loveland and Williams (1963) on simple addition.

For tasks requiring self-pacing, the research effort has been marginal by comparison with the voluminous literature on work-rest scheduling and the effects of the diurnal rhythm. The leisure and free play of children might be considered under the broad spectrum of self-paced activity. Under these conditions, subjects choose their own work-rest intervals and are not on a fixed schedule of time allotted for the particular activity. Studies by Plutchik and Petti (1964) and Gerben and House (1960), suggest both an optimum work-rest ratio for maximum performance, and that subjects tend to vary their rest periods rather than change the work rate.

Industrial Engineers and Human Factors Specialists have traditionally concerned themselves with the energy cost of industrial activity, and have frequently used heart-rate as a measure of mean activity level in terms of energy cost. The necessity for accurate, unobtrusive measurement of human performance has led to the popularity of heart-rate as a dependent variable in this kind of research. The development of printed circuitry has made possible small, reliable transmitters, which do not interfere with the subject's usual activity.

Kalsbeek and Ettema (1963) produced evidence that heart-rate data could be used as a measure of perceptual load. Further evidence of the value of heart-rate as a behavioral measure was reported by Hokanson and Burgess (1964). This study measured time to solve a coding task, and used heart-rate as a measure of arousal.

As an indirect measure of energy cost in social situations heartrate has proved relatively accurate and reliable. Bradfield, Huntzicker and Fruehan (1969) compared heart-rate, accumulated pulse, and respirometer data on subjects performing steady-state activities for four hours and reported less than ten percent variation among the three techniques. Further support for the use of heart-rate as an indirect measure of the energy cost of activity has been provided by Goldsmith (1969), Hunt (1969), and Wolf (1969). Grieco, Cardani and Motteni (1969) reported that long-term heart-rate telemetry is an accurate and reliable method of measuring muscular and circulatory workload of steel workers. Heart-rate was used as the measure of activity level and samples were taken from the continuous record at thirty second intervals. Docter, Wesseling and Ettema (1967) reported an average error of only 1–2% in heart-rate measurement when determined over thirty seconds.

Heart-rate has proven to be a reliable and accurate measure of activity level. Although limited by autonomic and psychic influences, the linear relationship with work output below 180 beats per minute (b.p.m.) in adults (about 200 b.p.m. in children) realistically reflects the activity profiles of the subjects in free activity. The great advantage of heart-rate telemetry as an indirect measure of activity is that subjects modify their behavior less in relation to the recording apparatus used and then provide more realistic data that reflects the ecological state of the organism. Leisure behavior has different psychological and sociological origin but the biological needs of the system do not discriminate between work or leisure both have energy demands which must be met—irrespective of the activity. The use of telemetry to quantify leisure and play activity has been a unique contribution of the Leisure Behavior Research Laboratory at the University of Illinois. My own research program in the early 1970's produced a series of studies (Wade, Ellis and Bohrer, 1973) (Wade and Ellis, 1971; Wade, 1973) that provided evidence of periodic elements (biorhythms) in childrens play behavior. For a complete review of these and other work on the role of energy systems in leisure activities see Ellis and Scholtz (1978). Suffice to say that cyclic or biorhythmic behaviors are a significant component of leisure behavior and further research of this aspect of leisure behavior is needed.

Periodicity

The biological basis of arousal illustrates an important bio-behavioral phenomenon which permeates both our leisure and non-leisure time. This is the phenomenon of periodicity; that is the rhythmic and regular ebb and flow of behavior that influence, and at times constrain, lifestyle and action.

Seasonal variations in temperature cause mammals to divide their time between periods of fairly intense activity and long periods of sleep. The activity of man and animals during the day (diurnal) and their behavior patterns during the hours of light and darkness (circadian) has produced a considerable body of research. Reviews by Cloudsley-Thomson (1961), Sollberger (1962) and Kleitman (1963) attest to this extensive literature relating circadian and diurnal periodicity to the various physiological parameters in both man and animals.

Sollberger (1965) classified three rhythmic mechanisms. The external rhythm of the universe (diurnal, seasonal and lunar) which exerts exogeneous influences on the organism. Second, the alternation between working for food and resting involves the capacity to expend, and the need to restore energy in the organism. Energy is needed for the smallest action, and as we cannot feed continuously, the result is a dynamic process of energy storage and depletion in the body. There are, however, limits to organic processes and this gives rise to the third mechanism, the concept of homeostasis (Cannon, 1929), by which the body counter-regulates excesses as it equilibrates the levels of internal activity by working essentially as a servo-mechanism. The homeostatic system regulates the internal environment and eliminates the disturbances created by the products of muscular activity. This system can run into debt due to local energy supplies that can be restored later, but in general works to depress activity level.

As well as the internal physiological regulatory system there seems to be a clearly demonstrated need for man to seek stimulation, that is to process information. This process is less well understood but, as already noted above, consists of a postulated neural system involving the RAS. The RAS arouses the organism in response to sensory information, and works to preserve an optimal range of arousal (Leuba, 1955; Maddi, 1961; Zubeck, 1964). The system elicits stimulus seeking behavior (epistemic behavior) to maintain the information flow and hence appropriate arousal. The process has been called sensoristasis (Schulz, 1965), and in general works to stimulate activity.

The inherent lag in the physiological system thus allows for bursts of high energy output before the body must restore its depleted energy store. Further, the tendency to seek stimulation and restore optimal arousal increases in strength with the duration of sub-optimal arousal. Thus, these two systems (homeostatic and sensoristatic) appear to act in countervailing fashion and produce oscillations in the activity level of subjects encountering environments that elicit gross muscular activity (Wade, 1971; Wade et al., 1973).

The homeostatic mechanisms exert a constraining influence on the activity of the organism. To take extreme cases, regardless of the occurrence of stimuli calling for increased action, if the individual is already operating at maximal oxygen consumption, a further increase in activity is possible, but no matter how stimulating the activity, there will come a time when the intensity of activity has to be reduced to allow the blood to become alkaline. Thus the internal and the external environments exert countervailing influences that cause an individual's activity to oscillate about some mean value. This mean value will be a function of the arousing action of stimuli, be they learned or innate, and the degree to which the individual has adapted physiologically to the stress involved in the activity. Thus, individuals will vary among themselves and the mean activity level will vary over time due to adaptation. The amplitude of the oscillation, resulting from the intensity of the arousal to action, is limited by the stress invoked by an action. The period appears to be a function of the interaction of the habituation curve (attention span) and the lag in the physiological system (Wade and Ellis, 1971). A finite stimulus situation becomes known and less arousing when for example, the uncertainty in play environments for children are reduced, or the homeostatic system is sufficiently disturbed that play activity is reduced. This system has some commonality with a surplus energy theory of play (Spencer, 1896), but goes beyond it, in that it can account for play to exhaustion, the surplus energy theory's major difficulty.

A traditional concept that has found its way into everyday industrial practice is that the more a worker is stressed above a comfort level of exertion, the more frequent and longer must be the compensatory rests (Edholm, 1967). Leisure is not "work" but as we have discussed it often involves activities that are self-paced and participants presumably select work-to-rest ratios individually. Thus, leisure-time activity patterns show (in stimulating environments) defined "work-rest" patterns with the oscillations being dampened as the situation becomes less arousing over time.

The above rationale for the existence of biorhythms in activity level led to research which has demonstrated the existence of such periodicities in the play of children. Spectral time series analysis has been used to discriminate intrinsic biorhythms in play activity from noise. The fact that interactions between homeostatic and sensoristatic mechanisms predict periodicity provides a means whereby the basis for an attempt to manipulate the phase of the recorded period via the stimulus level of play environment (play-group size and apparatus configuration); this relationship has heuristic value. Increased stimulus complexity produces an increased period length in the biorhythm and a change in the activity level of subjects. The behavior that generates a cycle has both a physiological and a psychological basis. It is the interaction between the physiological and psychological processes which may produce periodicities. Evidence forthcoming from the Illinois research program suggested that children exhibit periodic behaviors of both a physiological (work-rest) and a psychological (habituation) nature. Further, it has been demonstrated that such behaviors were not present in mentally handicapped children who were clearly constrained by a variety of cognitive deficits (Wade, 1973).

Finally it should be pointed out that explanations of periodicity in behavior is not new. Short-term biorhythms of approximately four to five minutes were reported by Wada (1922) on the feeding habits of 10-month-old babies and by Richter (1965) in rats. They reported the impression of simple cycle phenomenon by examining raw data. The cycle(s) therefore might well be artifactual or a combination of more than one rhythm. The research literature is devoid of material that concerns itself with non-circadian rhythms. Augenstine (1958) used spectral analysis to show periodicities of one hundred milliseconds (Msecs.) and two hundred and fifty Msecs. for vertical scanning tasks. The problem under attack was information processing time but the study is of interest because the techniques for data reduction were the same ones used in our research program. Frazier, Rummel and Lipscomb (1968) employed spectral analysis techniques to study the performance variability on vigilance task over a period of 7 days. Their results suggested sinusoidal fluctuations about an essentially twenty-four hour period. There were in addition to this, a complexity of lesser rhythms some less than one hour.

From the discussion presented above it is clear that a behavioral perspective of leisure must be viewed against the backdrop of a dynamic biological system that place broad constraints on all behaviors, because of its fundamental need for energy utilization and its optimal functioning in the environment.

When we talk of constraints on leisure it does not matter from which perspective these issues are discussed as all are inextricably interwoven with ecological demands. This view has been elegantly but controversially expressed by Gibson, (1979) in his Theory of Affordances. To Gibson affordances are what an environment "offers the animal, what it provides or furnishes, either for good or ill" (p. 127). The ecological concept of a niche is expanded in Gibson's view such that an "econiche" is the animal's style of living, rather than location, in the environment. Gibson suggests further a mutual "complementarity" between the animal and the environment in which it exists. This animal-environment interface is much like the ergonomic notion of optimizing the man-machine interaction, an important goal in industrial system. As Gibson (1979) noted:

"The possibilities of the environment and the way of life of the animal go together inseparably. The environment constrains what the animal can do, and the concept of a niche in ecology reflects this fact. Within limits, the human animal can alter the affordances of the environment but is still the creature of his or her own situation." (p. 143).

The individuals who have contributed the chapters in this volume have done so in relative isolation. It has been my task in this introductory chapter to provide a broad ecological context in which the contributions in this volume should be viewed. I operationally defined a perspective of leisure in the preface. Having provided a working definition of leisure I have presented here a biological perspective of the constraints on leisure behavior. What now follows are a series of psychological and sociological explorations into leisure behavior. I shall return in the epilogue for some final observations.

REFERENCES

Arai, T. (1912). Mental fatigue. *Teachers College Contributions to Education,* #54.

Augenstine, L. G. (1958, December). *Human performance in information transmission, Part VI. Evidences of periodicity in information processing* (Report #R-75). Urbana: University of Illinois, Control Systems Lab.

Berlyne, D. E. (1960). *Conflict, arousal and curiosity.* New York: McGraw-Hill.

Berlyne, D. E. (1966). Curiosity and exploration. *Science, 153,* 25–33.

Bohrer, R. E. *Modified Grenander-Rosenblatt tests.* Paper submitted to Technometrics. Copies available from the author. Urbana-Champaign: University of Illinois, Department of Mathematics.

Bradfield, R. B., Huntzicker, P. B., & Fruehan, G. J. (1969). Simultaneous comparison of respirometer and heart-rate telemetry techniques as measures of human energy expenditure. *American Journal of Clinical Nutrition, 22*(6), 696–700.

Bunning, E. (1964). *The physiological clock.* Heidelberg, Springer-Verlag.

Cannon, W. B. (1929). Organization and physiological homeostasis. *Physiological Reviews, 9,* 379–431.

Cloudsley-Thomson, J. L. (1961). *Rhythmic activity in animal physiology and behavior.* New York-London: Academic Press.

Coleman, W. M. (1921). The psychological significance in bodily rhythm. *Journal of Comparative and Physiological Psychology,* 213–220.

Colquhoun, W. P., Blake, M. J. F., & Edwards, R. S. (1968). Experimental studies of shift work I: A comparison of "rotating" and "stabilized" 4-hour shift systems. *Ergonomics, 11*(5), 437–453.

Docter, H. E., Wesseling, L. H., & Ettema, J. H. (1967). The accuracy of heart rate. Presented at the 3rd International Ergonomics Congress, Birmingham, England.

Edholm, O. G. (1967). *The biology of work.* Penguin Books.

Ellis, M. J. (1973). *Why people play.* Englewood Cliffs, NJ: Prentice-Hall.

Ellis, M. J., & Scholtz, G. J. L. (1978). *Activity and play of children.* Englewood Cliffs, NJ: Prentice-Hall.

Fiske, D., & Maddi, S. (1961). *Function of varied experience.* Illinois: Dersey Press.

Frazier, T. W., Rummel, J. A., & Lipscomb, H. S. (1968). Circadian variability in vigilance performance. *Aerospace Medicine, 39,* 383–395.

Freeman, G. L., & Wonderlic, E. F. (1935). Periodicity and performance. *American Journal of Psychology, 47,* 149–151.

Gerben, M. J., & House, J. L. (1960). Hypoxia and self-paced work. *Percept. and Motor Skills, 28,* 995–1002.

Gibson, J. J. (1979). *The ecological approach to visual perceptions.* Boston: Houghton Mifflin.

Goldsmith, R. (1969). Assessment of habitual physical activity from heart-rate. *Ergonomics, 12*(3), 477.

Grieco, A., Cardani, A., & Motteni, G. (1969). Heart-rate and energy expenditure in evaluatory muscular and circulatory work-load of oven workers in a steel factory. *Ergonomics, 12*(5), 814.

Hauty, G. T. (1962). Periodic desynchronization in humans under outer space conditions. *Annuals of the New York Academy of Sciences, 98*(4), 1116–1125.

Hokanson, J. E., & Burgess, M. (1964). Effects of physiological arousal level, frustration and task complexity on performance. *Journal of Abnormal and Social Psychology, 68,* 698–702.

Hunt, J. McV. (1965). Intrinsic motivation and its role in psychological development. In D. Levine (Ed.), *Nebraska Symposium on Motivation,* (Volume 13, pp. 189–282).

Hunt, T. J. (1969). The value of field measurements of heart-rate. *Ergonomics, 12*(3), 477.

Huxtable, Z. L., White, M. H., & McCarter, M. A. (1946). A re-performance and re-interpretation of the Arai experiment in mental fatigue with three subjects. *Psychological Monographs, 59*(5), 275.

Kalsbeek, J. W. H., & Ettema, J. H. (1963). Continuous recording of heart-rate and the measurement of perceptual load. *Ergonomics, 6,* 306–307.

Kleitman, N. (1949). Biological rhythm and cycles. *Physiological Reviews, 29*(1), 1–27.

Kleitman, N., & Kleitman, E. (1953). Effect on non-24 hour routines of living on oral temperature and heart-rate. *Journal of Applied Physiology, 6,* 283–291.

Kleitman, N. (1963). *Sleep and wakefulness.* Chicago: University of Chicago Press.

Leuba, C. (1955). Toward some integration of learning theories: The concept of optimal stimulation. *Psychological Reports, 1,* 27–33.

Lewis, P. R., & Lobban, M. C. (1957). Dissociation of diurnal rhythms in human subjects living on abnormal time routines. *Quarterly Journal of Experimental Physiology, 42,* 371–386.

Loveland, N. T., & Williams, H. L. (1963). Adding, sleep loss, and body temperature. *Perceptual and Motor Skills, 16,* 923–929.

Maddi, S. R. (1961). Exploratory behavior and variation seeking in man. In D. W. Fiske, & S. R. Maddi (Eds.), *Functions of varied experience.* Homewood, IL: Dorsey Press.

Martens, R. (1969). The effect of an audience on learning and performance of a complex motor skill. *Journal of Abnormal Social Psychology, 54,* 210–212.

Plutchik, R., & Petti, R. D. (1964). Rate of learning on a pursuit motor task as a constant work-rest ratio with varying work and rest ratios. *Perceptual and Motor Skills, 19,* 227–231.

Richter, C. P. (1965). *Biological clocks in medicine and psychiatry.* Springfield, IL: C. C. Thomas Co.

Schulz, D. D. (1965). *Sensory restriction: Effects on behavior.* New York: Academic Press.

Sollberger, A. (1962). General properties of biological rhythm. *New York Academy of Science, 98,* 757–774.

Sollberger, A. (1965). *Biological rhythm research.* Amsterdam-London-New York: Elsevier.

Spencer, H. (1896). *Principles of psychology.* 2 (2) 3rd Ed., New York: Appleton.

Taylor, D. W. (1960). Toward an information processing theory of motivation. In M. R. Jones (Ed.), *Nebraska symposium on motivation* (pp. 51–78). Lincoln, NE: Nebraska University Press.

Thor, D. H. (1962). Diurnal variability in time estimation. *Perceptual and Motor Skills, 15,* 451–454.

Wada, T. (1922). An experimental study of hunger in its relation to activity. *Archives of Psychological Monographs, 57,* 1.

Wade, M. G., & Ellis, M. J. (1971). Measurement of free range activity in children as modified by social and environmental complexity. *American Journal of Clinical Nutrition, 24,* 1457–1460.

Wade, M. G., Ellis, M. J., & Bohrer, R. E. (1973). Biorhythms in the activity of children during free play. *Journal of the Experimental Analysis of Behavior, 20,* 155–162.

Wade, M. G. (1973). Biorhythms and activity level of institutionalized mentally retarded persons diagnosed hyperactive. *American Journal of Mental Deficiency, 78,* 262–267.

Wolf, H. S. (1969). Socially acceptable monitoring. *Ergonomics, 12*(3), 477.

Zubeck, J. P. (1964). Effects of prolonged sensory and perceptual deprivation. *British Medical Bulletin, 20,* 38–42.

PART I
PSYCHOLOGICAL
CONSTRAINTS ON LEISURE

Chapter II

INTRAPERSONAL CONSTRAINTS TO LEISURE

DOUGLAS A. KLEIBER and GUY R. DIRKIN

Who are the baseball players, the art lovers, the travelers to exotic places? Who can relax most easily, create new alternatives and respond most readily to those created by others? The premise of this chapter is that choices to participate in certain leisure activities and the ability to have certain leisure experiences are dictated—to some extent—by stable individual differences. It is our contention that whatever else influences such behavior, there are constitutional and thoroughly conditioned characteristics of the individual which are either limiting or enhancing to various kinds of leisure behavior and experience. The focus here then is on characteristics which vary from individual to individual but which are consistent and relatively stable *within* the individual, defining and delimiting experience accordingly.

In proposing stable characteristics which operate across situations, it may be argued that we have failed to heed the criticisms of trait studies which have led to the more well-regarded "interactionist" approach to behavioral investigation (See for example, Endler and Magnussen, 1976). After all, as will be acknowledged throughout, factors other than individual differences are responsible for the greater portion of variability in leisure-related activity and experience. But the interactionist approach becomes reasserted by the manner in which "leisure" will be utilized as a construct. For while we will view leisure at some points as a *specific experience,* we will also be considering it as a *context for recreation,* wherein self-expression is minimally constrained.

As an experience itself, leisure has been defined as relaxation (Martin, 1975), as a sense of freedom (Neulinger, 1974), as enjoyment (Mannell, 1980) and as self-expansion (deGrazia, 1964). As

17

recreation, we include all those activities that people use in departure from the "real world," (i.e., work, school or other social
obligations) to create a change of experience, however much the
activities may in fact represent or re-create that real world. (For a
similar meaning see Dumazedier, 1974.) The activities of recreation may be those which are formally structured and defined by
the culture as "recreational" in purpose (e.g., church bingo), or
those such as storytelling and "homemade" enjoyable interactions
which are more individualistically conceived (See for example,
Lynch, 1979; Swanson, 1978). And, while much of leisure is social
we will also consider those activities such as resting and the
"escape" of a wilderness hike which reflect some degree of social
disengagement.

Some who have studied leisure behavior in relation to personality have tried to differentiate leisure types on the basis of the types
of activities or patterns of leisure behavior that individuals report
doing without reference to the personalities of the individuals
studied (Duncan, 1978; Witt, 1971). But such attempts do not take
into account the fact that people often do the same activities for a
multitude of purposes, and the research indicates that the amount
of variance accounted for by such factors is low and unstable.
Nevertheless, the activity dimensions identified (e.g., outdoor/
nature, status-oriented, mechanical, social, etc.) do suggest the
possibility of attraction to some activities which have the conditions and offer the experiences which are compatible with personal predispositions, or avoidance of the activities which are
made more difficult or less enjoyable by virtue of such factors.

Thus, while it might be possible to run through a list of leisure
experiences and activities trying to identify relevant personality
factors for each, the scope of such a task argues that we proceed
instead to identify a smaller, more manageable number of personality factors and factor sets which we think have special relevance
to some kinds of leisure preferences and experiences. And for the
purposes of further organization, these will be grouped into *leisure-
types* (but defined by leisure *styles* rather than activities) and those
personality traits which are conceptually significant to variations in
leisure behavior and experience.

LEISURE FOLKS

While it certainly depends on how one views leisure, the idea that there are types of people who are more positively predisposed to, or more capable of maximizing leisure experience is an intriguing one. One approach might be to envision a "leisure addict" as the antithesis of the "workaholic" (See Machlowitz, 1980), or to pursue Veblen's (1899) early characterization of the leisure class as the idle rich, the wealthy élite. But such approaches would only continue to perpetuate the idea of leisure as a condition of nonwork. In contrast, the four characterizations which follow, the leisure kind, the playful, the autotelic and the B type, describe individuals who are psychologically predisposed to leisure-like experiences wherever they occur. In this way we are using leisure not as a behavioral context as is done elsewhere (and as we will do in the next section on traits) but more as an individual experience which may transcend various life situations.

The Leisure Kind *(deGrazia, 1964)*

Contrasting it with Veblen's notion of the "leisure class" (p. 360), deGrazia proposed the "leisure kind" as a category of people who love ideas, imagination and "the play of thought," who invent stories and create the cosmos. He regarded such an orientation as a matter of temperament ("The daemon [of mental play] doesn't depend on environment" [p. 359]), but saw its particular manifestation—in artists, scientists or poets—as being determined by the times.

While it may seem grossly unreasonable to group people into two kinds—the "leisure kind" and all others—what is significant about deGrazia's treatment is that leisure is characterized within an intellectual orientation, i.e., where one feels the freedom to explore and manipulate meaning and has a "great love for activating the mind" (p. 359).

The Playful *(Lieberman, 1977)*

Perhaps the major difference between Lieberman's characterization of "Playfulness" and the leisure kind of deGrazia is in the focus of the former on childhood and adolescence and the latter on adulthood. Lieberman's discussion of the importance of "toying with ideas" and a sense of humor in the pattern of playfulness of some children and adolescents would suggest their emergence as "the leisure kind" in adulthood. But in her configuration of playfulness she adds to sense of humor and cognitive spontaneity the attributes of physical and social spontaneity and manifest joy. In other words, playfulness for her is decidedly social and physical as well as cognitive. She further described the playful child as showing "bubbling effervescence" and "glint in the eye" behavior. Still she does note a separation of qualities in adolescence where playfulness may be reflected in academic curiosity or socio-emotional playfulness, but not always both, and implies that physical spontaneity of early years either gives way with the expanding intellectual abilities of adolescence or works somewhat destructively, as "restlessness," on interpersonal relations in the school context. Thus, effective adaptation for the playful adolescent may involve evolution into something closer to deGrazia's "Leisure Kind," although the degree of constraint in the context of schools suggests that such an orientation may be more fully actualized outside of school.

In some contrast to deGrazia's scholarship, Lieberman's work is based on extensive observation and testing of children judged to be "playful" by their teachers. In addition to identifying the five components referred to earlier (physical, social and cognitive spontaneity, manifest joy and sense of humor), scores on the playfulness measure (1977) have been found to correlate with measures of creativity. Unfortunately, the influence of intelligence on both factors was not determined, and later work (Barnett & Kleiber, 1982) has established intelligence as a confounding influence, at least for boys. Creativity covaries with intelligence and with intelligence controlled statistically, the relationship between playfulness and creativity for boys virtually disappears. For girls on the other hand the relationship actually increases with the influence of intelligence held constant. Intelligence apparently mediates the relationship between playfulness and creativity for boys while suppressing (statistically) the relationship for females. The explanation offered for these relationships was that sex role orientation, as early as age five, may direct the manifestation of playfulness. In this case, specifically, it may be that the more intelligent girls at such an early age learn to suppress playfulness to a degree, as being "inappropriate" in school (with only the more flexible among them feeling free enough to play vigorously) while boys are exuberant and boisterous because that is what is expected of them. Speculation such as this always needs to be further tested, but it is offered here as an example of the interaction of leisure-related patterns and orientations with the demands of cultural contexts, a point elaborated on in other chapters of this volume (e.g., Iso-Ahola) and to which we will return again as well.

The Autotelic *(Csikszentmihalyi, 1975)*

While Lieberman's factor analysis of playfulness allowed for the possibility that the factors were not totally independent, it did call into question whether playfulness could in any way be regarded as a unified pattern of traits. But still common to all the characteristics and to deGrazia's leisure kind as well, is the readiness to find enjoyment in the action of the present. This is the orientation that Csikszentmihalyi (1975) sees in the "autotelic" person. Autotelic means that the purpose lies within the activity itself; i.e., it is inherently or intrinsically enjoyable; doing it is reward enough. Some activities (e.g., games) are created, designed, and entered into with this in mind. Optimal enjoyment is thought to occur when the skills, abilities and resources of a person are sufficient to meet the challenges available in the immediate environment; and the most autotelic activities are those where the demands can be modified to match lower or higher levels of skills. When the demands are too great in an activity a degree of stress or anxiety may result, just as boredom may be the effect when an activity is unchallenging. With demands and abilities fairly well matched, one can become totally immersed in the activity experiencing a kind of "flow" which leaves that person fully involved in the present, attending exclusively and effectively to the activity itself.

However, while this pattern can be predicted to some extent on the basis of the objective situational demands and individual abilities, the perception of challenge and opportunity is experienced subjectively and herein lies the potential influence of individual differences. Specifically, it is argued that one person with the same skills as another may be better able to create the enjoyable "match" in the activity by reinterpreting the challenge to fit his/her interests. This may mean the ability to find something to manipulate or play with, cognitively or physically, in an otherwise boring situation or to manage a more difficult situation by attending to only these elements of it that can be managed effectively. For example, two equally intelligent and articulate women engaged in conversation at a cocktail party may differ in their ability to isolate a topic of conversation, and manipulate it for maximum interest, especially while so much is going on around them. This may be, in part, a matter of attentional style, a factor which we will examine more closely in the next section on specific leisure-relevant personality factors. Before turning to those however, one more leisure type should be considered.

The "B" Type *(Friedman and Rosenman, 1974)*

The concern about the relationship between hypertension and heart disease in this country has led in the past to considerations of smoking, diet and other conditions of physical health. But in examining life style patterns more generally, physicians identified a pattern of behavior which seems more predictably related to heart disease than any other health related factors (Friedman & Rosenman, 1974). Calling it "Type A behavior," the authors describe a person who, with a high need for achievement, is in an incessant struggle against time and other people to produce and accomplish as much as possible. The "hurry sickness," as they also call it, results from the stress created mostly by two personality factors—competitiveness and time urgency.

Most people in this culture, according to the authors, are A types or reflect some degree of the Type A pattern; only 10% of people interviewed and tested in this research show the opposite, *Type B,* pattern. In contrast to the Type A person, the Type B person does things patiently and at a pace that is responsive to his/her natural rhythms. The Type B person is not found to do more than one thing or think more than one thing at a time as the Type A person is. The Type B person is able to relax without guilt. The Type B person does not feel challenged or threatened by others who present achievement-oriented patterns and therefore does not experience the insecurity and hostility of the Type A person.

Thus the Type B person embodies the characteristic of *relaxation,* considered by some to be the essence of leisure (e.g., Martin, 1975); but like the leisure kind, the playful and the autotelic, the Type B person may also be regarded as operating with an open system, with a sense of freedom for discovering new alternatives and the sense of confidence to be responsive to the conditions which exist. Such global typologies may only be useful in sketching an ideal (and in this case an ideal which is leisure-defined), but in so doing there are suggestions of the particular ingredients necessary for certain kinds of experiences in various leisure situations and activities. It is to those ingredients that we now turn.

LEISURE BEHAVIOR PREDICTORS

This section examines several psychological traits that have particular relevance for understanding individual dispositions to pursue differing forms of leisure activity and the experiences likely to be derived in turn. The examination will begin with biologically based traits such as extraversion-introversion and sensation-seeking and will end with a consideration of two traits— achievement motivation and locus of control—which are more socially than biologically determined but which may be equally as likely to influence leisure behavior. From the theoretical models cited and the experimental evidence, it should be apparent that the prediction of leisure choice and experience cannot be based solely on any single construct. However, matching psychological constructs to characteristics of recreation activities may be fruitful for understanding the variability of behavior and experience in the context of leisure.

BIOLOGICALLY-BASED CONSTRAINTS OF PERSONALITY

Activation Theory

Fiske and Maddi (1961) have described a theory of human behavior based upon the construct of activation and the homeostatic principle of motivation. *Activation theory* describes a class of behaviors characterized by the direction and approach to, or withdrawal from, stimulation. The homeostatic principle of motivation implies that a preferred level of stimulation exists for each individual and people will *seek or avoid stimulation to achieve those levels*. The latter point is of particular relevance for trait explanations of behavior and to individual differences in the selection of, and experience of, leisure activities. This should become apparent as we outline the activation perspective in more detail.

It is unpleasant when individuals are either under or over stimulated and various strategies may be employed to avoid such negative affect. If levels of stimulation are too high withdrawal from the proximity of the stimulus and physiological relaxation are appropriate options. Conversely, if stimulus levels are too low, approach towards the proximity of the stimulus until there is an increase of physical tension is an appropriate response. Cognitive and perceptual strategies can be employed to increase or decrease levels of stimulation. Stimuli can be screened or perceptually enhanced, or cognitive operations can be simplified or made more complex, depending on the need to magnify or reduce levels of activation.

Individuals may differ not only in the strategies for modulating tension but also in their normal operating amount (basal level) of activation and in the level of arousal which is experienced as optimal for them. For example, some individuals may find nearly all situations less inherently stimulating than other people do and this may be manifest in a kind of "stimulus hunger." These people seek sensation to modify stimulus impact to raise activation levels to acceptable levels, creating a state of positive effect. Maddi and

Scott-Propst (1971) contend that individuals only seek to modify stimulus intensity when it is outside (below or above) a "band" of acceptable limits of activation. Individuals with higher baseline levels of physiological activation are more concerned with avoiding high levels of stimulation than individuals who are at the opposite end of the continuum, the sensation seekers. Those initially high in baseline activation, might be expected to pursue relatively passive forms of leisure activity. They may also tend to remain engaged in single activities for longer periods of time. Individuals who take part in varied and intense activities, on the other hand, may be characterized by a relative insensitivity to stimulation with lower basal levels of activation.

Within the framework of activation theory, it might be predicted that dispositions to undertake specific forms of leisure activity arise as individuals recognize which environmental situations yield stimulus conditions congruent with their characteristic "band" (Maddi & Scott-Propst, 1971). Some individuals will be initially drawn toward highly stimulating activities while others may prefer less excitement. This does not mean that an individual will be continually satisfied with one activity, or one level of intensity within an activity. Response habituation will decrease the effective level of stimulation for anyone, regardless of basal activation level. Individuals will eventually change activities to seek increases in stimulation *or* manipulate the intensity and challenge of the activity itself. Some individuals prefer to seek stimulation outside the current activity while others prefer to manipulate demands within their activity. The extraversion-introversion dimension of personality (Eysenck, 1967) and Zuckerman's (1979) sensation seeking dimension are useful in clarifying which people may frequently change leisure activities to create greater stimulation and those who would stay with activities with which they were more familiar.

Extraversion-Introversion

The personality variable of extraversion-introversion has been widely used in the psychological literature and has meaningful use in common language. We will examine the trait as it relates to activation and its possible implications for leisure preference. It should be emphasized that other psychological dimensions such as reduction-augmentation (Petrie, 1967), repression-sensitization (Byrne, 1964) and field dependence-field independence (Witkin et al., 1962) are related in some respects to extraversion-introversion and are also of relevance to the choice of leisure activity. The dimension of extraversion-introversion is illustrative of the potential that such personality variables hold for determining leisure behavior, and it also provides a conceptual link between physiological conditions and personality.

Eysenck (1967) has proposed that extraverts have high cortical inhibition of stimuli and consequently low cortical arousal. Extraverts therefore have a "stimulus hunger" which creates a need to seek out stimulation extraceptively. The reticular activating system in the brain stem is analogous in function to a filter, which is complexly related to arousal regulation. In introverts neural inhibition develops more slowly and dissipates more quickly while for extraverts the converse is true. Introverts are considered to have lower thresholds for arousal activation than extraverts. Thus introverts require less stimulation at lower levels of intensity than extraverts to reach optimal levels of activation. In practice then, extraverts would be expected to modify stimulus impact by seeking out stimulation from external sources. Introverts, on the other hand, are characterized by higher degrees of baseline activation and responsiveness to stimulation. The need for the introvert to satisfy a stimulus hunger is not as much a problem as is the reduction of stimulus impact. To reduce negative affect and remain in the homeostatic bandwidth, one would expect extraverts to actively engage in seeking sensation in their leisure activities, while introverts may choose relatively unchanging activities and ones with which they are more familiar.

In their leisure preferences, then, it would be expected that extraverts would be more likely to engage in contact sports or pastimes with an element of risk. Research evidence supports this contention (Kane, 1972). Bishop & Jeanrenaud (1976) have also found that extraverts prefer both a greater number of activities and a greater frequency of participation than introverts. In their study, activity shifts were associated with positive mood states to a

greater degree with extraverts than introverts* This is consonant
with the prediction of activation theory that individuals with
lower levels of baseline activation will tend to change activities
more frequently to maintain positive affect.

It is important to understand that introverts, or those less prone
to seek sensation, may be found in activities that involve risk. It
would be incorrect to imply that introverts would not be found in
activities such as mountain climbing, race car driving or hang-
gliding. Csikszentmihalyi (1975) has pointed out, for example,
that experienced rock climbers report feelings of high challenge
but without the sense of danger that is commonly assumed
(pp. 82–84). One can speculate that to the introvert perceived
control over the activity would be especially important. Therefore,
the introvert may take part in overtly risky activities but would
probably display limited *risk-taking* behavior within that activity.

Sensation Seeking

A personality trait that is related to both activation and
extraversion-introversion is *sensation seeking* (Zuckerman, 1979).
Sensation seeking is concerned with the extent to which individuals need varied and novel sensations and take physical and social
risks merely for the experience. Sensation seeking behavior has a
biological basis. Studies of identical and fraternal twins have led
Zuckerman to state that between one-half and one-third of the
variability in the sensation seeking trait can be accounted for by
heredity.

But the trait of sensation seeking illustrates the complexity of
the human organism as much as it represents a stable personality
disposition. At first glance, Zuckerman's evidence on sensation-
seekers seems to be inconsistent with the stimulus insensitivity
and low levels of cortical activation found in Eysenck's extraverts
(1967); Zuckerman considers that sensation seekers are people
who are *easily* aroused by novel stimuli. Eysenck's (1967) theory
suggests that low basal levels of physiological activation are respon-

---

*It should be noted however that the relationship was true only with stable individuals.
The reverse was found with neurotic individuals.

sible for the need for extraverts to seek sensation, but Zuckerman (1979) offers experimental evidence that sensation seekers have a stronger response to stimuli of moderate intensity, as measured by galvanic skin tests. This finding seems inconsistent with activation theory; but sensation seekers, while showing increases in physiological arousal in response to novel stimuli, stop responding to those stimuli if they are repeated and recede to levels of activation similar to low sensation seekers. This latter finding by Zuckerman is consistent with the rapid build up of neural inhibition reported for extraverts (Eysenck, 1967). However, some sensation seekers, those high on a "disinhibition" factor, continue to respond to high intensities of stimulation and apparently lack a natural protective mechanism against high stimulation.

The emerging picture of the biologically based interpretations of behavior is one that is complex and resistant to categorization. A concept which assists in bridging our discussion of sensation-seeking with the earlier activation-based interpretations of behavior (Eysenck, 1967; Fiske & Maddi, 1961) is the orienting response (Sokolov, 1963). The orienting response is a primitive alerting mechanism. When someone unexpectedly slams a door shut the brain automatically responds with a "What's that?" response. Sensation seekers, even though they may have relatively low base-line levels of arousal, may also have a sensitive threshold response to novel stimuli. In some individuals a rapid return to base levels may occur. In others, those "disinhibitors" with a lesser degree of inhibiting function, the decline may take longer.

The conclusions that emerge from examination of the biological interpretations of human action reveal only general tendencies of directional behavior. As Maddi & Scott-Propst (1971) point out, the tendency of individuals to act in order to return to some homeostatic balance occurs only when extremely high or low levels of excitation are present. What is clearly evident is that unidimensional interpretations of behavior, based upon physiological levels of activation, are overly simplistic and of only limited usefulness at present. Thus, the prediction of leisure preferences and experience based upon individual differences in activation can only be made very generally: high seekers of sensation tend to participate in more adventurous, intense activities and demonstrate a preference for a varied number of leisure pursuits; individuals who are predisposed to avoid sensation from a biological standpoint will tend to be found in passive types of leisure activities. These dispositions give little predictive information about the *quality* of leisure experience that might be drawn from active or passive leisure participation. The quality of leisure experience in a given activity will be determined by the complete spectrum of dispositional tendencies, and certainly, any matching of activities to purely emotional needs would contribute only partially at best to leisure satisfaction.

Some improvement in such an approach might be effected by also considering the cognitive style of individuals. The following section deals with one of the styles that is closely related to emotional conditions and is particularly relevant to intrinsically motivated activities such as those found in leisure. This style is based upon individual differences in attention.

Attentional Style

From the previous discussion of biological dispositions to respond, it is clear that enhancement or inhibition of the flow of stimulus information is central for maintaining positive affect. Attention is a mediating mechanism primarily responsible for the selection of information from both external and internal sources. Attention has to be a selective process because the human capacity to process information is limited (Kahneman, 1973; Moray, 1967). To successfully process information, limited attentional capacity has to be allocated to selected stimulus sources at the expense of others; and the efficiency with which attention can be regulated to maintain an optimal level of processing differs between individuals (Keele & Hawkins, 1982). When highly involved in a game of tennis, for example, attentional resources are allocated to important informational cues present within the game. A concomitant decline in the perceptual monitoring of secondary information results. This decline would be experienced as a loss of awareness of the presence of spectators or unrelated sources of noise. Thus, a person who can more effectively screen out information is less likely to be distracted by a clicking camera or boisterous fans than a person who fails to screen information.

Earlier in the chapter we referred to "flow" as the enjoyable experience that occurs when people become highly involved in an activity. That experience has been thought to be very much a matter of focused attention (Csikszentmihalyi, 1975, 1978). It was argued elsewhere (Dirkin, 1982) that flow is an "altered state of awareness" and that the regulation of attention plays an important role in the engagement of such states. Accordingly, efforts to measure flow have utilized tests of peripheral awareness to examine levels of involvement in activities (Mannell, 1980).

We also argued earlier that the flow experience is more accessible to some types of individuals (e.g., the "autotelic type"); and research in attentional style suggests that some people are indeed better than others at framing their environment to engage in such states (Davidson, Schwartz and Rothman, 1976; Singer, 1975). Measures of attention that discriminate the ability to maintain episodes of high focus and stimulus exclusion are extremely important in understanding these individual differences. Absorption is a stable disposition for experiences that are perceptually intense and are characterized by total attention (Tellegren & Atkinson, 1974). High and low scoring subjects on the Tellegren Absorption Scale (TAS) have been differentiated in electroencephalographic (EEG) studies employing averaged evoked potentials (Davidson, 1976). High scoring subjects were found to have lower electrical activity in brain regions associated with a secondary task, demonstrating the ability to exclude stimulation. Hypnotic susceptibility and meditation, which require highly focused attention have also been correlated with absorption (Davidson, Goleman and Schwartz, 1976; Engstrom, 1976).

Such experimental evidence strongly suggests that individual differences exist which facilitate or reduce the potential for flow experiences in the context of leisure. But it bears repeating that environmental influences will condition the manifestation of those predispositions. Swanson (1978) has observed that the tendency for absorbing and self-altering experiences are related to patterns of decision-making in families and family size. Utilizing items from Josephine Hilgard's research on susceptibility to hypnosis and Tellegren and Atkinson's (1974) classification system, he examined the correlates of four kinds of absorbing experiences: 1) reality absorption, the ease with which a person can be "swept away" in a movie or a nature walk, for example; 2) fantasy absorption, the preference for imagined objects or situations; 3) dissociation, the experience whereby the body and/or an element of the personality is segmented from ordinary consciousness operations; and 4) openness to experience. While the pattern of relationships discovered is outside the scope of this chapter on individual differences, suffice it to say, first, that our notions of flow may be too simplistic, and secondly, that we must recognize the importance of environmental influences on the predispositions for flow-like experiences.

Hamilton (1981) presents an additional consideration that is particularly pertinent to leisure behavior. She argues that a relationship exists between absorption and its correlated indices and intrinsic enjoyment. The successful regulation of attention and the prolongation of positive mood states leads to reports of high degrees of intrinsic enjoyment and positive expectation in leisure activities. Also of interest at this point is evidence that introverts perform better on tests of attention than extraverts (Bakan et al., 1963; Thackery et al., 1974). Introverts are less susceptible to vigilance decrement, for example, than extraverts. These findings offer additional support to the contention that some personality dispositions may facilitate the manipulation of attentional strategies to the extent that positive mood states and high involvement in leisure activities are more easily effected.

Csikszentmihalyi's work (1975, 1978) further implies that intrinsic enjoyment *within* an activity may be prolonged, offsetting the effects of habituation, by shifting attention to other cue locations. This shift in attention may *not* be overtly recognizable but provides a means of adjustment to stimulation. Singer (1975) points out that some individuals have the cognitive capacity to generate information in almost any situation through fantasy and imagery. One might expect such people to restructure boring work tasks into "games," for example (Hamilton, 1981). Singer's (1975) work on imagery and daydreaming indicates that some individuals may possess a "cognitive skill" with which to manipulate levels of stimulation over longer periods of time, lengthening periods of enjoyment. These would appear to be the patterns of the leisure kind, the playful or the autotelic types referred to earlier. Other individuals, less adept at structuring their environment with covert adjustments, may need to regulate information input by overtly changing activities to seek sensation. Such people may, in the context of leisure, lose interest in the activity and seek sensation and entertainment from other sources. This may not mean a complete change of leisure activity. Increases in "off-task" behaviors could be observed, some of which may be loosely described as "goofing off" or "playing around."

There is still other empirical work on attentional style which is relevant to our discussion. Mehrabian (1977) has developed a procedure for measuring individual differences in stimulus screening and associated differences in arousability. Screening is defined as the tendency to "screen out less relevant parts of the environment, thereby effectively reducing the environmental load and the (person's) arousal level" (Mehrabian, 1977). People who are good at screening extraneous stimulation have an ability clearly related to engagement in autotelic activities. The screener is also more likely to suffer less from distraction once engaged in a leisure activity. The nonscreener on the other hand shows a more rapid arousal response to environmental change. As such the nonscreener deals less effectively with aversive environments. However, nonscreeners potentially can get more out of a positive environment, "approaching it with a passion" (Mehrabian, 1976, p. 31). Mehrabian's approach is particularly useful therefore for predicting how individuals would react to environments that are more or less pleasant and preferred. As leisure activities implicitly involve choice and enjoyment, the screening-nonscreening dimension could be useful for further research.

From a somewhat similar perspective Nideffer (1976) suggests that just as different activities demand different attentional patterns, some individuals may be stylistically more capable of selecting an appropriate attentional strategy than others in a given situation. Using his "Test of Attentional and Interpersonal Style," he groups individuals along two dimensions from external to internal focus and from broad to narrow focus. Among the various performance domains he considers is the deployment of sport skills. Thus, weight lifting requires a narrow focus while basketball requires a broader focus to deal with the complexity of the situation. And the focus in running is more on internal cues while external cues are more important in hitting a baseball.

Recently, MacNeil & Dunn (1981) employed the Group Embedded Figures Test (Oltman, Raskin & Witkin, 1971) as a measure of field dependence/independence and correlated the results with the Dunn Leisure Preference Survey (DLPS). In so doing, they attempted to establish a relationship between perceptual style and leisure preference. The DLPS consists of four categories of activities: individual competitive, individual noncompetitive, group competitive and group noncompetitive. It was hypothesized that field dependent people would prefer group-oriented activities while field independent people would prefer individually-oriented activities. Also of interest was the relationship between field-independence-dependence and preference for competitive vs. non-competitive activities. Contrary to expectations the results indicated that field dependent subjects were more likely to prefer individual-competitive activities while field independent subjects were more likely to prefer group oriented, non-competitive activities.

The preference of field dependent subjects for individual activities and field independent for group activities was a complete reversal of the hypothesized relationship. Previous research (Witkin & Goodenough, 1976) would suggest that field dependent people generally do prefer socially oriented group situations. MacNeil and Dunn (1981) suggest that the intrinsic nature of leisure activities creates a different situation than those of previous research. An alternative explanation and one more in line with the position of this chapter centers on the stimulus environment. Field dependent people are characterized by the inability to select salient information (figure) from complex stimulus fields (ground). Therefore, it could be speculated that in a dynamic group/social situation field dependent people would be less able to ignore secondary social cues in order to focus in on salient sources of enjoyment. In individual activities the field dependent person has the opportunity to create the setting needed for intrinsic satisfaction. In any case, the study by MacNeil and Dunn is noteworthy for its contribution of linking perceptual style to leisure preference.

Earlier in the section we referred to a study by Davidson, Schwartz and Rothman (1976) which demonstrated individual differences in attentional style as measured by EEG data. It is feasible that differences in brain wave activity may be associated with stable traits of stimulus enhancement and exclusion. We have argued that these traits are consistently related to differences in environmental preference and, as a consequence, to choices of leisure activity. However, it should be recognized that different measures of attentional style tap similar traits but not necessarily identical traits. A greater proportion of the variance could be accounted for if an attention test battery was constructed. In the areas of driver/accident involvement (Mihal and Barrett, 1976) and pilot selection (Gopher, 1982) combined attentional and perceptual tests have been useful in increasing predictive sensitivity. Such a multiple test approach may also be a more useful way of predicting leisure preference or leisure activity persistence.

From the literature we have reviewed on the psychobiology of trait behavior it is apparent that different individuals seek different levels of stimulation to facilitate positive affect and that they do it in different ways. We have noted that through the regulation of attention some individuals can achieve deep leisure states more easily than others. The point we wish to emphasize in concluding this section concerns the *quality* of the leisure experience. From a theoretical and practical standpoint the realization that individuals will attempt to manage their environment to create optimal levels of stimulation implies that the specific form of leisure activity is of secondary importance to the subjective experience that it generates.

SOCIALLY-BASED TRAITS

In the previous section we argued that there are some personality factors influencing leisure behavior which are based on the particularly unique physiology of individuals. In this section we will consider traits which are shaped primarily in the course of early socialization. Given that they are environmentally rather than biologically conditioned they may be regarded as less stable and immutable. Nevertheless we will argue that their are some socialized dimensions of personality which are relatively resilient, determining the experience across numerous situations including, and perhaps especially, those associated with leisure. While there are a number of traits which might be considered, we will limit our attention here to two: achievement motivation and locus of control.

Achievement Motivation

The need for achievement (See Atkinson and Raynor, 1974) is consistent with many types of leisure behavior. Inherent in the flow model referred to earlier is a challenge-seeking orientation which results from feelings of competence associated with the experiences of flow and the need to progress to higher levels of difficulty and complexity to recreate that experience (Csikszentmihalyi 1975, 1978). In fact, Tinsley and Kass (1979) identify achievement need as a primary component of the self-actualization factor which accounted for the greatest amount of variance in their assessment of leisure needs and satisfactions. It is easy to see the sense of achievement that one gets from building a table or successfully raising daffodils. And it is predictable that a person with a relatively low need for achievement would use free time for other activities, where concentrated effort, a goal orientation and persistence—the basic components of achievement motivation—are unimportant.

The need for achievement is also fundamental to *competition* and may be what draws some people to sports while it draws others to dog shows. Also contingent upon successful competition, in addition to a sense of accomplishment, are such things as recognition, status, popularity and even financial reward. But it is in response to these outcomes that the more intrinsically-satisfying aspects of leisure experience may become diminished in importance. There is a rather substantial literature indicating that rewarding people extrinsically (with money, trophies, etc.) for behaviors (activities) that have previously been enjoyed for their own sake may change the focus in those activities to more external, payoff-oriented outcomes (e.g., Lepper & Greene, 1978).

There is also some reason to think that competitiveness is more a matter of *power* orientation than an achievement need. But that such satisfactions are sought in the context of leisure is undeniable. In the study referred to before, Tinsley & Kass (1979) found a power orientation (for status, recognition, etc.) to be another significant factor in leisure participation. But as the achievement need shades into the power need at least some types of leisure experience become constrained. Where the pursuit of payoffs serves to "overjustify" play, thereby making it work-like in purpose, the potential for present-centered enjoyment may be threatened. And characteristic of the A-type personality referred to earlier, the pursuit of achievement may become an insatiable need that precludes enjoyment and relaxation at any time other than when the payoff is made (Friedman & Rosenman, 1974).

Additionally, highly achievement-oriented individuals are necessarily future-oriented. The present is but a pathway to future accomplishment. And while personal direction, effective time management and a progressively ordered existence are generally associated with positive mental health, they may in the extreme impose a kind of mechanical tyranny on the ideal experience of leisure (see for example, Godbey, 1976; Linder, 1970).

Locus of Control *(Rotter, 1966)*

Fundamental to an achievement orientation is the belief that one can effectively influence those factors which bring success and failure, wealth and wisdom. The construct of "locus of control" has been utilized in research to differentiate those who believe themselves to be capable of directing their own consequences (internals) from those (externals) who feel relatively more at the mercy of luck, fate and other forces beyond their control (Rotter, 1966; See also Lefcourt, 1976). Since a perception of control brings a perception of freedom and since the sense of freedom is thought to be central to the experience of leisure, it is quite natural that locus of control has been considered as a likely determinant of leisure attitudes and experiences (Neulinger, 1974). For one thing, those with a more internal locus of control are likely to take greater risks, and play, exploration and the pursuit of varied experience, as patterns of recreation, generally involve some degree of risk-taking.

However, there is evidence that internals are less rather than more likely to have an affinity for leisure (Kleiber, 1979; Kleiber & Crandall, 1981). This may be due in part to the sense among many internals that a "leisurely" existence is inconsistent with progressive achievement; but the converse may also be true that externals are attracted to leisure precisely because the need for control seems somehow less important there. This represents a kind of existential acceptance of things as they are, an appreciation of life for whatever it brings with the assumption that one can and/or should do little about it. Perhaps we are returning here in part to the Type A–Type B distinction. Further research should be clarifying.

At the extreme end of the continuum, however, a person with an external locus of control feels relatively helpless in the face of changing circumstances. And leisure as we have described it in both the experiential and contextual sense requires an exercise of self with an inherent perception of freedom. Not only is the extreme external unlikely to take risks, but he or she may be unable to see even the potential for utilizing a given activity or situation to effect some level of enjoyment or satisfaction.

IMPLICATIONS FOR RESEARCH AND PRACTICE

There are many other personality characteristics which may have an influence on leisure behavior—directing leisure choices or determining leisure experience. Further attention might thus be given to impulsivity-reflectivity, anxiety and guilt, conformity, sociability and nurturance among others. Those discussed above represent only a sampling of possible predictors, albeit those more likely to show some differences.

In the last two decades techniques have been developed that have increased the sensitivity of measurements of stable individual differences. Physiological, behavioral and questionnaire measures, used singularly or in conjunction with one another, have increased predictive capabilities. Current research in the area of individual differences commonly involves matching a particular trait with the demands on a particular activity or task. For example, in an attempt to improve decision-making performance, the matching of a person's cognitive style with the specific types of decision environment (e.g., well-structured versus ill-structured) has achieved moderate success (Davis, 1982). A similar matching strategy may be applied in studying leisure behavior. Analysis of the structure of a leisure activity may provide valuable information as to what cognitive qualities would be needed to maximize levels of enjoyment. The matching, then, of the most appropriate individual dispositions with these activity characteristics may help to identify which people may be predisposed to engage in a selected leisure pursuit and to what extent the activity will be enjoyed.

Nevertheless, it must be reiterated that studies have shown and will continue to show that personality traits alone, even in combination with one another, are rather limited in their potential for predicting leisure behavior and experience. This is due in part to the fact that different activities are chosen for different purposes and in response to various needs, and also that an activity is very often less important than are the people with whom it is done (Kelly, 1982). There is also certainly the influence of learning history and socialization. Leisure patterns and sport preferences are often established in early childhood in response to the influence of significant others (i.e., families and friends). But another important source of variance—perhaps the major one—is the context of the leisure opportunity. However individual differences dictate tendencies to choose one type of activity or another, the flexibility of human beings makes them enormously responsive to environmental influences. For example, it is not unreasonable to expect that after a long day in a boring, isolated work role, even an introvert will seek stimulation and company, or that even the most open and playful child may be resistant to the leadership of an overbearing camp counselor. In sum, to the extent that individual differences are examined, it must be recognized that their influence is tempered by environmental conditions, and thus the argument is for an interactive approach to the study of leisure behavior (see Endler & Magnussen, 1976). However, it will be important to give ample attention to stable individual difference if that approach is to be effective.

Finally, by way of implication, it is important to note that individual differences may be even more important in the practice of "leisure service delivery" than in leisure research. First, when it comes to suggesting leisure alternatives for those looking for direction, an understanding of individual differences may be useful in helping someone move beyond the limits of past experience. Secondly, while an interactive approach is necessary to understand leisure choices and preferences, effective intervention, supervision and leadership within a given context (e.g., a waterfront, a library) may depend on a differential approach. Just as public schools have struggled with the task of individualizing instruction, so too should recreation programs. But while schools operate with compulsory attendance and a fixed curriculum, recreation programs can and should be more responsive to the vicissitudes of individual expression.

REFERENCES

Atkinson, J., & Raynor, J. (1974). *Motivation and achievement.* Washington, D.C.: Winston & Sons.

Bakan, P., Belton, J. A., & Toth, J. C. (1963). Extraversion-introversion and decrement in an auditory vigilance task. In D. N. Buckner, & J. J. McGrath (Eds.), *Vigilance: A symposium.* New York: McGraw-Hill.

Barnett, L. A., & Kleiber, D. A. (1982). Concomitants of playfulness in early childhood: Cognitive abilities and gender. *Journal of Genetic Psychology, 141,* 115–127.

Bishop, D., & Jeanrenaud, L. (1976). End-of-day moods on work and leisure days in relation to extraversion, neuroticism, and amount of change in daily activities. *Canadian Journal of Behavioral Science, 8*(4), 388–400.

Byrne, D. (1964). Repression and sensitization as a dimension of personality. In B. Maher (Ed.), *Progress in experimental personality research.* New York: Academic.

Csikszentmihalyi, M. (1975). *Beyond boredom and anxiety.* Washington: Jossey-Bass.

Csikszentmihalyi, M. (1978). Attention and the wholistic approach to behavior. In K. S. Pope, & J. L. Singer (Eds.), *The stream of consciousness.* New York: Plenum.

Davidson, R. J., Schwartz, G. E., & Rothman, L. P. (1976). Attentional style and the self-regulation of mode-specific attention: An electroencephalographic study. *Journal of Abnormal Psychology, 85,* 611–621.

Davidson, R. J., Goleman, D. J., & Schwartz, G. E. (1976). Attentional and affective concomitants of meditation. *Journal of Abnormal Psychology, 85,* 235–238.

Davis, D. L. (1982). Are some cognitive types better decision makers than others? An empirical investigation. *Human Systems Management, 3,* 165–172.

de Grazia, S. (1964). *Of time, work and leisure.* Garden City, NY: Doubleday & Co.

Dirkin, G. R. (1982, October). Stress management, leisure activity and attention. Paper presented at the SPRE symposium of the National Parks and Recreation Association, Louisville, Kentucky.

Dumazedier, J. (1974). *Society of Leisure.* Amsterdam: Elsevier.

Duncan, D. J. (1978). Leisure types: factor analyses of leisure profiles. *Journal of Leisure Research, 10,* 113–125.

Endler, N. S., & Magnussen, D. (1976). Toward an interactional psychology of personality. *Psychological Bulletin, 83,* 956–974.

Engstrom, D. R. (1976). Hypnotic susceptibility, EEG-alpha, and self-regulation. In G. E. Schwartz, & D. Shapiro (Eds.), *Consciousness and self-regulation.* New York: Plenum.

Eysenck, H. J. (1957). *The dynamics of anxiety and hysteria.* London: Routledge and Kegan Paul.

Eysenck, H. J. (1967). *The biological basis of personality.* Springfield: Thomas.

Fiske, D. W., & Maddi, S. R. (1961). *Functions of varied experience.* Homewood: Dorsey Press.

Friedman, M., & Rosenman, R. H. (1974). *Type A behavior and your heart.* New York: Fawcett.

Godbey, G. (1976, October 16–17). Time deepening and the future of leisure. *Leisure Today* (JOPER).

Gopher, D. (1982). A selective attention test as a predictor of success in flight training. *Human Factors, 24*(2), 173–183.

Hamilton, J. A. (1981). Attention, personality, and the self-regulation of mood: Absorbing interest and boredom. *Progress in Experimental Personality Research, 10,* 281–315.

Huizinga, J. (1955). *Homo ludens.* Boston: Beacon.

James, W. (1980). *The principles of psychology.* New York: Hall.

Kahneman, D. (1973). *Attention and effort.* Englewood Cliffs: Prentice-Hall.

Kane, J. E. (1972). *Psychological aspects of physical education and sport.* London: Routledge and Kegan Paul.

Keele, S. W., & Hawkins, H. L. (1982). Explorations of individual differences relevant to high level skill. *Journal of Motor Behavior, 14,* 3–23.

Kelly, J. R. (1982). *Leisure.* Englewood Cliffs: Prentice-Hall.

Kleiber, D. A. (1979). Fate control and leisure attitudes. *Leisure Sciences, 2,* 239–248.

Kleiber, D. A., & Crandall, R. (1981). Leisure and work ethics and locus of control. *Leisure Sciences, 4,* 477–485.

Lefcourt, H. M. (1976). *Locus of control.* New York: Wiley.

Lepper, M. R., & Greene, D. (1978). *The hidden costs of reward.* Hillsdale: Lawrence Erlbaum.

Lieberman, J. N. (1977). *Playfulness: Its relationship to imagination and creativity.* New York: Academic Press.

Linder, S. (1970). *The harried leisure class.* New York: Columbia University Press.

Lynch, R. L. (1979). *Social play: An interactional analysis of play in face-to-face social interaction.* Unpublished doctoral dissertation. Urbana-Champaign: University of Illinois.

Machlowitz, M. (1980). *Workaholics.* Reading: Addison-Wesley.

MacNeil, R. D., & Dunn, G. E. (1981, October). The relationship of cognitive style to leisure preference: A preliminary investigation. Paper presented at the SPRE leisure symposium, Minneapolis.

Maddi, S. R., & Scott-Propst, B. (1971). Activation theory and personality. In S. R. Maddi (Ed.), *Perspectives on personality.* Boston: Little, Brown and Company.

Mannell, R. C. (1980). Social psychological techniques and strategies for studying leisure experiences. In S. Iso-Ahola (Ed.), *Social psychological perspectives on leisure and recreation.* Springfield: Thomas.

Martin, A. R. (1975, March). Leisure and our inner resources. *Parks and Recreation* (Supplement).

Mehrabian, A. (1976). *Public places and private spaces: The psychology of work, play and living environments.* New York: Basic Books.

Mehrabian, A. (1977). A questionnaire measure of individual differences in stimulus screening and associated differences in arousability. *Environmental Psychology and Nonverbal Behavior, 1,* 89–103.

Mihal, W. L., & Barrett, G. V. (1976). Individual differences in perceptual information processing and their relation to automobile accident involvement. *Journal of Applied Psychology, 61*(2), 229–233.

Moray, N. (1967). Where is capacity limited? A survey and a model. *Acta Psychologica, 27,* 84–92.

Neulinger, J. (1974). *The psychology of leisure.* Springfield: Thomas.

Nideffer, R. M. (1976). Test of attentional and interpersonal style. *Journal of Personality and Social Psychology, 34*(3), 394–404.

Oltman, P. K., Raskin, E., & Witkin, H. A. (1971). *Group embedded figures test.* Palo Alto: Consulting Psychologists Press.

Petrie, A. (1967). *Individuality in pain and suffering.* Chicago: University of Chicago Press.

Rotter, J. (1966). Generalized expectancies for internal versus external control of reinforcement. *Psychological Monographs, 80*(609).

Singer, J. L. (1975). *The inner world of daydreaming.* New York: Harper.

Sokolov, E. N. (1963). *Perception and the conditioned reflex.* New York: Macmillan.

Swanson, G. E. (1978). Travels through inner space: Family structure and openness to absorbing experiences. *American Journal of Sociology, 83,* 890–919.

Tellegren, A., & Atkinson, G. (1974). Openness to absorbing and self-altering experiences ("absorption"), a trait related to hypnotic susceptibility. *Journal of Abnormal Psychology, 83,* 268–277.

Thackeray, R. I., Jones, K. N., & Touchstone, R. M. (1974). Personality and physiological correlates of performance decrement on a monotonous task requiring sustained attention. *British Journal of Psychology, 65,* 351–358.

Tinsley, H. E. A., & Kass, R. A. (1979). The latent structure of the need satisfying properties of leisure activities. *Journal of Leisure Research, 11,* 278–291.

Veblen, T. (1899). *The theory of the leisure class.* New York: Viking Press.

Witkin, H. A., Dyk, R. B., Faterson, H. F., Goodenough, D. R., & Karp, S. A. (1962). *Psychological differentiation.* New York: Wiley.

Witkin, H. A., & Goodenough, D. R. (1976). Field-dependence and interpersonal behavior. TB 76-12. Princeton, NJ: Educational Testing Service.

Witt, P. A. (1971). Factor structure of leisure behavior for high school age youth in three communities. *Journal of Leisure Research, 3,* 213–219.

Zuckerman, M. (1979). *Sensation-seeking: Beyond the optimal level of arousal.* Hillsdale: Lawrence Erlbaum Associates.

Chapter III

INDIVIDUAL CONSTRAINTS ON CHILDREN'S PLAY

Lynn A. Barnett and Mary Jo Kane

INTRODUCTION

Picture young Benjie, a three-year-old boy sitting on the floor one morning at preschool, surrounded by a chaotic assortment of multi-colored wooden blocks and plastic beads. He is busily engaged in some constructive activity—carefully placing one block on top of, next to and adjoining the others. He attentively scrutinizes his construction at regular intervals and then proceeds with the next step. His actions appear systematic and progressively organized, his countenance is "serious" and directed, he appears oblivious to his surroundings and he shows little hesitation as he mounts each successive block. From these observations can we label Benjie's activity as play? Suppose we then ask Benjie what he's building and he answers, "an XQ-50 missile." Does his response give us additional information in defining the behaviors as playful? Does the goal-directed nature of his activity impact upon our judgment as to the play encounter? Clearly, we, as observers, cannot proffer the play characterization. Benjie must solely make this determination and it is based upon the nature, extent and direction of his internal motives.

While contemporary theoretical formulations of play agree that any behavioral response can only be labeled as play by the individual (as opposed to a description of the activity), there are specific constituent factors which consistently underlie playful self-reports.

This chapter was supported in part by a grant from National Institute of Child Health and Human Development, No. HD 05951.

43

The most encompassing of these concerns the intent of the individual for engaging in the behavior: play is not motivated by any other goal than seeking the reward inherent immediately in the activity itself. The motive for play is seen to be intrinsic, that is, inherent in the process of the activity itself. Play behavior is thus initiated for the internal rewards associated with the process and sustained by the continued expression and realization of these rewards.

We may further delineate the intrinsic motive by describing the prevailing environmental climate in which it appears. Definitions of play repeatedly utilize words such as, "voluntary," "freedom," and "choice." Thus, if the behavior appears independent of externally applied contingencies and consequences, if it appears that individual choice motivates the onset of activity, and if positive affect accompanies the process, we may presume the encounter to be a playful interaction. The focus, then, is on the source of control over the immediate environment—in play, the individual controls the initiation and direction for enjoyment. We may thus conclude, from the above, that the antithesis of play is external mediation. To the extent that external forces guide or shape the behavior, the playful experience becomes minimized. As others place restrictions or contingencies on the range of choices available to the individual, the freedom to choose and the individual's perceived control over the environment wanes. Thus, we may say that there is an inverse relationship between playful expression and contextual constraints, such that the greater the degree of extrinsic factors impinging upon the individual, the less the opportunity for play to occur and be sustained.

Recent research has demonstrated that free play is important to the developing child. Play has been shown to be positively related to creativity, problem solving, divergent thought processes, emotional stability, social judgment, effective peer interaction, and language development. Investigations of play sequences and interactions have thus focused upon ways in which playful expression may be promoted and facilitated in attempts to foster its cognitive, social and emotional correlates. While little effort has been undertaken to specify the constraints to playful expression, it seems crucial at this stage to identify these inhibiting variables. It is only through careful delineation of the constraints on play that we can more fully understand the behavior itself, maximize the playful interaction between the individual and his/her environment, and provide for its effective management in intervening with those individuals deficient in developmental processes.

INDIVIDUAL DIFFERENCES

Psychological Variables

A new way of thinking about play has received a great deal of attention in recent years. Early thinking and research about play has focused on topological analysis of the play activity in attempts to describe and categorize the domain of play bouts. More recent focus represents a shift away from this perspective and emphasizes the qualities of the player in bringing to an environment a unique propensity to play. Lieberman (1964, 1965, 1977) was among the first to promulgate the existence of a personality predisposition which she labeled "playfulness." She further suggested that this trait is comprised of five constituent components: physical spontaneity, social spontaneity, cognitive spontaneity, manifest joy and sense of humor. Research by Cattell (1950, 1979) and others (e.g., Meehl, Lykken, Schofield and Tellegen, 1971) has indicated that these playfulness factors may be distributed across and correlated with other personality factors in adults. One of the correlates is "surgency" which is comprised of attributes such as "cheerful," "joyous," "humorous," "witty," and "energetic." A second factor which incorporates the playfulness dimensions is "siza-affectia" (Cattell, 1979), which includes the characteristics, "good natured," "laughs readily" and "likes to participate with people." The existence of the playfulness quality and its five component factors has been replicated and confirmed in other investigations (Barnett and Kleiber, 1982; Singer and Singer, 1978; Singer, Singer and Sherrod, 1980). Singer et al. (1980) also recorded behaviors at several points in time and found that the playfulness factor was relatively stable over a one-year period.

Singer and his colleagues (Singer and Singer, 1978; Singer,

Singer and Sherrod, 1980) attempted to further delineate characteristics of the child which were related to the playfulness quality. We
may interpret his findings as suggestive of a constraining influence of the individual's internal psychological make-up in initiating playful activities. Through factor analysis of behavioral
observations, a descriptive picture of the less playful child emerged.
Children who were identified as low in playfulness were characterized as showing little positive affect, being physically inactive,
exhibiting low degrees of social and imaginative play and being
less verbal than their preschool peers.

Children who are less playful are also less creative and less
imaginative than their more playful peers. This finding has been
substantiated over the past ten years across a variety of play
contexts and activities (Dansky, 1980; Dansky and Silverman,
1973, 1975; Lieberman, 1965; Rosen, 1974; Singer and Rummo,
1973; Sutton-Smith, 1968). Singer (1973) found that children who
were less imaginative in their play performed more poorly later
in school and were more aggressive and less joyful than their more
imaginative counterparts. Singer and Rummo (1973) reported that
less creative boys were also less communicative, curious, humorous and expressive. Pulaski (1973) demonstrated that children who
showed a low disposition to fantasy in free play were also less
likely to be imaginative in a task situation. Hutt (1966) and Hutt
and Bhavnani (1972) categorized young children by the degree of
inventiveness and exploration they showed in play. They found
that the nonexploring children were lower in creativity than those
children who were more active initiators and explorers in play. In
addition, self report data indicated that the nonexploring girls
rated themselves as tense, reserved, and conforming while nonexploring boys saw themselves as unadventurous and less physically active.

There is support for the notion that individual children may
exercise their capacity for imaginative play in different ways
(Hudson, 1966; Matthews, 1977; Minuchin, Biber, Shapiro and
Zimiles, 1969; Singer, 1973; Winner, McCarthy, Kleinman and
Gardner, 1979). The types of play materials available as well as the
amount of previous experience with certain toys influences the
appearance and form of creative and imaginative play. Pulaski

(1973) found that highly structured play materials, and those with which the child has had little previous acquaintance, constrained fantasy play. Pepler (1979; Pepler and Ross, 1981) showed that certain types of toys labeled as "convergent" play materials produced play forms with little creative involvement. Dreyer and Rigler (1969) summarized, that structured materials provide such strong direction for children's activity that they inhibit the behaviors that might facilitate the child's creative expression.

Recent investigations have noted a strong relationship between the child's playful characteristics and cognitive processing. Support for the relationship between play and divergent thinking ability has been substantiated in recent years (Barnett and Kleiber, 1982; Bruner, 1972; Cheyne and Rubin, 1981; Dansky, 1980; Dansky and Silverman, 1973, 1975; Hutt, 1979; Hutt and Bhavnani, 1972; Johnson, 1976; Li, 1978; Lieberman, 1965; Pepler, 1979; Pepler and Ross, 1981; Smith and Dutton, 1979; Sutton-Smith, 1968; Sylva, 1977; Sylva, Bruner and Genova, 1976; Vandenberg, 1978, 1981). Dansky and Silverman (1975) explain this relationship by noting that, "play creates a set, or attitude, to generate associations to a variety of objects whether or not these objects are encountered during play activity" (p. 104).

The implication from this research is that children who are low in playfulness and who incorporate less creative and imaginative styles into their play activities may be poorer at divergent modes of thought. Dansky (1980) hypothesized that certain cognitive processes involved in make-believe or fantasy play, such as free association and symbolic thinking, are similar to those involved in divergent thinking. Hutt and Bhavnani (1972) demonstrated that children who were low in exploration and invention in play performed at lower levels on divergent thinking tasks. Pepler (1979) and Pepler and Ross (1981) found that children who had fewer divergent play experiences also gave fewer unique responses and were less imaginative on a divergent thinking task. Lieberman (1965) demonstrated that children who were less spontaneous and joyful in their play and who had little or no sense of humor performed at lower levels on divergent thinking tasks than those who showed more of these playful qualities. All of these findings suggest that there is a positive relationship between play, creativity and divergent thinking, such that children who are low in creativity or who exhibit more immature modes of thought are also less playful.

Gender Differences

Consistent sex differences in play have been reported from infancy through adolescent years. Children experience significant constraints on their play solely as a function of their gender, and these arise from parents, peers, teachers, other adults and societal expectations in general. The rigidity with which children are expected to adhere to differential sex-role stereotypes has not drastically changed in recent years, and results in differential opportunities and avenues for play in boys and girls. Gender differences are thus reviewed and included here as a constraint in recognition that other agents play a predominant role in influencing and restricting the range of play for boys and girls.

Minimal sex differences in the play of infants have been recorded, in activity level (Kagan, 1971; Kagan and Lewis, 1965; Rheingold and Eckerman, 1969) and toy or activity preference (Brooks and Lewis, 1974; Kaminski, 1973). However, following the child's first year, differences in play as a function of gender begin to appear. At thirteen months, boys tended to be more rigorous and active in their style of toy play and time spent generally at play is greater (Goldberg and Lewis, 1969; Jacklin, Maccoby and Dick, 1973; Maccoby and Jacklin, 1973; Messer and Lewis, 1972). By preschool, major differences can be found in play whether at home, in school, or in outdoor play areas (Blakemore, La Rue and Olejnik, 1979; Guttentag and Salasin, 1977; Hartup, Moore and Sager, 1963; Masters, Ford, Arend, Grotevant and Clark, 1979; Serbin, Connor and Citron, 1981; Serbin, Connor, Burchardt and Citron, 1979; Vance and McCall, 1934). Boys have reliably been found to display a higher activity level and motility during play (Pulaski, 1970; Smith and Connolly, 1972) and to show more fantasy and vocalization during play and games (Emmerich, 1971; Marshall, 1961; Mueller, 1972; Singer, 1973; Szal, 1972). Preschool girls tend to show more passive play forms and their play is generally characterized as more cognitive and manipulative in format (Emmerich,

1971; Pederson and Bell, 1970; Vance and McCall, 1934). Distinct sex-role toy and activity preferences have been well established by this age (Brown, 1956; Clarke, Wyon and Richards, 1969; Connor and Serbin, 1977; Eaton, von Bargen and Keats, 1981; Fagot, 1977; Fagot and Patterson, 1969; Fauls and Smith, 1956; Giddings and Halverson, 1981; Halliday and McNaughton, 1982; Lamb and Roopnarine, 1979; Rabban, 1950; Rheingold and Cook, 1975; Schwarz, 1972; Sears, Rau and Alpert, 1965; Smith, 1980; Wohlford et al., 1971) and these behavioral preferences have been found to reflect children's understanding of sex-role identification and standards (Eisenberg, Murray and Hite, 1982; Flerx, Fidler and Rogers, 1976; Maccoby and Jacklin, 1974; Schlossberg and Goodman, 1972; Teglasi, 1981). Pressures for sex-role typing children's play contribute to the young child's understanding of differential expectation and opportunities from a variety of sources, other than parental pressures. Children's writers (Weitzman, Eifler, Hokada and Ross, 1972), television programmers (Levinson, 1975), the toy industry in general (Kutner and Levinson, 1978) as well as sales personnel in toy stores (Ungar, 1982) all converge upon the child's world to influence play materials and opportunities. It is clear, then, that by school age children respond to, mimic, conform to and rationally verbalize sex-role stereotypic preferences and behaviors in play.

These patterns continue throughout childhood. During the school years and through adolescence, reliable differences between boys and girls are readily observed. Masculine and feminine toy choices are equally pronounced (De Lucia, 1963, 1972; Hilton and Berglund, 1971; Honiz, 1951; Laosa and Brophy, 1972; Liebert et al., 1971; Nelson and Rosenbaum, 1972; Walberg, 1969; Ward, 1969) and, with the maturation of social skills and development of morality and social conscience, games show these same trends as well. Rosenberg and Sutton-Smith (1960) investigated the game preferences of nine to eleven-year-old preadolescents and found that boys preferred more forceful and physical contact in their play and more complex team games with major conflicts between male roles. Girls' games, in contrast, tended to be more static, verbal and noncompetitive. Lever (1978) replicated and extended these findings with a similar age group using observations, interviews and daily logs of play activities. She found substantive sex differences within this sample in that girls' play was more spontaneous, imaginative, less structured and rule-governed and tended to occur in small groups. Games were less competitive and leadership roles were either nonexistent or were randomly assigned.

From this literature a very different picture emerges of the play of boys and that of girls. Significant differences in the characteristics of play style, format and preferences can be documented almost solely as a function of gender. While recognition is given to the fact that genetic factors do account for some variation, the position adopted here has been that structural mechanisms play a minor role in accounting for these differences. Rather, the environment in which the child lives and plays significantly influences playful behaviors toward sex-appropriate lines. Play is thus modulated by others and constrained to the effect that violation of normative societal role-governed standards is not liberally tolerated. Boys and girls thus have restricted avenues for play available from which to choose and it is the freedom of choice factor which underlies playful definition.

Contextual Influences

Psychologists have long suggested that the environment can have an important influence on people's behavior (Lewin, 1931). Indeed, play, however defined, does not take place in a vacuum. The environment in which a child plays, whether literal or figurative, consists of a setting that is populated with objects, others or both. Opportunities for play are often precluded by a sterile environment and the nature of play interactions are shaped by the opportunities available to the child. Playful behaviors may be constrained by an environment which offers little opportunity for exploration or creative exercise. In this section, the literature is examined which identifies constraints on play brought by structural environmental features. These may be viewed as classes of constraint as a function of the play environment in general: of play objects and play things which foster or debilitate the richness of the play experience, and play areas which are typically regarded as spaces specifically designed to facilitate individual playful expression.

Recent evidence suggests that the most widely used play areas are those which are not specifically designated for play. Public park or recreation facilities are often not reported to be "prime" play areas (Hole, 1966; Martensson, 1972; Maurer and Baxter, 1972; Sanoff and Dickerson, 1971). While city streets often inhibited a variety of play activities, they were also viewed by children as rich in play opportunities (Barker and Wright, 1955; Benjamin, 1974; Gans, 1962; Jacobs, 1961; Lynch et al., 1977; Opie and Opie, 1969). It has been argued that the reason for such minimal usage of designated play areas is that they are overly structured in design and dictate potential activity patterns. Unplanned play areas meet different needs that developed play areas do not, among which are the need for areas which facilitate natural and creative exercise (Cobb, 1959; Cooper, 1975; Opie and Opie, 1969). The child's tendency to seek undeveloped, unplanned open space for play activities can be viewed as his/her search for unique playful experiences, exploratory and manipulatory expression, a challenging environment in which to express the internal desire to master and control (White, 1959) and the need for privacy from adults (Coates and Bussard, 1974; Matterson, 1966, 1968; Pintler, 1945; Vlietstra, 1980).

One of the characteristics of the setting which has been found to influence play concerns the quantity and quality of materials available to the child. The general findings from research examining toys and their mediating effect on play has been that toys may have a debilitating effect (Dreyer and Rigler, 1969; Goldman and Chaille, 1981; Pepler, 1979; Pepler and Ross, 1981; Phyfe-Perkins, 1980; Pulaski, 1973; Smith and Connolly, 1980). Social play is more likely to occur when there are only a few toys available (Bjorkland, 1979) or no toys present at all (Eckerman and Whatley, 1977). Tizard (1977) found that more social games occur without toys and that a surplus of toys serves to inhibit extended play with preschool children. These findings have been confirmed by others in experimental and naturalistic investigations of various types of toys on social play forms (Rubin and Seibel, 1979; Turner and Goldsmith, 1976). Along similar lines, the amount and type of toys available to the child also effects cognitive play styles

(Rubin and Seibel, 1979). Toys designed with certain task demands and those which are relatively familiar and low in novelty and complexity detract from symbolic and creative play activities (Berlyne, 1966; Bjorkland, 1979; Elder and Pederson, 1978; Frost and Campbell, 1978; Gower, 1978; Gramza, 1976; Hughes, 1978; Hutt, 1970, 1979; Pepler, 1979; Ross, 1970; Vlietstra, 1980). Other aspects of the play environment which have been found to influence play behavior include the number of children present (McGrew, 1972), the age and sex of play partners (Garvey, 1974; Jacklin and Maccoby, 1978) and adult control and direction over play activities (Carpenter, 1979; Huston-Stein, Freidrich-Cofer and Susman, 1977). It thus appears that the degree of structure contained within the setting, either by the quantity of materials, the nature of these materials, or the more general definition of the setting constrains social and cognitive playful expression.

EXCEPTIONAL INDIVIDUALS

The phenomenon of play is often considered to be a natural and spontaneous process. Observations of children in free range settings note natural developmental play sequences which can be reliably documented from infancy through adolescence. Choice of play materials, play environments and playmates correspond to these developmental stages and compositely indicate that children naturally initiate, sustain and modulate playful interaction. There is some indication that special, or atypical, children do not play in the same way that normal children do and the implication is that the natural cognitive, social and emotional benefits of play experiences are thus altered. Indeed, a wealth of literature has recently emerged which reports the use of play as a context in which therapeutic intervention can be facilitated (for reviews, see Schaefer, 1976; Schaefer and O'Connor, 1983; Wehman, 1977). Many of these "training studies" assume atypical play patterns for the population under study yet a systematic determination of the extent to which play is different with special individuals has not been undertaken. This section reviews the empirical evidence on the play of handicapped and accelerated children in an attempt to delineate the nature of these differences. The assumption is made that one of the major constraints on play arises from etiological factors which inhibit "natural" play and this limits the special child from realizing the full potential of playful expression to healthy development.

The Mentally Retarded Child

A crucial difference between the play of normal and mentally handicapped children is the absence of spontaneous play in the mentally retarded (Copeland and Golden, 1979; Hillman, 1966; Horne and Philleo, 1942; Paloutzian, Hasazi, Streifel and Edgar, 1971). Mentally retarded children appear unable to initiate a play bout without some adult guidance (Kirk and Johnson, 1951; Phemister, Richardson and Thomas, 1978; Thomas, Phemister and Richardson, 1981; Zigler, 1966), and the need for adult direction becomes more exaggerated as the functioning level of the retarded child is more depressed (Jeffree and McConkey, 1976; Odom, 1981; Wing, Gould, Yeates and Brierley, 1977).

Several authors have speculated that it is the exploratory component of the play experience which contributes most strongly to learning and development (for reviews, see Hutt, 1966; McCall, 1974; Rubin, Fein and Vandenberg, 1982; Vandenberg, 1978, 1980a, b). Observations of retarded children at play indicate that less exploration of objects and setting occurs, in contrast to normal peers (Haywood and Burke, 1977; Vanderkooij, 1979; Weisler and McCall, 1976; Woodward and Hunt, 1972). Retarded children have been shown to be more disruptive, less organized (Schachter, Meyer and Loomis, 1962), more variable (Wing, Gould, Yeates and Brierly, 1977) and less attentive (Cooper and Henderson, 1973; Hannam, 1975; Phemister, Richardson and Thomas, 1978; Rosenzweig, 1954) in their play. Normal children play longer than retarded children and their play is relatively more stable and less chaotic (Horne and Philleo, 1942; Takata, 1971). In a study contrasting one to two-year-old normal with matched handicapped children, the handicapped children were shown to have "empty" days, i.e., longer periods of unobligated time devoted to self-stimulating behaviors and staring or wandering, rather than playful or interactive activities (Phemister, Richardson and Thomas, 1978). In general, the play of mentally handicapped children has been characterized as repetitive and stereotypic (Flavell, 1973; Hopper and Wambold, 1978; Mogford, 1977; Wehman, 1977), lacking in imagination and originality (Kirk and Johnson, 1951) and accompanied by apathetic or neutral expressiveness (Richardson, Reid, Phemister and Thomas, 1981).

One of the earliest forms of play beyond infancy is object manipulation, the concrete representation of objects and their use in the construction of new play forms and environments. Comparisons of the manipulative play styles of young normal and retarded children seem to be at variance in their observations. In a series of studies with severely handicapped and normal children of the same mental age, findings indicated that as many handicapped children were as quick to contact and manipulate a novel object, and that the amount and types of manipulative play with a wide range of conventional toys was similar to that of the normal children (Phemister, Richardson and Thomas, 1978). In a follow-up comparative study (Thomas, Phemister and Richardson, 1981), manipulative play depended on the setting: both groups showed the same duration of contact with objects and play materials but handicapped children in motivational settings were not as attentive to the objects as those who were in their home environment. In contrast, mentally handicapped children of similar chronological age have been shown by other investigators to lack the motivation to approach and persist with an activity involving novel or familiar objects (Cooper and Henderson, 1973; Hannam, 1975; Jones, 1976; Tilton and Ottinger, 1964; Weiner, Ottinger and Tilton, 1969). Weiner and Weiner (1974) attempted to categorize the nature of manipulative play behavior and to contrast noninstitutionalized handicapped children with normal controls on both chronological and mental age. Normal children of comparable chronological age (six years) were found to show more combinations of play objects, separation and manipulation of toy parts and pushing and pulling of toys, and less personalized uses of toys than the matched retarded children. Fewer differences were observed in manipulative play when subjects were matched on mental age (three years): again, retarded children combined play objects less and showed fewer incidences of throwing or tossing about the toys in the free play room. These same results were obtained in earlier research (Tilton and Ottinger, 1964; Weiner, Ottinger and Tilton, 1969) whereby normal children exhibited more combinatorial toy play, and more pushing, pulling and pounding of toys. Retarded children showed fleeting contact with toys which typically consisted of merely touching a toy or picking up and either dropping or setting a toy down without manipulating it. The conclusion from these studies was that specific toy play usage is a valid means of differentiating between normal and mentally handicapped children.

Other investigators have also observed differences in toy play preferences and usage patterns. Handicapped children tend to have fewer play companions, show shorter total playtime and spend much of their time playing alone (Gralewicz, 1973). Horne and Philleo (1942) earlier noted that normal subjects preferred constructing play objects and creating new "games" with those objects in contrast to retarded subjects, who showed a stronger preference for games and toys which were more structural and clearly defined. Switzky, Ludwig and Haywood (1979) concurred and found that moderately retarded children spend more time playing with less complex objects. Gramza and his colleagues (Gramza and Witt, 1969; Gramza, Witt, Linford and Jeanrenaud, 1969) found similarities for color preferences in play objects but different preferences for positioning of play materials in young mongoloid children. Keeran, Grove and Zachofsky (1969) found severely and profoundly retarded children to be very limited in their ability to use conventional playground equipment, a finding which may be explained by the observation that these children have marked coordination and movement problems (McCoull, 1971).

Piaget (1952, 1962) stressed the importance of the acquisition of symbolic representation in the development of language and intelligence. His schema theory delineated play stages which closely approximated levels of cognitive and intellectual maturity. Perhaps the most striking and frequently investigated feature of the retarded child's play is the virtual absence of symbolic play forms. In a variety of studies contrasting normal play development with that of the retarded child, symbolic fantasy play has been found to be severely depressed if not virtually non-existent (Cooper, Moodley and Reynell, 1978; Hulme and Lunzer, 1966; Jeffree and and McConkey, 1974, 1976; Whittaker, 1979, 1980; Wing et al., 1977). Jeffree and McConkey (1976) and Hill and McCune-Nicolich (1981) found a significant relationship between the frequency and variety of symbolic play and mental age in normal and retarded samples. Whittaker (1979) investigated the onset of doll play and found that it was strongly correlated with the transition to simple relational play with nonsymbolic toys. In a later study, Whittaker (1980) compared the symbolic play of young profoundly retarded children with normative play observations (Lowe, 1975; Sheridan, 1975) and found similar play patterns. He thus concluded that changes in the progression of play forms are caused by developmental levels rather than determined by experience or environmental factors. In contrast, Phemister, Richardson and Thomas (1978) demonstrated that attentive play in handicapped children varies markedly with the environment and that, under appropriate circumstances, there can be as much spontaneous contact with objects in handicapped children as in normal children at a similar developmental level (although the play of normal children was not found to vary with the setting).

The importance of play to the development of social competence has received much critical attention (for reviews, see Anderson and Messick, 1974; Harter, 1982; Shantz, 1975; Suomi, 1979; Wright, 1980). The child is naturally intrinsically motivated to engage in social encounters (Piaget, 1970), and the beginnings of socialized thought are largely determined by interactions and conflicts with peers (Damon, 1978; Hartup, 1979; Piaget, 1932). Many authors (c.f., Borke, 1971; Flavell, 1970; Piaget, 1967; Urberg and Docherty, 1976) stress the playful context as the primary and critical means by which children forfeit their egocentricity and test their awareness of moral judgment, perspective-taking and reciprocal role relationships. The social play patterns and progression of young children is thus an important variable to study as it is highly suggestive of successful adaptation to the adult world. Several authors have noted the social play deprivation of mentally retarded children (Capobianco and Cole, 1960; Ross, 1970; Tizard, 1960a, b). In comparisons between normal and handicapped children, the play of handicapped children tends to be more solitary, independent and variable, with very little cooperative play interaction with peers and almost no competitive social play (Knapczyk and Yoppi, 1975; Rosenzweig, 1954; Wehman, 1977; Whitman, Mercurio and Caponigri, 1970). Rosenzweig (1954) found that with increases in age, retarded children begin to enjoy the company of peers but with little social reciprocity displayed in their play interactions. More recent research contradicts the above findings, by proposing that there is a similar relationship between the child's developmental level and his/her level of social play. Schlottman and Anderson (1975) compared the social interactions during free play of mongoloid and two groups of normal subjects matched on chronological and mental age. Results indicated that the mongoloid children showed more social play and social object manipulation and were more likely to participate with peers in activities involving toys and other objects. However during social play, these children exhibited more negative verbal behavior—they expressed dislike or dissatisfaction verbally and reprimanded other children during play interactions. Odom (1981) compared the free play of preschool-aged moderately and severely retarded children and found that categories of social play (Barnes, 1971; Parten, 1932) showed a linear progression similar to that shown by a normal population. It is unclear why this study should result in such conflicting findings to earlier work, but it may be argued that without a matched group of normal control subjects, comparisons can be regarded as speculative, at best.

The Autistic Child

Descriptive accounts of autistic children at play bear some similarity to those of retarded children. While clinical diagnoses of childhood schizophrenia sometimes include some degrees of mental retardation, current practice indicates that multiple diagnosis of this type only occurs in a small percentage of the autistic population (Kanner, 1951; White, DeMyer and DeMyer, 1964). Similarly, the vast majority of play research with this population is conducted with children with the single diagnosis, and as such, only that data will be reported here.

Play observations of children characterized as autistic have been of interest for some time (Jahoda and Goldfarb, 1957; Loomis, Hilgeman and Meyer, 1957; Schachter, Meyer and Loomis, 1962; Streisel, Weiland, Denny, Smith and Chaiken, 1960) and the vast majority indicate play in general, to be comprehensive, preservative, restrictive, sterile and repetitious (Despert and Sherwin, 1958; Eisenberg and Kanner, 1956; Ferrara and Hill, 1980). Playful interactions tend to be fixated on a singular play object (Bakwin, 1954; Bender, 1947; Black, Freeman and Montgomery, 1975) or often involve only self-stimulatory behaviors with no toy play at all (Brown, 1960; Gralewicz, 1973; Koegel, Firestone, Kramme and Dunlap, 1974; Ungerer and Sigman, 1981). Black, Freeman and Montgomery (1975) found that autistic children would only play under adult direction and presentation of a limited number of play objects. Schachter, Meyer and Loomis (1962) found schizophrenic children to be similar to retarded children at play: both groups exhibited less transportation play, more disruptive play, and less organization in their general play styles than normal children.

Indeed, autistic children appear to be the most handicapped in all aspects of play. Tilton and Ottinger (1964) observed normal, retarded and autistic children ranging in age from three-and-a-half to six-and-a-half years as they played in a free range setting with a variety of toys. Their findings indicated that the autistic children showed the least amount of toy play and significantly less variety and creativity than either the retarded or normal children. The play of the autistic children was predominantly oral and repetitive, a finding which has been confirmed by others (Despert and Sherwin, 1958; Sigman and Ungerer, 1981; Weiner, Ottinger and Tilton, 1969).

Most autistic children never advance beyond simple manipulative play. The appearance of symbolic play forms is virtually absent in the autistic child's repertoire (Riguet, Taylor, Benaroya and Klein, 1981; Rutter, 1978; Wing, 1978; Wing et al., 1977). Of the few autistic children who have been observed to exhibit some rudimentary symbolic play forms, play tends to be repetitive and stereotypic, lacking in the typic innovation and variety found in normal symbolic play (Clune, Paolella and Foley, 1979; Wing et al., 1977).

One of the defining characteristics of autism is the inner-directedness and social withdrawal (Hutt, Hutt, Lee and Ounsted, 1965) observed in the presence of peers and adults. The speech impairment so typical of this population severely limits social opportunities for play and reduces the opportunity for coopera-tive play interactions (Mogford, 1977). Observational reports of autistic children focus on the infrequent occurrence of social play forms (Boer, 1968; DeMyer, Mann, Tilton and Loew, 1967; Kanner, 1944; Lovaas, Koegel, Simmons and Long, 1973; Rimland, 1964; Romanczyk, Diament, Goren, Trunell and Harris, 1975; Tilton and Ottinger, 1964). Group play participation is severely lacking in autistic play (Gralewicz, 1973; Ritvo, 1976; Rutter, 1978; Rutter, Bartak and Newman, 1971), even when opportunities for such play are provided and encouraged (Kanner, 1943, 1973).

The Language and Hearing Impaired Child

Verbal communication skills are critical components of the expression of cognitive and social play in normal children (Garvey and Hogan, 1973; Kretschmer, 1972; Rosenblatt, 1977). It is widely recognized that there is a strong linkage between the ability to pretend and the ability to use language (Bates, 1979; Escalona, 1979; Nicolich, 1977; Piaget, 1951; Rocissano, 1979; Vygotsky, 1962; Werner and Kaplan, 1963). As language develops in the maturing child, verbal interaction becomes critical for peer interaction and for sustaining the cooperative play of the older preschool child (Garvey, 1974). Thus, language deficiencies in the young child often show differences in playful development and expression (Brackett and Henniges, 1976; Gorrell, 1972; Mindel and Vernon, 1971; Rutter, 1972).

Luria and Yudovitch (1971) described in detail the play activi-ties of twin boys with severe delays in language comprehension and expression. These authors report "peculiarities which sharply differentiated (their play) from the play of their counterparts" —little organization or systematic progression was shown and play was generally found to be simplistic and repetitive. Kretschmer (1972) compared the solitary play of hearing impaired and normal hearing preschool children in a laboratory setting and found the hearing impaired showed less object-focused play than their peers. Hulme and Lunzer (1966) found language delayed children to be equivalent to normal agemates in their organization of play, and Lovell, Hoyle and Siddal (1968) found such qualitative differences in play to be observable only in older children (four years and older).

The literature reporting differences in symbolic play appears to be at variance. Lennenberg (1967) found the play of the congenitally deaf child to be rich in symbolic play and representation, although as the child gets older, play becomes more restricted (Heider and Heider, 1941). Gregory (1976) reported mothers' observations of their deaf child's play, supporting the evidence that extended imaginative sequences are characteristic of their play, and that hearing impaired children show the same tendency as normal four-year-olds to have an imaginary playmate (Newson and Newson, 1970). Hulme and Lunzer (1966) concurred with the above findings that language delayed and normal children are equivalent in the degree of imaginative content shown in play episodes. In contrast to this research is the finding by several others that symbolic play is depressed in children with language handicaps. Rutter (1972) compared children suffering from profound language disabilities and found little make-believe/pretend play involving stories or complex symbolic interactions. Kretschmer (1972), Darbyshire (1977) and Lovell, Hoyle and Siddal (1968) found fewer imaginative play sequences and the need for concrete objects to sustain play interactions.

Insufficient communication experiences have been found to interfere with participation in social play, which, in turn, contributes to the characteristic rigidity ascribed to the hearing impaired child's social behavior (Kretschmer, 1972; Mindel and Vernon, 1971). Gorrell (1972) observed that small play groups of hearing impaired children lacked the social play skills of children with normal hearing. They vocalized less, responded to and approached each other less, and attended to themselves more in group play. Darbyshire (1977) found that children with the greatest communication impairments were less likely to play in group situations or to interact with others generally while at play. Higginbotham and

Baker (1981) compared levels and types of social participation of severe to profoundly hearing impaired and normally hearing children during preschool free play activities. They found the hearing impaired children demonstrated significantly less cooperative play, favoring solitary construction play as the most preferred play mode.

The Visually Impaired Child

The effects of visual handicaps on play behavior have received relatively little empirical attention. Indeed, research investigations comparing the cognitive and social behaviors of blind to sighted children have been equivocal in identifying similarities or differences in daily functional level. Several investigators have reported that although blind children appear to follow the same pattern of cognitive development as do sighted children, their development is more protracted (Gottesman, 1971, 1973; Miller, 1969; Singer and Streiner, 1966). Several investigators have found that blind preschool and kindergarten children show no particular interest in play and their intensity and personal involvement in play activities is substantially less than that of sighted children (Tait, 1972a, 1973; Wills, 1972). Still others have reported either no delay between the sighted and the blind (Cromer, 1973) or much more variability in the daily behaviors of blind children (Tobin, 1972).

Sandler and Wills (1965) studied the play development of congenitally blind children who have no additional handicaps. From their extensive observations they were able to identify several major areas of divergence in play development. Blind infants were found to be delayed in early play experiences which usually consist of exploring, reaching for and locating objects in their environment. The blind infant typically has difficulty in locating playthings and the motivation to do so is often lacking since many objects, at this stage of development, are often sought because of their visual appeal. Sandler and Wills (1965) suggested that blind infants may react more to sound for satisfaction and in stimulating exploration of their environment. Gerhardt (1982) more recently confirmed these observations in describing the early object play development of a blind child to 18 months old.

The next stage in normal play development is imitation and again, differences between sighted and blind children have been observed. Traditional role play is virtually nonexistent in children with visual handicaps and the child's early imitative play forms are restricted to the imitation of sound. The visually impaired child often repeats the verbal exchanges which s/he has heard or in which s/he has participated, often assessing different roles in the dialogue.

The blind child also shows divergence in imaginative play, so typically characteristic of the play activities of sighted preschool children (Frampton, Kerney and Schattner, 1969; Rogow, 1981). Fraiberg (1968; Fraiberg and Adelson, 1973) found a delay in progression to doll play with little imaginative or fantasy components to be exhibited. The doll play which was shown by these children tended to be fairly rudimentary and concrete, dolls often had little personality or imaginative lifestyle assigned to them and children appeared unable to extend beyond their own self-preoccupation. In general, the fantasy play of the visually handicapped child seems confined to dealing with the concrete, showing very little dramatic play (Tait, 1972b) and lacking in the richness, variety and flexibility characteristic of the play of sighted children of comparable age (Singer and Streiner, 1966).

The Behavior Disordered Child

The behavior of young children is highly variable and directly susceptible to characteristics of the immediate environment (Behar and Rapaport, 1983; Routh, Schroeder and O'Tuama, 1974). It is unclear, at this point in time, why some children respond inappropriately or maladaptively to their environment (for reviews see Michaels, 1955; Soddy, 1960; Thomas, Chess and Birch, 1968), yet play has been used as an effective intervention technique for working with these children (for reviews see Levitt, 1971; Redl and

Wineman, 1951; Schaefer, 1976; Schaefer and O'Connor, 1983; Winnicott, 1965, 1971). While the success of play programs is receiving much attention, it appears to be founded on only a handful of research studies which illustrate differences in the play behavior of the psychologically disturbed child.

Factor and Frankie (1980), in a recent study, conducted one of the first empirical investigations addressing the play of this population. They observed nineteen socially maladjusted preschool children and compared them with the same number of normal controls, each in their natural classroom setting. During free play opportunities, the maladjusted children displayed a significantly greater number of nonsocial play activities and their social play interactions were directed almost entirely at teachers and other attending adults. The normal children, in contrast, exhibited more "unoccupied" and "onlooker" behaviors during play and were involved to a greater extent in longer periods and more occurrences of group play. Roberts (1979) hypothesized, following an earlier investigation (Kantosky, 1976), that differences in play between behaviorally disordered and normal children were a function of the degree of structure imposed by the setting on the child. They observed differences in three groups of disturbed children (pure aggressive, pure hyperactive, combined hyperactive) by setting up two experimental play conditions. In the first, children were allowed to play in an unrestricted manner with any or all of a variety of toys available in a room; in the second, the children were allowed to play with only one toy presented to them. The findings indicated that few differences between these groups could be observed during free play, but large differences were observed during the restricted play session. The authors concluded (as did Kantosky, 1976) that the behavioral problems so frequently observed in the classroom, or other structural settings, all but disappeared in an informal atmosphere. Children often considered unmanageable by parents and teachers appear quite "normal" when at play.

In the few studies which have measured the fantasy play of hyperactive children, the results have been equivocal. Malone (1963) found almost no fantasy play, Guerney (1979) observed less use of fantasy play by hyperactive learning disabled children, and

Thompson and Wade (1974) found that eight to ten-year-old hyperactive subjects displayed higher levels of fantasy play than their normal peers. It is difficult to reconcile these conflicting findings, although it should be noted that the populations under study differed slightly with respect to age and etiology. The Thompson and Wade (1974) study used older subjects and while the age of the children participating in the Malone (1963) and Guerney (1979) studies were approximately the same, subjects in the latter study also had learning disabilities of various origin. Thus, at this point in time, we are able to conclude little about the nature of imaginative play styles in behaviorally disordered children.

The Gifted Child

It has often been suggested that to understand the "why's" and "hows" of play we must examine the playful activity of "special" individuals. Although research has typically chosen, albeit for pragmatic reasons, to observe children who are in some way physically or mentally deficient, the picture would not be complete without looking at the play of those individuals who approximate the other end of the developmental continuum.

There is only some validity to the stereotype of the oval-headed, horn-rimmed glasses, overly serious gifted child who would much prefer reading the Encyclopedia Brittanica to romping about with playmates on the ballfield or at pretend tea parties. Terman's (1926) early extensive longitudinal investigation of California children with intelligence quotients between 140 and 200 included a survey of play interests and gaming activities. Several differences between the play of the gifted child and their contemporaries of normal intelligence were noted. The play interests of gifted children tended to be more intellectual as opposed to physical in play activity levels and the gifted child seemed less interested in boisterous or competitive games, showing a greater preference for quiet play pursuits. These findings were also obtained by Lehman and Witty (1927) and Boynton and Ford (1933), the latter authors finding that highly intelligent children showed more "mental" forms of play—reading, looking at atlases, encyclopedias and almanacs as their favorite chosen activity. The play of gifted children seemed to be more developmentally advanced, often resembling the play patterns of older children of normal intelligence (Terman, 1926). Although the specific activities chosen for play appear to be different, the gifted child shows the same amount of pleasure and "glee" in approaching their play as normal children do (Carter, 1958).

Gifted children have often been popularly seen as "loners" who would much prefer the company of an interesting book to that of a human companion. Terman (1926) found that a good deal of the gifted's time is spent playing with others but they were observed to play alone more than the normal control group. Gifted children tended to be as popular as their normal counterparts with their peers, yet they preferred the company of older playmates and show less of a preference for one or the other sex in choosing a play companion. Gifted children show equivalent amounts of quarrelling and fighting with peers during play but they recover from these skirmishes faster and more completely (Carter, 1958). The appearance of imaginary playmates and playful themes involving living in imaginary countries was common among gifted children.

CONCLUSION

Mergen (1977) recently wrote that, "play, and later recreation and leisure, were symbols for a whole complex of values and attitudes about opportunity, creativity and self-fulfillment" (p. 55). Play is of critical import to the individual as it allows for the expression of the self and provides response feedback for such developing processes as cognition and socialization. Play has thus been identified as a "person" variable whose tempo, format and mode of interaction stems from internal wishes and needs. Examination of an individual's playful encounters thus represents a mirror through which we can learn much about the individual. In this chapter we explored the "uniqueness" of play by focusing on the individual and the ways in which his/her "self" variables modulate playful interaction. In the same way that certain person types seem to be more prone to playful engagement, others appear to have individual characteristics which constrain their ability to play and the multitude of ways in which play might be approached, sought and sustained.

Playfulness, as a personality trait, appears related to individual predispositions. Children who are less creative show more "sterile" play patterns and appear restricted in their playful interactions with peers and play objects. The child's propensity to introduce imaginative themes into playful manipulations strongly correlates with more mature problem solving styles in later life and the ability to perform well on divergent-thinking tasks. The "richness" which the child weaves throughout his/her play in early years appears to be a good predictor of later academic success and with the general affect which the individual carries into other activities and interactions. It thus appears that children who lack several of the above psychological characteristics are at a distinct disadvantage. The child who is fearful or reticent in play often lacks the exploratory style which fosters creative thought and contributes to intellectual growth. Play interactions which are stereotypic or vacuous in imaginative content do little to facilitate active environmental observation and manipulation and thus constrain specific and divergent learning. The qualities which the child possesses, mirrored in playful behavior, represent a graphic perspective by which we may predict later performance and adaptive adjustment.

The child's play is greatly effected by social and genetic influences which arise almost solely on the basis of gender. It is clear that boys and girls play differently and that the same opportunities for play are not comparably available to both sexes. By the first year of life, boys' play appears to be more physically active and energetic, while the play of young girls is more confined in motoric expression. Masculine and feminine toy preferences and play styles are differentially pronounced by preschool years and continue throughout middle childhood and into adolescence. External agents exert a strong influence on sex-role stereotyping children's play, and thus serve to limit the range of playful alternatives available to the child. The freedom to choose, an underlying dimension in defining playful behavior, is severely restricted as a function of gender, and thus exerts a constraining influence on the child's natural playful expression.

The immediate context in which the child finds him/herself

may have an impact upon playful engagement. Play environments which are highly structured dictate playful usage and hence constrain possibilities for varied play interactions. Play objects often dictate functional uses and allow minimal opportunities for transposition activities and imaginative imposition. The design of play materials and play areas thus necessitates incorporation of manipulable components to allow the same child, over repeated time intervals, and different children, within the same developmental stage, the wealth of opportunities for active and enriching play experiences.

REFERENCES

Anderson, S., & Messick, S. (1974). Social competency in young children. *Developmental Psychology, 10,* 282–293.

Bakwin, H. (1954). Early infantile autism. *Journal of Pediatrics, 45,* 492–497.

Barker, R. G., & Wright, H. F. (1955). *Midwest and its children.* Evanston, IL: Row, Peterson.

Barnes, K. (1971). Preschool play norms: A replication. *Developmental Psychology, 5,* 99–103.

Barnett, L. A., & Kleiber, D. A. (1982). Concomitants of playfulness in early childhood: Cognitive abilities and gender. *Journal of Genetic Psychology, 141,* 115–127.

Bates, E. (1979). *The emergence of symbols: Cognition and communication in infancy.* New York: Academic Press.

Behar, D., & Rapoport, J. L. (1983). Play observation and psychiatric diagnosis. In C. E. Schaefer, & K. J. O'Connor (Eds.), *Handbook of play therapy.* New York: Wiley.

Bender, L. (1947). Clinical study of 100 schizophrenic children. *American Journal of Orthopsychiatry, 17,* 40–56.

Benjamin, J. (1974). *Grounds for play.* London: National Council of Social Service.

Berlyne, D. E. (1966). Curiosity and exploration. *Science, 153,* 25–33.

Bjorkland, C. (1979). *The effects of toy quantity and qualitative category on toddlers' play.* Paper presented at the meeting of the Society for Research in Child Development, San Francisco, CA.

Black, M., Freeman, B. J., & Montgomery, J. (1975). Systematic observation of play behavior in autistic children. *Journal of Autism and Childhood Schizophrenia, 5,* 363–371.

Blakemore, J. E. O., La Rue, A., & Olejnik, A. B. (1979). Sex-appropriate toy preference and the ability to conceptualize toys as sex-role related. *Developmental Psychology, 15,* 339–340.

Boer, A. P. (1968). Application of a simple recording system to the analysis of free play behavior in autistic children. *Journal of Applied Behavior Analysis, 1,* 335–340.

Borke, H. (1971). Interpersonal perception of young children: Egocentrism or empathy? *Developmental Psychology, 5,* 263–269.

Boynton, P. L., & Ford, F. A. (1933). The relationship between play and intelligence. *Journal of Applied Psychology, 17,* 294–301.

Brackett, D., & Henniges, M. (1976). Communicative interaction of preschool hearing-impaired children in an integrated setting. *Volta Review, 78,* 276–285.

Brooks, J., & Lewis, M. (1974). Attachment behavior in thirteen-month-old, opposite-sex twins. *Child Development, 45,* 243–247.

Brown, D. F. (1956). Sex role preference in young children. *Psychological Monographs, 70.*

Brown, J. (1960). Prognosis from presenting symptoms of preschool children with atypical development. *American Journal of Orthopsychiatry, 30,* 382–390.

Bruner, J. S. (1972). The nature and uses of immaturity. *American Psychologists, 27,* 687–708.

Capobianco, R. J., & Cole, D. A. (1960). Social behavior of mentally retarded children. *American Journal of Mental Deficiency, 64,* 638–651.

Carpenter, C. (1979). *Relation of children's sex-typed behavior to classroom and activity structure.* Paper presented at Society for Research in Child Development, San Francisco, CA.

Carter, T. M. (1958). The play problems of gifted children. *School and Society, 86,* 224–225.

Cattell, R. B. (1950). *Personality.* New York: McGraw-Hill.

Cattell, R. B. (1979). *Personality and Learning Theory.* New York: Springer.

Cheyne, J. A., & Rubin, K. H. (1981). *Playful precursors of problem-solving in preschoolers.* Paper presented at Society for Research in Child Development, Boston.

Clarke, A. H., Wyon, S. M., & Richards, M. P. M. (1969). Free play in nursery school children. *Journal of Child Psychology and Psychiatry, 10,* 205–216.

Clune, C., Paolella, J., & Foley, J. (1979). Free-play behavior of atypical children. *Journal of Autism and Developmental Disorders, 9,* 61–72.

Coates, G., & Bussard, E. (1974). Patterns of children's spatial behavior in a moderate density housing development. In R. W. Moore (Ed.), *Childhood city: Man-environment interactions.* Milwaukee: EDRA.

Cobb, E. (1959). The ecology of imagination in children. *Daedalus, 88,* 537–548.

Connor, J. M., & Serbin, L. A. (1977). Behaviorally based masculine and feminine activity preference scales for preschoolers: Correlates with other classroom behaviors and other cognitive tests. *Child Development, 48,* 1411–1416.

Cooper, C. (1975). *Easter hill village.* New York: Free Press.

Cooper, J., Moodley, M., & Reynell, J. (1978). *Helping language development.* Bath, England: Arnold.

Cooper, L., & Henderson, R. (1973). *Something Wrong?* London: Arrow.

Copeland, A. P., & Golden, D. B. (1979). Possessing and facilitating play in handicapped children. *Child Care, Health and Development, 5,* 335–346.

Cromer, R. (1973). Conservation by congenitally blind children. *British Journal of Psychology, 64,* 241–249.

Damon, W. (1978). *The social world of the child.* San Francisco: Jossey-Bass.

Dansky, J. L. (1980). Make-believe: A mediator of the relationship between play and associative fluency. *Child Development, 51,* 576–579.

Dansky, J. L., & Silverman, I. W. (1973). Effects of play on associative fluency in preschool-aged children. *Developmental Psychology, 9,* 38–43.

Dansky, J. L., & Silverman, I. W. (1975). Play: A general facilitator of associative fluency. *Developmental Psychology, 11,* 104.

Darbyshire, J. (1977). Play patterns in young children with impaired hearing. *Volta Review, 79,* 19–26.

DeLucia, L. A. (1963). The toy preference test: A measure of sex-role identification. *Volta Review, 79,* 19–26.

DeLucia, L. (1972). Stimulus preference and discrimination learning. In J. F. Rosenblith, W. Allinsmith, & J. P. Williams (Eds.), *The causes of behavior.* Boston: Allyn and Bacon.

DeMyer, M. K., Mann, N. A., Tilton, J. R., & Loew, L. H. (1967). Toy-play behavior and use of body by autistic and normal children as reported by mothers. *Psychological Reports, 21,* 973–981.

Despert, J. L., & Sherwin, A. C. (1958). Further examination of diagnostic criteria in schizophrenic illness, and psychoses of infancy and early childhood. *American Journal of Psychiatry, 114,* 784–789.

Dreyer, A., & Rigler, D. (1969). Cognitive performance in Montessori and nursery school children. *Journal of Educational Research, 62,* 411–416.

Eaton, W. O., von Bargen, D., & Keats, J. G. (1981). Gender understanding and dimensions of preschooler toy choices: Sex stereotype versus activity level. *Canadian Journal of Behavioral Science, 13,* 203–209.

Eckerman, C., & Whatley, J. (1977). Toys and social interaction between infant peers. *Child Development, 48,* 1645–1656.

Eisenberg, L., & Kanner, I. (1956). Early infantile autism. *American Journal of Orthopsychiatry, 26,* 556–566.

Eisenberg, N., Murray, E., & Hite, T. (1982). Children's reasoning regarding sex-typed toy choices. *Child Development, 53,* 81–86.

Elder, J., & Pederson, D. (1978). Preschool children's use of objects in symbolic play. *Child Development, 49,* 500–504.

Emmerich, W. (1971). *Structure and development of personal-social behaviors in preschool settings.* Princeton: Educational Testing Service.

Escalona, S. (1979). *The emergence of symbolic functioning through pictures and words.* Paper presented at New York Child Language Conference, New York.

Factor, D. C., & Frankie, G. H. (1980). Free-play behaviors in socially maladjusted and normal preschool children: A naturalistic study. *Canadian Journal of Behavioral Science, 12,* 272–277.

Fagot, B. I. (1977). Consequences of moderate cross-gender behavior in preschool children. *Child Development, 48,* 902–907.

Fagot, B. I., & Patterson, G. R. (1969). An *in vivo* analysis of reinforcing contingencies for sex-role behaviors in the preschool child. *Developmental Psychology, 1,* 563–568.

Fauls, L. B., & Smith, W. D. (1956). Sex-role learning in 5-year-olds. *Journal of Genetic Psychology, 89,* 105–117.

Ferrara, C., & Hill, S. D. (1980). The responsiveness of autistic children to the predictability of social and nonsocial toys. *Journal of Autism and Developmental Disorders, 10,* 51–57.

Flavell, J. H. (1970). Role-taking and communication skills in children. In W. W. Hartup, & N. L. Smothergill (Eds.), *The young child.* Washington, D.C.: National Association for the Education of Young Children.

Flavell, J. H. (1973). Reduction of stereotypes by reinforcement of toy play. *Mental Retardation, 11,* 21–23.

Flerx, V. C., Fidler, D. S., & Rogers, R. W. (1976). Sex-role stereotypes: Developmental aspects and early intervention. *Child Development, 46,* 339–347.

Fraiberg, S. (1968). Parallel and divergent patterns in blind and sighted infants. *Psychoanalytic Studies of the Child, 23,* 264.

Fraiberg, S., & Adelson, E. (1973). Self-representation in language and play: Observations of blind children. *Psychoanalytic Quarterly, 42,* 359.

Frampton, M., Kerney, E., & Schattner, R. (1969). *Forgotten children.* Boston: Porter Sargent.

Frost, J. L., & Campbell, S. D. (1978). *Play and equipment choices of conserving and preconserving children on conventional creative playgrounds.* Paper presented at World Congress of the International Playground Association, Ottawa.

Gans, H. (1962). *Urban villagers.* New York: Random House.

Garvey, C. (1974). Some properties of social play. *Merrill-Palmer Quarterly, 20,* 163–180.

Garvey, C., & Hogan, R. (1973). Social speech and social interaction: Egocentrism revisited. *Child Development, 44,* 562–568.

Gerhardt, J. B. (1982). The development of object play and classificatory skills in a blind child. *Visual Impairment and Blindness, 76,* 219–223.

Giddings, M., & Halverson, C. F. (1981). Young children's use of toys in home environments. *Family Relations, 30,* 69–74.

Goldberg, S., & Lewis, M. E. (1969). Play behavior in the year old infant: Early sex differences. *Child Development, 40,* 21–32.

Goldman, J., & Chaille, C. (1981). *Object use in the preschool: An under-developed resource.* Paper presented at Society for Research in Child Development, Boston.

Gorrell, S. (1972). Group data. In R. Kretschmer (Ed.), *A study to assess the play activities and gesture output of hearing handicapped preschool children.* Cincinnati Speech and Hearing Center, U.S. Department of Health, Education and Welfare, Office of Education, Bureau of the Handicapped.

Gottesman, M. (1971). A comparative study of Piaget's developmental schema of sighted children with that of a group of blind children. *Child Development, 42,* 573–580.

Gottesman, M. (1973). Conservation development in blind children. *Child Development, 44,* 824–827.

Gower, J. (1978). *Structural elements of symbolic play of preschool children.* Paper presented at American Educational Research Association, Toronto.

Gralewicz, A. (1973). Play deprivation in multihandicapped children. *American Journal of Occupational Therapy, 27,* 70–72.

Gramza, A. F. (1976). Responses to the manipulability of a play object. *Psychological Reports, 38,* 1109–1110.

Gramza, A. F., & Witt, P. A. (1969). Choices of colored blocks in the play of preschool children. *Perceptual and Motor Skills, 29,* 783–787.

Gramza, A. F., Witt, P. A., Linford, A. G., & Jeanrenaud, C. (1969). Responses of mongoloid children to colored block presentation. *Perceptual and Motor Skills, 29,* 783–787.

Gregory, H. (1976). *The deaf child and his family.* London: Allen and Unwin.

Guerney, L. (1979). Play therapy with learning disabled children. *Journal of Clinical Child Psychology, 28,* 303–310.

Guttentag, M., & Salasin, S. (1977). Women, men and mental health. In L. A. Carter, A. F. Scott, & W. Martyna (Eds.), *Women and men: Changing roles, relationships and perceptions.* New York: Praeger.

Halliday, J., & McNaughton, S. (1982). Sex differences in play at kindergarten. *New Zealand Journal of Educational Studies, 17,* 161–170.

Hannam, C. (1975). *Parents and mentally handicapped children.* Hammondsworth: Penguin.

Harter, S. (1982). The self system and self control. In E. M. Hetherington (Ed.), *Carmichael's manual of child psychology: Social development.* New York: Wiley.

Hartup, W. W. (1979). Peer relations and the growth of social competence. In M. W. Kent, & J. E. Rolf (Eds.), *Social competence in children.* Hanover: University Press of New England.

Hartup, W. W., Moore, S. G., & Sager, G. (1963). Avoidance of inappropriate sex-typing by young children. *Journal of Consulting Psychology, 27,* 467–473.

Haywood, H. C., & Burke, W. P. (1977). Development of individual differences in intrinsic motivation. In I. C. Uzgiris, & F. Weizmann (Eds.), *The structuring of experience.* New York: Plenum.

Heider, F., & Heider, G. M. (1941). Studies in the psychology of the deaf: The language and social behavior of young deaf children. *Psychological Monographs, 242.*

Higginbotham, D. J., & Baker, B. M. (1981). Social participation and cognitive play differences in hearing-impaired and normally hearing preschoolers. *Volta Review, 83,* 135–149.

Hill, P. M., & McCune-Nicolich, L. (1981). Pretend play and patterns of cognition in Down's syndrome children. *Child Development, 52,* 611–617.

Hillman, W. A., Jr. (1966, April). Therapeutic recreation with the profoundly retarded. *Recreation for the Ill and Handicapped.*

Hilton, T. L., & Berglund, G. W. (1971). *Sex differences in mathematics achievement—a longitudinal study.* Princeton: Educational Testing Service.

Hole, V. (1966). *Children's play on housing estates.* London: HMSO.

Honiz, M. P. (1951). Sex differences in the occurrence of materials in the play constructions of preadolescents. *Child Development, 22,* 15–35.

Hopper, C., & Wambold, C. (1978). Improving the independent play of severely mentally retarded children. *Education and Training of the Mentally Retarded,* 42–46.

Horne, B., & Philleo, C. (1942). A comparative study of the spontaneous play activities of normal and mentally defective children. *Journal of Genetic Psychology, 61,* 33–46.

Hudson, L. (1966). *Contrary imaginations.* New York: Schocken.

Hughes, M. (1978). Sequential analysis of exploration and play. *International Journal of Behavioral Development, 1,* 83–97.

Hulme, I., & Lunzer, E. A. (1966). Play, language and reasoning in subnormal children. *Journal of Child Psychology and Psychiatry, 7,* 107.

Huston-Stein, A., Freidrich-Cofer, L., & Susman, E. I. (1977). The relationship of classroom structure to social behavior, imaginative play and self recognition of economically disadvantaged children. *Child Development, 48,* 908–916.

Hutt, C. (1966). Exploration and play in children. *Symposium of the Zoological Society of London, 18,* 61–81.

Hutt, C. (1970). Specific and diverse exploration. In H. Reese, & L. Lipsitt (Eds.), *Advances in child development and behavior.* New York: Academic Press.

Hutt, C. (1979). Exploration and play. In B. Sutton-Smith (Ed.), *Play and learning.* New York: Gardner Press.

Hutt, C., & Bhavnani, R. (1972). Predictions from play. *Nature, 237,* 71.

Hutt, S. J., Hutt, C., Lee, D., & Ounsted, C. (1965). A behavioral and encephalographic study of autistic children. *Journal of Pediatric Research, 3,* 181–197.

Jacklin, C., & Maccoby, F. (1978). Social behavior at thirty-three months in same-sex dyads. *Child Development, 49,* 557–569.

Jacklin, C. N., Maccoby, E. E., & Dick, A. E. (1973). Barrier behaviors and toy preference: Sex differences (and their absence) in the year old child. *Child Development, 44,* 196–200.

Jacobs, J. (1961). *Death and life of great american cities.* New York: Random House.

Jahoda, H., & Goldfab, W. (1957). Use of a standard observation for the psychological evaluation of non-speaking children. *American Journal of Orthopsychiatry, 27,* 745–753.

Jeffree, D., & McConkey, R. (1974). Extending language through play. *Special Education, 1,* 13–16.

Jeffree, D., & McConkey, R. (1976). An observation scheme for recording children's imaginative doll play. *Journal of Child Psychology and Psychiatry, 17,* 189–197.

Johnson, J. E. (1976). Relations of divergent thinking and intelligence tests scores with social and nonsocial make-believe play of preschool children. *Child Development, 47,* 1200–1203.

Jones, O. (1976). Prelinguistic communication in Down's syndrome and normal infants. In H. R. Schaffer (Ed.), *Mother-infant interaction.* London: Academic Press.

Kagan, J. (1971). *Change and continuity in infancy.* New York: Wiley.

Kagan, J., & Lewis, M. (1965). Studies of attention in the human infant. *Merrill-Palmer Quarterly, 11,* 95–137.

Kaminski, L. R. (1973). *Looming effects on stranger anxiety and toy preferences in one-year-old infants.* Unpublished master's thesis, Stanford University, Stanford, CA.

Kanner, L. (1943). Autistic disturbances of affective contact. *Nervous Child, 2,* 217–250.

Kanner, L. (1944). Early infantile autism. *Journal of Pediatrics, 25,* 211–217.

Kanner, L. (1951). A discussion on early infantile autism. *Digest of Neurological Psychiatry, 19,* 158–159.

Kanner, L. (1973). *Childhood psychosis: Initial studies and new insights.* Washington: Winston.

Kantosky, M. A. (1976). *A behavioral method for assessing overactivity in hyperactive children.* Unpublished master's thesis, University of Wisconsin.

Keeran, C. V., Jr., Grove, F. A., & Zachofsky, T. (1969). Assessing the playground skills of the severely retarded. *Mental Retardation,* 29–32.

Kirk, S. A., & Johnson, G. O. (1951). *Educating the retarded child.* Cambridge: Houghton-Mifflin.

Knapczyk, D. R., & Yoppi, J. O. (1975). Development of cooperative and competitive play responses in developmentally disabled children. *American Journal of Mental Deficiency, 80,* 245–255.

Koegel, R. L., Firestone, P. B., Kramme, K. W., & Dunlap, G. (1974). Increasing spontaneous play by suppressing self-stimulation in autistic children. *Journal of Applied Behavior Analysis, 7,* 521–528.

Kretschmer, R. (1972). *A study to assess the play activities and output of hearing handicapped preschool children.* Cincinnati Speech and Hearing Center, U.S. Department of Health, Education and Welfare, Office of Education, Bureau of the Handicapped.

Kutner, N. G., & Levinson, R. M. (1978). The toy salesperson: A voice for change in sex-role stereotypes? *Sex Roles, 4,* 1–7.

Lamb, M. E., & Roopnarine, J. L. (1979). Peer influences on sex-role development in preschoolers. *Child Development, 50,* 1219–1222.

Laosa, L., & Brophy, J. E. (1972). Effects of sex and birth order on sex-role development and intelligence among kindergarten children. *Developmental Psychology, 6,* 409–415.

Lehman, H. C., & Witty, P. A. (1927). The play behavior of fifty gifted children. *Journal of Educational Psychology, 18,* 259–265.

Lennenberg, E. H. (1967). *Biological foundations of language.* New York: Wiley.

Lever, J. (1978). Sex differences in the complexity of children's play and games. *American Sociological Review, 43,* 471–483.

Levinson, R. M. (1975). From Olive Oil to sweet Polly Purebread: Sex-role stereotypes and televised cartoons. *Journal of Popular Culture, 9,* 561–572.

Levitt, E. E. (1971). Research on psychotherapy with children. In A. E. Bergin, & S. L. Garfield (Eds.), *Handbook of psychotherapy and behavior change.* New York: Wiley.

Lewin, K. (1931). Environmental forces in child behavior and development. In C. Murchison (Ed.), *A handbook of child psychology.* Worcester: Clark University Press.

Li, A. K. F. (1978). Effects of play on novel responses of preschool children. *Alberta Journal of Educational Research, 24,* 31–36.

Lieberman, J. N. (1964). *Playfulness and divergent thinking: An investigation of their relationship at the kindergarten level.* Unpublished doctoral dissertation, Columbia University, New York.

Lieberman, J. N. (1965). The relationship between playfulness and divergent thinking at the kindergarten level. *Journal of Genetic Psychology, 107,* 219–224.

Lieberman, J. N. (1977). *Playfulness: Its relationship to imagination and creativity.* New York: Academic Press.

Liebert, R. M., McCall, R. B., & Hanratty, M. A. (1971). Effects of sex-typed information on children's toy preference. *Journal of Genetic Psychology, 119,* 133–136.

Loomis, E. A., Hilgeman, L. M., & Meyer, L. R. (1957). Play patterns as nonverbal indices of ego functions: A preliminary report. *American Journal of Orthopsychiatry, 27,* 691–700.

Lovaas, O. I., Koegel, R., Simmons, J. Q., & Long, J. S. (1973). Some generalization and follow-up measures on autistic children in behavior therapy. *Journal of Applied Behavior Analysis, 6,* 131–166.

Lovell, K., Hoyle, H. W., & Siddal, M. Q. (1968). A study of some aspects of play and language of young children with delayed speech. *Journal of Child Psychology and Psychiatry, 9,* 41.

Lowe, M. (1975). Trends in the development of representational play in infants from one to three years—an observational study. *Journal of Child Psychology and Psychiatry, 16,* 33–48.

Luria, A. R., & Yudovitch, F. (1971). *Speech and the development of mental processes in the child.* Harmondsworth: Penguin.

Lynch, K. (1977). *Growing up in cities.* Cambridge, MA: Institute of Technology Press.

Maccoby, E. E., & Jacklin, C. N. (1973). Stress, activity and proximity seeking: Sex differences in the year old child. *Child Development, 44,* 34–42.

Maccoby, E. E., & Jacklin, C. N. (1974). *The Psychology of sex differences.* Standord: Stanford University Press.

Malone, C. A. (1963). Some observations on children of disorganized families and problems of acting out. *Journal of the American Academy of Child Psychiatry, 2,* 22.

Marshall, H. (1961). Relations between home experiences and children's use of language in play interactions with peers. *Psychological Monographs, 75,* 1–77.

Martensson, B. (1972). *Observator of outdoor activities in some housing areas.* Stockholm: Swedish National Institute of Building Research.

Masters, J. C., Ford, M. E., Arend, R., Grotevant, H. D., & Clark, L. V. (1979). Modeling and labeling as integrated determinants of children's sex-typed imitative behavior. *Child Development, 50,* 364–371.

Matterson, E. M. (1966). *Play with a purpose for under-sevens.* Harmondsworth: Penguin.

Matterson, E. M. (1968). *Play and playthings for the preschool child.* Baltimore: Penguin.

Matthews, W. S. (1977). Modes of transformation in the initiation of fantasy play. *Developmental Psychology, 13,* 211–216.

Maurer, R., & Baxter, J. C. (1972). Images of the neighborhood and city among Black, Anglo and Mexican-American children. *Environment and Behavior, 4,* 351–388.

McCall, R. B. (1974). Exploratory manipulation and play in the human infant. *Monographs of the Society for Research in Child Development, 39,* 1–87.

McCoull, G. (1971). *Newcastle upon Tyne regional aetiological survey (mental retardation).* Newcastle upon Tyne, Newcastle upon Tyne Regional Health Committee.

McGrew, W. (1972). *An ethological study of children's behavior.* New York: Academic Press.

Meehl, P. E., Lykken, D. T., Schofield, W., & Tellegen, A. (1971). Recaptured—in technique (RIT): A method for reducing somewhat the subjective element in factor naming. *Journal of Experimental Research in Personality, 5,* 171–190.

Mergen, B. (1977). From play to recreation: The acceptance of leisure in the United States. In P. Stevens (Ed.), *Studies in the anthropology of play.* New York: Leisure Press.

Messer, S. B., & Lewis, M. (1972). Social class and sex differences in the attachment and play behavior of the year-old infant. *Merrill-Palmer Quarterly, 18,* 295–306.

Michaels, J. J. (1955). *Disorders of character: Persistent enuresis, juvenile delinquency and psychopathic personality.* Springfield, IL: Thomas.

Miller, C. K. (1969). Conservation of the blind. *Education of the Visually Handicapped, 1,* 101–110.

Mindel, E., & Vernon, M. (1971). *They grow in silence.* Silver Springs, MD: National Association of the Deaf.

Minuchin, P., Biber, B., Shapiro, E., & Zimiles, H. (1969). *The psychological impact of school experience.* New York: Basic Books.

Mogford, K. (1977). The play of handicapped children. In B. Tizard, & D. Harvey (Eds.), *Biology of play.* London: William Heinemann Medical Books.

Mueller, E. (1972). The maintenance of verbal exchanges between young children. *Child Development, 43,* 930–938.

Nelsen, E. A., & Rosenbaum, E. (1972). Language patterns within the youth subculture: Development of slang vocabularies. *Merrill-Palmer Quarterly, 18,* 273–285.

Newson, E., & Newson, J. (1970). *Four year olds in an urban community.* Hammondsworth: Penguin.

Nicolich, L. (1977). Beyond sensorimotor intelligence: Assessment of symbolic maturity through analysis of pretend play. *Merrill-Palmer Quarterly, 23,* 89–101.

Odom, S. L. (1981). The relationship of play to developmental levels in mentally retarded, preschool children. *Education and Training of the Mentally Retarded, 16,* 136–141.

Opie, I., & Opie, P. (1969). *Children's games in street and playground.* London: University Press.

Paloutzian, R. F., Hasazi, J., Streifel, J., & Edgar, C. (1971). Promotion of positive social interaction in severely retarded young children. *American Journal of Mental Deficiency, 75,* 519–524.

Parten, M. B. (1932). Social play among preschool children. *Journal of Abnormal and Social Psychology, 28,* 136–147.

Pederson, F. A., & Bell, R. Q. (1970). Sex differences in preschool children without histories of complications of pregnancy and delivery. *Developmental Psychology, 3,* 10–15.

Pepler, D. J. (1979). *The effects of play on convergent and divergent problem solving.* Unpublished doctoral dissertation, University of Waterloo.

Pepler, D. J., & Ross, H. S. (1981). The effects of play on convergent and divergent problem solving. *Child Development, 52,* 1202–1210.

Phemister, M. R., Richardson, A. M., & Thomas, G. V. (1978). Observations of young normal and handicapped children. *Child Care, Health and Development, 4,* 247–259.

Phyfe-Perkins, E. (1980). Children's behavior in preschool settings: A review of research concerning the influence of the physical environment. In L. Katz (Ed.), *Current topics in early childhood education.* Norwood, NJ: Ablex.

Piaget, J. (1932). *The moral judgment of the child.* New York: Free Press.

Piaget, J. (1962). *Play, dreams and imitation in childhood.* New York: Norton.

Piaget, J. (1952). *The origin of intelligence.* New York: Norton.

Piaget, J. (1967). *Six psychological studies.* New York: Random House.

Piaget, J. (1970). Piaget's theory. In P. H. Mussen (Ed.), *Carmichael's manual of child psychology.* New York: Wiley.

Pintler, M. H. (1945). Doll-play as a function of experimenter-child interaction and initial organization of the materials. *Child Development, 16,* 146–166.

Pulaski, M. A. (1970). Play as a function of toy structure and fantasy predisposition. *Child Development, 41,* 531–537.

Pulaski, M. A. (1973). Toys and imaginative play. In J. Singer (Ed.), *The child's world of make-believe.* New York: Academic Press.

Rabban, M. (1950). Sex-role identification in young children in two diverse social groups. *Genetic Psychology Monographs, 42,* 81–158.

Redl, F., & Wineman, D. (1951). *Children who hate: The disorganization and breakdown of behavior controls.* New York: Free Press.

Rheingold, H. L., & Cook, K. V. (1975). The content of boys' and girls' rooms as an index of parents' behavior. *Child Development, 46,* 459–463.

Rheingold, H. L., & Eckerman, C. O. (1969). The infant's free entry into a new environment. *Journal of Experimental Child Psychology, 8,* 271–283.

Richardson, A. M., Reid, G., Phemister, M. R., & Thomas, G. V. (1981). Play materials for mentally handicapped children. *Child Care, Health and Development, 7,* 317–330.

Riguet, C. B., Taylor, N. D., Benaroya, S., & Klein, L. S. (1981). Symbolic play in autistic, Down's and normal children of equivalent mental age. *Journal of Autism and Developmental Disorders, 11,* 439–448.

Rimland, B. (1964). *Infantile autism.* New York: Appleton-Century-Crofts.

Ritvo, E. R. (1976). *Autism: Diagnosis, current research and management.* New York: Spectrum Press.

Roberts, M. A. (1979). *A behavioral method for differentiating hyperactive, aggressive and hyperactive plus aggressive children.* Unpublished doctoral dissertation, University of Wisconsin, Madison.

Rocissano, L. (1979). *Object play and its relation to language in early childhood.* Unpublished doctoral dissertation, Columbia University, New York.

Rogow, S. M. (1981). Developing play skills and communicative competence in multiply handicapped young people. *Visual Impairment and Blindness, 75,* 197–202.

Romanczyk, R. G., Diament, C., Goren, E. R., Trunell, G., & Harris, S. L. (1975). Increasing isolate and social play in severely disturbed children: Intervention and postintervention effectiveness. *Journal of Autism and Childhood Schizophrenia, 5,* 57–70.

Rosen, C. E. (1974). The effects of sociodramatic play on problem solving behavior among culturally disadvantaged children. *Child Development, 45,* 920–927.

Rosenberg, B. G., & Sutton-Smith, B. (1960). A revised conception of masculine-feminine differences in play activities. *Journal of Genetic Psychology, 96,* 165–170.

Rosenblatt, D. (1977). Developmental trends in infant play. In B. Tizard, & D. Harvey (Eds.), *Biology of play.* London: William Heinemann Medical Books.

Rosenzweig, L. (1954). Report of a school program for trainable mentally retarded children. *Journal of Mental Deficiency, 59,* 181–205.

Ross, D. (1970). Incidental learning of number concepts in small group games. *American Journal of Mental Deficiency, 74,* 718–725.

Routh, D. K., Schroeder, C. S., & O'Tuama, L. A. (1974). Development of activity level in children. *Developmental Psychology, 2,* 163–168.

Rubin, K. H., & Seibel, C. (1979). *The effects of ecological settings on the cognitive and social play behaviors of preschoolers.* Paper presented at American Educational Research Association, San Francisco.

Rubin, K. H., Fein, G. G., & Vandenberg, B. (1982). Play. In E. M. Hetherington (Ed.), *Carmichael's manual of child psychology.* New York: Wiley.

Rutter, M. (1972). The effects of language delay on development. In M. Rutter, &

J. A. M. Martin (Eds.), *The child with delayed speech: Clinics in developmental medicine.* London: SIMP.

Rutter, M. (1978). Diagnosis and definition. In M. Rutter, & E. Schopler (Eds.), *Autism: A reappraisal of concepts and treatment.* New York: Plenum.

Rutter, M., Bartak, L., & Newman, S. (1971). Autism: A central disorder of cognition and language. In M. Rutter (Ed.), *Infantile autism: Concepts, characteristics and treatment.* Edinburgh: Churchill Livingstone.

Sandler, A., & Wills, D. M. (1965). Preliminary notes on play and mastery in the blind child. *Journal of Child Psychotherapy, 1,* 7.

Sanoff, H., & Dickerson, J. (1971). Mapping children's behavior in a residential setting. *Journal of Architectural Education, 25,* 98–103.

Schachter, F. F., Meyer, L. R., & Loomis, E. A. (1962). Childhood schizophrenia and mental retardation: Differential diagnosis before and after one year of psychotherapy. *American Journal of Orthopsychiatry, 32,* 584–595.

Schaefer, C. E. (1976). *Therapeutic use of child's play.* New York: Aronson.

Schaefer, C. E., & O'Connor, K. J. (1983). *Handbook of play therapy.* New York: Wiley.

Schlossberg, N. K., & Goodman, J. A. (1972). Woman's place: Children's sex stereotyping of occupations. *Vocational Guidance Quarterly, 20,* 266–270.

Schlottman, R. S., & Anderson, V. H. (1975). Social and play behaviors of institutionalized mongoloid and nonmongoloid children. *Journal of Psychology, 91,* 201–206.

Schwarz, J. C. (1972). Effects of peer familiarity on the behavior of preschoolers in a novel situation. *Journal of Personality and Social Psychology, 24,* 276–284.

Sears, R. R., Rau, L., & Alpert, R. (1965). *Identification and child rearing.* Stanford: Stanford University Press.

Serbin, L. A., Connor, J. M., & Citron, C. C. (1981). Sex-differentiated free play behavior: Effects on teacher modeling, location and gender. *Developmental Psychology, 17,* 640–646.

Serbin, L. A., Connor, J. M., Burchardt, C. J., & Citron, C. C. (1979). Effects of peer presence on sex-typing of children's play behavior. *Journal of Experimental Child Psychology, 27,* 303–309.

Shantz, C. U. (1975). The development of social cognition. In E. M. Hetherington (Ed.), *Review of child development research.* Chicago: University of Chicago Press.

Sheridan, M. D. (1975). The Stycar language test. *Developments in Medicine and Child Neurology, 17,* 164–174.

Sherman, J. A. (1967). Problems of sex differences in space perception and aspects of intellectual functioning. *Psychological Review, 74,* 290–299.

Sigman, M., & Ungerer, J. (1981). Sensorimotor skills and language comprehension in autistic children. *Journal of Abnormal Child Psychology, 9,* 149–165.

Singer, D. G., & Singer, J. L. (1978). *Some correlates of imaginative play in preschoolers.* Paper presented at American Psychological Association, Toronto.

Singer, D. G., & Rummo, J. (1973). Identical creativity and behavioral style in kindergarten aged children. *Developmental Psychology, 8,* 154–161.

Singer, J. L. (1973). *The child's world of make-believe: Experimental studies of imaginative play.* New York: Academic Press.

Singer, J. L., & Streiner, B. F. (1966). Imaginative content in the dreams and fantasy play of blind and sighted children. *Perceptual and Motor Skills, 22,* 475–482.

Singer, J. L., Singer, D. G., & Sherrod, L. R. (1980). A factor analytic study of preschoolers' play behavior. *American Psychology Bulletin, 2,* 143–156.

Smith, A. B. (1980). The family, schools and sex roles. In G. H. Robinson, & B. T. O'Rourke (Eds.), *Schools in New Zealand societies — a book of readings.* Auckland: Longman Paul.

Smith, P. K., & Connolly, K. (1972). Patterns of play and social interaction in preschool children. In N. Blurton-Jones (Ed.), *Ethological studies of child behavior.* Cambridge: Cambridge University Press.

Smith, P. K., & Connolly, K. (1980). *The ecology of preschool behavior.* Cambridge: Cambridge University Press.

Smith, P. K., & Dutton, S. (1979). Play and training in direct and innovative problem-solving. *Child Development, 50,* 830–836.

Soddy, K. (1960). *Clinical child psychiatry.* London: Bailliere, Tindall and Cox.

Streisel, I. M., Weiland, I. H., Denny, J. V., Smith, K., & Chaiken, N. (1960). Measuring interaction in nonverbal psychotic children. *American Journal of Orthopsychiatry, 30,* 405–411.

Suomi, S. J. (1979). Peers, play and primary prevention in primates. In M. W. Kent, & J. E. Rolf (Eds.), *Social competence in children.* Hanover: University Press of New England.

Sutton-Smith, B. (1968). Novel responses to toys. *Merrill-Palmer Quarterly, 14,* 151–158.

Switzky, H. N., Ludwig, L., & Haywood, H. C. (1979). Exploration and play in retarded and nonretarded preschool children: Effects of object complexity and age. *American Journal of Mental Deficiency, 83,* 637–644.

Sylva, K. (1977). Play and learning. In B. Tizard, & D. Harvey (Eds.), *Biology of play.* London: William Heinemann Medical Books.

Sylva, K., Bruner, J., & Genova, P. (1976). The role of play in the problem-solving of children 3–5 years old. In J. Bruner, A. Jolly, & K. Sylva (Eds.), *Play — its role in development and evolution.* New York: Penguin.

Szal, J. A. (1972). *Sex differences in the cooperative and competitive behaviors of nursery school children.* Unpublished master's thesis, Stanford University.

Tait, P. (1972a). The implications of play as it relates to the emotional development of the blind child. *Education of the Visually Handicapped, 10,* 52–54.

Tait, P. (1972b). Behavior of young children in a controlled play session. *Perceptual and Motor Skills, 34,* 963–969.

Tait, P. (1973). Play and the intellectual development of blind children. *New Outlook for the Blind, 66,* 361–369.

Takata, N. (1971). The play milieu: A preliminary appraisal. *American Journal of Occupational Therapy, 25,* 281–284.

Teglasi, H. (1981). Children's choices of and value judgments about sex-typed toys and occupations. *Journal of Vocational Behavior, 18,* 184–195.

Terman, L. M. (1926). *Genetic studies of genious: Mental and physical traits of a thousand gifted children.* Stanford: Stanford University Press.

Thomas, A., Chess, S., & Birch, H. G. (1968). *Temperament and behavior disorders in children.* New York: New York University Press.

Thomas, G. V., Phemister, M. R., & Richardson, A. M. (1981). Some conditions affecting manipulative play with objects in severely mentally handicapped children. *Child Care, Health and Development, 7,* 1–20.

Thompson, A. R., & Wade, M. G. (1974). Real play and fantasy play as modified by social and environmental complexity in normal and hyperactive children. *Therapeutic Recreation Journal, 8,* 160–167.

Tilton, J. R., & Ottinger, D. R. (1964). Comparison of the toy play behavior of autistic, retarded and normal children. *Psychological Reports, 15,* 967–975.

Tizard, J. (1960a). Residential care of mentally handicapped children. *British Medical Journal, 1,* 1040–1046.

Tizard, J. (1960b, July). *The residential care of mentally handicapped children.* Paper presented at London Conference on the Scientific Aspects of Mental Deficiency.

Tizard, B. (1977). Play: The child's way of learning? In B. Tizard, & D. Harvey (Eds.), *Biology of play.* London: William Heinemann Medical Books.

Tobin, M. U. (1972). Conservation of substance in the blind and partially sighted. *British Journal of Educational Psychology, 42,* 192–197.

Turner, C. W., & Goldsmith, D. (1976). Effects of toy guns and airplanes on children's antisocial free play behavior. *Journal of Experimental Child Psychology, 21,* 303–315.

Ungar, S. B. (1982). The sex-typing of adult and child behavior in toy sales. *Sex Roles, 8,* 251–260.

Ungerer, J., & Sigman, M. (1981). Symbolic play and language in autistic children. *Journal of the American Academy of Child Psychiatry, 20,* 318–337.

Urberg, K. A., & Docherty, E. M. (1976). Development of role-taking skills in young children. *Developmental Psychology, 12,* 198–203.

Vance, T., & McCall, L. (1934). Children's preferences among play materials as determined by the method of paired comparisons of pictures. *Child Development, 5,* 267–277.

Vandenberg, B. (1978). Play and development from an ethological perspective. *American Psychologist, 33,* 724–738.

Vandenberg, B. (1980a). Play, problem-solving and creativity. In K. H. Rubin (Ed.), *Children's play: New directions for child development.* San Francisco: Jossey-Bass.

Vandenberg, B. (1980b). *Play: A causal agent in problem solving?* Paper presented at the American Psychological Association, Montreal.

Vandenberg, B. (1981). The role of play in the development of insightful tool-using strategies. *Merrill-Palmer Quarterly, 27,* 97–110.

Vanderkooij, R. (1979). Study of the play behavior of retarded children. *Acta Paedopsychiatrica, 45,* 25–42.

Vlietstra, A. (1980). Effects of adult-directed activity, number of toys and sex of child on social and exploratory behavior in young children. *Merrill-Palmer Quarterly, 26,* 231–238.

Vygotsky, L. S. (1962). *Thought and language.* Cambridge: MIT Press.

Walberg, H. J. (1969). Physics, femininity and creativity. *Developmental Psychology, 1,* 47–54.

Ward, W. D. (1969). Process of sex-role development. *Developmental Psychology, 1,* 1963–1968.

Wehman, P. (1977). *Helping the mentally retarded acquire play skills.* Springfield: Thomas.

Weiner, B. J., Ottinger, D. R., & Tilton, J. R. (1969). Comparison of the toy play behavior of autistic, retarded and normal children: A reanalysis. *Psychological Reports, 25,* 223–227.

Weiner, E. A., & Weiner, B. J. (1974). Differentiation of retarded and normal children through toy-play analysis. *Multivariate Behavioral Research,* 245–252.

Weisler, A., & McCall, R. B. (1976). Exploration and play. *American Psychologist, 31,* 492–508.

Weitzman, L., Eifler, D., Hokada, E., & Ross, C. (1972). Sex-role socialization in picture books for preschool children. *American Journal of Sociology, 77,* 1125–1150.

Werner, H., & Kaplan, B. (1963). *Symbol formation: An organismic-developmental approach to language and the expression of thought.* New York: Wiley.

White, P. T., DeMyer, W., & DeMyer, M. (1964). EEG abnormalities in early childhood schizophrenia: A double-blind study of psychiatrically disturbed and normal children during promazine sedation. *American Journal of Psychiatry, 120,* 950–958.

White, R. W. (1959). Motivation reconsidered: The concept of competence. *Psychological Review, 66,* 297–323.

Whitman, T. L., Mercurio, J. R., & Caponigri, V. (1970). Development of social responses in two severely retarded children. *Journal of Applied Behavior Analysis, 3,* 133–138.

Whittaker, C. A. (1979). *Piagetian sensori-motor level activities in relation to language and symbolic play in profoundly retarded hospitalized children.* M. Ed. Thesis, University of Newcastle upon Tyne.

Whittaker, C. A. (1980). A note on developmental trends in the symbolic play of hospitalized profoundly retarded children. *Journal of Child Psychology and Psychiatry, 21,* 253–261.

Wills, D. M. (1972). Problems of play and mastery in the blind child. In E. P. Trapp, & P. Himelstein (Eds.), *Readings on the exceptional child.* New York: Appleton-Century-Crofts.

Wing, L. (1978). Social, behavioral and cognitive characteristics. In M. Rutter, & E. Schopler (Eds.), *Autism: A reappraisal of concepts and treatment.* New York: Plenum.

Wing, L., Gould, J., Yeates, S., & Brierley, L. (1977). Symbolic play in severely mentally retarded and in autistic children. *Journal of Child Psychology and Psychiatry, 18,* 167–178.

Winner, E., McCarthy, M., Kleinman, S., & Gardner, H. (1979). First metaphors. *New Directions in Child Development, 1,* 29–41.

Winnicott, D. W. (1965). *The maturational processes and the facilitating environment.* London: Hogarth.

Winnicott, D. W. (1971). *Playing and reality.* London: Tavistock.

Wohlford, P., Santrock, J. W., Berger, S. E., & Liberman, D. (1971). Older brother's influences on sex-typed, aggressive and dependent behavior in father-absent children. *Developmental Psychology, 4,* 124–134.

Woodward, M., & Hunt, M. (1972). Exploratory studies of early cognitive development. *British Journal of Educational Psychology, 42,* 248–259.

Wright, M. J. (1980). Measuring the social competence of preschool children. *Canadian Journal of Behavioral Science, 12,* 17–32.

Zigler, E. (1966). Mental retardation: Current issues and approaches. In L. W. Hoffman, & M. L. Hoffman (Eds.), *Review of child development research.* New York: Sage.

Zigler, E. (1967). Familial mental retardation: A continuing dilemma. m1122ience, *155,* 292–298.

Chapter IV

MENTAL RETARDATION AS A CONSTRAINT ON LEISURE

MICHAEL G. WADE AND JOHN H. HOOVER

Introduction

Where possible, the present chapter focusses on the leisure behavior of people in the moderate and severe ranges of mental retardation. An exception to this generalization is when research undertaken with mildly handicapped subjects generalizes to the lower ranges of the disability. Neither the construct of mental retardation nor the "border" between levels of mental handicap lend themselves to non-controversial definition, and it is not our purpose to expand on these debates here. However, the nature of mental retardation will be examined to the extent that it pertains to use of leisure-time by persons with the disability. An example of this distinction would be the case where mentally handicapped persons were being taught to play a game that contained a considerable cognitive component (cf. Spitz, 1979). Here, the nature of retardation may constrain the ability to play (and, we will argue, to enjoy) the game. Primarily, the population of concern here consists of those persons with moderate and severe mental retardation—that is to say, those with IQ's below about 55.

The chapter is divided into three sections; the first deals with what might be termed "external" constraints on effective leisure pursuits by mentally handicapped individuals. Under this heading fall the topics of institutionalization and societal attitudes. The second section is concerned with leisure-constraints that may be posited "within" the individual; here we discuss physical constraints, such as fitness and motor skill deficits; another "internal" constraint that will be addressed is the role of cognitive disabilities in constraining the ability of mentally handicapped individuals to beneficially utilize non-work time. A discussion of the capacity of mentally retarded persons to experience enjoyment is included in the "internal constraints" subheading. Finally, the third section considers training and trainability in leisure-oriented skills. We recognize the arbitrary nature of the "internal-external" dichotomy; observed behavior in leisure settings clearly represents an interaction between those elements contained "in" the environment and those abilities brought to particular ecologies by individuals. Thus, chapter headings merely represent an operationally useful way to categorize information about these interactions.

I. External Constraints

A. Institutionalization

According to Wade and Gold (1978), who were primarily addressing the vocational domain, the dominant clinical opinion of the '50's and '60's was that moderately and severely mentally handicapped individuals were unable to perform basic skills. This sense of hopelessness was due to the observed difficulty of training mentally handicapped persons to perform moderately complex tasks and reflected the ethos of treatment in general at that time. Many mentally retarded individuals were warehoused in large institutions, where "care" (though dubious, at best) was stressed over training and education. Though the trend has, of late, been away from institutionalization (and toward "training"), the issue remains with us (Thompson, 1977). Thus, we may ask: What is the effect of institutionalization upon leisure behavior?

There is some evidence to suggest that institutionalization, of itself, may have a negative impact on residents. Thompson (1977), in a literature review, concluded that—"institutionalization can actually cause, or promote the development of retardation" (p. 7). While this is debatable there is little doubt that the various factors inherent in an institutional setting, such as size (Baroff, 1980), aggregate living and group dining are different than community life; certainly, these factors will impact upon the use of free time. Raw and Erickson (1977) noted, for example that large institutions will "generate obstacles to the establishment of recreational and other programs designed to promote maximum development" (p. 380). Wehman (1975) reported that institutionalized retarded children engaged in few play behaviors; he attributed this to the ward staff's attitude.

Institutional settings appear to generate considerable free time for their clients. Klaber (1969), felt that these nonprogrammed hours were inefficiently utilized; he reported that severely retarded residents did nothing or very little 33 to 50 percent of the time. Scheer (1968) stated that, "one of the most brutally true criticisms of institutional life is the boredom that takes place within the dormitory existence of the residents" (p. 26). Some writers have argued that lack of stimulation on wards produces self-stimulatory and self-injurious behaviors (Ball, Hendrickson, & Clayton, 1974; Frankel & Simmons, 1976). Nesbitt, Neal, and Hillman (1974) argued that if this "free time" is to exist, it should be put to use by encouraging mentally handicapped persons to develop and learn.

Oblique evidence for the pejorative impact of institutionalization on leisure can be found in studies where levels of "boredom" were systematically reduced. Ball, Hendrickson, and Clayton (1974) reported a feeding technique that decreased occurrences of chronic regurgitation to near zero:

> The attendant's technique . . . emphasized the subjects' active participation in the feeding process. The bottle remained in his mouth and he engaged in active biting movements. At times the nipple was playfully thrust in and out between the teeth and a teasing "tug of war" ensued—(Ball et al., p. 488).

Ball's feeding technique can be interpreted as producing a reduction in the boring conditions under which many institutional activities take place; it was playful.

Finger biting and face slapping behaviors in profoundly retarded subjects have been reduced via toy use (Strain, 1975). The effect produced by access to toys in this study was further enhanced when one subject was differentially reinforced for interacting with the playthings. Similar results with self injurious behaviors have been elsewhere reported (Hewson, McConkey, & Jeffree, 1980; Horner, 1980; Mulick, Hoyt, Rojan, & Schroeder, 1978).

Favell (1976) reduced stereotypic behaviors in institutionalized children by replacing them with reinforced toy play. Similarly, Quilitch and Gray (1974) found that purposeful activity increased on a state hospital ward among profoundly mentally handicapped residents as a function of the introduction of activities centered around toys and simple crafts. Most interesting is that the new, more directed actions noted by investigators generalized to such domains as attention span, eye contact, and pro-social behavior.

Rowe (1976) conducted a study of institutional environments in an English hospital where, she argued, the living conditions could be characterized as non-stimulating. When the general level of stimulation was increased by means of training in recreation and leisure activities, an accompanying increase in adaptive behavior was noted.

Institutional environments may be characterized by a great deal of unstructured time, minimal training in leisure-oriented skills, and staff attitudes that may be resistant to programming. To the extent that these factors are true for a given program, it is clear that the ability of handicapped residents to enjoy fruitful leisure time there will be reduced. However, as society becomes more enlightened regarding these issues, the leisure-oriented problems encountered by handicapped persons will move out of the institution and into the community. The attitudes held by members of society toward mentally retarded persons will be primary among these factors.

B. Societal Attitudes

Whether because of increased favorable publicity or as a result of more contact with handicapped persons, lay persons appear to hold more benevolent attitudes toward retarded persons than in past years. The passage of P.L. 94-142 is a case where improved attitudes have been translated into public policy. However, several issues must be raised about this observation.

First, there is a question whether people are willing to reveal how they really feel about a *weak* group in attitude surveys. Perhaps, many respondents view mentally handicapped persons as intrinsically weak and will thus "protect" them by answering opinion surveys more benevolently than they really feel. Second, even if attitudes are deeply held, and the respondents really believe that they "feel that way" about handicapped persons, these factors may not be sufficient to motivate behavior. It is interesting that in a society awash in good feelings about mentally handicapped individuals, neighbors will still resist the advent of group homes near them and large, austere state hospitals still house thousands of retarded persons. So while it is difficult to induce householders to say pejorative things about retarded people, it is worthwhile to examine the *reality* of the leisure experience in communities; the mere presence of retarded persons in a community does not imply that meaningful and enjoyable opportunities become magically available to them.

Stanfield (1973) investigated the community lives of 120 special education high school graduates. These individuals ranged in age from 19 to 21 years, and all fell within the moderate range of mental retardation. Ninety-four percent of the adults were living with their families. When interviewed about the leisure-oriented activities of their offspring, parents related most often that the graduates participated in activities like "watching television, listening to records and the radio, and looking at books and magazines" (p. 551).

Interestingly, it appears that the noted lack of integration during leisure hours that mentally handicapped persons experience is a phenomenon of western culture, not only a North American one. Katz and Yekutiel (1974) attained similar results in an Israeli study, including the intuitive finding that "a lack of interest in leisure time activity was especially conspicuous among the institutionalized" (p. 55). Owen (1977), in Britain, concluded that mentally handicapped persons held leisure interests, "in line with those of the population as a whole" (p. 151). He noted also, however, that more of their life-style revolved around the place of residence than appears to be true in the general population. Owen ascribed this finding to a "disconcerting continuation of the same life-style as that previously practised in hospital" (p. 151).

It is disarmingly simple to accept Owen's hypothesis for the American data reported by Stanfield and others; that is, to blame institutional life for a lack of preparation for recreation in the community. But none of Stanfield's subjects had been institutionalized. Obviously, the complex factors determining leisure behaviors cannot be entirely explained via institutionalization. Given that the public attitude towards "appropriateness" impacts upon opportunity, these attitudes will go a long way toward explaining any differences noted between the mentally handicapped population and their age-peers in leisure life-style. It appears that mentally retarded people are not getting to the park. We must ask: Why not? Part of the blame must be placed on limiting factors in the public's attitude. This is particularly the case if retarded persons report similar leisure interests to the rest of society (Owen, 1977), but participate in different activities. It is impossible to escape the conclusion that societal attitudes are a constraining influence on leisure for deinstitutionalized retarded persons.

Like that of institutionalization, the attitude explanation for constraints on leisure is too simple. We would argue that, even in a perfect world, a Utopia where no conscious or unconscious roadblocks were placed in the way of handicapped persons, some differences in leisure orientation would exist. In Owen's study, for example, it was reported that retarded persons at all levels held leisure interests not unlike those of the general population. However, some significant differences were noted, even between the levels of mental retardation. For example, more mildly handicapped individuals were interested in reading during their spare time than were moderately retarded persons. To the extent that reading is a worthwhile leisure pursuit, then retardation itself probably represents a constraint on this class of behaviors. Of course the "interaction" with social values remains important, in that attitudes preventing retarded persons from learning to read (for example, the belief that they are unable to do so), would be significant, over and above the absolute effect(s) of ability. We believe, however, that ability *is* important; and that leads us to the section on "internal constraints" wherein physical fitness, motor skills, and cognitive factors are discussed in the context of their potential to constrain leisure behavior.

II. Internal Constraints on Leisure Behavior

This section of the chapter focuses on three elements of behavior. One of these is the physiological make-up of the mentally handicapped individual and how that is reflected in a limitation on the expression of physical activity, as well as the role of physical fitness in leisure time activities. A second element discussed is the constraints placed on the leisure experience by poor motor skill expression. A third element is the constraints placed on the leisure behavior of the mentally handicapped individual by the integrity of his or her cognitive apparatus. This final section, of course, assumes a hierarchical control over the development of, and expression of, motor skills. All forms of action are representative of cognitive intent and, therefore, motor skill expression will be affected by cognitive disability. Even the ability to become physically fit may be governed by cognitive processes.

A. Physical Fitness

There can be little doubt that the literature of the past decade clearly indicates the enormous benefits of physical fitness activities for maintaining the efficiency, and some would claim the longevity, of the human physiological system. Despite the benefits of vigorous physical activity, it should not be assumed that such activities are automatically enjoyable. The use of vigorous activities with mentally handicapped individuals, while perhaps being physiologically beneficial, may not be spiritually uplifting!

We are currently in an era of obsession with our health and our appearance. It seems only a matter of weeks go by when yet another svelte movie star brings out either a book or record on physical fitness which is designed to exort his or her fans to even greater heights of physical activity and thereby open the doors to all kinds of wonderful opportunities. It is not surprising, therefore that physical fitness programs for mentally handicapped persons are also in their own ways quite popular and regarded as beneficial for participants; there is probably no dissuading argument from a physiological perspective. The vast majority of those labeled mentally handicapped have essentially intact physiological systems and therefore are subject to the simple laws of progressive resistance overload. Heart rates can be lowered, muscle tone can be improved, and the overall physiological status of the individual may be upgraded. The question for the mentally handicapped individual is whether these undoubted physiological benefits are in concert with his or her own personal feelings of well being. This, in large part, is dealt with later in this section when we talk about the ability of the mentally retarded to experience enjoyment, a feeling many of the nonretarded proponents of physical fitness say they experience!

In a recent review of physical fitness of the mentally handicapped, Moon and Renzaglia (1982) trace completed research on the physical fitness of mentally retarded persons from the early work of Brace (1927) up to more recent reviews (cf. Londeree & Johnson, 1974). They reported that beyond a general agreement that maintaining levels of physical fitness was desirable for mentally handicapped individuals, there was a need for systematic research in three areas: replication of earlier studies, self-initiation and maintenance of fitness levels by the mentally retarded, and integration of the retarded into community based programs. The most comprehensive evaluation of the physical fitness of mentally handicapped individuals was reported by Rarick, Widdop, and Broadhead (1970). They evaluated 4235 educably mentally retarded (EMR) boys with a modified version of the American Association for Health Physical Education, Recreation and Dance (AAHPERD), Fitness Test. The sample was not only large, but was stratified across geographical lines. The data from this study suggested that all age groups scored below the national norms on the AAHPERD Youth Fitness Test and the relationship of change in level to age was essentially the same for the mentally handicapped sample as it was for their normal peers.

Generally, it has been shown that the mentally handicapped person's abilities to score on a battery of physical fitness tests places them below the mean level of their age-peers. In fact, this tendency to score below the norms seems to be stable across a wide range of physical and motor tests. However, the reasons for these observed low scores are unclear. It is partly due to delayed physical development and a lack of opportunity to participate in the activities that promote fitness. This, coupled with a decreased expectancy to perform may explain the reported results. Since the inception of Public Law 94-142, the legal grounds that ensure mentally handicapped individuals the right to participate in physical fitness activities have existed. Whether or not this has translated into a wider participation on the part of mentally handicapped individuals in local community and school physical fitness programs seems to be a question that remains unanswered. The integration of mentally handicapped persons into regular programs offered community-wide is of critical importance. The issue of integration is one* criticism of Special Olympics because of the possible deleterious effects of participation in a segrated program. This is particularly true for mildly handicapped athletes. For this group, it seems more important to find integrated alternatives between two extreme options: interscholastic sports programs on the one hand and a completely segregated sports program for the handicapped on the other (Polloway and Smith, 1978). The whole question of integration into regular physical fitness programs is beyond the control of mentally handicapped individuals and rests in large part on community attitudes and education, issues raised in this chapter. Attitudes may not only determine the level at which retarded persons are integrated into community-based physical fitness programs but, to an extent, also controls the behavior of professionals in their interactions with mentally retarded persons. Thus, when considering constraints on the leisure behavior of mentally handicapped individuals, physical fitness is probably not a constraint in the physiological sense but rather, it is a question of "opportunity" for mentally handicapped persons to participate at school and in the community in what might be called regular physical fitness activities (i.e., physical fitness classes, aerobic dance, three-, six- and ten kilometer runs, softball, swimming, etc., etc.). There are problems that relate to the methods adopted to teach physical fitness skills to retarded persons, but by far the greatest problem constraining the involvement of mentally

---

*Another has been the nature of the Special Olympics i.e. not promoting continuous, community based athletic opportunities for its participants.

handicapped individuals in physical fitness activities is one of attitude by both professionals and the community relative to their ongoing participation. As in so many domains, "opportunity" rather than "ability" is the real constraint on physical fitness participation for mentally retarded folks.

B. Motor Skills Deficits

In sharp contrast to the physical fitness of mentally handicapped persons, the acquisition of that broad range of motor skills which require anticipation, temporal judgement, and the control and coordination of movement presents a constraint upon activities in which they may participate, even though leisure time pursuits are broad enough in their offerings to accommodate individuals with the lowliest of motor skill levels. The pertinent question is the level at which retarded persons might be expected to participate relative to their ability to acquire, express and maintain a broad range of motor skills.

It is not only mentally retarded individuals who exhibit low levels of skilled behavior; there are many individuals, defined as normal in terms of cognitive development, who possess poor motor skills. Nevertheless, the overwhelming body of research (see, for example, Wade, Newell and Wallace, 1978; Wade and Gold, 1978; Wade, Hoover & Newell, 1983; Wade, 1977), points to a sizeable negative correlation between global intelligence and motor skill acquisition.

The two general features which reflect the motor skill performance of mentally handicapped persons, when compared with their nonretarded peers, are below average scores and comparatively high variability (Wade, 1977). This should not be construed to mean that retarded persons are unable to acquire motor skills, or further that given appropriate training they cannot perform motor skills at a higher level of sophistication.

The theoretical ideas regarding the cognitive involvement in the acquisition of skill would require a considerable allotment of space in this chapter and is inappropriate for the present discussion. Suffice to say that one interesting and dominant notion that has been advanced by Atkinson and Shiffrin (1968) promotes a view that cognitive skills (memory) may be classified to be either structural or control processes. The former (structural) seem not amenable to any serious change and, in fact, may be regarded as "hard-wired" components of a neural network, while the latter (control) are elements in the cognitive makeup of the individual which are amenable to modification via training and development. We have based much of our research on an extension of this idea relative to the training of motor skills (memory for movement?) in mentally handicapped persons (cf., Hoover, Wade, and Newell, 1981; Wade, Newell and Hoover, 1982; Wade, Hoover, and Newell, 1983 Wade, Hoover, and Newell, in press). It is, nevertheless, true to say that no one theoretical position has demonstrated, beyond a doubt, any distinction between what may or may not be trained in the realm of motor skill learning. It would be true to say, that retarded individuals experience difficulties in acquiring motor skills, particularly those that require enhanced levels of precision, and anticipation. Depending on the particular level of this developmental disability, appropriate training methods can, in many instances have dramatic effects on the level at which skill performance may be improved and it would seem, from our research, maintained over reasonable periods of time (Hoover, Wade, and Newell, 1981).

The question, then, arises as to what implications do observed deficits have and how do these deficits constrain leisure behavior? Obviously, leisure activities require different levels of motor skill expression. It is not difficult to imagine that those individuals with certain developmental disabilities will, without appropriate training, be unable to acquire the necessary skills which will allow them to participate in a given leisure activity. The important role that research in motor behavior can play in expanding the range of leisure time participation of mentally handicapped people is to determine precisely the potential of those with developmental disabilities to participate in appropriate leisure time activities.

Those individuals who label themselves as Therapeutic Recreators concern themselves with enhancing leisure participation of developmentally disabled persons (among other groups). It would behoove them to understand fully the appropriate training methods that have been designed and recommended from the considerable research on motor skills. This will optimize the skill level of mentally handicapped individuals and encourage them to use those skills in appropriately-devised leisure time activities. A word of caution is important: It would be foolish not to encourage mentally handicapped persons to participate in leisure time activities, but nevertheless it should be recognized that cognitive deficits may preclude participation in certain activities as they are usually designed to be performed. What is important, therefore, is to make sure that developmentally disabled individuals are encouraged to participate in a social milieu in which they can make a contribution to the activity at hand and not be embarrassed or excluded from the activity by virtue of the motor skill constraints that are inherent as a function of the cognitive deficits of that person. As Welford (1975) has noted. "One cannot make a silk purse out of a sow's ear, but training can considerably improve the quality of the leather."

C. Cognitive Skills

This section extends the special notion of the interrelatedness motor and cognitive behavior. Viewing cognitive development within a skills context is not a new idea. Bartlett (1932) coined the term "skill" as a useful metaphor to discuss his ideas about thinking and remembering. It's not surprising, therefore, that a discussion of cognitive skills would form part of this section on internal constraints. The development of cognitive skills or rather the lack of such development plays an important role in the nature, scope, and involvement in leisure by the mentally handicapped.

Favell and Cannon (1977) found that severely retarded individuals (ages 11 to 26, X = 14) favored certain toys over others. Preferred toys appeared to elicit significantly more interaction from experimental subjects than non-preferred items. Derived from very systematic observations and relatively high interobserver reliability, two significant findings made this an interesting study. First, investigators attempted a post hoc validation of their findings via independently presenting most- and least-preferred toys to subjects. It was found that popular toys produced engagement at roughly twice the rate of least-preferred toys. Engagement was defined as "manipulating, visually attending to, or listening to an item." The fact that toys preferred by subjects increased levels of activity lends further validity to the rating system. There was no significant correlation between cost of the toys and their popularity; further, staff persons in daily contact with subjects were unable to predict which toys would be preferred.

A second implication of the study lies in the nature of preferred toys. Manipulative and interactive toys tended to be preferred, though not overwhelmingly. It may be significant that two of the most popular toys (spring mounted rocking horse and rocking chair) are items that produce sensations of vertigo. Generally speaking, these severely retarded subjects tended to select and favor toys more age appropriate for much younger children. Thus, one cognitive constraint implied by mental retardation is the altering of the relationship between age and "toy preference." In fact, the topology of play in the severely retarded population is quite similar to that of non-retarded infants. Their play is, at worst, self centered—at best centered around the world of manageable and manipulative toys (Frankel & Simmons, 1977).

Extant studies support the notion that retarded adolescents and adults are comparatively unskilled at procuring age-appropriate leisure- activities (Stanfield, 1973). One possible generalization to be drawn is that mentally handicapped persons do not efficiently utilize environments which they encounter. This, of course, includes leisure-oriented settings. As mentioned, several authors have made the same argument for the case of retarded adults in the community (Andron & Sturm, 1973; Corcoran & French, 1977).

Spitz (1979) maintained that number games and games of strategy represent a nearly universal (one might say "normative") form of entertainment for older children and adults. He has further argued that, in nearly every culture, expertise in strategic games has been taken as evidence of superior intelligence. The two games he identified in most cultural groups were mancala type and three-in-a-row games, which both, Spitz argued, require planning and logical foresight. He and his colleagues have provided experimental evidence (Spitz & Winters, 1977) pointing to a $1\frac{1}{2}$ to 4 year mental-age lag in these skills by retarded persons. This lag has been found in both institutionalized and non-institutionalized samples and impulsivity was ruled out as a source of such deficits.

The performance of mentally handicapped persons in playing tic-tac-toe was one specific game-skill examined by Spitz and Winters (1977). They argued that both trainable handicapped and educably retarded children could be taught the basics of tic-tac-toe, and to recognize when they had won. However, a group of non-handicapped third graders performed better than either group of retarded adolescents. Noted differences in performance between retarded and non-retarded subjects increased as a function of task difficulty, despite the fact that the EMR subjects were mental-age matched to the third grade group. These findings have been approximated in other settings which require strategic performance (cf. Spitz, 1979). This observed developmental lag probably represents a significant cognitive constraint on the leisure of retarded persons. They appear to demonstrate a developmental lag in the ability to meaningfully play games which require strategy and forethought for their denouement. The characteristics found in sports and games that non-retarded persons find enjoyable may, therefore, be intellectually inaccessible to moderately and mildly retarded adolescents. An inability, as described, to usefully participate in culturally normative activities constitutes a constraint on leisure for this population. Consider, also, the level of cognitive planning required to gain access to typical activities in a community setting. To join a softball league, for example, a mentally handicapped person would need to check the newspaper for the formation of leagues, make contact with league officials, and organize transportation to the park (or parks) where games were to be played. Obviously, these rather mundane tasks might well prove to be a serious barrier to a person whose very disability is premised on difficulty in making foresightful decisions.

Over and above the constraints on leisure here listed, which might be termed "logistical" cognitive constraints, we think the intriguing possibility exists that retarded persons may occasionally be unable to *enjoy* the leisure activities they do attain. There is a glaring absence of reference in the literature to the qualitative nature of leisure experiences provided mentally handicapped persons. The good intentions of all recreation professionals are for nought if programmed activities do not prove to be enjoyable for participants; at least this is true if one includes subjective, experiential phenomena in a definition of leisure. Inappropriate decisions might be made for retarded persons just as we adults are frequently guilty of deciding what activities are "enjoyable" for children irrespective of their level of physical or intellectual development.

Perhaps due to the relative success demonstrated by research which has induced change in leisure behavior through training and the manipulation of environments, efforts in the area of leisure (and recreation) with retarded subjects are becoming increasingly centered on training and trainability.

We devote a section on training and trainability next, but for now we must consider the pay-off of such training—enjoyment! Moderately retarded children have been guided through developmental play stages (Knapczyk & Yoppi, 1975). Peterson and McIntosh (1973) have taught severely retarded youngsters to ride tricycles, and Day and Day (1977) have reported techniques that successfully encouraged mentally handicapped youngsters to use toys and games independently. Typically, however, the nature of the experience for the mentally handicapped person participating in his new skill is not mentioned. This is, of course, appropriate, because the focus of the above papers, and those in a similar vein, is specifically skill acquisition. But of interest to us here is whether retarded individuals, once trained, really enjoy and value the chance to participate in an activity.

One difficulty in attempting to answer questions about enjoyment is one of definition; another is one of operational and experimental considerations. Depending upon one's definition of enjoyment, varying answers would be forthcoming regarding the possibility that "lack of enjoyment" is a constraint on leisure for retarded persons. Further, a definition cannot be so qualitative or nebulous that it allows no possibility for quantitative investigation (see Mannell, 1979 for an excellent statement of this particular consideration). Finally, it is our bias that the definition of "enjoyment" should hearken to the nature of the act as experienced by the individual (retarded) participant.

Berlyne (1960) developed the term "epistemic" to describe the class of behaviors where organisms seek out particular external stimuli, imagery, and thought. According to Berlyne, attention plays two roles in eliciting exploratory behavior. In the first, finite aspects of environmental stimuli primarily novelty, complexity, and uncertainty, serve to elicit and alter exploratory behavior. The second roll is more of a transformation; the stimuli have their effect upon the organism by increasing arousal level.

Berlyne's postulation does not unequivocally state that in play, or exploratory behavior, the organism experiences enjoyment. It is however implied. Organisms work to achieve a comfortable level of arousal; for example, during periods of high stimulation, relaxation is sought and during periods of low stimulation arousal is sought. This postulation has been tested and confirmed in free play in nonhandicapped subjects by Wade, Ellis and Bohrer (1973), and the lack of such behavior has been reported in mentally handicapped children (Wade, 1973).

"Aimless" behaviors often appear during boredom as an increased arousal level is sought via active environmental manipulation. In its motivating properties this optimal comfort level of arousal is congruent with enjoyment (in an instrumental sense) to the extent that when it follows behaviors the mathematical chances of their reoccurrence increases. It might be argued that terms like "enjoyment" and "fun" refer to the existence of such a phenomenon (the Premak principal may be taken as another example).

An excellent construct for enjoyment, which fits the above-stated requirements, has been suggested by Csikszentmihalyi (1975). Csikszentmihalyi referred to what he termed the "flow experience" that occurs when persons perform certain activities. Individuals have reported the experience of accelerated time, a merging of action and awareness, and the centering of attention on a limited stimulus field. Csikszentmihalyi suggested that flow occurs when challenge and ability are roughly matched during an autotelic activity. Another component of this conceptualization is that challenge levels can be quite low and individuals may still experience a form of "microflow" by engaging in activities such as pencil tapping and idle conversation. Unlike the deep flow represented by the challenge-ability match, microflow is characterized by manipulative behavior designed to occupy idle moments and, in effect, "use up" excess attention. It may be useful to consider "flow" insofar as it represents the ability to experience enjoyment.

We would hypothesize the relationship between low intelligence-level and the ability to experience enjoyment, as follows:

> To the extent that they are intellectually disabled, retarded individuals may be less able to enjoy traditional flow-producing activities.

There is ample evidence that some activities that can be thought of as "flow producing" and that are engaged in by non-handicapped persons for the purpose of having fun, may not prove to be enjoyable for retarded individuals. As has already been mentioned, intellectual level by itself may preclude the use of strategic games with members of this population. Using Csikszentmihalyi's model, it might also be argued that these activities would not be experienced as enjoyable—particularly when challenge far outstrips expertise.

Games, as with many other activities, can be manipulated so that the challenge can be modified, such as is the case of wheelchair basketball. In chess or checkers, an opponent could "ease up" on a retarded adversary, and matches could be arranged between opponents of like skill level. No one can say whether artificially diminished challenge (modified games) or enhanced ability (training) would increase the likelihood that experiences are made more enjoyable for handicapped participants; training probably increases the enjoyment of performance—but this proposition is currently debatable.

In light of these considerations, particular care must be taken when manipulating difficulty level; the absolute difference between the original and modified activity may have the potential to reduce the amount of enjoyment experienced by mentally handicapped participants. Wolfensberger (1976), for example, warned that normalization can be undermined by symbolic issues. By this he was suggesting that situations and objects that are institutional, odd, or age-inappropriate may, of themselves, pejoratively lable a handicapped individual who becomes associated with them. Utilizing this perspective to analyze a "leisure" situation, it might be noted that it would be unusual, and therefore inappropriate, for a retarded adult to play a childrens' game. Of more concern here, of course, is the next logical question: Are mentally handicapped persons able to make the discrimination between culturally normative and nonnormative leisure pursuits, apply negative labels to participation in modified ones, and hence, enjoy them less? If this phenomenon were found to occur it would have widespread implications for leisure counseling.

It is evident from the work of Levine and Longness (1983) that the issues raised regarding cerebral games also have application in leisure-time athletics. Their systematic and naturalistic observation of a mentally handicapped basketball team coincide with the point made earlier in this chapter from laboratory studies, that the cognitive component of an otherwise physical skill will be problematic for members of this group. Levine and Longness compare the performance of a non-retarded team (Hot Shots) and a team made up of mildly retarded young people (Spirit):

> The hot shots were in good physical shape. They played with intensity, passing hard, shooting aggressively, running fast, and taking risks. In contrast, the Spirit players were in relatively poor physical condition and played basketball in a style that was at once both slower and more impulsive (p. 533).

While all the categories of skill examined by Levine and Longness favored the non-retarded players, only "free throws made" proved to be statistically significant. We cannot help but think that larger samples would have produced significant results given the dimension of the trends reported. In addition to the ability data, Levine and Longness administered a 20 item anxiety scale to subjects just before games. Retarded participants manifested significantly more anxiety before games than non-retarded players on the dimensions of tension, worry, anxiety, upset, and happy vs. sad. In terms of the present discussion, the possibility exists that the challenge level presented by a recreational basketball game may militate against the experience of enjoyment. Another implied outcome, though one not treated empirically, was that feelings about the game may be more closely tied to the outcome in retarded participants. The authors reported severe reactions by retarded athletes to both winning and losing.

In the case of strategic games, there may be two classes of

variables which contribute to the experience of enjoyment by moderately handicapped persons. First, the match between challenge and ability, which is the central theme in Csikszentmihalyi's construct, may predict the level of enjoyment for participants in a freely-chosen activity. Second, social-comparison may also lend variability to the experienced degree of pleasure. That is to say, there may be situations where (in Csikszentmihalyi's terminology) the retarded performer evaluates challenge, not in terms of the absolute difficulty of a task, but by comparison to a larger notion of normative competence.

Csikszentmihalyi did not maintain that low levels of ability prevent flow; this is a slight modification of his perspective that is being examined here. His model implies, on the contrary, that as long as ability and challenge are roughly equivalent, enjoyment can eventuate. As it has been demonstrated that mentally handicapped individuals will avoid activities in which they are unskilled (Day & Day, 1975), it must be assumed that either there is an absolute level of skill below which no challenge will be welcomed, or as mentioned above, challenge may be judged subjectively. Personality and motivational variables probably influence the willingness of individuals to attempt new activities—where, obviously, their skill-level will be initially quite low.

The relationship between the experience of flow and participation in modified games is another domain deserving of empirical attention. To the extent that "flow" is a function of normative performance or treatment, the modification of games, and to a lesser extent training (or coaching), might be seen as intrusive by handicapped performers. The "overjustification hypothesis," which states that external rewards for an otherwise intrinsic activity may reduce the frequency of its emission (Deci, 1975; Ross 1976), suggests that nominally "harmless" intrusions on leisure activity may well alter the experience. Consider Iso-Ahola's (1980) statement regarding the effect of similar factors on the subjective experience of little league baseball:

> ... players are likely to think that the reason for their playing is not so much fun and enjoyment as the possible rewards. The less the children think of external consequences of the game, the

> more likely they are to enjoy the game. It is also likely that very
> authoritative coaching causes players to shift their perception of
> focus of casuality from themselves to the environment, which
> should therefore reduce players' intrinsic motivation in the game
> (p. 201).

There is no reason to believe that similar intrusions won't be seen
as annoying by mentally handicapped athletes as well.

III. Training Issues in Leisure-Oriented Skills

The leisure behavior of handicapped children and adults appears
to be highly modifiable via training and the various feedback and
motivational techniques. As a result, there may be great advantage
to pursuing interventions in this area with retarded persons. As
has been mentioned, however, certain quality-of-life questions
need to be asked before a training effort is undertaken: Is the
activity age appropriate? Is the activity commensurate with the
student's ability? Is the activity culturally-normative? Is it enjoyable,
and how will training itself impact on the experience for this
individual?

Despite these caveats there is a good chance that increased
leisure skills will benefit retarded persons. The increased adaptive
behavior and reduced stereotypyc noted earlier are examples of
potential benefits. Increased play skills brought about by training
might produce better overall learning in moderately retarded
preschoolers; this will eventuate to the extent that these skills help
the child to organize experience. However, the relationship between
intervention in play-behaviors and cognitive performance has
proved to be equivocal to this point. It should be pointed out that
increased rates of play provide the clear advantage of producing
adaptive behavior with which to occupy free time (Hewson,
McConkey, & Jeffree, 1980; Hopper & Wamboldm, 1978; Strain,
1975).

One defining characteristic that is generally given for play is
that it is motivated internally—that it is self-directed. Obviously
there is some degree of tension between notions of free play and
efforts to train so-called "leisure behaviors." A potential solution

to this dilemma is to consider the random nature of free-play in retarded children (Wade, 1972), and to assume that there exists an absolute skill level below which any approach to the environment is too random to be considered play. Retarded children and adults may, indeed, be "starving amidst plenty," as suggested by Finkelstein, Gallagher, and Fahan (1973) if they are not taught the intellectual and motor approach skills that would enable them to "attack" and explore an environment via play (epistemic behavior).

To the extent that play proves to be adaptable without changing in topography, theorists may need to reexamine strict application of intrinsic motivation as a defining characteristic of play-behavior. Hewson et al. (1980) summarized one aspect of this position as follows:

> Our resolution to the dilemma is not to devalue the significance of free play. On the contrary, we have argued strongly for the role of spontaneous play in the young child's development . . . Just as free play promotes future development it is also dependent on past learning. We have in mind such skills as being able to organize one's own actions, being able to explore one's surroundings constructively, as well as the more advanced capabilities such as imaginitive play. Children who, for whatever reason, are developmentally delayed may lack such skills and, thereby, the enjoyment and benefits of free play (p. 74).

Once the decision has been reached that intervention in the general area of leisure behavior is appropriate, certain technological issues will follow. There is considerable uncertainty in the literature as to the nature of skill and the relative ability of mentally handicapped persons to learn skills of varying descriptions (Wade, Hoover, & Newell, 1983). One clear trend, however, has been the elucidation of more and more skill-domains that are accessible to retarded individuals (Wade & Gold, 1978; Wade, Hoover, & Newell, 1983). At this point we would briefly like to raise a few of the technical issues inherent in skill training.

Task analysis has become the primary tool in teaching skills to mentally handicapped individuals (Wade & Gold, 1978). Task analysis is essentially a method whereby a task, and its requirements, can be operationally defined for teaching purposes. A task analysis can be more or less accurate or efficient in terms of the topology of the actual skill in question. It is, in the end, a training document. Gold (1975) advocated a task analysis process which may be of use to therapists planning to teach complex leisure-skills to handicapped persons. In Gold's model, the instructor examines the actual topography of the task at hand, the division of the task into instructional components (steps), and the strategies for inculcating the various steps in specific trainees.

There are many examples of the use of task analysis for teaching play, sport, and leisure skills to retarded persons. We have already mentioned the work of Knapczyk & Yoppi (1975), Peterson and McIntosh (1973), and Day & Day (1977). Wehman (1974) conducted a study in which play behaviors were taught to severely retarded adults. Previous to the study, clients displayed very minimal levels of play behavior, defined here as interaction with toys. Wehman's procedures were designed to increase "touching, holding, or manipulation of the play objects" (p. 100). Utilizing task analysis and modeling procedures, trainers were able to produce a marked increase in the frequency of appropriate toy use. Similarly, Wehman, Renzaglia, Berry, Schutz and Karan (1978) trained severely retarded adolescents to self-initiate the use of table games.

In another experiment, task analysis and motivational procedures were successfully employed to increase the frequency of "independent use of leisure time in a group setting" (Wambold & Bailey, 1979). Based on a pretest—posttest design, it was concluded that all but one of the children gained significantly in percent of time engaged in appropriate play. The children generalized their training to other toys and sustained play with single items for longer periods of time. Task analytic procedures, teamed with other teaching technologies such as prompting and modeling, are obviously a useful set of tools with which to teach leisure skills to handicapped persons (Hewson, McConkey, & Jeffree, 1980; Horst, Wehman, Hill, & Bailey, 1981; Wehman, 1975).

Unfortunately, there is, as yet, little systematic evidence available regarding the exact nature of the interaction between the task analysis and a specific trainee (Wade & Gold, 1978; Wade, Hoover, & Newell, 1983). More work is clearly needed on delimiting qualitative limits to the performance of retarded persons on complex tasks and the effect of systematic training on these factors. As has been noted previously, the structure-control distinction (Atkinson and Shiffrin, 1968) may provide a useful framework for posing these questions. Wade, Hoover & Newell (1983) argued that, despite confusion regarding the structure-control dichotomy, the model retains its usefulness because a component of a task which cannot be successfully taught, given current technology, can be thought of as "environmentally structural." This distinction, for example, would hold for the observations of Spitz (1979), where it was impossible to teach even mildly retarded individuals to employ strategy in a game setting. In a case such as this, the utility of the task as a leisure-pursuit is questionable.

Borkowski and Cavanaugh (1979), however, have concluded that mentally handicapped persons can be taught to employ strategy in problem-solving situations, with maintenance and generalization of these behaviors specifically planned in the training process. Brown (1974), on the other hand, reported that strategic behaviors were seldom maintained over time or generalized by retarded persons. Here is a clearly-defined controversy that awaits solution — particularly within the domain of games, sport and leisure. Most sports, thought of typically in "gross motor" terms, also include major strategic components. Think of a shortstop in baseball who must decide whether or not to "charge" a grounder in order to throw the runner out at first base. Can these skills be summarized in a traditional task analysis? Can the game be modified in such a way that participants do not find the alterations annoying?

Some qualitative differences between the performance of mentally handicapped and nonhandicapped learners have been noted in tightly controlled laboratory settings. Many of these may have application in "real world" leisure and sport settings. For example, increasing the distance between a signal and the setting for the required response (stimulus- response compatibility) appears to seriously impede the performance of mentally handicapped learners (Brewer, 1978; Mulhearn & Baumeister, 1971). This may have direct implications for training.

In a series of experiments undertaken by the present authors, it has been demonstrated that performance on even very minute tasks can be improved with the application of systematic training efforts (Hoover, Wade, & Newell, 1981; Wade, Hoover, & Newell, in press). In these experiments simple reaction time (RT) when an aiming movement was required, and movement-to-target time, were significantly reduced in moderately and severely retarded adults. The least that can be drawn from these studies is that the boundary-level of performance by members of this population remains uncertain—at it appears possible that even quite subtle timing requirements in skilled motor performance are trainable.

There exists a grey area, in leisure services, between "allowing" for skill level in the choice of activity and the desire of trainers to intervene in the play and leisure of retarded persons. Favell and Cannon's (1977) results, imply that selection of toys for retarded persons can be based on empirical observations of player's preferences. However, using such a toy-selection procedure might exascerbate delays already manifest in the development of these children. Further, retarded children might select age-inappropriate toys and activities and thereby "label" themselves retarded. There is, for example, nothing age-appropriate about a fifteen-year-old girl merrily bouncing on a rocking horse (see Favell & Cannon).

Ultimately, the solution to the dilemma between age-appropriateness and play-style will likely represent a compromise. Practitioners will realize that there will be a degree of delay in the development of retarded persons, and allow these individuals time to pursue enjoyment in activities that match their abilities. On the other hand, it should be expected that these persons will grow and develop. Developmental models may provide practitioners with a picture of "what should happen next." Training in play-oriented behaviors can then proceed along these lines.

The quality of leisure experienced by mentally handicapped persons will be affected by many variables. Whether or not the person resides in an institution—and the nature of that institution, will likely have an impact on the quality of free time. The attitudes held by society probably define, in some ways, opportunities for attempting leisure-pursuits that are age-appropriate and culturally normative. The abilities of the individual client will be at issue—and that client will be, in turn, affected by the technical expertise and creativity of his teachers and counselors. Finally, if Csikszentmihalyi (1975) is to be believed, the "experience" will be partially a function of the activity itself and, we might add, the person's perception(s) of that event.

Mental retardation, of itself, may well be the *least* significant constraint to leisure examined here. As it has been stated elsewhere, regarding the motor skills domain, the opportunity to attempt new activities may be all these individuals require to constrain the constraints.

REFERENCES

Andron, L., & Sturm, M. (1978). Is "I do" in the repertoire of the retarded? A study of the functioning of retarded married couples. *Mental Retardation, 11,* 31–34.

Atkinson, R. E., & Shiffrin, R. M. (1968). Human memory: A proposed system and its control process. In K. W. Spence, & J. T. Spence (Eds.), *The psychology of learning and motivation* (2nd ed., pp. 189–195). New York: Academic Press.

Ball, T., Hendrickson, H., & Clayton, J. (1974). A special feeding technique for chronic regurgitation. *American Journal of Mental Deficiency, 78,* 486–493.

Balla, D. Relationship of institution size to quality of care: A review of the literature. *American Journal of Mental Deficiency, 81,* 117–124.

Baroff, G. S. (1980). On "size" and the quality of residential care: A second look. *Mental Retardation, 18*(3), 113–117.

Bartlett, F. C. (1932). *Remembering: A study in experimental and social psychology.* Cambridge University Press.

Berlyne, D. E. (1960). *Conflict, arousal, and curiosity.* New York: McGraw-Hill Book Company.

Borkowski, J., & Cavanaugh, J. (1979). Maintenance and generalizability of skills and strategies by the retarded. In N. R. Ellis (Ed.), *The handbook of mental deficiency* (2nd ed.). Hillsdale, NJ: Lawrence Erlbaum.

Brace, D. R. (1927). *Measuring motor ability.* New York: A. S. Barnes & Company, Inc.

Brewer, N. (1978). Motor components in the choice reaction time of mildly retarded adults. *American Journal of Mental Deficiencies, 82,* 37–43.

Brown, A. L. (1974). The role of strategy behavior in retardate memory. In N. R. Ellis (Ed.), *International review of research in mental retardation* (Volume 7, pp. 55–111). New York: Academic Press.

Cocoran, E. L., & French, R. W. (1977). Leisure activity for the retarded adult in the community. *Mental Retardation, 12,* 21–23.

Csikszentmihalyi, M. (1975). *Beyond boredom and anxiety.* San Francisco: Jossey-Bass.

Day, R., & Day, M. (1977). Leisure skills instruction for the moderately and severely retarded: A demonstration project. *Education and Training of the Mentally Retarded, 2,* 128–131.

Deci, E. L. (1975). *Intrinsic motivation.* New York: Plenum Publications.

Favell, J. E. (1976). Reduction of stereotypes by reinforcement of toy play. In

D. Gibson, & R. D. Brown (Eds.), *Managing the severely retarded: A sampler.* Springfield, IL: Charles C Thomas.

Favell, J. E., & Cannon, P. (1977). Evaluation of entertainment materials for severely retarded persons. *American Journal of Mental Deficiency, 84,* 357–362.

Finklestein, N. W., Gallagher, J. J., & Fahan, D. (1973). Attentiveness and responsiveness to auditory stimuli of children at risk for mental retardation. *American Journal of Mental Deficiency, 78,* 323–330.

Frankel, F., & Simmons, J. (1977). Self-injurious behaviors in schizophrenic and retarded children. *American Journal of Mental Deficiency.*

Gold, M. W. (1975). Vocational training. In J. Wortis (Ed.), *Mental retardation and developmental disabilities: An annual review* (pp. 344–364). New York: Brunner Mayel.

Hewson, S., McConkey, R., & Jeffree, D. (1980). The relationship between structured and free play in the development of a mentally handicapped child. *Child Care, Health and Development, 6,* 73–82.

Hoover, J. H., Wade, M. G., & Newell, K. M. (1981). The trainability of reaction time and movement time in moderately mentally handicapped workers. *American Journal of Mental Deficiency, 85,* 389–395.

Horner, R. D. (1980). The effects of an environmental "enrichment" program on the behaviors of institutionalized, profoundly retarded children. *Journal of Applied Behavioral Analysis, 13,* 473–491.

Horst, G., Loehman, P., Hill, J. W., & Bailey, C. (1981). Developing age-appropriate leisure skills in severely handicapped adolescents. *Teaching Exceptional Children, 14,* 11–15.

Iso-Ahola, S. E. (1980). A social psychological analysis of little league baseball. In S. E. Iso-Ahola (Ed.), *Social psychological perspectives on leisure and recreation.* Springfield, IL: Charles C. Thomas.

Katz, S., & Yekutiel, E. (1974). Leisure time problems of mentally retarded graduates of training programs. *Mental Retardation, 12*(3), 54–57.

Klaber, M. M. (1969). The retarded and institutions for the retarded: A preliminary report. In S. B. Soranson, & J. Doris (Eds.), *Psychological Problems in Mental Deficiency.* New York: Harper and Row.

Knapczyk, D. R., & Yoppi, J. O. (1975). Development of cooperative and competitive play responses in developmentally disabled children. *American Journal of Mental Deficiency, 80,* 245–255.

Levine, H. G., & Langness, L. L. (1983). Context, ability, and performance: Comparison of competitive athletics among mildly mentally retarded and nonretarded adults. *American Journal of Mental Deficiency, 87*(5), 528–538.

Londeree, B. R., & Johnson, L. E. (1974). Motor fitness of TMR vs. EMR and normal children. *Medicine and Science in Sport, 6,* 247–252.

Mannell, R. C. (1979). A conceptual and experimental basis for research in the psychology of leisure. *Society and Leisure.*

Moon, M. S., & Renzaglia, A. (1982). Physical fitness and the mentally retarded: A critical review of the literature. *Journal of Special Education, 16*(3), 269–287.

Mulhearn, T., & Baumeister, A. A. (1971). Effects of stimulus-response compatability and complexity upon reaction times of normals and retardates. *Journal of Comparative and Physiological Psychology, 75,* 459–463.

Mulick, J. A., Hoyt, P., Rojan, J., & Schroeder, S. R. (1978). Reduction of a "nervous habit" in a profoundly retarded youth by increasing toy play. *Journal of Behavior Therapy and Experimental Psychiatry, 9,* 381–385.

Nesbitt, J., Neal, L., & Hillman, A. (1974). Recreation for exceptional children and youth. *Focus on Exceptional Children, 6*(3), 1–12.

Owen, J. P. W. (1977). An investigation of the quality of life of expatients in the community in terms of interests and leisure activities. *Research Exchange and Practice in Mental Retardation, 3,* 147–152.

Peterson, R. A., & McIntosh, E. J. (1973). Teaching tricycle riding to retarded children. *Mental Retardation, 11,* 32–34.

Polloway, E. A., & Smith, J. D. (1978). Special Olympics: A second look. *Education and Training of the Mentally Retarded, 13,* 432–433.

Quilitch, H., & Gray, J. (1974). Purposeful activity for the profoundly mentally retarded: A demonstration project. *Mental Retardation, 12*(6), 28–29.

Rarick, G. L., Widdop, J. H., & Broadhead, G. D. (1970). *Exceptional Children, 35,* 509–519.

Raw, J., & Erickson, E. (1977). Behavioral techniques in therapeutic recreation. In T. Thompson, & J. Grabouski (Eds.), *Behavior modification of the mentally retarded.* New York: Oxford University Press.

Ross, M. (1976). The self-perception of intrinsic motivation. In J. H. Harvey, W. J. Ickes, R. F. Kidd (Eds.), *New directions in attribution research* (Volume 1, pp. 121–141). Hillsdale, NJ: LEA.

Rowe, D. (1976). The effect of a more stimulating environment on the behavior of a group of severely subnormal adults. In D. Gibson, & R. J. Brown (Eds.), *Managing the severely retarded: A sampler.* Springfield, IL: Charles C Thomas.

Scheer, R. (1968). Fusion of social group work and recreational skills in providing services to the mentally retarded. *Training School Bulletin, 65,* 21–27.

Spitz, H. H. (1979). Beyond field theory in mental retardation. In N. R. Ellis (Ed.), *Handbook on Mental Deficiency.* Hillsdale, NJ: Lawrence Erlbaum.

Spitz, H. H., & Winters, G. (1977). The tic tac toe performance of trainable and educable retarded junior high school students. *Intelligence, 4,* 31–40.

Stanfield, J. S. (1973). Graduation: What happens to the retarded child when he grows up? *Exceptional Children, 39,* 548–553.

Strain, P. (1975). Increasing social play of severely retarded preschoolers with socio-dramatic activities. *Mental Retardation, 3*(6), 7–9.

Thompson, T. (1977). History of treatment and misconceptions concerning the mentally retarded. In T. Thompson, & J. Gragowski (Eds.), *Behavior modification of the mentally retarded.* New York: Oxford University Press.

Wade, M. G. (1973). Biorhythms and activity level of institutionalized mentally retarded persons diagnosed hyperactive. *American Journal of Mental Deficiency, 78,* 262–267.

Wade, M. G. (1977). Categories of disabilities and their influence on the motor performance of children. In R. E. Stadulis (Ed.), *Research and practice in physical education* (pp. 77–88). Champaign, IL: Human Kinetics Press.

Wade, M. G., Ellis, M. J., Bohrer, R. E. (1973). Biorhythms in the activity of children during free play. *Journal of the Experimental Analysis of Behavior, 20,* 155–162.

Wade, M. G., & Gold, M. W. (1978). Removing some of the limitations of MR workers by improving job design. *Human Factors, 20,* 339–348.

Wade, M. G., Hoover, J. H., & Newell, K. M. (in press). Training RT and MT of moderately and severely retarded persons in aiming movements. *American Journal of Mental Deficiency.*

Wade, M. G., Newell, K. M., & Hoover, J. H. (1982). Coincidence timing behavior in young mentally handicapped workers under varying conditions of target velocity and exposure. *American Journal of Mental Deficiency, 86*(6), 643–649.

Wade, M. G., Newell, K. M., & Wallace, S. A. (1978). Decision time and movement time as a function of response complexity in retarded persons. *American Journal of Mental Deficiency, 83,* 135–144.

Wambold, C., & Bailey, R. (1979). Improving the leisure time behaviors of severely/profoundly mentally retarded children through toy play. *AAESPH Review, 4*(3), 237–250.

Wehman, P. (1975). Establishing play behaviors in mentally retarded youth. *Rehabilitation Literature, 36*(8), 238–246.

Wehman, P., Renzaglia, A., Berry, G., Schutz, R., & Karan, O. (1978). Developing a leisure skill repertoire in severely and profoundly handicapped persons. *American Association for the Education of the Severely/Profoundly Handicapped Review, 3,* 162–172.

Welford, A. T., (1975). What can be trained? Paper read at the 18th International Congress of Applied Psychology, Montreal, Canada, August.

Wolfensberger, W. (1976). The origin and nature of our institutional models. In Kugel, & Shearer (Eds.), *Changing patterns in residential services for the mentally retarded* (pp. 35–82). Washington, D.C.: Presidents Committee on Mental Retardation.

Chapter V

SOCIAL AND PSYCHOLOGICAL CONSTRAINTS ON LEISURE

SEPPO E. ISO-AHOLA and ROGER C. MANNELL

I. INTRODUCTION

The leisure and recreation service system is regarded as a helping profession. By the definition of their profession, recreation providers and practitioners are therefore expected to remove barriers to leisure participation and facilitate the obtaining of satisfying leisure experiences. Thus, the mere existence of this profession implies that people's leisure behavior is constrained by personal, social and cultural factors. On the surface, this is surprising because the very idea of leisure means the absence of external sanctions and controls (Ellis, 1973; Iso-Ahola, 1980a). Leisure represents the "realm of freedom" in which "the development of human personality for its own sake" begins (Marx, 1894). But as we know, human beings do not live in ideal societies, and their leisure is often not a realm of freedom.

While no one's leisure participation is totally free from constraints, the social environment of some individuals limits their leisure behavior considerably more than others. It is therefore important to identify those social-psychological barriers that hinder individually rewarding leisure experiences. Such identification is an important step in attempts to understand why these constraints develop in the first place. The resultant information can be applied directly through education and counseling, and less directly through programming and advocacy activities. It can, in the best possible circumstances, free individuals from many of the constraints on their leisure.

In theory, many different types of constraints exist, but social

111

and psychological ones are perhaps the most important among them. While such physical constraints as lack of money and of recreational opportunities may be real hindrances, the social nature of human beings is the most pervasive of all constraints. People are "social animals" (Aronson, 1972), they depend on their fellow persons. Therefore, their leisure choices and actions are socially affected. Their leisure cognitions and behaviors influence and are influenced by those of others (Iso-Ahola, 1980a). This social influence process implies continuous change—be it slow or rapid—in leisure behavior. To put it another way, people continuously revise their leisure goals, patterns and habits in response to their social environment. As a consequence, an individual's leisure is never totally free of social constraints.

The constraining effect of the social environment on leisure is attested to by the very fact that most people do or like to do certain leisure activities. At times some activities explode in popularity. Such explosions reflect people's concern about social deviancy. That is, to be "normal," people engage in those activities that are known to be participated in by others. Any deviation from the norm puts constraints on leisure. Of course, people can construct their own idiosyncratic leisure repertoires, but the activities that comprise these leisure repertoires are known to have been participated in by others. For example, *most* business people play golf during their free-time. Since it is inconceivable that they all are inclined to play golf, the predominance of this activity reflects their acceptance of the stereotype that business people are supposed to play golf. Thus, this cultural stereotype limits the leisure behavior of certain individuals.

It is important to note that constraints are subjective and psychological, meaning that they reside in a person's mind. Constraints become constraints only when a person perceives them as such. One individual may have a chronic lack of money but may not regard it as an obstacle to his leisure participation, whereas another individual has more money than needed for participation in any leisure activity but nevertheless does not know how to spend his free-time, mainly due to the fact that he perceives money providing too many and confusing options. Although certain standards may be established, such as, the number of paid holidays or the range of recreation opportunities available in a community which will supposedly reduce the constraints on an individual's leisure, such objective criteria are meaningless unless they correspond to individual perceptions of constraint.

Even if, at a given time, we were able to remove all the barriers to a person's leisure participation, it is unlikely that he would be completely satisfied and happy with his leisure and life for two reasons. First, people continuously revise their definitions of satisfaction and happiness "on the basis of what they have seen and heard others to have or to be," meaning that "this revision process is endless as long as human beings are 'social animals'" (Iso-Ahola, 1980a, p. 392). Second, satisfaction or happiness is a peak or flow experience rather than a lasting one (Mannell, 1980). This then suggests that the removal of constraints increases the *frequency* of satisfying and happy experiences. We therefore postulate that of two persons, one who perceives fewer constraints on his leisure experiences satisfaction or happiness more frequently than the other who perceives more constraints, other things being equal.

The above hypothesis forms the foundation of this chapter. That is, if the removal of barriers increases the quality of life even on a temporary basis, it is important to examine the formation and development of such barriers. Therefore, the purpose of this chapter is to identify major social and psychological constraints on leisure behavior and review relevant empirical evidence. Since constraints must be perceived to affect the individual, we approach this topic purely from a psychological perspective.

II. CONCEPTUALIZATION OF LEISURE CONSTRAINTS

When conceptualizing leisure constraints, perhaps the most obvious distinction to be made is the one involving biologically and environmentally-induced constraints on leisure behavior. It has been shown empirically that "there is a small but reliably heritable influence on the *patterning* of interests in individuals" (Grotevant, Scarr & Weinberg, 1977, pp. 673–675). The results of this study indicated that the leisure interests of members of biological families correlated positively and significantly (ranging from .19 to .34), whereas the leisure interests of members of adoptive families were unrelated. The data can therefore be taken to indicate that the biological family members are moderately (but significantly) similar in their leisure interest styles, and that genetic factors influence individual activity patterns.

Does this mean that people's leisure choices and actions are genetically programmed, determined and constrained? No, because genetic factors do not determine one's participation in specific activities but rather set the stage for certain types of social experiences which subsequently determine and constrain an individual's involvement in specific activities. As the Grotevant, et al. data showed, the same-sex siblings (.36) were much more similar over the leisure interest dimensions than the opposite-sex siblings (.08) and parent-child pairs (.17). These correlations provide strong evidence of the effects of the social environment on leisure behavior. Since like-sex pairs have more similar rearing environments than do opposite-sex or parent-child pairs, they are therefore more similar on their leisure interests dimensions. As a whole, these findings are important because they clearly document that while biological factors set the foundations for one's interests, his/her leisure choices and behaviors ultimately depend on social factors and influences. This fact alone demonstrates the importance of studying social psychological constraints on leisure behavior. The question then is: What are these constraints?

In principal, constraints stem from one of two factors: a perceived deficiency or an abundance of something. In other words, a person's feelings of being incapable to perform certain leisure activities are rooted either in feelings of (1) *not having or being* something or in feelings of (2) *having or being* something. Thus, in the former case a person may feel constrained because of lack of ability or money, while in the latter a person may feel constrained by his social role and the norms associated with it. For example, the latter person would like to play golf on Saturdays and Sundays but because of being a father, he thinks he is expected to spend weekends playing with his children, or simply, because of the demands of his wife. Another example of the latter category would be a girl who feels constrained by the fact that she is female. She would like to play baseball, but cannot because it is *boys'* and *men's* activity.

To develop a model of constraints on leisure behavior, several questions must be answered. First, what are the perceived causes of such constraints? Second, what types of constraints are there? Constraints can be divided into three categories: social-personal, social-cultural and physical. Third, how enduring are they? In principal, constraints can be stable or variable. Based upon these dimensions, leisure constraints may be conceptualized as follows:

Type/Locus

		Social-Personal	Social-Cultural	Physical
	Permanent	Abilities, Competencies, Control	Social Norms, Roles, Obligations	Resources, Finances, Facilities
	Temporary	Attitudes, Motives, Needs	Social Interaction	Time

Stability/Permanence Variable/ Stable/

Figure V-1. Conceptualization of Sources of Constraints on Leisure (from Iso-Ahola, 1981).

According to Figure 1, there are six major categories or sources of constraints, one-half of which is considered fairly stable and permanent and the other more variable and temporary. These constraints are "social-personal" when personal abilities and motives are in question. They are "social" because the evaluations and perceptions of personal abilities and motives are influenced by social environments and forces (Deci, 1975; Festinger, 1954; Suls & Miller, 1977). Perceived lack of ability or competence is perhaps the most serious of all constraints because it readily leads to a state of perceived uncontrollability and helplessness (Seligman, 1975). It is well established by social psychological research that the perception of abilities is stable. That is, once a person gets an idea, whether justifiably or not, that he is incompetent to perform a given task it is difficult to change such a perception (Seligman, 1975). On the other hand, the perception of motives is more variable because motives and needs in themselves are unstable and because they can be easily altered by a social environment.

As Figure 1 shows, constraints are "social-cultural" when social norms and social interactions are in question. While human behavior is changeable, social norms nevertheless regulate what is desirable and unacceptable. For example, it is not usually socially acceptable that a husband and wife spend their Saturday evenings dancing in different nightclubs; they are expected to go and dance together. Such social norms are stable and resistant to change and can, therefore, become permanent constraints on one's leisure behavior. Social interaction, on the other hand, forms an unstable source of constraints on leisure. Both the quantity and quality of social company can become constraining. For example, a person may be unsatisfied with his leisure because he does not have a lot of friends to interact with it, or he may have enough but not the type of friends who share similar interests. Besides lacking the right types of friends, social interaction can be constraining for the opposite reason: a person has too many friends and relatives with whom he must interact on a regular basis. If these friends are many and interaction frequent, much of his free-time is committed, and the feelings of freedom of choice are lost. Patterns of social interaction, however, can be changed, and it is for this reason that social interaction is viewed as an unstable and variable source of constraints on one's leisure behavior.

Finally, such factors as a lack of money, facilities and opportunities can form real obstacles to leisure behavior and become permanent sources of constraints. In a similar vein, too little or too much time is often perceived as a constraint on leisure behavior. Campbell, Converse and Rodgers (1976, p. 357) reported data indicating an inverted-U relationship between the availability of discretionary time and leisure satisfaction. In other words, leisure satisfaction was at its highest when subjects felt they had an optimal amount of discretionary time available for their activities and at its lowest when there was a feeling of plenty of free-time or very little free-time available for leisure activities. Thus, it appears that too much or too little free-time is constraining.

When conceptualizing constraints, it is possible to examine them in relation to *before, during* or *after* leisure participation.

Constraints can be inhibitory and therefore prevent one from participating in certain activities. Such obstacles reduce a person's leisure repertoire, that is, the range of activities available to him. On the other hand, some factors become constraints while one is involved in a leisure activity. For example, the behavior of onlookers may often inhibit one's leisure behavior and may subsequently disrupt that behavior. Mannell (1980) has suggested that there may be factors, operating after the occurrence of the leisure behaviors which affect the recall and memory of this experience, and hence the satisfaction derived from it. The above model, however, presents constraints in relation to the inhibitions or constraints felt before actual involvement rather than during or after it.

III. PERCEIVED INCOMPETENCE AS A CONSTRAINT

"While recreational activities are pursued for a variety of reasons, the underlying cause is perceived competence within the individual confines of optimal arousal. Those activities which help to satisfy a person's need for competence are greatly preferred to those which are not congruent with individual competencies" (Iso-Ahola, 1980a, p. 197). If a person attributes his leisure behavior or its outcomes to personal dispositions (abilities, competencies), such attributions imply personal control over the environment. It is known that human beings "strive for personal causation, to be the primary focus of causation, or the origin of, their behavior" (deCharms, 1968, p. 269). This, then, suggests that people prefer and participate in those leisure activities that allow dispositional attributions, because such participation implies personal causation and control over the environment and brings about feelings of competence and satisfaction (Iso-Ahola, 1980a, p. 330).

It follows from the above that perceived incompetence is the major obstacle to one's leisure involvement. Empirical data indeed corroborate this hypothesis. Spreitzer and Snyder (1976) found that perceived ability was the strongest predictor of adult leisure involvement for both men (.35 = standardized regression coefficient) and women (.32). This means that as perceived incompetence increased, involvement in leisure activities decreased. In a related study, Csikszentmihalyi, Larson and Prescott (1977) obtained data suggesting that the least enjoyable forms of leisure were associated with perceived incompetence. In this study, adolescent subjects carried for a week a pocket-size electronic paging device which signaled them to self-report at random times what they were doing, why they were doing it, etc. It appeared that the activities which provided the most positive experiences were playing games and sports because they were perceived to offer the greatest amount of challenge, required a relatively high level of skill, and provided a strong feeling of control over their actions. At the same time, watching TV was the activity related to the least positive overall mood, because it was perceived to offer no challenge and require a low level of skills and provide the least amount of personal control.

These findings clearly suggest that perceived incompetence is a major constraint on individual leisure behavior. Its consequences are severe and lasting: reduced involvement in or complete withdrawal from a range of activities. This in turn may lead to apathy, helplessness and depression. Since human beings seem to be "born generalizers" (Seligman, 1975), perceived incompetence in one activity or area is probably generalized to other similar activities. For example, if a person, for some reason, believes that he is incompetent to play tennis, he is likely to generalize this belief to all racquet sports and perhaps to all sport activities, thereby excluding a wide range of activities from his leisure repertoire. Another bothersome aspect of such beliefs is that they are persistent. It has been shown experimentally (Seligman, 1975) that once a person has developed a feeling and inference of helplessness, as a result of perceived incompetence, it is difficult to change his self-perceptions; in fact, it is much easier to sink into a state of helplessness than climb out of it.

Given the importance of perceived incompetence as a constraint on leisure, a question immediately arises about its determinants. How do people come to infer that they are incapable of performing certain tasks or activities? These determinants can be broken into six major categories: (1) individual differences, especially in terms of locus of control, (2) exposure to failures and uncontrollable events, (3) modeled failures, (4) social judgements and labeling, (5) relinquishing personal control and (6) environmental constraints.

Individual Differences in Feelings of Control and Competence

This first determinant suggests that individuals differ in their general tendency to evaluate personal competencies. Regardless of the conditions, some people are more inclined to view themselves competent than are others. This difference in personality reflects past experiences and the effects of socialization. "Induction from past experience determines how strong the sense of helplessness or mastery is" (Seligman, 1975, p. 137). If a person has grown up in an environment where he has experienced little mastery, he is more likely to infer a personal lack of control and helplessness in novel situations than a person who has learned, *by his own actions,* to master difficulties and frustration. As Seligman (1975, p. 158) puts it: "Unless a person confronts anxiety, boredom, pain and trouble, and masters them by his own actions, he will develop an impoverished sense of his own competence." Thus, obstacles and difficulties and competition should not be removed from the lives of young people, but instead, children should be taught to overcome these problems by their own actions. Reared under such conditions, children's ego strength emerges and self-esteem increases (Seligman, 1975).

A vast amount of research conducted on the validity of "locus of control" supports the above speculation. Lefcourt (1976) reviewed past studies and concluded that opportunities for "contingent responses" in the home and the larger social environment are necessary for the development of a sense of personal control and competence. Citing the experimental evidence, Lefcourt found that parents' acceptance, warmth, supportiveness, and encouragement of their children is essential for the growth of the sense of personal control. Children who have been reared under the attentive, responsive, critical, and contingent home and social environment have a greater internal locus of control than children who have repeatedly met with rejection, hostile control, inconsistent discipline and withdrawal from their parents and the social milieu.

It follows from the above that a sense of incompetence, lack of personal control, and low self-esteem become a major constraint on one's leisure behavior. Empirical data support this contention.

In a study planned to determine the relationship between the locus of control construct and preferences for participating in skill vs. chance-related leisure activities, Schneider (1968) found that preference for skill activities was positively related to an internal locus of control and that preference for chance activities was associated with an external locus of control. This finding, however, was true only for men but not for women. Individuals character-ized with an internal locus of control have a strong sense of personal control over their actions, behaviors and environment, whereas persons with an external locus of control do not have such a sense of personal control but instead believe themselves inca-pable of controlling the important events in their life space (Lefcourt, 1976; Rotter, 1966). Thus, it appeared that "internal" men preferred such skill-oriented leisure activities as football, soccer and golf, whereas "external" men chose chance-related activities like dice-throwing, playing slot machines and horse betting. In a similar vein, Gold (1967) found that internal men chose skill-oriented tasks more often than chance tasks, while the opposite was true for external men. Again, internal and external females did not differ significantly in their preferences, presumably because of the use of predominately "masculine" activities in these studies. Schneider (1968), however, reported that females picked a greater number of chance activities than did males, though the difference was statistically nonsignificant.

Taken together, these findings suggest that "internals" partici-pate more frequently in skill-oriented leisure activities than do "externals", presumably because participation in such activities permits them to confirm their expectancy of internal control. Because of their generalized expectancy to control outcomes by their own actions, internals expect to succeed in skill activities, and when they do succeed they attribute their performance to personal abilities and effectiveness. Even if they do not im-mediately succeed, they do not give up easily because of their generalized expectancy of internal control. This, in turn, means that they will succeed eventually. On the other hand, "externals" participate more often in chance activities, presumably because participation in these activities minimizes the risk of failure or because they value success on chance activities. Due to their perceived incompetence, externals believe that they cannot perform well on skill activities and thus control outcomes; and even if they succeed on such tasks they think it is due to external forces rather than their own capabilities. In support of this theorizing, Witt and Goodale (1981) found that external persons saw most of a list of barriers to leisure enjoyment as significantly more constraining than did internal persons.

The above results indicate that externally oriented personality constrains leisure behavior. Due to their generalized expectancies for personal incompetence and lack of personal control, externals avoid skill activities and consequently exclude these activities from their leisure repertoire. If many chance activities (e.g., horse betting, lottery) are not available, externals' leisure repertoire may be greatly limited. Even if externals do not completely exclude skill activities from their repertoire, the frequency and intensity of their participation in these activities, however, may be adversely affected and their liking of skill activities is significantly decreased.

Studies (e.g., Ryckman, 1979) have shown that externals have lower self-esteem, higher anxiety levels, are less cognitively active and less motivated to succeed, take less pride in accomplishments and are generally less adjusted than internals. Thus, we tentatively conclude that an external locus of control constrains leisure behavior by reducing the leisure repertoire (a range of potentially satisfying leisure experiences available), the frequency and intensity of involvement, and liking of activities. Research is needed to determine if this restriction in the leisure repertoire impedes an individual's capacity to cope with psychological problems (Iso-Ahola, 1980a, p. 88).

Direct Personal Failures and Competence

The second major category of determinants of perceived incompetence deals with failures, and exposure to uncontrollable events. Uncontrollable events are events which the individual feels to be potentially controllable, but which he/she seems unable to influence. While it is true that internals are more resistant to the detrimental effects of failures and uncontrollable events (Hiroto, 1974), it is also true that failure, as opposed to success, negatively affects all people. In terms of its psychological effects, the success-failure variable is one of the most powerful social psychological factors, and its influences have been widely investigated. It has been well established that failure in various tasks and activities, as opposed to success, reduces self-confidence and self-evaluation of personal abilities (Feather, 1968), increases attributions of failure to lack of personal ability (Bradley, 1978), lowers expectations of success (Feather, 1966) and generally produces negative feelings (Isen, 1970). Women seem to be more sensitive than men to the effects of failure, in that they are more inclined than men to attribute their failure to lack of ability and success to such external factors as good luck (Deaux, 1976). Similar differences have been found between externals and internals (Lefcourt, 1976).

Increased feelings of incompetence resulting from failures undermine one's involvement in activities in which the negative outcome is experienced. If a person attributes his failure to a lack of personal ability, his persistence at and liking of the activity is reduced and he is likely to withdraw from the activity. The problem becomes compounded if a person is repeatedly exposed to failures and uncontrollable events. Iso-Ahola, MacNeil and Szymanski (1980) have theorized that if feelings and inferences of personal helplessness, as a result of exposures to uncontrollable events or outcomes, are attributed to personal incompetence and lack of control, a state of *generalized helplessness* is the inevitable consequence. This state at its worst is characterized by decreased leisure participation, withdrawal, apathy, and depression. Given that individuals are *continuously* seeking knowledge about their abilities by means of social comparison (Festinger, 1954), it is clear that repeated failures or negative experiences represent a severe blow to perceived personal competence. Especially in an achievement oriented society, people are very sensitive about their abilities in comparison to others' and are therefore greatly hurt by failing or performing poorly. It, therefore, takes a psychologically strong individual to be able to resist the psychological consequences of direct failures. Internal persons are stronger than external persons in this respect (Lefcourt, 1976). Like externals, females have been found to be more susceptible to direct personal failures than males (Dweck & Bush, 1976).

Since repeated failure constrains leisure behavior by increasing the sense of incompetence, what then can be done to eliminate this constraining factor? The most obvious solution, of course, would be to remove competition from leisure activities. Such solutions, however, are far too simpleminded and unrealistic. While there certainly is a need to de-emphasize competition and the importance of winning and perhaps even organize certain leisure activities into noncompetitive forms, competition and winning cannot be eliminated from the face of the earth. Even if we were able to throw out all the objective criteria and standards needed for declaring winners and losers, people still would continue to compete by using subjective criteria and standards—because of their need and desire to evaluate their personal abilities relative to those of others. Furthermore, recent empirical evidence (Langer, 1979) suggests that subtle and indirect social comparison can be as powerful as a direct failure in creating the illusion of incompetence. So, rather than spending energy in all-out attacks against competition and winning, it would seem more useful to train people to tolerate failures and uncontrollable events. Such immunization against helplessness would make for more resilient individuals (Seligman, 1975).

Immunization against failure may be achieved in several ways. First, when engaged in leisure activities in which competition and winning outcomes are salient, a person may participate with individuals who are approximately at the same ability level. This similarity in the activity-related ability guarantees that no repeated and constant failures will occur. Also the similar abilities of the participants result in the outcomes being more unpredictable, making it easier for a person to avoid always attributing failures to personal incompetence. Second, people may be encouraged to place the importance of outcomes into perspective when confronted with a failure. Usually others have also failed under similar conditions. As a last resort, the importance of not only the outcome but also of the whole leisure activity in which failures are experienced can be minimized; simultaneously, the importance of leisure activities in which the individual is more proficient can be maximized: "Everyone can play golf, but it's only a few who can play the piano." Thus, the idea is to encourage people to "discriminate" or limit their feelings of incompetence and helplessness resulting from failures to a set of "unusual" or specific conditions occurring at a specific time. "While I did not play golf especially well *today*, I am a good player, not to mention my highly talented piano-playing." Of course, a balance must be found between internalizing all failures as evidence of incompetence, and the total rationalization of all failures through the above strategies. Leisure participation should aid people in learning about and coming to terms with their strengths and weaknesses.

Modeled Failure and Competence

It is interesting and significant that self-perceptions of ability and leisure motivation can be undermined not only by direct personal failures but also by exposures to *modeled* failures. Such vicarious influences can have similar adverse effects as the direct experiences of failure and uncontrollability: increased perceived incompetence which makes people shun certain leisure activities and results in the failure to exert the effort needed for acquiring basic skills in these activities. Decreased competence through modeling may occur if a person is strongly associated with a peer group and observes failure by members of the group. Perceived similarity in competence between the performer and the observer is an important determinant of whether a sense of incompetence and uncontrollability develops as a result of modeled failure.

Brown and Inouye (1978) showed experimentally that observers' persistence in the task and expectations of personal efficacy in it were strongly undermined by exposure to modeled failure or uncontrollability. After witnessing another person fail in an experimental task, subjects' persistence in performing the same task, especially when confronting difficulties in it, was significantly lower if they had been informed that the observed ineffectual model was similar in ability, than if they had been told that the failed model was superior in ability. Likewise, subjects who observed the "similar" model fail exhibited a very low sense of personal efficacy for performing and solving the task; on the other hand, subjects who were told that they are more competent than the ineffectual model expressed high expectations of self-efficacy.

Another experiment (Brown, 1979) qualified these results by indicating that in general, girls are more vulnerable than boys to the negative influences of modeled failure.

The above findings have clear implications for leisure behavior. If, for example, our friends who are thought to be similar in leisure skills and interests perform poorly in novel activities, we are inclined to think that we too will perform badly in the same leisure activity. Consequently, we may prematurely hurry to exclude that activity from our leisure repertoire. If the activity were not immediately abandoned, at least such vicarious influences would decrease expectations of self-efficacy, which is known to reduce persistence and effort expenditure in the face of task difficulty. These adverse effects in turn would impede the acquisition of essential skills or the rehearsal of old ones.

To eliminate these constraints created by the observation of modeled failure, two principal strategies exist. First, if the observer attributes the performer's failure to a lack of effort, such attribution implies that failure had nothing to do with the lack of ability and therefore suggests that success is possible next time—assuming that the performer will expend the effort needed for successful performance. Second, if the observer assumes that he is superior to the performer in competence, the performer's failure should increase the observer's expectations of self-efficacy, enhance his persistence, and boost his motivation (Brown & Inouye, 1978). Finally, vicarious influences of modeled failure can, of course, be avoided by eliminating competition from leisure activities or by arranging leisure activities so that the distinction between success and failure or between good and poor performance becomes hazy and relative. If it is emphasized that everybody fails while acquiring new leisure skills and that everybody succeeds if he is willing to expend a sufficient amount of effort and time in the activity, most of the negative influences described above can be avoided. The idea is that at his own stage of skill learning, the person is performing well, even if his objective performance may be lower than others'. However, as noted earlier, it is not possible to totally eliminate competition from leisure activities because (1) people have a need to socially compare their performances and (2) because "people develop expectations about how well they will perform on tasks at which they have had no direct experience" (Brown, 1979, p. 108). But it is clear that the more we emphasize skills and competencies in leisure activities in terms of objective standards and criteria, the more important we make the winning and thus the more vulnerable we make people for such negative influences as those created by modeled failures.

Social Judgements, Labeling and Competence

An individual's perception of his competencies is undermined not only by direct personal failures or exposures to uncontrollable events and vicarious influences, but also by others' social judgements of his capabilities. Two different lines of research support this conjecture. First Hiroto (1974) showed experimentally that if people are told, through externally provided instructions, that they have no direct control over an aversive stimulus they become helpless more easily than people who are told that they have direct control over the stimulus. In this study, "chance instructions" emphasized that this is a "guessing game", whereas "skill instructions" pointed out that the amount of unpleasantness to be received is dependent on personal skills and capabilities to find the solution to the problem. The results showed that the former instructions decreased subjects' ability to escape the aversive stimulus more than did the latter instructions.

These findings suggest that simply telling people that their actions cannot control the outcome in a given task brings about feelings of incompetence and helplessness, which in turn drastically reduces motivation to perform the task. It is therefore logical to suggest that if our "significant others" inform us directly or indicate by implication, that our abilities are inadequate or insufficient for performing well in a leisure activity, then such social judgments strongly undermine our interests, efforts and motivation to participate in this leisure activity. This possibility is particularly relevant when learning new skills because people are very sensitive and vulnerable to outside influences and social judgments about their competence to acquire the skill in question. It is therefore reasonable to propose that "chance instructions" delivered by whoever and whenever, present severe constraints on the acquisition of novel leisure skills.

Another line of research is consistent with the above suggestions. Langer and Benevento's (1978) experiments showed that if people are assigned an inferior label they develop an illusion of incompetence which leads to performance decrements and lowered persistence. The tendency to erroneously infer incompetence from interpersonal situational factors was termed "self-induced dependence." The existence of this tendency was demonstrated by two experiments. In three phases, subjects first performed successfully a task "A," then were given an inferior label ("assistant," "worker") or superior label ("boss") or no label and performed a task "B," and finally performed the task "A" again. The results revealed that regardless of their earlier success on the task, those subjects who were given the inferior label ("dependency experience") performed significantly worse than those who were not labeled or those who had the superior labels. The authors argued that the performance debilitation was due to "negative expectations induced by the label" and the accompanying illusion of personal incompetence.

In various interpersonal situations, people often assign labels to leisure performers as well as leisure activities. When a leisure performer is assigned a label that connotes inferiority relative to other leisure performers, such a label is likely to lead to an illusion of incompetence and thereby reduce motivation to engage in the activity. Another but more subtle way of assigning labels to others is often done by categorizing activities: active vs. passive, old vs. novel, smart vs. stupid, etc. When a person hears another person saying that such mentally and physically challenging leisure activities as racquetball are "smart," "good," and "wholesome," he, by implication, may infer that he is incompetent to engage in these activities if he currently participates in such physically or mentally unchallenging activities as reading, jogging and TV-watching. Not only may he conclude personal incompetence to engage in those "smart" activities but may also begin demeaning those activities in which he is presently involved. As desirable as it would be, it is difficult to eliminate this kind of labeling because it is an essential part of impression formation about people and their actions. In this process, individuals form stereotypes about leisure performers and leisure activities—not because of intention-ally putting constraints on or undermining other people and their interests but because of human incapacities to process information. Stereotypes like "business persons play golf," are economical ways of classifying information about people and their social environment. Unfortunately, such categorizing and stereotyping becomes constraining.

Relinquishing Personal Control and Competence

Another way of developing an illusion of incompetence and thereby putting constraints on leisure behavior is to allow some-one else to perform an activity or task for oneself and conse-quently become a passive observer. This is particularly relevant when performing leisure activities with an overtly confident indi-vidual and when learning leisure skills. It is fairly common to hear people say: "Go ahead, you do it, I'll watch." Of course, a self-confident individual does not hesitate to take the initiative: "Let me do it. I'll show how to perform this activity." The "you-do-it-I-watch" attitude is especially detrimental in the process of acquiring new leisure skills. To relinquish too much control to another person (e.g., teacher) in a learning situation hampers a person's attempts to acquire leisure skills, because it makes him a passive recipient of services. Besides slowing down the learning process, passive participation induced by a lack of perceived control is deleterious to one's physical and psychological health (Langer & Rodin, 1976; Rodin & Langer, 1977). Furthermore, passive recrea-tional participation has been shown to be associated with the least positive overall mood, because it offers virtually no challenge and requires little, if any, mastery (Csikszentmihalyi, et al., 1977).

Thus, it appears that the absence of active involvement—whether induced by an overtly confident performer and other social or situational factors—is accompanied by feelings of lack of compe-tence and mastery. The sequence of events may be as follows:

Social or Situational Factors (e.g., overtly con-fident partner)		Relinquish Personal Control	$\rightarrow$	Illusion of Incompetence	$\leftarrow$ $\rightarrow$	Passive Leisure Partici-pation
	$\rightarrow$					

As shown earlier, an illusion of incompetence is psychologically detrimental because it can lead to feelings of helplessness, apathy, withdrawal and depression. Thus, even though the above sequence describes an illusion of incompetence as an end product, it means that such illusions further strengthen the pattern of passive leisure participation. The latter in turn strengthens the former, thereby creating a self-perpetuating circle. The above paradigm is important because it demonstrates that an illusion of incompetence is not only followed by passive leisure involvement but under certain circumstances can be preceded by it.

Environmental Constraints and Competence

The discussion thus far indicates that a feeling or the illusion of incompetence is a major constraint on leisure. It undermines one's leisure repertoire, reduces activity levels and decreases leisure and life satisfaction. Does this then mean that a competence-enhancing intervention will always be beneficial? Recent experimental evidence suggests a negative answer to this question. Schulz and Hanusa (1979) reported two experiments which indicated that the benefits of the competence-enhancing intervention depend on existing environmental constraints on one's opportunities to exercise mastery and competence. The data revealed that those subjects whose competence was enhanced in an experimental task afterwards engaged in significantly more leisure activities than those subjects who received a low competence manipulation. Similarly, the former subjects were judged by a trained clinician more socially adjusted and competent than the latter subjects. However, these positive effects occurred only in an environment where the subjects had a multitude of opportunities to accommodate different levels of personal competence, that is, on college campuses. But when the same experiment was done on the institutionalized aged, no positive gains were recorded for the subjects whose competence was enhanced experimentally; in fact, the low-competence subjects were more satisfied than the high-competence subjects. Thus, increasing an individual's level of perceived competence does not always facilitate functioning.

These two groups of subjects differ in one critical respect.

"A college environment provides infinite opportunities for exercising individual competencies, and there may therefore be no
upper limit on the impact of competence- and control-enhancing
interventions. The opportunities to exercise individual competencies in a long-term care facility for the aged are undoubtedly
more limited. With the exception of participating in some recreational activities and interacting with other patients, there are
few opportunities that would challenge persons of moderate or
high levels of perceived competence" (Schulz & Hanusa, 1979,
p. 335).

The institutionalized aged are captives of their environment and
can do little with their leisure skills and competencies. Thus, we
can rhetorically ask: what good does it do to have skills and
competencies if you cannot do anything with them? It then follows that the externally elevated feelings of competence in a
constraining environment are likely to backfire and constrain
rather than liberate.

IV. ATTITUDINAL CONSTRAINTS

Motives and attitudes are highly interrelated. Since leisure
attitude is defined "as the expressed amount of affect toward a
given leisure-related object" (Iso-Ahola, 1980a, p. 251), a positive
attitude means liking and a negative attitude connotes disliking
of a leisure-related object. Because people do not generally participate in the activities they dislike, it then follows that there must
be a positive correlation between leisure attitudes and leisure
motivation. In other words, the more positive attitude a person
has toward a leisure activity, the more motivated he is to participate in it. This, in turn, means that negative leisure attitudes
constrain leisure motivation and actual leisure behavior.

Our overall attitudes about people, objects and ideas are influenced by our beliefs about these and our feelings toward them. In
fact, to hold positive or negative feelings about leisure, we must
first hold some beliefs about what leisure is and does. If we are
interested in the determinants of constraining leisure attitudes,

the factors determining belief formation are therefore relevant to our discussion also. These factors are three-fold (Fishbein & Ajzen, 1975): (1) informational, (2) descriptive, and (3) inferential.

First, beliefs can be formed on the basis of externally provided information. This includes reading newspapers, watching television or simply receiving leisure-related information from another person. Whether such information is judged accurate depends on many factors such as credibility of the communicator, content of the message and the type of audience the message is directed to (Fishbein & Ajzen, 1975). Second, direct leisure experiences result in the formation of descriptive beliefs about an object. Third, beliefs are also formed by making logical inferences. For examples of these, see Iso-Ahola (1980a, p. 256). Any of these three processes of forming beliefs can become a source of constraining leisure attitudes. Let's consider some of these possibilities next.

Lack of Information as a Constraint

An important "informational" and motivational constraint on leisure behavior is caused by the lack of information itself. This deficiency may stem from a lack of knowledge on available recreation programs, activities and environments. Alternatively, a leisure participant may have no or little idea about potential benefits of engagement in certain leisure activities. And, of course, these deficiencies can work interactively; for example, a person may know that a certain leisure activity is available in his community but thinks that it is not conducive to the psychological rewards he expects of his leisure activities. Or, another person may be so accustomed to hiking in national parks that he overlooks similar opportunities nearby his community. In short, people can lack *specific* information about whether or not certain leisure opportunities exist and/or *diversive* information about what they can do and gain by participating in certain forms of leisure. Either deficiency constrains leisure behavior.

To combat such informational deficiencies and resultant constraints on leisure, three principal courses of action exist. First and most obviously, practitioners can immediately inform people about the existing leisure programs, activities and resources in their community, and the potential benefits associated with utilization of these opportunities. In fact, this is probably the most important function and task for practitioners to undertake. To simply build excellent programs and facilities is inadequate. Practitioners have to reach out to their residents and provide positive and well-documented information about leisure in general and about specific programs in particular. Second, leisure education should be started in childhood and continued throughout the adult life-span. The primary function of such education is to initiate or increase *cognitive awareness* of leisure in general as well as specific leisure skills and opportunities. For example, people have typically been taught to view outdoor recreation environments in terms of a "setting for action"—a place for activity. Yet a summary of recent research indicates that the same environment can be experienced in a variety of ways, for example, as emotional territory in which certain moods and experiences are triggered producing one brand of leisure satisfaction. (Iso-Ahola, 1980a). This, then, calls for leisure education to increase environmental knowledge and ecological consciousness, so as to de-emphasize the need to always see leisure in terms of activities and products (e.g., winning) and emphasize it also as a process and form of experience (Mannell, 1980).

Third, exposure to a wide variety of leisure activities and experiences is essential through childhood and adolescence. Empirical evidence (Brooks & Elliott, 1971; Bruner, 1975) indicates that the lack of a variety of active and stimulating play experiences in childhood not only constrains leisure behavior presently and in the future, but is psychologically detrimental to adults 20 years later.

Past experiences can be both constraining and liberating. They are constraining in that they may limit the individual to choosing the familiar, and liberating in the sense that they provide a springboard for seeking new leisure experiences—whether "within" familiar leisure activities or totally new forms of leisure. The reported positive and significant correlation between childhood recreation experiences and adult leisure behavior (Kelly, 1977; Sofranko & Nolan, 1972; Yoesting & Burkhead, 1973) shows that adults participate in many of those activities they learned in childhood. But this potentially constraining effect is greater, the more limited the early experiences are in the first place. In other words, if a person has acquired only a few leisure skills in childhood, his adult leisure behavior will be doubly hurt because he is limited to the few previously learned skills; this in turn undercuts his predisposition and readiness to acquire new leisure experiences as an adult. However, if a person has acquired a large leisure repertoire in childhood and adolescence, as an adult he perceives more opportunities for substituting various learned activities should he be constrained by accidents, lack of facilities or other reasons. The person who has a predisposition to learn new skills continues to seek novel leisure experiences. The resultant cognitive flexibility safeguards and contributes to his psychological well being.

Biased Information as a Constraint

In a work-oriented society, one may be exposed to information that glorifies work and demeans leisure. Mass media and politicians stress the importance of work, employment and productivity, but one may hear little about leisure. This may create the impression that leisure is an evil and does not contribute to the quality of life. Many people feel guilty about their participation in leisure. Such a negative attitude toward leisure is bound to constrain leisure behavior and undermine leisure and life satisfaction.

Externally provided information can also become constraining if it is stereotypical or prejudicial in nature. Unfortunately, much of the leisure information transmitted by the mass media gives a misleading or false picture of adults' leisure patterns and ethics. For example television's beer commercials promote the idea that people work hard and spend the remaining free-time drinking beer: "Weekends are made for Michelob!" One of the authors (Iso-Ahola) is presently collecting data to determine the effects of such commercials on the development of work and leisure ethics and leisure aspirations in children and adolescents. It is hypothesized that the information transmitted through these commercials perpetuates the work-ethic philosophy and undercuts leisure ethic, suggesting that leisure can only be earned through hard work. Leisure is therefore pictured as secondary to the primary human function—to work, and the earned leisure is equated with resting and drinking. If this conjecture proves correct, it is clear that such public portrayal of work and leisure is devastating to human development and undermines the importance of leisure to quality of life. If leisure becomes equated with drinking, even if only partially and unconsciously, this concept of leisure shuts off people from a wide variety of leisure experiences. Incidentally, it is worth noting that there are few, if any, females in typical beer commercials, which implies that such leisure is considered appropriate for men but not for women.

A study recently completed by one of the authors (Mannell) and a student, Nancy Renner, based on a content analysis of selected magazines found that 50 percent of the full-page ads in men's magazines used images or a background of people at leisure to sell non-leisure related products in 1979. For the same year, in women's magazines, this percentage was 38 percent, though it had been steadily increasing through-out the 1970s. With this kind of information presented in the mass media it seems inevitable that leisure and consumer consumption are associated, again creating biased beliefs about leisure.

Whether acquired through the mass media or other external sources, it appears that children and adolescents hold stereotypical views of sex-role appropriate leisure behaviours. Stein and Smithells (1969) found that artistic, social and reading skills and activities were considered as the most feminine and the least masculine; on the other hand, athletic, spatial and mechanical, and arithmetic skills and activities were viewed the most masculine and the least feminine. These differences in sex-role standards became gradually, though not linearly, more pronounced with age (from the second to the twelfth grade). The results also showed that boys' ratings of reading (activity considered appropriate for girls) changed more than their ratings of other activities, whereas girls' ratings of athletic and arithmetic activities (considered appropriate for boys) shifted more than their ratings of other activities. The authors, therefore, concluded that "the major learning which occurs during the school years may be learning what is *inappropriate* for one's own sex rather than what is appropriate."

These results are also consistent with Iso-Ahola's (1980a) contention that elementary and secondary schools in the U.S. are failing in educating for leisure because they put a premium on few masculine activities, namely football and baseball. Such narrow education and socialization not only limits males' leisure repertoire but seriously impedes females' leisure aspirations and pursuits. Fortunately, there are signs that sex-role stereotypes of leisure behavior are being broken, as attested to by the fact that many girls are playing Little League sports. But we still have a long way to go for eliminating constraints on leisure behavior due to the sex-role stereotyping education.

Finally, it should be noted that leisure information becomes constraining if it arouses needs that cannot be satisfied. A case in point is the media advertisement of vacation trips to exotic places. Iso-Ahola (1980a, pp. 197–198) has suggested that the constant bombardment by the mass media stressing the necessity and desirability of visiting such glamorous places as Acapulco and the Bahamas makes people believe that their recreational needs can only be satisfied in exotic places. Since the majority of people cannot afford such trips, their sense of freedom may be constrained and psychological well-being threatened by the commercials. Whether these "false" recreational needs are psychologically harmful would make an interesting subject for study.

V. SOCIAL-CULTURAL CONSTRAINTS

As noted in the introduction, constraints on leisure cannot totally be eliminated as long as human beings are "social animals." Due to his/her social nature, an individual's leisure choices and behaviors influence and are influenced by those of others. Thus, the individual is tied to the immediate social environment. This does not automatically mean that an individual's leisure is constrained greatly. Whether the social environment becomes predominantly constraining or liberating depends on several factors. Among these are social roles and norms.

Social Obligations and Constraints

Social roles and norms impose obligations on people. This type of constraint is compounded by the fact that they are fairly permanent and stable in nature. Due to these obligations, people have to spend their free-time, or at least portions of it, in activities they do not like. Csikszentmihalyi, et al.'s (1977) data indicated that 34 percent of adolescents' activities contain some form of obligation or coercion, while only 38 percent of their time is taken up with purely voluntary activities. Kelly (1976) found that 26 percent of all leisure activities were perceived as having "some obligation" and 29 percent as having "considerable obligation." Thus, one-half of personal leisure activities are perceived obligatory in nature. While all of this constraint is probably not due to social obligations, it is nevertheless fair to assume that social roles and norms are major contributors.

Social obligations are psychologically deleterious because they reduce one's perceptions of freedom (Iso-Ahola, 1979a, b) and actual involvement in and liking of leisure activities (Mannell, 1979a, b). These obligations may turn play and recreation into work, by changing intrinsic leisure motivation into extrinsic motivation. This change in the perceived locus of causality of one's leisure behavior from personal to environmental (social) factors means that a person comes to believe the reason why he engages in a leisure activity is not because he wants to but because he is compelled to do it. The "overjustification" research (Deci, 1975; Lepper & Greene, 1978) has shown that extrinsic rewards undermine intrinsic motivation and leisure behavior. In other words, when a person who is initially intrinsically motivated by a given activity is asked to perform the same activity for rewards or other extrinsic reasons, or is simply put under constant surveillance or given a deadline by which to finish the activity, his interest in and liking of the activity considerably decreases and may die. Recently Williams (1980) and Bradley and Mannell (1982) have provided evidence to suggest that the behavioral constraint component of an extrinsic reward may be more important in undermining intrinsically motivated behavior than the reward value itself. For example, social obligations such as playing with one's children may be rewarding, but also reduce personal choice to engage in other more preferred leisure pursuits. At times, then, playing with one's children may be work and not leisure. In short, extrinsic rewards, sanctions and controls severely constrain leisure behavior and reduce leisure satisfaction.

Familial Constraints

While examples of the constraining effects of social obligations can be found everywhere, they are perhaps most readily observable in the family. In this context, constraints are reciprocal, parents constraining each other and children, and children in turn constraining their parents. Although there is a set of reciprocal constraints between parents and children, it is clear that parents, due to their authority, are more constraining than children; parents can order and dictate children's play activities, whereas children can only influence and constrain their parents' leisure patterns by their mere presence or personal "powers of persuasion." The issue, however, is not who is actually more constraining. What is important is to understand the process of how parents and children constrain each other's play and leisure and what the psychological consequences of such constraints are.

Marriage Partners Constraining One Another.

We first consider the possible constraining effects of marriage on the partners' leisure behavior and the resultant satisfaction. The question is: Would people express more marital satisfaction, if they perceived more freedom in the relationship to pursue personal leisure interests? In general, it is true that the greater the perceived freedom to engage in varied activities, the greater the perception of leisure and enjoyment associated with participation in those activities (Iso-Ahola, 1980a; Mannell, 1979b). This, therefore, suggests that the sense of freedom in regard to personal leisure behavior is important to marital satisfaction. On the other hand, if this freedom translates into the pursuit of "individual" activities during the first five years of marriage, the marital satisfaction will significantly decrease (Orthner, 1975). But involvement

in "joint" activities during the same period is positively related to
marital satisfaction. If a couple's leisure interests are incompatible,
they may have to develop a system which allows both of them to
have as much freedom as possible to pursue personal leisure
interests plus a few common interests. In any case, it seems clear
that marriage considerably constrains individual leisure behavior
and forces the partners to make leisure compromises to keep the
marital satisfaction high.

Parents Constraining Children.

From their birth onward children show a rapidly increasing
capacity for understanding the world around them. Their thirst
for knowledge and novel experiences appears insatiable. But at
the same time children lack the capacity to completely control
their actions and to understand what is and is not safe for them.
Consequently, parents often have to severely restrict children's
play. But with growing age, parents' role as a constrainer changes
from physical safeguarding to psychological tutoring of what is
appropriate and inappropriate. Although this probably means
that parents' direct orders and restrictions decrease with children's
age, it does not mean that parents' concern and influence over
their children's leisure activities wane. Restrictions may become
less direct (more implicit), but they still exist.

Concern about children's extracurricular activities has increased
in recent years because of the availability of drugs and the increase
in teenage sexual behavior. To prevent these "destructive forms"
of recreation, many parents have come to emphasize the role of
Little League sports to the extent that these activities have become
an institution as American as apple pie. "Too many parents feel
that if their sons and daughters do not go through this institution,
they will miss an essential aspect of education and socialization.
Too many of them feel that Little League is the only or major
activity that strengthens their children psychologically" (Iso-Ahola,
1980b, p. 77). Although a need for such sports activities seems
legitimate in light of the "dangers" of drugs and premature sex,
this emphasis on youth sports seems to occur at the expense of
other leisure activities. Consequently parents' guiding of their

children into sports is overly one-sided and constraining.

Another way of constraining children's leisure in the context of Little League sports is to turn their initially intrinsic motivation into extrinsic motivation. By their mere presence the spectators and coaches may turn a Little League sport activity into work. "Performing under the keen eyes and in front of the open mouths of authoritative coaches and spectators, it is almost impossible for players to get intrinsically motivated by Little League baseball. They are working hard to excel, mainly to satisfy their coaches and parents. They are working but not playing" (Iso-Ahola, 1980b, p. 52).

Besides imposing upon children value judgments of what constitutes appropriate and inappropriate leisure activities, parents constrain children's leisure in other ways as well. First, depending on their "cognitive style," some parents are considerably more restrictive than others. Bishop and Chace (1971) found that those mothers who are rigid, simple, concrete, conventional and authoritative in their cognitive performance create a less playful engendering environment for their children than those mothers who can be characterized in their everyday behavior as abstract, flexible, unorthodox and nonauthoritarian. The former types of mothers' attitudes toward their children's play were less flexible, they encouraged less play and reported actual conditions of the home play environment to be less conducive to play than did the abstract mothers. Thus, parents' own cognitive style or capacity is significantly linked to the quality of their children's home play environment. But the importance of this study does not end here. Bishop and Chace demonstrated empirically that the home play environment affects children's potential creativity. Specifically, children's creativity declined as the playfulness (i.e., greater variety, novelty, complexity and autonomy for the child) of the home play environment decreased. In conclusion, it appears that parents' own cognitive limitations constrain their children's home play and consequently are psychologically very detrimental to them.

Another more insidious way by which parents constrain their children's leisure activity has to do with a lack of time spent together. The unbelievable fact is that about half of the American parents of 0 to 13 year old children never spend time with them in such important leisure activities as reading, playing games or outing trips (Pratt, 1976). At the same time, it is known that most children (80 percent in Pratt's study) greatly enjoy doing things with their parents. Parents' lack of interest in and/or time for joint activities not only reduces children's repertoire of leisure skills and interests but prevents strong and psychologically healthy bonds from developing between parents and children. On the other hand, "extended periods of shared time have considerable potential for facilitating family cohesion" (Orthner & Mancini, 1980).

Children Constraining Parents.

As for children's constraining their parents' leisure, there is an inverted U-relationship between family stage and too many family obligations as a barrier to leisure enjoyment, as illustrated in Figure 2 based upon Witt and Goodale's (1981) data. In other words, "too many family obligations" as a barrier is at its highest when the youngest child is still at home but at its lowest when the family does not yet have a child or when the youngest is old enough to have left home. But Figure 2 also indicates considerable sex differences. Specifically, the family stage (i.e., the age of the youngest child) makes a much bigger difference to females' feelings of "too many family obligations" than to those of males. This result probably reflects the fact women carry the main burden of child rearing and consequently suffer more from it than men as a barrier to leisure enjoyment.

When children are very young, they become the major restrictive factor on adults' (particularly women's) leisure by demanding constant surveillance. Ryder, Kafka and Olson (1971) found that the coming of a baby restricted parental activities outside the home. Similarly, Bollman, Moxley and Elliott (1975) documented that the presence of a preschool child in the home limited parents' leisure behavior to homecentered activities and was "a greater inhibitor of community participation than lack of financial resources." This means that home-centered leisure activities become easier and cheaper and may explain the large amount of time young couples spend in watching television. While parents can leave their children with a babysitter, in order to engage in personal leisure activities, this soon becomes too expensive for young

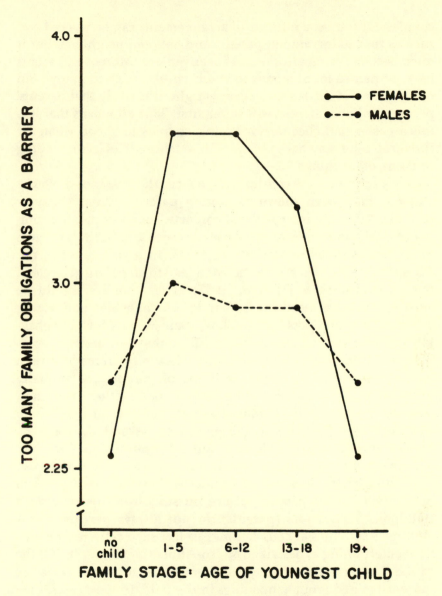

Figure V-2. Relationship Between Family Stage and Too Many Family Obligations as a Barrier to Leisure Enjoyment (from Witt and Goodale, 1981).

couples. Of course, a number of arrangements can be worked out, such as turntaking among parents and between neighbors, but it often becomes cumbersome and inconvenient. Moreover, parents have to spend a lot of money for their children's clothes, toys and other things. If the family budget is tight, it is likely that parents' personal leisure interests will suffer first. This all means that it is much easier and cheaper for young couples to spend whatever little free-time they have at home, in watching television, reading or doing other things.

In addition to these constraining effects, the presence of young children have been shown to modify parents' sexual behavior (Harper, 1975) and interpersonal contacts. For example, the coming of a baby increases mothers' contacts with and feelings towards their own mothers (Ryder, et al., 1971). In a similar vein, the adoption of a child has been shown to lead to an enlarged circle of friends (Massarik & Franklin, 1967). These studies should be extended to determine the extent to which babies and young children limit and possibly facilitate, their parents' leisure behaviors and how parents resolve any conflicts that may arise.

When children are older, they constrain their parents' leisure in different ways. For example, millions of parents are annually involved in their children's Little League sports either as coaches, referees or spectators. Parents have to make arrangements to transport their children to the games on several days a week for two months, and they have to put off vacations until the end of July when the games are over. It is important to note, however, that although these kinds of children's leisure activities seem to severely restrict parents' leisure pursuits from the observer's standpoint, the actors (parents) do not always perceive their children's activities as constraining; in fact such activities may be very entertaining as described by Iso-Ahola (1980b, p. 77): "Of the games I observed, only a few of them failed to make spectators (parents) exited about happenings in the field. In most cases, they screamed, yelled, commented, and analyzed performances and performers. It looked like spectators were having a good time while modern gladiators battled among themselves and sorted out the fittest." But even if these activities are enjoyable to parents, it is likely that parents would spend considerably less of their free-time in watching Little League games should they have no children.

To this end, then, children's leisure activities constrain parents' leisure.

Social Norms

So far, in this section, we have discussed the psychological mechanisim underlying the effects of social obligations on leisure and given examples of the most obvious social obligations — familial roles. Another important group of social roles is associated with occupation, meaning that one's occupation constrains his leisure. The degree of constraint and certainly the nature of the leisure activities constrained vary with the socio-economic status of an occupation. Both blue collar and white collar workers are expected to participate in certain leisure activities, which therefore constrains their leisure. Such social constraints may be stronger for white collar than blue collar workers. Persons with high status jobs have much more responsibility than persons with low status jobs. Certain leisure activities are viewed to interfere with the conduct of such high responsibility jobs. For example, if an academic dean and an assembly line worker went to drink beer in a tavern after their work, it probably would not take long before the dean would feel pressure to drop this leisure activity — especially if the tavern was not particularly reputable — no matter how brilliantly he performed his duties on the job. On the other hand, the blue collar worker likely would have fewer constraints on his drinking behavior. Of course, a blue collar worker who frequented the ballet would likely feel similar sanctions from his peer group. In many cases, leisure is constrained not only by what is socially undesirable but also by what is socially desirable to do during free-time. For example, the white collar worker is expected to participate in various organizations and service clubs.

Another more striking example of the powerful constraining effects of social norms on leisure behavior occurred while this was being written. The following incident made headlines in Iowa newspapers. In short, a Dubuque high school swimming coach faced the possibility of being fired for sharing a room with his fiancee on a recent team trip. The coach admitted he spent one night at a Cedar Rapids motel with his fiancee while he was accompanying members of the girls' diving team to a meet in

Cedar Rapids. Dubuque School Superintendent immediately suspended the coach and recommended to the school board that he be dismissed. The incident stirred a furor in Dubuque, which ultimately saved the coach's job. But he was reprimanded by the Board and suspended for a month without pay, costing the coach about $3,000. This example clearly illustrates how social norms associated with certain social roles (e.g., teacher) can constrain leisure behaviors of those who occupy these roles. The norms dictate directly by suggesting what is socially undesirable leisure and indirectly by making the distinction between work and leisure hazy. The situations like the one described above make it difficult for people to tell where their leisure begins and job ends.

We suggest that the pressure to comply with and conform to social norms concerning leisure behavior is greater in small than large communities. This follows because in small communities almost everyone knows each other and what everybody is capable of doing and can afford to do. On the other hand, it is easy to disappear and get lost in the mass in heavily populated communities and not worry about others when selecting leisure activities.

Social Interaction as a Constraint

Social interaction is the central component of leisure. Studies have shown that social interaction is one of the three underlying dimensions of leisure needs (London, Crandall & Fitzgibbons, 1977), that the best leisure activities are those that involve both friendly interaction *and* an activity (Crandall, 1979), that social interaction significantly contributes to the physical and psychological health of the elderly (Schulz, 1976), and that social participation and happiness are positively and significantly related to one another (Graney, 1975). A lack of social interaction manifests itself in the perceived infrequency of social contacts (quantitatively) and/or in the lack of preferred and desired friends and interactions (qualitatively).

Too much social interaction may be constraining as well. Leisure behavior is a dialectical, optimizing process which regulates social interaction with others to provide a person with a desired level of privacy and social contacts. Thus, "leisure behavior is a continuous interplay of opposing forces to shut oneself off from others at one time and to open oneself up for interpersonal contacts at another time, to achieve an optimal amount of social interaction" (Iso-Ahola, 1980c, p. 32). While people strive for a desired level of social interaction, this does not mean that they will actually achieve it. Often, they have more social interaction and contacts than they would like to have. This excess, therefore, becomes a burden and limits their leisure choices, with the result of reduced leisure satisfaction and decline in the overall quality of life.

A recent study supports this theorizing. Csikszentmihalyi and Graef (1979) used electronic beepers to page 107 subjects several times a day to ask them to report, among other things, what they were doing and why. The subjects' age ranged from 19 to 63 and their occupations included a variety of blue and white collar jobs. The results indicated that people were most cheerful when they were at such public leisure settings as restaurants. However, when they "had to be there to please a friend or member of the family" they felt more irritable than in work. Clearly, then, social interaction is annoying when it is unwanted and performed for extrinsic reasons. Unfortunately, unwanted social interaction is the rule rather than an exception among many white collar workers. It is common that people in varied white collar jobs are expected to entertain and be entertained by other workers during their free time. Such social interaction can easily become a burden, especially if both husband and wife work. Frequent parties for the sake of formality with people who are not genuine friends take away free-time otherwise spent in personally rewarding activities or in the "right" type of social interaction.

The problem is compounded by the fact that such forms of social interaction as parties have to be scheduled days and perhaps weeks beforehand. This, of course, means that even if a person wants to have a party tonight, he may have no desire for it next Saturday. He may simply be physically and mentally tired on Saturday due to the requirements of daily activities, so that he would much rather do something else than spend the evening at a social party. But the prior commitment would force him to attend. While it is impossible for practical reasons to completely avoid scheduling social get-togethers ahead of time, it is also clear that prior commitments constrain and undermine the very essence of leisure—freedom. What is needed is what has been called "improvised" leisure (Iso-Ahola, 1980a), social interaction in this case. Improvised leisure is based upon personal freedom, on the spur of the moment, to choose and control involvement in activities, including the time, place and social company of participation.

VI. A CONCLUDING NOTE

Whatever the constraints are, they are psychologically detrimental because they undercut the sense of freedom—the very essence of leisure. While people "feel most free when engaged in leisure activities" (Csikszentmihalyi & Graef, 1979), the aforediscussed constraints can turn leisure into work and destroy leisure enjoyment. But freedom to choose one's leisure activities is not enough. It can be deduced from past research that people feel they have less freedom in regard to leisure if their leisure activities provide few challenges, little variety and responsibility and if participation does not bring about feelings of competence. Thus, feelings of freedom (and of lack of constraints) are affected not only by the initial freedom to choose an activity in which to engage but also by the process and products of leisure involvement. This in turn means that to understand the psychology of leisure constraints, one has to consider the perceived blocks to one's freedom to choose leisure activities as well as factors that become inhibitory during the course of leisure behaviors. For example, repeated failure in a leisure activity may be generalized to similar activities. As a result, a person may altogether drop these activities from his leisure repertoire or at least, feel less enthusiastic about participation in them. This, of course, means that his initial freedom to choose from a range of leisure activities is narrowed and undermined considerably.

Finally, it should be noted that the more routine leisure behaviors become, the more inhibitory and constraining they are and thus less conducive to leisure enjoyment. Routine takes away uncertainty, which reduces the feeling of freedom. It has been shown (Harvey, 1976) that the more uncertain people are about the alternatives from which to choose, the greater their feeling of freedom. There seems to be sex differences in these feelings, however, as research has shown that what is work for women is leisure to men. Csikszentmihalyi and Graef (1979) reported that men felt much freer than women in domestic and household chore activities, presumably because these activities had become routinized for women while they provided diversion for men. A need for optimally arousing leisure experiences underlies leisure behavior. Factors that hinder the pursuit and fulfillment of this need are the major constraints of leisure behavior.

VII. SUMMARY

This paper presents a conceptualization of leisure constraints and examines how these constraints develop, what their psychological consequences are, and what can be done to combat them. Research indicates that perceived incompetence is a major obstacle to rewarding leisure experiences, because it reduces involvement in or leads to a complete withdrawal from a range of leisure activities. Increased passivity at its worst is accompanied by apathy, helplessness and depression. The second major group of constraints has to do with attitudinal variables, including motives and needs. In this respect, it appears that a lack of information is an important constraint on leisure. Leisure involvement can be constrained by a lack of specific information about whether or not certain leisure opportunities exist or by a lack of diversive information about what can be done and gained by participating in certain forms of leisure. To combat such informational deficiencies and the resultant constraints on leisure, three principal courses of action were discussed. In addition to the lack of information itself, biased information can become a constraint on leisure behavior. In a work-oriented society, one may be continuously exposed to biased information that glorifies work and demeans leisure. Furthermore, much of the leisure information transmitted by the mass media gives a false picture of adults' leisure patterns and values by promoting the idea that "weekends are made for Michelob!" The externally provided information can also become constraining if it is stereotypical in nature, as in the case of the sex-role stereotyping of certain leisure activities.

Finally, "social-cultural" constraints were discussed. Research indicates that various types of social obligations turn play and recreation into work, by changing intrinsic leisure motivation into extrinsic motivation. Particular attention was paid to familial constraints, addressing how parents constrain each other and their children and how the children in turn constrain their parents. In addition, the effects of other social roles and norms were discussed. It was suggested that social norms dictate one's leisure directly by suggesting what is socially undesirable leisure and indirectly by making the distinction between work and leisure hazy, meaning that it is difficult for people to tell where their leisure begins and job ends. Social interaction was shown to constrain leisure when there is too little or too much of it and when social interaction is not of the desired type. One way of combatting such constraining social interaction is to begin to "improvise" social contacts.

REFERENCES

Aronson, E. (1972). *The social animal.* San Francisco: W. H. Freeman and Company.

Bishop, D. W., & Chace, C. A. (1971). Parental conceptual systems, home play environment, and potential creativity in children. *Journal of Experimental Child Psychology, 12,* 318–338.

Bollman, S. R., Moxley, V. M., & Elliott, N. C. (1975). Family and community activities of rural nonfarm families with children. *Journal of Leisure Research, 7,* 53–62.

Bradley, G. W. (1978). Self-serving biases in the attribution process: A reexamination of the fact or fiction question. *Journal of Personality and Social Psychology, 36,* 56–72.

Bradley, W., & Mannell, R. C. (1982, August). *The effects of extrinsic rewards and reward procedures on intrinsic motivation and the experience of flow during play.* Paper presented at the American Psychological Association's Annual Convention, Washington, D.C.

Brooks, J. B., & Elliott, D. M. (1971). Prediction of psychological adjustment at age thirty from leisure time activities and satisfactions in childhood. *Human Development, 14,* 51–61.

Brown, I., Jr. (1979). Learned helplessness through modeling: Self-efficacy and social comparison processes. In L. C. Perlmuter, & R. A. Monty (Eds.), *Choice and perceived control* (pp. 107–120). Hillsdale, NJ: LEA.

Brown, I., Jr., & Inouye, D. K. (1978). Learned helplessness through modeling:

The role of perceived similarity in competence. *Journal of Personality and Social Psychology, 36,* 900–908.

Bruner, J. (1975, January). Play is serious business. *Psychology Today,* pp. 81–83.

Campbell, A., Converse, P. E., & Rodgers, W. L. (1976). *The quality of american life: Perceptions, evaluations, and satisfactions.* New York: Russell Sage Foundation.

Crandall, R. (1979). Social interaction, affect and leisure. *Journal of Leisure Research, 11,* 165–181.

Csikszentmihalyi, M., & Graef, R. (1979, December). Feeling free. *Psychology Today,* pp. 84–90, 98–99.

Csikszentmihalyi, M., Larson, R., & Prescott, S. (1977). The ecology of adolescent activity and experience. *Journal of Youth and Adolescence, 6,* 281–294.

Deaux, K. (1976). Sex: A perspective on the attribution process. In H. J. Harvey, W. J. Ickes, & R. F. Kidd (Eds.), *New directions in attribution research* (Volume 1, pp. 335–352). Hillsdale, NJ: LEA.

deCharms, R. (1968). *Personal causation: The internal affective determinants of behavior.* New York: Academic Press.

Deci, E. L. (1975). *Intrinsic motivation.* New York: Plenum Press.

Dweck, C. S., & Bush, E. S. (1976). Sex differences in learned helplessness: I. Differential debilitation with peer and adult evaluators. *Developmental Psychology, 12,* 147–156.

Ellis, M. J. (1973). *Why people play.* Englewood Cliffs, NJ: Prentice-Hall.

Feather, N. T. (1966). Effects of prior success and failure on expectations of success on subsequent performance. *Journal of Personality and Social Psychology, 3,* 287–298.

Feather, N. T. (1968). Change in confidence following success or failure as a predictor of subsequent performance. *Journal of Personality and Social Psychology, 9,* 38–46.

Festinger, L. (1954). A theory of social comparison processes. *Human Relations, 7,* 117–140.

Fishbein, M., and Ajzen, I. (1975). *Belief, attitude, intention, and behavior: An introduction to theory and research.* Reading, MA: Addison-Wesley.

Gold, D. (1967). Preference for skill or chance tasks in ambiguous situations. *Psychological Reports, 20,* 877–878.

Graney, M. J. (1975). Happiness and social participation in aging. *Journal of Gerontology, 30,* 701–706.

Grotevant, H. D., Scarr, S., & Weinberg, R. A. (1977). Patterns of interest similarity in adoptive and biological families. *Journal of Personality and Social Psychology, 35,* 667–676.

Harper, L. V. (1975). The scope of offspring effects: From caregiver to culture. *Psychological Bulletin, 82,* 784–801.

Harvey, J. H. (1976). Attribution of freedom. In J. H. Harvey, W. J. Ickes, & R. F. Kidd (Eds.), *New directions in attribution research* (Volume 1, pp. 73–96). Hillsdale, NJ: LEA.

Hiroto, D. S. (1974). Locus of control and learned helplessness. *Journal of Experimental Psychology, 102,* 187–193.

Isen, A. (1970). Success, failure, attention and reaction to stress: The warm glow of success. *Journal of Personality and Social Psychology, 15,* 194–201.

Iso-Ahola, S. E. (1979a). Basic dimensions of definitions of leisure. *Journal of Leisure Research, 11,* 28–39.

Iso-Ahola, S. E. (1979b). Some social psychological determinants of perceptions of leisure: Preliminary evidence. *Leisure Sciences, 2,* 305–314.

Iso-Ahola, S. E. (1980a). *The social psychology of leisure and recreation.* Dubuque, IA: Wm. C. Brown.

Iso-Ahola, S. E. (1980b, June). Who's turning children's Little League play into work? *Parks and Recreation,* pp. 50–54, 77.

Iso-Ahola, S. E. (Ed.). (1980c). *Social psychological perspectives on leisure and recreation.* Springfield, IL: Charles C Thomas.

Iso-Ahola, S. E. (1981). Leisure counseling at the crossroads. *The Counseling Psychologist, 9,* 71–74.

Kelly, J. R. (1976). *Two orientations of leisure choices.* Paper presented at the Annual American Sociological Association Convention, New York.

Kelly, J. R. (1977). Leisure socialization: Replication and extension. *Journal of Leisure Research, 9,* 121–132.

Langer, E. J. (1979). The illusion of incompetence. In L. C. Perlmuter, & R. A. Monty (Eds.), *Choice and perceived control* (pp. 301–313). Hillsdale, NJ: LEA.

Langer, E. J., & Benevento, A. (1978). Self-induced dependence. *Journal of Personality and Social Psychology, 36,* 886–893.

Langer, E. J., and Rodin, J. (1976). The effects of choice and enhanced personal responsibility for the aged: A field experiment in an institutional setting. *Journal of Personality and Social Psychology, 34,* 191–198.

Lefcourt, H. M. (1976). *Locus of control.* Hillsdale, NJ: LEA.

Lepper, M. L., & Greene, D. (Eds.). (1978). *The hidden costs of reward: New perspectives on the psychology of human motivation.* Hillsdale, NJ: LEA.

London, M., Crandall, R., & Fitzgibbons, D. (1977). The psychological structure of leisure: Activities, needs, people. *Journal of Leisure Research, 9,* 252–263.

Mannell, R. C. (1979a). A conceptual and experimental basis for research in the psychology of leisure. *Leisure and society, 2,* 179–196.

Mannell, R. C. (1979b). Leisure research in the psychological lab: Leisure a permanent and/or transient cognitive disposition. In E. Avedon, M. LeLievre, & T. Stewart (Eds.), *Contemporary leisure research.* Waterloo, Ontario: Ontario Research Council on Leisure.

Mannell, R. C. (1980). Social psychological techniques and strategies in studying leisure experiences. In S. E. Iso-Ahola (Ed.), *Social psychological perspectives on leisure and recreation* (pp. 62–88). Springfield, IL: Charles C Thomas.

Marx, K. (1967). *Capital: A critique of political economy. Vol. III: The process of capitalistic production as a whole.* (Originally published in 1894.) New York: International Publishers.

Massarik, F., and Franklin, D. C. (1967). *Adoption of children with medical conditions.* Los Angeles, CA: Children's Home Society of California.

Orthner, D. K. (1975). Leisure activity patterns and marital satisfaction over the marital career. *Journal of Marriage and Family, 37*, 91–102.

Orthner, D. K., & Mancini, J. A. (1980). Leisure behavior and group dynamics: The case of the family. In S. E. Iso-Ahola (Ed.), *Social psychological perspectives on leisure and recreation* (pp. 307–328). Springfield, IL: Charles C Thomas.

Pratt, L. (1976). *Family structure and effective health behavior: The energized family.* Boston, MA: Houghton Mifflin.

Rodin, J., & Langer, E. J. (1977). Long-term effects of a control-relevant intervention with the institutionalized aged. *Journal of Personality and Social Psychology, 35*, 897–902.

Rotter, J. B. (1966). Generalized expectancies for internal versus external control of reinforcement. *Psychological Monographs, 80*(1).

Ryckman, R. M. (1979). Perceived locus of control and task performance. In L. C. Perlmuter, & R. A. Monty (Eds.), *Choice and perceived control* (pp. 233–261). Hillsdale, NJ: LEA.

Ryder, R. G., Kafka, J. S., & Olson, D. H. (1971). Separating and joining influences in courtship and early marriage. *American Journal of Orthopsychiatry, 41*, 450–467.

Schneider, J. M. (1968). Skill versus chance activity preference and locus of control. *Journal of Consulting and Clinical Psychology, 32*, 333–337.

Schulz, R. (1976). Effects of control and predictability on the physical and psychological well-being of the institutionalized aged. *Journal of Personality and Social Psychology, 33*, 567–573.

Schulz, R., & Hanusa, B. H. (1979). Environmental influences on the effectiveness of control- and competence-enhancing interventions. In L. C. Perlmuter, & R. A. Monty (Eds.), *Choice and perceived control* (pp. 315–337). Hillsdale, NJ: LEA.

Seligman, M. E. P. (1975). *Helplessness: On depression, development and death.* San Francisco, CA: W. H. Freeman and Co.

Sofranko, A. J., & Nolan, M. F. (1972). Early life experiences and adult sports participation. *Journal of Leisure Research, 4*, 6–18.

Spreitzer, E., & Snyder, E. E. (1976). Socialization into sport: An exploratory path analysis. *Research Quarterly, 47*, 238–245.

Stein, A. H., & Smithells, J. (1969). Age and sex differences in children's sex-role standards about achievement. *Developmental Psychology, 1*, 252–259.

Suls, J. M., & Miller, R. L. (Eds.). (1977). *Social comparison processes.* Washington: Hemisphere Publishing Co.

Williams, B. W. (1980). Reinforcement, behavior constraint, and the overjustification effect. *Journal of Personality and Social Psychology, 39*, 599–614.

Witt, P. A., & Goodale, T. L. (1981). The relationships between barriers to leisure enjoyment and family stages. *Leisure Sciences, 5*, 29–49.

Yoesting, D. R., & Burkhead, D. L. (1973). Significance of childhood recreation experience on adult leisure behavior: An exploratory analysis. *Journal of Leisure Research, 5*, 25–36.

PART II
SOCIO-ECONOMIC
CONSTRAINTS ON LEISURE

Chapter VI

WORK CONSTRAINTS ON LEISURE: A SOCIAL PSYCHOLOGICAL ANALYSIS

ROGER C. MANNELL and SEPPO E. ISO-AHOLA

INTRODUCTION

The nature of work and leisure have been changing and will likely continue to change in the years to come. Achieving an understanding of how they are related in modern life has proven difficult, and predicting their future relationship is a perilous enterprise. A variety of scenarios have been suggested for the future of work and leisure, ranging from world collapse with no leisure, to post-industrial utopias where the distinction between work and leisure has disappeared (Kando, 1980). Certain social analysts have been predicting for decades that modern automated technology will make work obsolete. Most recently it has been argued that the rapidly developing microelectronic technology is evolving so rapidly that a society with large portions of the population permanently unemployed is not only inevitable but imminent (Jenkins and Sherman, 1981).

Research seems to suggest that the work ethic is declining and the leisure ethic increasing (Campbell, Converse and Rodgers, 1976; London, Crandall and Seals, 1977; Yankelovich, 1978; Iso-Ahola and Buttimer, 1981). From his examination of the empirical research, Zuzanek (1978) concludes that while leisure has become more positively valued, "verbal" commitments to work values are still strong. However, "unwillingness to take jobs for minimal pay, a high element of choosiness, attempts to weight commitment toward a job against other rewards and trade-offs—all indicate that we have probably entered the stage where traditional ethic of work is giving way to a more personal cost-benefit approach to work" (p. 675).

155

The issue of work and leisure relationships is also beginning to enter into public consciousness through a variety of popular writings. Lefkowitz (1979) examined American workers who voluntarily rejected work and chose leisure as a means of providing the purpose and meaning in their lives. On the other hand, Machlowitz (1981) has written about, not those who have rejected work, but those persons who have embraced work as the most important and all-consuming activity in their lives.

Theory concerning the relationship between the work and the leisure in our lives has typically painted a picture of our work constraining our leisure. Social analysts and researchers have viewed free or discretionary time to be not unlike a Rorschach inkblot, that is, an amorphous entity on which the psychological consequences of work are projected independent of other social influences. While economic, social and political conditions in society are held responsible for the conditions of work, leisure has been seen as completely dependent on or shaped by work. After all, is not work by definition somewhat constraining, limiting the freedom to choose ones activities, participation times, rate of activity and companions? On the other hand, leisure is conceptualized as occurring during free or discretionary time, and therefore our choices are supposedly unconstrained or in research parlance — free to vary.

The present chapter will begin with an overview of the traditional theories of the work-leisure relationship, and an analysis of the empirical research that has been reported testing these various conceptualizations. At first glance, it would seem that the impact of work constraints on leisure should be relatively straightforward to establish. Work can be considered an independent variable and leisure a dependent variable. People in most societies do something that they identify as work and most have some amount of discretionary time that they perceive as their own, and that they feel can be used according to their personal dictates. Unfortunately, cause and effect relationships in human affairs are seldom this simple, as the difficulties of empirically establishing work-leisure relationships suggest. The work-leisure theories that have been forwarded have successfully evaded attempts to provide support for them.

These theories, for the most part, have been provided by sociologists who, ironically, have suggested that the causal mechanisms or linking processes between what we do on the job and what we do in our free time are primarily psychological (e.g., alienation, frustration-aggression). However, these processes have been expressed in the form of sweeping generalizations about the psychopathology of work which supposedly creates in the individual an inability to engage in meaningful leisure. Social scientists have paid only lip service to these psychological processes and no attempts have been made to confirm their actual operation, or establish their role in mediating or linking work and leisure. The remaining sections of the chapter will discuss and analyze the "psychology" implicit and untested in most discussions of work-leisure relationships. What are the psychological mechanisms linking work and leisure, what support exists for these mechanisms, and what are alternative ways of conceptualizing the manner in which work and leisure are related in peoples lives? Directions for future research will also be discussed.

THE PROBLEMS OF WORK AND LEISURE

Psychological Consequences of Work for the Worker

The roots of the concern with work-leisure relationships can be found in the social criticism that emerged at the beginning of the industrial revolution directed at the negative effects of work on the quality of life of the worker. For example, Engels (1892) observed what he felt was the demoralization of English textile-mill workers.

> Nothing is more terrible than being constrained to do some one thing every day from morning until night against one's will. And the more a man the worker feels himself, the more hateful must his work be to him, because he feels the constraint, the aimlessness of it for himself. Why does he work? For love of work? From a natural impulse? Not at all! He works for money, for a thing which has nothing whatsoever to do with the work itself. . . . (Engels, 1892, p. 118–119)

The "constraint and aimlessness" of work was seen to be due to the development, on the one hand, of technology for work (tools and machines) and, on the other, the division of labor or human organization of work. The division of labor increased dramatically when work was reorganized in the form of assembly-line production groups. The single craftsman who incorporated his skills, experience and knowledge of materials in an artifact made with his own tools was no longer needed.

> It was encouraged during the nineteenth century by a further specialization of machine and by the firm belief — one might almost call it a semi-mystical belief — which took possession of the engineering world . . . that all 'scientific' rationalization of labour would imply a breaking down of jobs, increasing the output of the 'semi-skilled' worker and the volume of production with a lowering of the cost of such mass-produced goods. (Friedmann, 1961, Introduction)

From the beginning of the industrial revolution to the present day, social commentators have expressed concern over the harmful effects believed to result from the specialized, routinized work of the factory. Smith (1937, p. 734) noted that a factory worker "whose whole life is spent in performing a few simple operations . . . becomes as stupid and ignorant as it is possible for a human creature to become." Marx did not view all labor as alienating but felt that much of it was because of the way in which it was organized. "The division of labor," he explained, "only becomes a real division from the moment when the distinction between material and mental labor appears." As a consequence, "enjoyment and labor, production and consumption devolve on different individuals, coming into contradiction" (1964, p. 92). It is therefore "the detail-worker of today, the limited individual, the mere bearer of a particular social function, produced by large-scale industry" (1964, p. 252) who is engaged in alienating labor.

The "assembly line," such as those in North American automobile factories, became a symbol of the purported evils of impersonal, dehumanized, goalless, robotlike performance. The consequences of years spent in such jobs, it has been asserted, "range from mild boredom and discontent to passive resignation and stunted personal development or to bitter despair, violent revolt, severe psychoneuroses, and even outright psychotic break-down" (Kornhauser, 1965, Introduction).

Taylor is frequently called the father of "scientific" management. His approach was based on the conviction that the interests of the employer and the employee are the same, and that the division of labor makes it possible to give the worker what he wants—high wages—and the employer what he wants—low costs (Taylor, 1947). Drucker (1950) criticized this approach to work, and argued that the traditional methods of mass-production produce three types of disturbances in the worker. The fragmentation of labor increases fatigue and leads to physiological and neurological damage. The worker is yoked to the pace of the slowest man on the line and is not allowed to work according to his personal rhythm; the result fatigue and irritability.

More recently, Argyle (1972) has argued that of the very important social psychological problems in industry today alienation and low job satisfaction of workers are major ones. Many workers report that they are alienated through a lack of control over the work process, that the work is meaningless, and that the work is not an important part of their personalities or lives. Workers are seen to suffer from high blood pressure, ulcers, heart disease, and mental stress supposedly as as result of their work.

Leisure as Problematic

According to critics like de Grazia (1964), modern leisure is simply mass consumption and therefore also problematic. Critics of this bent believe that modern technology and affluence prom-ised a leisure society but instead produced a consumer society. Associated with mass consumption are the generally passive and mindless forms of activity given labels such as mass culture, mass leisure and mass sport, denoting "mere entertainments" for a mindless and unthinking population. At the roots of this criticism, is the belief that leisure or free time should be used for personal growth and development, and active involvement in ones social and political world. Concerns for the passivity of much of contem-porary leisure activity has led to the discussion and development of theory and strategies for the encouragement of more active and involving uses of leisure. In many European countries and in Canada, for example, government policy and funds have attempted to actively encourage greater participation in the cultural arts and physical activity. The former programs are often seen as contributing to the "democratization of culture" (e.g., Mennell, 1979; Zuzanek, 1979), and the latter go under a variety of titles, for example, in Canada a government sponsored agency called Participation, has been responsible for promoting physical fitness among Canadians.

Theories of Work-Leisure Relationships

The problems of work and the problems of leisure were linked together by sociologists. Wilensky (1960) provided the initial analysis which has led social scientists to conceptualize alternative work-leisure relationships—one called "spillover," and the other "compensation." From his analysis of Engels (1892), deTocqueville (1954) and other classic social philosophers, Wilensky reduced the potential impact of work on leisure to these two effects. As well as Engels' powerful and eloquent indictment of industrial work quoted earlier, he also made a causal connection between this dehumanizing work and the leisure engaged in by the worker.

> Next to intemperance in enjoyment of intoxicating liquor, one of the principle faults of English working men is sexual license. But this too follows with relentless logic that the working men, in order to get something out of life, concentrate their whole energy upon these two enjoyments, carry them to excess. (Engels, 1892, p. 128)

Wilensky saw this type of argument as the "compensatory hypothesis" and it appears very similar to the catharsis or surplus energy theories of play (see Ellis, 1973). Leisure as compensation was viewed as a release in the form of "excessive" attempts to make up for the deprivations experienced at work—an explosive letting off of steam built up under the constraints of the work setting. The spillover hypothesis, as suggested by Wilensky, is a generalization of alienation from work into alienation from leisure.

> ...where the technical and social organization of work offers much freedom—for example, discretion in methods, pace or

schedule, and opportunity for interaction with fellow workers
... then work attachments will be strong, work integrated with
the rest of life, and ties to community and society solid. Conversely, if the task offers little workplace freedom ... then work
attachments will be weak, work sharply split from leisure,
and ties to community and society uncertain. (Wilensky, 1961,
p. 522)

A review of the literature since Wilensky's analysis shows that
spillover is typically viewed as the extension of work habits, attitudes and interests into one's leisure. People supposedly choose
leisure activities that are characteristically similar to their jobs. If
their jobs are monotonous, unchallenging, and provide little or
no autonomy and control over work, their leisure behavior becomes
passive, idle amusement. Compensation, on the other hand, is the
opposite, namely involvement in leisure activities that possess the
opposite characteristics of those of one's job. For example, someone employed in a sedentary occupation and who engages in
active physical leisure activities may be said to exemplify the
compensatory work-leisure relationship. Such a person's leisure
activities compensate for deprivations suffered on the job (Kando,
1980, p. 68).

Parker (1971) has also discussed a third logical possibility—
neutrality. Instead of compensation or spillover, a person's work
and leisure may be two separate and unrelated spheres in his or
her life. The third hypothesis has also appeared in the writings of
Bacon (1975) and Meissner (1971), and more recently Kabanoff
(1980).

However, some confusion exists concerning the actual predictions of these theories. First, whether compensation and spillover
are viewed as positive or negative would actually seem to depend
on the nature of an individual's work. If challenging and fulfilling,
spillover should be viewed positively, yet as we have discussed
above, spillover is typically viewed as a negative effect. If work is
of the stereotypic assembly-line variety, compensation should be
positive. Theorists have not disentangled these issues. However,
what is the nature of compensation if work is meaningful, challenging and satisfying? Is it conversely negative? Engels viewed
compensation and spillover as both having negative outcomes for

the workers' leisure. On the other hand, other authors have discussed the compensatory mechanism as a potentially positive adaptation to dehumanizing work.

Zuzanek (1976) has recognized this confusion and has proposed an elaboration of the spillover-compensation dichotomy. His four cell matrix adds to the basic dimensions either a "pessimistic" or "optimistic" perspective depending upon the assessment of the overall trends in industrial work.

The spillover-pessimistic hypothesis is based on the belief that industrial and clerical work have become segmented into a series of mini-operations. As we have already seen, this type of mechanized and fragmented work is viewed as dull and alienating rather than a meaningful work experience. The pessimism of the spillover hypothesis comes from the suggestion that the quality of leisure can not vary from that of the work day. As Howe (1957) has suggested:

> It [leisure] must provide relief from work monotony without making the return to work too unbearable ... (p. 496).

The spillover-optimistic view differs in that it is based on a more positive view of the humanizing potential of technology. As Zuzanek points out, automation is viewed as reversing the long trend toward the fragmentation of human work. The worker in the automated plant has become a supervisor, one who oversees the whole operation and one who is required to have greater skill, greater knowledge and understanding of the total work process. Presumably this process will upgrade leisure as well. Culture will cease to be an unnecessary luxury, rather it will become an important part of one's life style. This view of spillover should also apply to those who currently have challenging and meaningful jobs.

The compensatory-aggressive hypothesis suggests that the worker compensates for a lack of excitement in his work by outbursts of uncontrolled spontaneity which in an overly repressed society takes antisocial and deviant forms (e.g., Wilensky, 1961; Bacon, 1975).

Finally, the compensatory-upgrading hypothesis follows from Friedmann (1961) who argued that even automated work could not be upgraded as a positive compensation for the dissatisfaction with the monotonous work. Leisure to Friedmann appeared more readily subject to modification and humanization than technologically constrained work. Of course, this raises the issue of whether you can have meaningful leisure while having meaningless work and avoid becoming schizophrenic.

PROBLEMS OF RESEARCH ON WORK-LEISURE RELATIONSHIPS

Testing Work-Leisure Relationships

Considering the extensive discussion of work-leisure relationships in the published literature, the volume of empirical research is surprisingly small. This research has been engaged in irregularly over the last two and a half decades, little of it building on previous work or generating active enthusiasm and debate among scholars. Following his review of the past research, Champoux (1975, p. 56) concluded that "the empirical research directed at the work-nonwork relationship is best described as inconclusive." He attributes this to the fact that almost all theoretical and empirical work has been done by sociologists and proposes that an interdisciplinary approach to the issues would improve the quality of future research. Two more recent reviews of the literature on the relationship between work and nonwork have been published (Staines, 1980; Kabanoff, 1980).

Staines (1980) includes in the category of nonwork activities leisure pursuits, family and home activities, and he concludes that while there is some support for both the notions of spillover and compensation, the evidence favors spillover. Arguing that investigations of experiences on and off the job seem fragmented and in need of a conceptual framework to integrate the research findings, Staines develops a typology for classifying the research. Treating work and leisure as roles, he classifies work-leisure research on the basis of three role-related concepts: degree of role involvement, types of role activities, and subjective role reactions. For example, degree of involvement in work refers to subjective feelings of involvement, as well as to objective factors such as time and energy invested in the job and range of work activities undertaken. Degree of involvement in nonwork activities invokes the same criteria as applied to work activities. Types of activities that various jobs and nonwork pursuits entail may be measured along dimensions such as degree of complexity, autonomy and social interaction. Subjective reactions to work experiences, as well as leisure experiences, may be scored in a positive or negative direction along common dimensions such as satisfaction and enjoyment.

The typology developed by Staines is created by classifying how each of the studies reviewed measured both work and leisure according to the three role-related concepts. Staines found no studies that measured degree of involvement (subjective or objective) in work and leisure. The studies he does examine focused primarily on family involvement and off-the-job political activity. It would seem that most of the research reviewed by Staines that examined work-leisure relationships fell into that category represented by the relationship between "types of work and nonwork activities." Staines concludes that the relationship between work and leisure activities seems to be positive (supporting the spillover hypothesis) for most dimensions on which researchers have compared work and leisure activities: interpersonal interaction (Bishop and Ikeda, 1970; Meissner, 1971; Staines and Pagnucco, 1977), autonomy (Karasek, 1976; Meissner, 1971), and mental effort (Karasek, 1976; Kohn and Schooler, 1973; Staines and Pagnucco, 1977). Only for the dimension of physical effort expended have investigators reported negative or compensatory relationships (Bishop and Ikeda, 1970; Karasek, 1976; Staines and Pagnucco, 1977). Research which Staines found to examine the relationship between the subjective reactions to work and nonwork roles comprises the third major category of research completed. Consistent with the spillover hypothesis, Rousseau (1978) reported a significant positive correlation between job satisfaction and satisfaction with life outside work. Positive correlations have been reported in several other studies (Kornhauser, 1965; London, Crandall and Seals, 1977).

Kabanoff (1980) focuses on research that exclusively examines work-leisure relationships. His analysis of the literature identified eight studies that collected quantifiable data, and he subjected this research to a much more critical analysis than did Staines. He concluded that there was no clear support for any of the three major work-leisure hypotheses. A number of reasons were advanced for this, dealing mainly with conceptual and methodological inadequacies in the studies. Kabanoff feels that the major problem has been the lack of consistency in the way that both work and leisure have been defined. Of course, this in itself is not all bad, even though it is difficult to make comparisons across studies. If similar patterns of results emerge with different operationalizations of work and leisure greater confidence can be placed in the results. Unfortunately, the relationships and linkages between the various measures, lack of rationale for their choice and the level of rigor in their specification and collection lend support to Kabanoff's conclusions.

Measuring Work and Leisure

In any research undertaking, consensus among researchers concerning how the important variables representing the phenomena under study are to be measured or operationally defined is critical to progress in the field of study. It is well documented in the study of leisure that definition has been and is still a contentious issue (Ennis, 1968; Zuzanek, 1976; Iso-Ahola, 1980; Mannell, 1980). Industrial psychologists and sociologists have also disagreed on the most useful way to operationalize work (Argyle, 1972; Landy and Trumbo, 1980). Little serious attention has been given the issue of measurement in the area of work-leisure relationships. The theories that have guided research are rather vague and lack specifics on what it is about work and leisure that they see as related. Probably because these theories emerged from broad and general social criticism aimed at illustrating the deficiencies and excesses of existing social orders, no attempt was made to make them more precise or specify the conditions under which different outcomes might be expected. As a consequence, the studies that have been reported show a wide range of operationalizations of the work and leisure constructs. This not only makes it difficult to compare the results of various studies, but difficult to evaluate the research in terms of the adequacy with which the various work-leisure hypotheses are tested.

Indicators of work and leisure. What indicators or dimensions of work and leisure should be tapped or measured to adequately capture the intent of the work-leisure hypotheses? The nature of the job and work environment can be characterized with a multitude of criteria. The criteria can be restricted to the "objective" features of the job and work environment, such as, physical features including noise and the presence of toxic substances; social features including the amount of social interaction and autonomy allowed in carrying out the job; physical and psychological demands, such as, the level of challenge, variety, physical exertion and demand for skill. The conditions of leisure could be characterized in a similar manner.

It is also possible that the psychological experience of work and leisure may be important measures. Examples, of these types of measures include assessments of satisfaction and psychological involvement with the job and leisure. London, Crandall and Seals (1977) provide an example of a study that asked survey respondents to indicate their level of satisfaction with both the work and leisure spheres of their life. They found, as did Mannell and McCarville (1979), that the evaluations of the two spheres of life were fairly independent of each other.

Most of the empirical research though, has attempted to assess the similarities or dissimilarities of the "objective" features of work and leisure environments. The objective characteristics of work and leisure have been measured by assessing the individual's own perceptions, recollections and subjective judgements. However, work has been operationalized much more consistently than leisure in terms of its various attributes. Workers have been asked to evaluate their job activities on a number of dimensions thought to characterize all work. Studies by Kornhauser (1965), Parker (1965), Meissner (1971), Bacon (1975), Bishop and Ikeda (1971), Pennings (1976), Rousseau (1978) and Kabanoff and O'Brien (1980) all attempted to measure at least some characteristics of the work environment deriving their specific criteria on the basis of their interpretations of the work-leisure theories. The dimensions of work examined include: skill level demanded, variety of tasks on the job, degree of responsibility and level of remuneration

(Kornhauser, 1965); technical constraints (machine pacing, spatial confinement, task dependence, work type) and social interaction — with nonworkmates, number of people free to interact with, content of discussion (Meissner, 1971); monotony on the job, degree of involvement in the job, degree of constraint, and level of demand and frustration (Bacon, 1975); physical energy required and social interaction (Bishop and Ikeda, 1970); autonomy, work variety, and group cohesiveness (Pennings, 1976); ability of the job to challenge, autonomy, and commitment to the job (Parker, 1965); task significance, task identity, feedback from the job, skill variety, autonomy and dealing with others (Rousseau, 1978); and skill utilization, influence, variety, pressure and interaction (Kabanoff and O'Brien, 1980).

These various studies vary with respect to the adequacy and rigor with which they conceptualize and measure these dimensions. The majority required the workers to rate their perceptions of their jobs on scales to characterize the work environment. Pennings' (1976) study is one of the few which actually had observers make independent ratings of the objective work environment and the job. Bishop and Ikeda (1970) had their respondents record their job or occupation and then they had independent judges assess (from published job descriptions) the job in terms of the amount of social interaction allowed and the physical demand required. Only two of the studies (Rousseau, 1978; Kabanoff and O'Brien, 1980) have used standardized instruments to assess work attributes — instruments which had some previous usage for the purpose of assessing the task attributes of jobs, and therefore had some proven validity.

Leisure has only rarely been subjected to such a task analysis. Usually, the leisure activities reported by respondents are grouped or categorized into a few types in an ad hoc manner on the basis of unsupported assumptions made about the similar nature of the activities. The following are some examples from the literature: self-development, self-expression and volunteer activities collected by questionnaire and personal interview (Kornhauser, 1965); organized purposeful discretionary activities (e.g., volunteering, active sports, hobbies), sociable activities, expressive activities low in their demand for discretionary and social skills (e.g., television viewing, driving for pleasure, fishing), moonlighting, reading and loafing collected by questionnaire and time budget diary (Meissner, 1971); "false" consumption obsessions (e.g., owning a house, car, record player, second car), passive leisure life style (e.g., watching television, reading, motoring, resting), and violent compensatory leisure behavior (visiting pubs, visiting social or recreation clubs, playing bingo) collected with a questionnaire survey (Bacon, 1975).

Two studies have used multivariate statistical procedures to group activities. Bishop and Ikeda (1970) measured leisure by asking the respondents in their survey to indicate their frequency of participation on 32 leisure activities. Discriminant analysis of this data and the occupational and demographic information collected revealed certain patterns of leisure participation—upperbrow leisure (e.g., theatre), popular activities (e.g., card playing, picnicking, walking), amount of mental and physical energy required and interpersonal-orientedness. Pennings (1976) factor analyzed frequency data on leisure participation and derived several types of recreation categories (social recreation, highbrow recreation, individual recreation and friendship activities).

Common dimensions of work and leisure. Another issue in adequately testing work-leisure relationships, however work and leisure are measured, concerns whether they should be measured and related on similar dimensions. Kando and Summers (1971) were probably the first to argue that common or similar dimensions, for work and leisure, needed to be used when examining work and leisure relationships. They suggested assessing work and leisure along common dimensions by asking respondents parallel sets of questions about their work and leisure behavior. If work is conceptualized as varying in the amount of autonomy available to the worker in carrying out the job should our measure of leisure allow an assessment of the amount of autonomy the worker typically chooses to have in his/her leisure? If compensation and/or spillover occur, we are more likely to detect this relationship if comparable dimensions of work and leisure are assessed.

Only two studies clearly operationalize both work and leisure along common dimensions. Kabanoff (1980) recommends an approach to measuring both work and leisure based on some of the strategies used by industrial and organizational psychologists to study work. Work, according to Kabanoff (1980), traditionally refers to:

> the set of prescribed tasks that an individual performs while occupying a position in an organization . . . A task-based definition of work is the appropriate and common one. (p. 67–68)

Kabanoff also adopts an activity or task definition of leisure. His "task analysis orientation" leads him to suggest the selection of activities that are "clearly leisure," so that he can apply task analysis to leisure as well as work. By "clearly leisure" we are left to assume that social or cultural consensus regarding whether an activity is leisure is to be the criteria used. By defining both work and leisure in terms of task attributes, it is possible to specify a limited number of task dimensions for describing work and leisure. Kabanoff argues that the strength of this type of approach is that it should allow a more adequate test of the various hypothesized work-leisure relationships.

Rousseau (1978) was the first researcher to attempt a task analysis of both work and leisure. She used the Job Diagnostic Survey which required respondents to judge their work on six dimensions: task significance, task identity, feedback from others and the job itself, skill variety, autonomy and interaction with others. She also had her respondents rate their "off work" experiences along the same dimensions. Kabanoff and O'Brien (1980) and Kabanoff (1980) criticize Rousseau's study for two reasons. It is guilty of common method variance since the same scales were used by the respondents to rate work and nonwork spheres of life, and since the data were collected in the same manner on a single questionnaire. This increases the chances that the respondent will rate both work and leisure similarly on common dimensions, and "artifically" increase the likelihood of finding the spillover effect which Rousseau did find. Second, Rousseau did not have the respondents rate specific leisure activities as they did their work activities. They made a global rating of their "leisure," leaving us with no idea of what it was that was actually rated.

Kabanoff and O'Brien (1980) measured job attributes by having their respondents rate their jobs on additive scales that provided scores on the dimensions of skill utilization, influence, variety, pressure and interaction. This approach to defining work is the same as that used by Rousseau. Conceptualizing leisure as a set of "tasks" but distinguished from work by the worker's freedom to choose in which of these tasks he/she will participate, the researchers had the respondents indicate which of 93 leisure activities they had taken part in at least three times during the previous year without obligation. Independent raters then classified all the leisure activities on the same five task dimensions used by the respondents in characterizing their own work. While this technique solves some of the problems of common method variance, it ignores the variations and differences that likely exist in the way in which each of the respondents experienced and participated in these "same" leisure activities.

The measurement of the task attributes of work by organizational and industrial psychologists has stemmed from the research of Turner and Lawrence (1965). The set of perceived task characteristics on which most attention has focused includes skill variety, task identity, task significance, autonomy and feedback (e.g., Sims, Szilagyi and Keller, 1976). Rousseau (1978) and Kabanoff (1980) by advocating the application of this measurement approach to both work and leisure have made a valuable contribution to work-leisure research methodology. However, there are several problems. First, a satisfactory method of applying the task analysis to leisure must be found. Rousseau by simply asking her subjects to rate their "leisure" in general on the various task dimensions can not be sure what it is that is that is being rated. Also, Kabanoff and O'Brien (1980) by having independent raters make these task dimension ratings based on knowing only the name of the leisure activity, introduce a large amount of error into their measures — error that could be accounted for by differences in the way in which individuals perceive the activity. Unless the researcher uses some measure assessing the relative importance and investment of time and energy in the activity, pursuits that are engaged in with little or moderate frequency and intensity, and which may bear a different relationship to work, for a given individual, will be given too much weight in determining overall work-leisure relationships.

To avoid these pitfalls and the problems of "common method

variance" a variety of studies need to be undertaken which measure the objective and perceived (subjective) characteristics of people's work and leisure "tasks." However, it should be noted that the task attribute approach has not definitively established a consistent relationship between the nature of the job and such psychological consequences as motivation, satisfaction, performance, alienation, etc. (Aldag, Barr and Brief, 1981). Other approaches for measuring task characteristics should be explored.

Meanings and perceptions of work and leisure. The problem of establishing the meaning of both work and leisure activities when studying work-leisure relationships was initially identified by Kando and Summers (1971). The difficulty for:

> ... a systematic theory relating work to nonwork has been the widespread tendency to overlook the complexity of the possible relationships between the outward appearances, or *forms* of work and leisure, and the way they are experienced and interpreted by participants in them ... *meaning* whether they are sources of sociability, creativity, tension release, or some form of alienation. (p. 312)

Iso-Ahola (1980) has made a similar point. The idea of compensation is typically presented by saying that the constraints and social isolation of the job are compensated for through discretionary free-time activities and activities involving social interaction. However, any free-time activity has elements of constraint and freedom, and social isolation and social interaction. Activities in themselves are not socially isolating or interactive, but rather it is the individual who attaches certain meanings to various activities.

Studies by Parker (1965), London, Crandall and Seals (1977), Kelly (1975) and Hunt and Weiner (1982) have touched on the problem of the perceived or personal meaning of work and leisure. Parker (1965) asked his respondents to indicate the functions or meanings leisure held for them, that is, did they enjoy leisure because of the difference between it and work, etc. Kelly (1975) had his respondents report their most important leisure activities and then each respondent was asked to check any of 35 reasons for their participation in the five activities in which they were most active. A variety of these reasons reflected compensation. Compen-

sation was found as a primary reason infrequently but as a secondary reason in 22.3 percent of the cases. In a related study, Hunt
and Weiner (1982) used the semantic differential technique to assess
the personal meanings of work and leisure to their respondents.
They interpret the significantly positive correlations between the
various meanings of work and leisure they provided as supporting
the spillover hypothesis. However, our confidence in these results
is reduced because the size of the correlations could in part be due
to common method variance associated with using the same scales
and meaning statements within the same questionnaire to assess
work and leisure meanings. Furthermore, as Iso-Ahola and Buttimer
(1982) have shown, the correlation between work and leisure varies
substantially, depending on the wording of the items of the selected
instruments, that is, whether or not the items pit work and leisure
against each other.

While the question of individual or personal meanings of both
work and leisure needs to be taken into consideration in testing
work-leisure relationships, it is questionable to assume that people
are able to accurately assess their own motives or reasons for
engaging in the leisure they choose. Our culture provides us with
certain rationales (lay-theories) which may influence our choice of
leisure but not relfect the real reasons or relationships between
work and leisure.

Kabanoff (1980) has attacked the notion that leisure can be
usefully defined subjectively. A "subjective approach to the definition of leisure ultimately makes it extremely difficult, if not
impossible, to distinguish between work and leisure activities"
(p. 68). If the same activity for a given individual may change its
classification as often as the individual's feelings change, how does
one monitor individual feeling states? The answer to this question
is not to retreat from it or ignore leisure as subjective experience,
however. It requires that we determine the factors that cause these
shifts in personal definitions of what constitutes a leisure activity
(Iso-Ahola, 1979) and the associated changes in intrinsically motivated experience (Mannell, 1979).

Establishing Links Between Work and Leisure

Now that we have considered the problems and issues of defining work and leisure, that is, considering "what it is that may be related," the equally important but ignored problem becomes, "what are the processes or intervening mechanisms by which they are linked. Since most of the theory and research has been contributed by sociologically oriented scholars, one might expect that the relationship between work and leisure would be conceptualized as an institutionalized relationship, the result of social influences outside both work and leisure. However, it is quite clear that not only have the role of these social structural variables been ignored, but that the relationship has been conceptualized as simple "cause and effect"—work the cause and leisure the effect. A review of the research literature seems to suggest that even if a cause-effect relationship exists between work and leisure, it is unlikely to be a simple or obvious one as suggested by the various work-leisure hypotheses. The relationship, that is, the impact of work on leisure, may take different forms depending on any of a variety of moderating and/or mediating factors.

Psychological processes as linking mechanisms. A variety of psychological processes have been hypothesized to intervene between man's environment and his behavior. Moods, emotions, biological and social drives, perceptions, memories, beliefs and attitudes are all psychological dispositions seen to inhabit our psychological world. These dispositions can only be indirectly observed through the behavior and verbal reports of individuals. Schools of psychology differ in their view of the value of using constructs representing "invisible" internal psychological processes. For example, behaviorism, which has ruled out the validity of internal psychological processes as legitimate and useful in the study of human behavior, argues that it is only necessary to consider external, directly observable, and quantifiable stimuli and responses. On the other hand, much of contemporary psychology has adopted an approach that allows the use of cognitive constructs in theory building and testing, and the collection of data that reflects the operation of these cognitive processes.

In a sense, discussions of work-leisure relationships have been behavioristic in their orientation by giving little more than lip-service to the nature of the causal linking processes. From the discussions of most researchers and theorists one gains the feeling that the impact of work on leisure is so automatic and invariable that the study of the intervening processes is unnecessary. Where intervening psychological processes are mentioned, their discussion is typically superficial. When research is carried out no attempt has been made to measure and monitor these processes to determine whether they conform to theoretical expectations.

When the various suggestions for the link between work and leisure are translated into psychological terms, the impact of work on leisure can be conceptualized as being mediated by either *temporary* or *permanent* changes in the individual's motives, attitudes or personality. The psychological linking mechanisms underlying *spillover* seem to have been generally conceived of as relatively permanent psychological changes. Work has been viewed as creating changes in attitudes and personality, skills and abilities, and mental health. These changes in psychological dispositions lead individuals to engage in leisure similar to their work. For example, people who have a general tendency to become heavily involved in their work—people Machlowitz (1981) labels workaholics—may tend to approach their leisure in the same manner. Staines (1980) has made a similar observation, suggesting that the Type A personality (Rosenman et al. 1966) is a candidate for spillover.

Another relatively permanent change hypothesized by several authors to contribute to spillover is work-created changes in skills and abilities (Kando and Summers, 1971; Meissner, 1971; Staines, 1980). Workers may acquire skills on the job that are transferred to leisure to influence the types of activities chosen. This mechanism appears to be what learning psychologists often refer to as "transfer of training." A final mechanism that is sometimes mentioned suggests that the permanent change mediating spillover from work to leisure is mental health, or rather, the psychopathology caused by the job. The conditions of work are seen to create psychopathologies and this psychopathology somehow compels the individual to engage in leisure having the same aberrant characteristics as their work. This type of psychopathology is usually given the label of "alienation." People whose "work does not reward their motivational investments, who experience a lack of interest, control, or autonomy in their work, learn the lesson of retreatism" (Bacon, 1975, p. 180). This retreatism is carried over into the nonwork sphere. Consequently, the leisure of the alienated worker is characterized by passive, home-centered, idle amusement with the aim being fun, relaxation and a good time (Marx, 1964; Baran and Sweezy, 1966). Wilensky (1960) used the term "mental stultification" to suggest some kind of permanent limitation or impairment of the workers' ability to be creative and use their intellectual abilities.

The psychological processes of *compensation* linking work to leisure seem to consist of both permanent and temporary changes, though the explanations given seem to lean more toward the notion that compensation is caused by temporary changes in the individual's motivational or need states. The assumption appears to be that there are a variety of social psychological needs that all humans must meet in order to achieve happiness and full psychological growth (e.g., Maslow, 1954; Rogers, 1959), and that the activities of work vary in their ability to satisfy these needs. Work then influences leisure by activating, on a temporary basis, each individual's motivational state, thereby leading the individual to seek the satisfaction of these needs in leisure. The need for competence, self-determination or autonomy, challenge, achievement, variety, affiliation and the opportunity for self-development are some that have been suggested. The compensatory process is essentially motivational.

Regardless of the quality of work, at first glance, this apparently homeostatic process would seem to be a beneficial one. However, various theorists have seen in the compensatory process negative outcomes. The compensation process, if positive, will satisfy these needs and manifest itself in a choice of activities that remediate these deficiencies. Kando and Summers (1971), Kelly (1975) and Friedmann (1961) have described compensation as potentially positive. On the other hand, compensation has been viewed as a negative outcome in the forms of "false" consumption needs (Bacon, 1975) and violent or explosive leisure behavior (Wilensky, 1960; Bacon, 1975; Kando and Summers, 1971). The violent or explosive compensation is predicted to result from an internal build-up of frustration and disaffection with work that is undemanding, repetitive, and unrewarding (Bacon, 1975). The extent to which these modes of adaptation are internalized in the form of attitude and personality change will determine how permanent the change will be. Generally, though little is said about permanent change with the compensation theory. We can only assume that long term "deprivation" may result in psychopathology and consequently permanently aberrant leisure behavior.

There has been no discussion or theoretical analysis that attempts to make predictions concerning which of these many possible, and in some cases, competing alternatives is the predominant process, or under which conditions various outcomes will occur. The advantage of specifying the nature of the linking processes between work and leisure are that they would allow for more precise predictions to be made, and perhaps more importantly, the intervening processes themselves can be examined and tested to determine if these linking processes themselves are operating as expected. Greater consideration of the actual linking mechanisms between work and leisure is essential for the advancement of theory and research.

Constructs, such as, alienation, basic human needs and mental health have been frequently and loosely used to label these hypothetical processes. While they have not been examined as linking mechanisms in the work-leisure research, the relationship between work and these factors has been subjected to considerable research. In the last few decades much social psychological research has been undertaken with the explicit aim to study human conditions at work from the point of view of health and satisfaction (Landy and Trumbo, 1980).

The empirical evidence suggesting links from various aspects of work environment to mental health and job satisfaction is enormous. There exist a number of reviews of this literature (e.g., Kasl, 1973; Locke, 1976; Porter and Steers, 1973; Strauss, 1974). Kasl (1978) points out, that while there is a convergence of evidence from this literature, we should not be blind to the fact that we are talking about modest correlations. Data on the association between job satisfaction and indices of mental health suggest a variety of relationships. Behavioral indicators such as drug use, alcohol consumption, and cigarette smoking, show no association with job satisfaction. Alienation at work does not seem to generalize (i.e., that it does not correlate to other areas of life). Measures of physical complaints correlate with job satisfaction in the −0.10 to −0.30 range. Measures of affect (e.g., anxiety-tension, depression) yield moderate correlations, while indices of life satisfaction tend to provide the strongest associations with job satisfaction — though, still falling in the low 0.40s. Due to the relatively small size of these associations, the effects of the work environment on job satisfaction and mental health are still somewhat unclear (Kasl, 1978).

If the causal links in our work-leisure model include job satisfaction and mental health, then it would be helpful if the relationships at the "front end" of the model, between work conditions and these linking processes, were consistent and strong. However, with the evidence of these tentative relationships, it is not surprising that the impact of work on the more "distal" leisure behaviors and experiences, especially if mediated by these psychological processes, are even less reliable and consistent.

The need to more closely examine the psychological processes assumed to link work and leisure is reinforced when the psychological research into alienation and human needs is taken into account. For example, Seeman's (1971) critique of the alienation construct in social science theory suggests to us that caution should be taken in rashly assigning it an explanatory role in the work-leisure relationship. Even the time-honored notion of "basic human needs," particularly Maslow's (1954) hierarchy of needs, is far from proven indisputable fact. A number of studies have yielded data that contradict the Maslow model (e.g., Hall and Nougaim, 1968; Lawler and Suttle, 1972). Landy and Trumbo (1980) state that findings such as these are "more than bothersome — they are terminal" (p. 339). A more cautious and careful examination of the operation of the assumed psychological bridges between work and leisure is called for.

Work and leisure relationships dependent on social influences. Moderator variables affect the degree and kind of relationship between two other variables without necessarily being correlated with either of the other two variables (Blum and Naylor, 1968). Sociologists often use moderator variables such as race, social class, occupation, etc. when considering the relationship between two social phenomena, for example, religion and suicide. There is the expectation that a relationship does exist between them, but that it varies systematically with the level of the moderating variable. The influence of work on leisure, while detectable, may be overwhelmed by the effects of a variety of social processes which may shape work-leisure patterns. This is the segmentalist hypothesis (Parker, 1971). Individual differences, due to socialization experiences, may predispose the individual to select work with the same qualities as the leisure selected or, for that matter, with different qualities. Particularly in contemporary western society, where entry into the job market is delayed, the individual's personality orientation—activeness, feelings of powerlessness and control, activity preferences, etc. are likely already established by the time a job is taken. Any systematic relationship that exists between work and leisure, therefore, may be the result of socialization forces which dictate both the individual's work and leisure choices and style of participation.

As we have seen, the sociological theories of work-leisure relationships that we have reviewed are really psychological in their emphasis. As typically conceptualized, an individual's leisure is viewed to be structured or directly influenced by what he/she does on the job, seeming to suggest that what is done during free time is not governed by social norms and is fairly independent of the socializing forces to which the individual has been and continues to be subjected. It seems odd that sociological theory has not argued more strongly that the work-leisure relationship is more of an institutional arrangement, that different patterns exist as a result of socialization experiences in various subcultures, where the meaning and purpose of the relationship within a particular culture has its own ideology and function. Sociological research on leisure and social structure (see Kando, 1980; Zuzanek, 1976) has demonstrated that leisure (types of activities and time spent on leisure) vary with a number of sociodemographic variables—education, sex, occupation, etc. The relationship between work and leisure has often been confounded when the correlation of demographic indicators of work with leisure have been ignored. This leads Kando and Summers (1971) to argue that:

...we need to clearly specify both the effects that work has on nonwork and the effects that other variables have on the work/ nonwork relationship. (p. 312)

Pennings (1976) controlling for marital status, sex educational level, race, age of children, income, overtime, and numbers of hours worked per week, found that educational level was the single best predictor of leisure activities. Also when these variables were controlled for, the relationship of work to leisure decreased substantially.

While Bishop and Ikeda (1970) found that independent of occupation the degree of role involvement (masculinity-feminity of the work, physical energy required and degree of intimate personal contact) explained a small but significant portion of the variance in leisure behavior, they argued that:

Our present inclination is to view these relationships as stemming from more basic mediating variables, such as, values, motives, social attitudes, and the socialization practices underlying them, which probably influence both occupational and leisure choices. (p. 206)

Kabanoff and O'Brien (1980) with discriminant analysis determined that certain psychological and social characteristics differentiated among persons with different work-leisure patterns. The authors interpreted their results to show that different work-leisure relationships were exhibited by different groups of persons. Of the demographic variables used, different levels of education, income, sex and age tended to characterize groups of persons who displayed different work-leisure patterns. For example, those persons whose work was passive and also had passive leisure were predominantly males with low education, and low income. Those persons who compensated their passive work with active leisure were characterized by being older, female, and having a low income. Unfortunately the amount of variance accounted for and the levels of significance were quite low. These findings should be followed up with research to identify different work-leisure patterns and to discover the factors that determine these patterns. The nature of work-leisure relationships could then be construed as a personality variable and act as an "independent variable" in examining the impact of different relationships on general life satisfaction, mental health, etc.. For example, it has been suggested that alienating work and highly satisfying and rewarding leisure are incompatible, leading to what we might describe as a schizophrenic existence. Research could examine the actual effects of the "compensatory" work-leisure pattern, if it was found to exist among members of the population.

There is also a need for longitudinal research to determine if individuals with similar interests and leisure patterns at the beginning of different work careers, change as a consequence of long term involvement with their work. It is reasonable to expect that in certain professions and jobs, there emerge norms which exert an influence on workers to engage in leisure activities considered appropriate for them (Iso-Ahola, 1980).

Personality and attitudes as moderators of work constraints on leisure. Social psychologists have long viewed attitude, emotional and personality differences to be important moderator variables. In fact, current social psychology is predominantly a cognitive social psychology, at the heart of which is the assumption that the behavior and experience of an individual are the joint product of social situational (external) and cognitive (internal) factors. These internal psychological factors can be viewed as moderator variables*. If, as has already been suggested, the basic work-leisure hypotheses are psychological, not only have the operation of intervening cognitive processes been ignored, the "individual" (and hence individual differences) has typically been left out of theoretical and empirical studies of work-leisure relationships. Faithful to their characteristic approach, sociologists in their theoretical analyses have lumped individuals together, and in doing so, have assumed that the effects of work on leisure are so pervasive that individual differences do not matter. This assumption, however, has been unfortunate, because it has retarded progress in the area, as evidenced by frequent contradictions in the findings in the relevant literature (Champoux, 1975).

The role of psychological processes, particularly more permanent ones, such as attitudes and personality, is that they may act to

---

*Moderator variables can also be other situational variables. There are factors in the social environment that may supress or moderate the effects of other situational variables.

modify how the individual actually perceives, assesses and reacts to the work environment. The same objective work environment could be judged to have different characteristics by two individuals, and different objective work environments could be judged the same. "In short, to determine the effects of work (W) on leisure (L) and vice versa one must take cognitive variables (O) into account, the basic paradigm therefore being—W–O–L" (Iso-Ahola, 1980, p. 363). Of course, many of these psychological variables are developed or shaped through the socialization process.

This model of work-leisure moderator variables recognizes that people bring their individual differences to their jobs—differences already existing before the job was begun. Pennings (1976) tested the work-leisure hypotheses in the context of a "moderating variable model." Working conditions were measured by independent observers in terms of the amount of autonomy present or allowed, job variety and opportunity for social interaction. Moderator variables were questionnaire responses assessing each individual's need for autonomy, variety and social interaction. While the results supported the spillover hypothesis and the moderator variables contributed to the variance explained, the relationships were extremely weak.

The more recently published Kabanoff and O'Brien (1980) study used the psychological moderating variable internal/external locus of control. They hypothesized that persons who positively compensate for a low-quality working environment have an active, self-directed orientation toward their leisure. Internally oriented persons should act in the expectation that they can obtain satisfactions denied in their work by manipulating the leisure environment to meet their needs—hence compensating. On the other hand, externally oriented persons should tend to feel that factors beyond their personal control determine their leisure behavior. Given this expectation, externals should show evidence of spillover from low-quality work to low quality leisure, and compensation from high-quality work to low quality-leisure. Internals in high-quality jobs should show spillover. The results were disappointing. Only the attributes of variety and skill utilization showed any relationship between work and leisure, and even here the relationships were small. The authors conclusion though, that

work attributes on the whole have no strong or consistent relationship to leisure attributes is questionable in light of the earlier
discussed problems of their leisure measures. The limitations of
this study have been discussed above.

A FINAL NOTE

We will conclude this chapter with several observations. First,
theories of work-leisure relationships assume that people characteristically engage in either spillover or compensatory activities
during leisure. However, it is not at all unlikely that people
engage in activities that provide for compensation sometimes and
spillover at others, or activities that spillover in the sense of a
transfer of skills and interests but that provide compensation
along another dimension such as autonomy. Kando and Summers
(1971) have stressed the potentially shifting nature of the meaning
of the same activity over time. Researchers need to establish the
day-to-day circumstances which modify when work experiences
are compensated and when they tend to spill over into free time
participation. The impact of work likely varies as a function of a
person's job performance and experiences each day (Iso-Ahola,
1980).

> If, for example, a businessman has made excellent sales on one
> day, the good mood resulting from his successful job performance
> is likely to carry over into his leisure behavior. He may improvise
> ... and take his family to a good restaurant ... (p. 363)

Research could be undertaken to explore daily fluxuations in the
function and meaning of leisure in relation to work. Compensatory and spillover effects might be more readily detected by research
in the context of daily life.

Second, much of the discussion of work-leisure relationships
has focused on assembly-line work. Not only have white collar
workers been ignored for the most part, but also other blue collar
workers have received little research attention. Early theorists
concentrated on the "evils" of factory work, and ignored managers
who were seen to be among those exploiting the working class.
However, since the beginning of the industrial revolution the

division of labor has continued so that we have many white collar jobs, service personnel and middle management people who may have as little control over the final result of their work as the assembly-line worker.

Some awareness of the need to examine the impact of the work environment on white collar and management employees is now surfacing. For example, Cooper and Marshall (1980) have identified research that is beginning to examine a variety of white collar stressors. Many of these, for example, repetitive tasks, little autonomy and the necessity to work at a pace out of step with personal rhythm, are similar to those identified in assembly-line work. An additional source of stress includes role stresses. These are related to the lack of a clearly specified role for the worker within the organization, responsibilities for supervising others and lack of mangerial support. Career development stresses, such as, lack of job security, obsolescence and frustration at having reached one's career ceiling have also been identified. The emergence of this research suggests that their is a need for the parallel development of a more comprehensive work-leisure theory which expands its scope to include all types of work and leisure.

Finally, interest in the nature of the work-leisure relationship did not arise simply from scholarly curiosity, but rather from a overriding concern with the quality of life in society. The particular work-leisure perspective adopted will influence the policies and programs developed to enhance the individual's life in society. For example, a compensatory view of the work-leisure relationship seems to suggest that social planning that encourages the increase and enrichment of leisure and cultural opportunities is adequate to enhance the quality of life, regardless of the deficiencies of work. It is assumed that people will "automatically" seek out and engage in those activities that will remediate these deficiencies. Social policy that encourages the development of an extensive recreational and cultural opportunity spectrum would be both a necessary and sufficient condition for the improvement of social life and mass psychological well-being.

Of course, if a spillover perspective is adopted no amount of social planning for leisure will off-set the constraints of the job. Improvements in the quality of life must be sought through changes in work which then will allow an enriched form of leisure to emerge. However, if there is: (1) no systematic relationship between work and leisure, (2) a transient relationship which fluxuates with daily situational circumstances, or (3) the relationship is a personality difference resulting from socialization differences between people, the development of guidelines for social policy regarding work and leisure becomes more difficult. Clearly there is a need to reconceptualize the work-leisure problem and move away from efforts based on the traditional conceptualizations of the work-leisure relationship. The development of conceptualizations that allow researchers to explore the ways in which people integrate work and leisure in their daily lives, and assess the consequences for their psychological adjustment would be a useful manner in which to begin.

REFERENCES

Aldag, R., Barr, S., & Brief, A. (1981). Measurement of perceived task characteristics. *Psychological Bulletin, 90,* 415–431.

Argyle, M. (1972). *The social psychology of work.* London: Allen Lane the Penguin Press.

Bacon, A. (1975). Leisure and the alienated worker: A critical reassessment of three radical theories of work and leisure. *Journal of Leisure Research, 7,* 179–190.

Baran, P., & Sweezy, P. (1966). *Monopoly capital.* London: Pelican Books.

Bishop, D., & Ikeda, M. (1970). Status and role factors in the leisure behavior of different occupations. *Sociology and Social Research, 54,* 190–208.

Blum, M., & Naylor, J. (1968). *Industrial psychology.* New York: Harper and Row.

Campbell, A., Converse, P. E., & Rodgers, W. L. (1976). *The quality of american life: Perceptions, evaluations and satisfactions.* New York: Russell Sage Foundation.

Champoux, J. (1975). *Work and nonwork: A review of theory and empirical research* (Technical Report No. 31). Irvine: University of California, Graduate School of Administration.

Cooper, C. L., & Marshall, J. (Eds.). (1980). *White collar and professional stress.* Toronto: John Wiley and Sons.

Drucker, P. F. (1950). *The new society.* New York: Harper.

Ellis, M. (1973). *Why people play.* Englewood Cliffs, NJ: Prentice-Hall.

Engels, F. (1892). *The condition of the working-class in England in 1844* (translated by F. K. Wischnewetsky). London: Allen and Unwin.

Ennis, P. (1968). The definition and measurement of leisure. In E. Sheldon, & W. Moore (Eds.), *Indicators of social change.* New York: Harper and Row.

Friedmann, G. (1961). *The anatomy of work.* New York: The Free Press of Glencoe.

deGrazia, S. (1964). *Of time, work and leisure.* New York: Anchor Books.

Hall, D., & Nougaim, K. (1968). An examination of Maslow's need hierarchy in an organizational setting. *Organizational Behavior and Human Performance, 3,* 12–35.

Howe, I. (1957). Notes on mass culture. In B. Rosenberg, & D. White (Eds.), *Mass culture—the popular arts in America.* New York: The Free Press.

Hunt, S., & Weiner, A. (1982). Relationships between meanings of work and meanings of leisure in a retirement community. *Recreation Research Review, 9,* 29–37.

Iso-Ahola, S. (1979). Some social psychological determinants of perceptions of leisure: Preliminary evidence. *Leisure Sciences, 2,* 305–314.

Iso-Ahola, S. (1980). *The social psychology of leisure and recreation.* Dubuque, IA: Wm. C. Brown Co.

Iso-Ahola, S., & Buttimer, K. (1981). The emergence of work and leisure ethics from early adolescence to early adulthood. *Journal of Leisure Research, 13,* 282–288.

Iso-Ahola, S., & Buttimer, K. (1982). On the measurement of work and leisure ethics and resultant intercorrelations. *Educational and Psychological Measurement, 42,* 429–435.

Jenkins, C., & Sherman, B. (1981). *The leisure shock.* London: Methuen.

Kabanoff, B. (1980). Work and nonwork: a review of models, methods, and findings. *Psychological Bulletin, 88,* 60–77.

Kabanoff, B., & O'Brien, G. (1980). Work and leisure: A task attributes analysis. *Journal of Applied Psychology, 65,* 596–609.

Kando, T. (1980). *Leisure and popular culture in transition* (Second Edition). Toronto: Mosby Company.

Kando, T., & Summers, W. (1971). The impact of work on leisure: Toward a paradigm and research strategy. *Pacific Sociological Review* (Special Summer Issue), 310–327.

Karasek, R. (1976). *The impact of work environment on life outside the job.* Unpublished doctoral dissertation, Massachusetts Institute of Technology.

Kasl, S. (1973). Mental health and the work environment: An examination of the evidence. *Journal of Occupational Medicine, 15,* 509–518.

Kasl, S. (1978). Epidemiological contributions to the study of work stress. In C. L. Cooper, & R. Payne (Eds.), *Stress at work.* Toronto: John Wiley and Sons.

Kelly, J. (1975, August). *Leisure as compensation for work constraint.* Paper presented at the Annual Meeting for the American Psychological Association, Chicago.

Kohn, M., & Schooler, C. (1973). Occupational experience and psychological functioning: An assessment of reciprocal effects. *American Sociological Review, 38,* 97–118.

Kornhauser, A. (1965). *Mental health of the industrial worker.* New York: John Wiley and Sons.

Landy, F., & Trumbo, D. (1980). *Psychology of work behavior.* Homewood, IL: The Dorsey Press.

Lawler, E., & Suttle, J. (1972). A causal correlational test of the need hierarchy concept. *Organizational Behavior and Human Performance, 7,* 265–287.

Lefkowitz, B. (1979). *Breaktime.* New York: Penguin Books.

Locke, E. (1976). The nature and causes of job satisfaction. In M. Dunnette (Ed.), *Handbook of industrial and organizational psychology.* Chicago: Rand McNally.

London, M., Crandall, R., & Seals, G. W. (1977). The contribution of job and leisure satisfaction to quality of life. *Journal of Applied Psychology, 62,* 328–334.

Machlowitz, M. (1981). *Workaholics.* New York: New American Library.

Mannell, R. C. (1979). A conceptual and experimental basis for research in the psychology of leisure. *Society and Leisure, 2,* 179–196.

Mannell, R. C. (1980). Social psychological strategies and techniques for studying leisure experiences. In S. Iso-Ahola (Ed.), *Social psychological perspectives on leisure and recreation.* Springfield, IL: Charles C Thomas.

Mannell, R. C., & McCarville, R. (1979). *The independence of leisure and work attitudes: A study of their relationship to psychological well-being and recreation behavior.* Paper presented at the NRPA Leisure Research Symposium, New Orleans.

Maslow, A. (1954). *Motivation and personality.* New York: Harper.

Marx, K. (1964). *Selected writings in sociology and social philosophy.* New York: McGraw-Hill.

Meissner, M. (1971). The long arm of the job: A study of work and leisure. *Industrial Relations, 10,* 239–260.

Mennell, S. (1979). Social research and the study of cultural "needs." In J. Zuzanek (Ed.), *Social research and cultural policy.* Waterloo, Ontario: Otium Publications.

Parker, S. (1965). Work and nonwork in three occupations. *Sociological Review, 13,* 65–75.

Parker, S. (1971). *The future of work and leisure.* New York: Praeger Publishers.

Pennings, J. (1976). *Leisure correlates of working conditions.* Unpublished manuscript, Carnegie-Mellon University, Graduate School of Industrial Administration, Pittsburgh, PA.

Porter, L., & Steers, R. (1973). Organizational, work, and personal factors in employee turnover and absenteeism. *Psychological Bulletin, 80,* 151–176.

Rogers, C. (1959). A theory of therapy, personality, and interpersonal relationships as developed in the client-centered framework. In S. Koch (Ed.), *Psychology: A study of a science.* New York: McGraw-Hill.

Rosenman, R., Friedman, M., Straus, R., Wurm, M., Jenkins, C., Messinger, H., Kositchek, R., Hahn, W., & Werthessen, N. (1966). Coronary heart disease in the Western Collaborative Group Study. *Journal of the American Medical Association, 195,* 86–92.

Rousseau, D. (1978). The relationship of work to nonwork. *Journal of Applied Psychology, 63,* 513–517.

Seeman, M. (1971). The urban alienations: Some dubious theses from Marx to Marcuse. *Journal of Personality and Social Psychology, 19,* 135–143.

Sims, H., Szilagyi, A., & Keller, R. (1976). The measurement of job characteristics. *Academy of Management Journal, 19,* 195–212.

Smith, A. (1937). *An inquiry into the nature and causes of the wealth of nations.* New York: Modern Library.

Staines, G. (1980). Spillover versus compensation: A review of the literature on the relationship between work and nonwork. *Human Relations, 33,* 111–129.

Staines, G., & Pagnucco, D. (1977). Work and nonwork: Part II—an empirical study. In Survey Research Center, *Effectiveness of work roles: Employee responses to work environments* (Volume 1).

Strauss, G. (1974). Workers: Attitudes and adjustments. In the American Assembly, Columbia University, *The worker and the job: Coping with change.* Englewood Cliffs, NJ: Prentice-Hall.

Taylor, F. W. (1947). *Principles of scientific management.* New York: Harper.

deTocqueville, A. (1954). *Democracy in America.* New York: Vintage Books.

Turner, A., & Lawrence P. (1965). *Industrial jobs and the worker.* Cambridge, MA: Harvard Graduate School of Business Administration.

Wilensky, H. (1960). Work, careers and social integration. *International Social Science Journal, 12,* 543–560.

Wilensky, H. (1961). Orderly careers and social participation. *American Sociological Review, 24,* 522–529.

Yankelovich, D. (1978, May). The new psychological contracts at work. *Psychology Today, 11,* 46–50.

Zuzanek, J. (1976). *Leisure and social change.* Waterloo, Ontario: University of Waterloo.

Zuzanek, J. (1978). The work ethic: What are we measuring? *Industrial Relations, 33,* 666–677.

Zuzanek, J. (1979). Democratization of culture in a sociological perspective. In J. Zuzanek (Ed.), *Social research and cultural policy.* Waterloo, Ontario: Otium Publications.

Chapter VII

ENVIRONMENTAL CONSTRAINTS ON CHILDREN'S PLAY

LYNN A. BARNETT and MARY JO KANE

INTRODUCTION

Young Benjie, our three-year old prototype, has just finished his XQ-50 missile and is now busily engaged in constructing his "BQRX-9065718 Space Port." While Benjie's choice for this particular architectural play design has not been overtly directed by external factors, Benjie's play episode has been subtly influenced by several forces. Play behavior is largely determined by individual attributes which the child brings to his/her play. Variables such as age, sex, intelligence and creative capacity modulate the child's instigation and choice of playful activities. While the previous chapter extensively reviewed the relationship between these individual variables and play, we will now examine another salient force, the external environment, which impacts upon the nature and characterization of play. The environment in which the child finds him/herself interacts with these individual "person" variables and significantly shapes general attitudes, beliefs, feelings and behavior, and play in particular.

From an early age, the child is influenced by parental involvement —indirectly as parents shape the child's playful personality and more directly as they may influence particular choices for objects and activities chosen for play. The child-rearing practices which parents adopt may restrict the child in his/her playful exploration and manipulation. The differential expectations which parents

This chapter was supported in part by a grant from National Institute of Child Health and Human Development, No. HD 05951.

189

bring to their children constrain the child in the style and choice of play interactions and materials. At a later age, peers become a significant influence in fostering playful involvement. Peers provide feedback to the child about his/her role in society in general and this occurs primarily through play and games (Mead, 1934; Piaget, 1932). Children lacking in the appropriate age and sex-related physical skills are often excluded by their peers from play and, if this occurs at a frequent rate, a negative self-image often results. The child is often at the mercy of others for positive playful interactions and peers therefore serve as constraining agents on the child's play.

Throughout childhood, the educational system occupies much of the child's environment and thus may have a substantial impact upon development. Philosophical approaches to education, as reflected in classroom structure, tend to restrict active exploration and playful involvement. The goal-directed nature of many traditional curricula serves to transform the intrinsic motives underlying playful activity and often results in decreased involvement and negative affect. Such educational "styles" thus constrain playful expression and inhibit the positive cognitive and social correlates which naturally accompany children's play.

The importance of these environmental factors suggests that while they may have a facilitative role in fostering the child's play, they may also serve, to an equal or greater extent, to restrict or constrain playful expression. This chapter investigates the influence of the family, the peer group and the educational system as they exert an inhibiting effect on the child's natural freedom of expression through play.

THE FAMILY ENVIRONMENT: PARENTAL CONSTRAINTS

"The rule that parents should not play with the baby may seem hard, but it is without a doubt a safe one. A young, delicate and nervous baby needs rest and quiet, and however robust the child much of the play that is indulged in is more or less harmful. It is a great pleasure to hear the baby laugh and coo in apparent delight, but often the means to produce the laughter, such as tickling, punching or tossing, makes him irritable and restless. It is a regrettable fact that the few minutes' play that the father has when he gets home at night—may result in nervous disturbance of the baby and upset his regular habits." (Children's Bureau, Department of Labor, 1914; p. 59–60).

Although the above caution to parents to avoid play with their young appeared seventy years ago, more recent child-rearing theory and empirical evidence suggests that, indeed, parents may have a disrupting and deleterious influence on their children's play (Singer and Singer, 1977; Sutton-Smith and Sutton-Smith, 1974; Weininger, 1979). A natural evolution in play style, form and preference has been reliably observed as children mature developmentally (Barnes, 1971; Iwanaga, 1973; Parten, 1932; Piaget, 1951; Ross and Kay, 1980; Rubin and Pepler, 1980; Sachs, 1980) and adult imposition can disrupt this progression and foster play interactions which may be inappropriate or premature for the child's cognitive, social or physical maturity.

Play is a natural and spontaneous process whose underlying definitional consideration rests upon the intrinsic motivation which initiates the playful act. A wealth of literature (c.f., Barnett, 1980; Lepper and Greene, 1978, for reviews) has found that adult intervention can change the nature of this motivation to play from intrinsic to extrinsic. In a wide variety of situational contexts with a number of different reward incentives and across a varied age span, children will no longer freely choose to play with materials when they have either been offered a reward for doing so or directed by an adult to play in a certain manner. It appears that without the perception of the freedom to choose, and the motivation to be perceived as internally regulated, play ceases to continue. Thus, adult direction which guides the young child into play avenues which may not be initially sought, can be harmful to the child developmentally and also can severely hamper playful expression.

This portion of the chapter examines the roles parents assume in influencing their children during play. We will attempt to demonstrate, by reviewing the available empirical evidence, that children's play takes on different appearances and values as a direct function of parental involvement. In addition, it will become obvious that parents behave differently toward their children during play as a function of their sex and the gender of the child. As early as a few days after birth, parental intervention and direction occurs and serves to constrain the child's natural playful expression.

Parental Style

Young children's playful behavior is more different in the home than in other settings. The most pronounced discrepancies have been reported during social play interactions with infants (Becker, 1977; Castell, 1970) and with preschool children (Jeffers and Lore, 1979). These investigations report that children tend to display more aggressive and disruptive social play styles in the home and support the need to look more closely at parents as salient influences on young children's play. Parents need to be studied from early in the child's development since recent findings indicate that the differential role of parent-infant interactions occurs primarily in the play context. In most families, the majority of father-infant interactions occur during play (Clarke-Stewart, 1978; Kotelchuck, 1976; Lamb, 1976; Parke, 1979; Rendina and Dickerscheid, 1976) and when mother-father differences in parent-infant interaction style are found, they are generally observed in play, not in care-giving (Parke and Sawin, 1980; Power and Parke, 1981).

The psychological characteristics of the parents as well as their style of child-rearing practices influences the child's play styles and social play interactions. Researchers have found that less competent parents and those who exhibited high degrees of authoritarian control had children who were poorer in problem-solving games and showed less exploratory and curiosity behaviors in play (Mondell and Tyler, 1981). Children of parents who adhered to punitive child-rearing styles were extremely restricted in their play and showed little imagination or creative involvement (Cheyne et al., 1969). Parents who insisted on play with specific objects and who were more compulsive about cleanliness and tidiness had children who were generally less playful in quantity and quality of play activities (Pintler, 1945; Vlietstra, 1980). In addition, the presence of a parent during doll play games tends to facilitate fantasy aggression (Elder and Pederson, 1978; Fein, 1975; Golumb,

1977; Jeffree and McConkey, 1976; Levin and Turgeon, 1957; Pintler, 1945; Robinson, 1946; Watson and Fischer, 1977).

Several investigators have attributed individual differences in pretend play styles to child-rearing factors (Singer, 1973; Sutton-Smith, 1979). El'Konin (1966, 1969) suggested that parents do not play or model pretend games with their children. In an intensive longitudinal study, White and Carew-Watts (1973) found that pretend play was virtually nonexistent in the home for toddlers, a finding replicated with older preschool children (Carew, 1980; Dunn and Wooding, 1977). If the child attempted to initiate pretend play, it was rarely reinforced by parents (Dunn and Wooding, 1977; Hay, 1979). It has been suggested that parents function to inhibit pretense play rather than to reinforce it (Whiting, 1963). Although parents with training in early childhood education may play or model pretense with their children (Gershowitz, cited in Sherrod and Singer, 1977), such parents constitute a small segment of the general population. Rather than operating directly, child-rearing factors might influence other systems which in turn facilitate or restrict pretend play behaviors (Matas, Arend and Sroufe, 1978). Additional evidence for an indirect influence of child-rearing style on play comes from research suggesting that children whose parents use physical punishment as a disciplinary method or who come from homes in which there is marital discord are likely to show low levels of imaginativeness in their play (Hetherington, Cox and Cox, 1979d; Manosevitz, Prentice and Wilson, 1973; Marshall, 1961; Singer, 1973).

Sex-role Stereotyping

Parent-infant play has increasingly been recognized as a context in which a great deal of learning of social and cognitive skills may take place (Pawlby, 1977; Ross and Kay, 1980; Schaffer, 1977; Schaffer and Crook, 1978; Stern, 1977). Studies of parent-infant play have generally focused on the description of either face-to-face interaction patterns during the first four months of life (c.f., Blehar, Lieberman and Ainsworth, 1977; Brazelton, Koslowski and Main, 1974; Kaye and Fogel, 1980; Stern, 1977) or on the description of ritualized parent-infant games during the second half year (c.f., Crawley, Rogers, Friedman, Iacobbo, Criticos, Richardson and Thompson, 1978; Green, Gustafson and West, 1980; Gustafson, Green and West, 1979; Ross and Kay, 1980). One of the major findings of all of this research has been that mothers and fathers interact differently with their children, and from a very early age. Although early findings in child development found little support for the notion that infant boys and girls receive any significant differential treatment from either or both parents (Barry, Bacon and Child, 1957; Sears, Maccoby and Levin, 1957), such findings have recently been challenged (Kagan and Lewis, 1965; Lewis, 1972a, b). Whether this creates or merely reinforces typical gender differences is still unclear; it nonetheless appears that, from an early age, the type of learning that accompanies or results from play interactions channels play styles into traditional sex-role stereotypic patterns. Sex-typed play is associated with reinforcement, encouragement and especially disapproval from parents (Fagot, 1973, 1978; Fein, Johnson, Kosson, Stork and Wasserman, 1975; Frisch, 1977; Rheingold and Cook, 1975). Parent reinforcement of sex-typed play has been demonstrated in children as young as twenty-four months (Fagot, 1973, 1974, 1978). Doll play was one of the few behaviors consistently assigned to girls in parents' reports, reinforced by parent behavior and actually preferred by girls when children of both sexes were observed (Fagot, 1978). Disapproval was also a strong factor—both parents responded negatively when their sons played with dolls. By school age, sex-typed play is so well-established that teacher reinforcement of feminine-preferred toy play behavior in boys showed no effect (Fagot, 1978).

Differential expectations from parents exist based on the sex of their child (Aberle and Naegele, 1952; Hartley, 1959; Rothbart and Maccoby, 1966). Observational studies by Goldberg and Lewis (1969) showed that there are sex differences in the way a mother treats a child by the age of six months—the mother is more likely to pick up an infant daughter and thus restrict the range and area over which the daughter may explore.

Parents stimulate gross motor activity more with infant sons than with infant daughters (Fagot, 1974; Maccoby and Jacklin, 1974) and parents almost always give more verbal stimulation to their infant daughters (Clarke-Stewart, 1973; Maccoby and Jacklin,

1974). Parents buy different toys for their children (Rheingold and Cook, 1975), although it has not been shown that they offer different toys to other children in a laboratory playroom (Jacklin, Maccoby and Dick, 1973). Clarke-Stewart (1977) found that infant "father's play was relatively more likely to be physical and arousing rather than intellectual, didactic or mediated by objects—as in the case of mothers" (p. 37). Similarly, Lewis (1972a, b) found parents allowed boys more freedom to display aggressive behavior and to engage in more vigorous activities with toys. Absence of the father during the first five years of a male child's life has been associated with preadolescents who were significantly less aggressive, had more feminine play preferences and avoided competitive games (Biller, 1969, 1970; Santrock, 1970). Fathers tend to show more positive reactions when their son chooses "male" activities than when their daughters choose "female" activities (Fling and Manosevitz, 1972; Lansky, 1967; Mussen and Rutherford, 1963; Sears, Rau and Alpert, 1965).

Maternal Influences

Messer (1978) investigated maternal interactions with their infants from birth to two years as they engaged in a joint play session involving a number of toys. Results indicated that mothers played a significant role in directing the course of their infant child's play. The mother's frequent reference to a toy strongly coincided with the infant's manipulation of that toy and reference was particularly associated with actions which were likely to involve joint attention to a toy. Further evidence for the directing influence of mothers on their children's play comes from a study of toddlers in four play settings: mother and child playing together, peer and child playing together, mother, child and peer in play and the child playing alone. Again, findings confirmed earlier work and indicated that the mother directed the child's play toward a particular object of her choosing. Sex differences were also found in that boys engaged in their most creative play when interacting with a peer and showed the least creativity in play when the mother was present (Cohen and Tomlinson-Keasey, 1980). Similar results were obtained by others (Crawley, Rogers, Friedman, Iacobbo, Criticos,

Richardson and Thompson, 1978), all indicating that mothers provide more than merely a supportive role in facilitating their child's natural playful responses. Indeed, they serve to direct their offspring to play with specific objects and in specific ways. Udwin and Shmukler (1981) critically discussed the child's need for psychological space and maternal noninterference to foster acceptance and security to promote natural playful expression. Children appear to require the opportunity to explore and manipulate their environment through play, and it is the inherent freedom and flexibility contained in a free-range setting which fosters creative growth (Bishop and Chase, 1971).

Paternal Influences

Fathers appear to spend less time with their preschool children (Clarke-Stewart, 1977; Kotelchuck, 1975; Lewis and Weinraub, 1974; Pedersen and Robson, 1969; Rebelsky and Hanks, 1971) and are less frequently involved in caregiving activities than mothers (Kotelchuck, 1972; Lamb, 1977a). Lamb (1977a) and Yogman (1977) found differences in the specific content of maternal and paternal behaviors. Weinraub and Frankel (1977) observed children separately with both parents in a free play setting. They found that parents talked to, sat on the floor with, and tended to share play more with same-sexed than opposite-sexed offspring and the patterns of free play behaviors were different for mothers and fathers. Mothers were observed to be more nurturant in their play interactions and interacted verbally and conversationally more. Fathers, alternately, were relatively aloof and uninvolved—they sat on the floor and watched their children rather than interacting with them during play, and also tended to roughhouse more when play interactions did occur.

Contradictory findings have been reported when investigating differential parental play involvement with infant children. Greenberg and Morris (1974) found that "fathers begin developing a bond to their newborn by the first three days after birth and often earlier" (p. 526). While fathers participate less than mothers in caring for the young infant, they spend a greater percentage of time available for interaction in play activities (Kotelchuck, 1976). Richards,

Dunn and Antonis (1975) interviewed mothers concerning fathers' participation in a wide range of activities when the infant was thirty and sixty weeks old. At both ages, playing with their infant was the most common activity of the fathers in the sample, with over ninety percent of the fathers playing regularly with their offspring. A series of studies by Yogman and his colleagues (Yogman, 1980; Yogman, Dixon, Tronick, and Brazelton, 1977) examined the quality of these play interactions by comparing mothers, fathers and strangers interacting with infants in a play context. Adults differed in their play with infants, as indicated by vocalization and touching behaviors. Mothers tended to vocalize in soft, repetitive, initiative burst-pause talking more often than fathers, who did so significantly more than strangers. Fathers, however, touched their infants more often than either mothers or strangers. Further differences emerged not only in these discrete behaviors but also in the patterns of behavior. Yogman (1980) reported that games were more likely to occur during play sessions with fathers than with mothers, and the types of games that mothers and fathers played differed as well. Visual games were the most common type of mother's play, while tactile and limb movement games were the more frequent types of father-infant game. These stylistic differences in play have also been observed with older infants. Power and Parke (1981) videotaped mothers and fathers while playing with their eight-month-old infants in a laboratory playroom. Fathers were observed to play more bouncing, lifting and physically motoric games while mothers played more toy-watching games. Lamb (1977a, b) and Clarke-Stewart (1980) found fathers of similar aged infants engaged in more physical and universal play activities than mothers, who, in contrast, engaged in more conventional play activities, stimulus toy play and reading games. Overall, children appear to show a progression toward preferred play with fathers by the age of two years (Clarke-Stewart, 1977; Lamb, 1976).

Several factors influence both the quality and quantity of parent-child play interactions. Entwistle and Doering (1980) found that men who adhered to rigid stereotypes (e.g., "nurturing an infant is unmasculine") showed less interest in their new babies and less "fathering" behavior. However, other studies have failed to confirm this relationship between play and androgyny (Frodi and Lamb, 1980; Radin, 1976). Pederson, Cain, Zaslow and Anderson (1980) observed the play of single versus dual wage-earner families with their five-month-old infants. Consistent with earlier findings, fathers in single wage-earner families tended to play with their infants more than mothers. However, in the dual wage-earner families, the mother's rate of social play was higher (Parke and Tinsley, 1982).

Single Parent Families

The absence of a parent has a strong impact on a young child. Even children who are able to recognize that a divorce had constructive outcomes, at first undergo considerable emotional stress and problems with adjustment (Hetherington, Cox and Cox, 1979a; Kelly and Wallerstein, 1975, 1976; McDermott, 1968, 1970; Pemberton and Benady, 1973; Wallerstein and Kelly, 1974, 1975). Age-inappropriate play, disruptions in play activities and unpopularity with peers have consistently been found to be related to anxiety and emotional disturbance in children (Hartup, 1976; Roff, Sells and Golden, 1972; Singer, 1977). Play has been shown to assume an effective role in helping children work through or modify their problem behavior (Hartup, 1976, 1977a, b; Singer and Singer, 1976; Sutton-Smith, 1971). When differences in the social adjustment between boys in the mother-headed one-parent household and those from two-parent families are reported, boys in mother-headed families are described as more antisocial, impulsive and rebellious against adult authority and less self-controlled than boys in two-parent families (Douvan and Adelson, 1966; Felner, Stolberg and Cowan, 1975; Hetherington, Cox and Cox, 1979a, b, c; Hoffman, 1971; Mischel, 1961; Santrock and Wohlford, 1970; Siegman, 1966; Suedfield, 1967). Differences in the social adjustment of girls from one-parent families headed by a mother and those in two-parent families are reported less often than those for boys. Girls are less likely than boys to respond in an antisocial, aggressive manner to marital dissension or their parents' divorce (Gurin, Veroff and Feld, 1960; Hetherington, Cox and Cox, 1979d; Hoffman, 1971; Langner and Michael, 1963; Nye, 1957; Rosenberg,

1965; Rutter, 1971; Santrock, 1975; Tuckman and Regan, 1966). In addition, no differences in traditional measures of sex-role typing in young girls from one-parent families headed by a mother have been found (Bach, 1946; Lynn and Sawrey, 1959; Santrock and Wohlford, 1970).

Hetherington, Cox and Cox (1979d) examined children at two months, one year and two years after their parents divorced and compared their play to children of nondivorced families. In the first year after divorce, disruptions were found in the play and social relationships for the children from the divorced families. These adverse effects had largely disappeared for the girls by two years after the divorce, however the effects were more intense and enduring for the boys. The play patterns of the children from divorced families were less socially and cognitively mature when measured shortly following the divorce. Limitations and rigidity in fantasy play were particularly noticeable. At two months following divorce, children showed more functional and less imaginative play than their nondivorced counterparts. They also showed less associative and cooperative-constructive play and more onlooker and unoccupied play; the play episodes of divorced children were shorter in duration. By one year following divorce, divorced girls differed from nondivorced girls only in showing less associative-imaginative and cooperative-imaginative play and more onlooker behavior. By two years after divorce, these differences disappeared. In contrast, although divorced boys showed the most disruption in play at one year following divorce and more mature play patterns at two years after divorce, they still differed from nondivorced peers in many ways. At all three time periods, divorced boys showed more solitary and parallel functional play and less cooperative, constructive, imaginative or game play than boys from nondivorced families. They also showed more onlooker behavior and shorter durations of play episodes at all three points in time. Boys from divorced families spent an increasing amount of time playing with younger children and girls rather than exhibiting the more characteristic developmental pattern of a marked and increasing preponderance of time in play with same-sex and same-aged peers. Disturbances to play were also reflected in differences in affective expression. Angry, hostile, threatening affect and excitement were found more frequently in boys than in girls in both divorced and nondivorced families. At two years after divorce, both boys and girls showed less happy, affectionate and task-involved affect and more depressed, anxious, guilty and apathetic affective responses than children in nondivorced families. At one year after divorce, girls were still less happy and more anxious than girls in nondivorced families, but these differences disappeared by two years following divorce. Boys from divorced families showed more hostile affect in the first year following divorce and were still less happy and more anxious two years after the divorce. There was less imaginative play by divorced children and differences between the divorced and nondivorced groups in amount of fantasy play persisted for boys but not for girls. When divorced children became involved in fantasy play in the first year following divorce, it was more likely to have been instigated by a peer than to have been self-initiated. At two months following divorce, the children spent a larger proportion of their imaginative play time in fantasy involving object-related functions, functional changes in objects and object-related animation than children of nondivorced homes, and they spent less time interacting with imaginary people. There were no fantasy differences between divorced and nondivorced girls at one and two years following divorce, but some of the observed differences for boys remained. In all three time periods, divorced boys less often made major or minor transformations in the role of the "self" and markedly less often made identity transformations of the "self" than nondivorced boys. These boys appeared to have great difficulty in moving from emphasis on "I" to the assumption of another's role in fantasy play. Gould (1972) noted that continued focusing on the "I" in fantasy play in children beyond this age tends to be associated with a preoccupation with aggression and an inability to assume the role of providing or caring for others in imaginative play. The divorced children were involved with themes in which they were the recipients or agents of aggressive behavior, and boys showed a smaller percentage of prosocial play themes dealing with caring for others, affection, helping, sharing and sympathy. A certain rigidity and narrowness was also reflected in the fantasy play of both divorced boys and girls at two months after divorce and for a more sustained period for boys. At two months after divorce, boys and girls had fewer characters involved in their fantasy play, less frequently made different uses of the same object in play, and showed less diversity in either themes or affect in play. Except for less variation in themes and affect, these differences had disappeared for girls by one year following divorce and even the variability differences were gone by two years after divorce. However, these indicators of thematic and affective narrowness persisted for boys from divorced families (Hetherington, Cox and Cox, 1979d).

THE SOCIAL ENVIRONMENT: PEER INFLUENCES

The nature and quality of peer interactions in early childhood seem to contribute substantially to all spheres of development. The following section will focus primarily on the social development of young children by examining their interactions with peers during play. Play has particular relevance for this issue because from early to middle childhood, interaction with peers is carried out predominantly within a play setting. The significance of play in early childhood peer interactions seems therefore to have a major impact on developmental competence in young children.

There are a number of factors which tend to inhibit or constrain positive peer interactions. Because of the relationship between peer contact and social development, it can be argued that those factors which constrain the full range of potential interaction may have a detrimental effect on a child's development. As a result, this section will also focus on specific factors which may inhibit the quality of peer interactions in childhood: social and physical skills as they relate directly to contact with peers; and competition and cooperation in play and games.

Peer Interaction and Social Development

As we have seen repeatedly throughout this chapter, play is one of the primary mechanisms available to the child for understanding and revising different conceptions of the world (Cohen and Tomlinson-Keasey, 1980). Recently, a number of investigations have begun to explore the potential influence of peer contact among young children. Historically, preschoolers were perceived as having little interest or ability in relating to each other (Piaget, 1926). Several authors have strongly challenged this notion. For example, the role of peers was recognized by Mead as early as 1934. Mead believed that specific social skills develop through the opportunities for role playing provided by playful peer interaction. Other studies have since pointed out the importance of peer contact in enabling the child to reduce egocentrism and, at the same time, increase the child's role-taking skills (Konner, 1975; Rosen, 1974). Lewis and Rosenblum (1975) have argued that peers contribute as much or more than adults to children's development because peers create the opportunity for a "paced, slowly elaborating enlargement of communication skills—and for experimentation and learning without the potential or dire consequences of error" (p. 6).

In addition to the importance of peer contact for the development of role-taking, there is some evidence to suggest that peers provide for children's emotional needs (Asher, 1978; Mueller and De Stefano, 1973). Peer contact also appears to help children achieve a differentiation between the many social and physical objects present in their environment (Marcus, 1971). Moving beyond this ability to differentiate among play objects, Rubenstein and Howes (1976) suggested that peers contribute significantly to a child's mastery of objects. The authors found that the presence of peers in a free-play setting actually stimulated toddlers toward more mature forms of interacting with their environment: toddlers were more likely to exploit and manipulate unique properties of toy objects when other children were present. Mueller and De Stefano (1973), have emphasized the importance of the play setting in early childhood peer interactions. According to Mueller and De Stefano (1973) the playgroup environment is one which permits children to establish direct contact with their peers. The playgroup in fact both encourages and demands that children develop social interaction.

> The play environment impels the growth of social skills [among peers] in two different ways. On the one hand, the child is "invited" to discover the contingency between his own actions on toys and

its imitation by other children. At the same time, it is "demanded" that a child accommodate his behavior or face a repeated loss of desirable objects (Mueller and DeStefano, 1973; p. 15).

All of the above studies clearly indicate the importance of playful peer interaction to the social competence of the child. What is of crucial significance however, is how children establish and maintain positive peer interaction. Perhaps of even greater significance is how children *fail* to establish healthy and reciprocal relationships with their peers. It is to this important issue that we now turn.

Social Skills

Children vary considerably in their abilities to interact with their peers (Asher, 1978). We shall consider two general aspects of social skills that children need in order to have effective relationships with their peers: initiation skills and maintenance skills.

Initiation

Rubin (1980) has argued that one of the primary skills needed to establish friendships with peers is the ability to successfully initiate contact. There are a number of initiation strategies that children employ during play. Corsaro (1979) focused on "access" or "entry" strategies of newcomers and found that one successful method for outsiders was the ability to be cautious and subtle in approaching unfamiliar peers. One example of a typical "cautious" strategy was the ingratiating statement, "we're friends, right?" Gottman, Gonso and and Rasmussen (1975) demonstrated that within a free-play setting, popular children knew significantly more about how to make friends than did unpopular children, i.e., popularity ratings were strongly associated with social knowledge scores. This "social knowledge" about friendships was most apparent in the strategies employed by popular children. For example, popular children were more likely than unpopular children to offer a greeting, give or request information, or suggest inclusion when first meeting a newcomer (Gottman et al., 1975).

One final initiation skill which has been investigated has been the ability to handle rejection. Dweck and Goetz (1979) looked at attributions given by children whose initiation attempts during play had failed. Some children would tend to take responsibility for the rejection because they would attribute the unsuccessful interaction to their own inadequacies. In contrast, other children would attribute that same rejection to an external variable such as a misunderstanding or temporary "bad mood" on the part of the other child. Not surprisingly, the authors conclude that it is the resilient child who will be more successful in initiating friendships because he/she will continue to initiate interaction.

Maintenance

Once a relationship with a peer is established, a child still needs a variety of skills to maintain or strengthen the relationship (Asher, 1978). Lee (1973) suggested that children who are able to maintain successful friendships with their peers have different styles of interacting than do children who have trouble maintaining friendships. For example, popular children tend to display a wide range of playful interaction strategies; they are emotionally and physically responsive, friendly, adaptive and seldom terminate contact initiated by others (Lee, 1973). In contrast, unpopular children seemed to be belligerent and unfriendly, and when others did initiate contact, these children tended to be passive and unresponsive. Hartup, Glazer and Charlesworth (1967) found very similar results. In their study on the social participation of children as measured by associative play, popular children were the ones who were most attentive to their peers. These "successful" children praised others, showed affection and cheerfully accepted requests from others. Unpopular children often ignored other children and were uncooperative or frequently blamed and threatened their peers (Hartup et al., 1967).

One final maintenance skill is the ability to manage conflict. Rubin (1980) found that children's disputes often center around sharing and playing with toys or objects. His findings suggest that the more successful children are those who are able to talk over hurt feelings and re-establish good will when these sorts of disputes arise during playful activity.

Physical Ability

One area which has received little attention in the literature is the way in which physical development contributes to peer acceptance or rejection. Marlowe (1980) argued that socially isolated children in particular tend to be deficient in terms of mature physical development. In addition, Gruber and Kirkendall (1974) suggest that socially isolated children have trouble relating in a reciprocal manner with their peers because they are lacking in motor abilities and certain physical skills which become increasingly important during play and games with peers. Ausbel and Sullivan (1970) found that retardation in motor competence often contributes to a young child's social maladjustment. Not surprisingly, Smoll (1974) discovered that children with poor movement ability have very low prestige with their peers and as a result, are frequently left out of play and game activities.

As Rubin (1980) points out, one critical point that cannot be overlooked is the fact that children can only establish friendships with those whom they have the opportunity to interact with. As we have seen, there are a number of social and physical skills which seem to influence a child's competence in peer interaction during play.

Competition and Cooperation

From a developmental standpoint, as children begin to reach the school age years, there is a parallel growth between involvement in organized play and games and interaction with peers. According to Asher (1978), it is during this stage that solitary and imaginative play give way to more structured and formalized play forms such as organized sports. Mueller and Lucas (1975) viewed structured peer games as emerging from socially blind activities (i.e., a child's focus is centered on toys rather than peers) to structured social activities which gradually become more sophisticated.

The sheer number of children interacting with their peers in organized games is staggering. Recent estimates indicate that 20 million children between the ages of 6 and 15 are involved in competitive sports programs alone (Scanlan and Passer, 1978). A number of authors have argued that the emphasis on organized, adult sponsored programs is inhibiting or programming out altogether the spontaneous and informally organized free play activities of young children (Devereux, 1972; Eifermann, 1971; Seagoe, 1962). There has been a great deal of concern expressed in the youth sport literature on the influences of organized, competitive sports on children. The primary focus of concern involves the debate on competition versus cooperation and how these two factors effect the development of young children. We will outline these two opposing points of view and show how critics of organized, competitive play and games have focused on the detrimental aspects of youth sports. In addition, we will show how recent evidence suggests that competition and cooperation are not necessarily polar opposites and that their impact appears to be dependent upon the experience *within* the sport activity itself. Finally, although the competition-cooperation debate has focused on all aspects of a child's development, we will limit our discussion to how organized games may inhibit or constrain play activities during peer interaction.

Historically, physical activities of a competitive nature have been seen as possessing great developmental value for children (Seefeldt, Gilliam, Blievernicht and Bruce, 1978). Proponents of youth sports have frequently advanced the notion that competition instills character development, discipline, courage, loyalty, social adjustment and self-confidence (Hale, 1959; Larson, Spreitzer and Snyder, 1976). Organized sport competition for youth also serves as a critical arena for social evaluation, particularly for young boys (Scanlan and Passer, 1978).

Few would argue that sport competition has significant impact on children involved in organized activities. There is considerable disagreement however, on the nature of that impact. Critics have argued that there is a tremendous overemphasis on winning in this culture and that competition (rather than cooperation) fosters this winning-at-all-costs approach to organized play and games. As early as 1949, Deutsch noted that in a competitive social situation there is a zero sum condition where the gain or reward of one individual (or team) reduces the rewards available to others. According to sport critics, this zero sum condition is at the heart of competitive peer interaction and is ultimately the cause of much of the negative impact on children (Hyland and Orlick, 1975; Orlick, 1974; Orlick and Botterill, 1975). Orlick (1974) in particular argues that competitive, structured sport activities for children creates only winners and losers and that this system is beneficial to only a small minority of participants:

> There is an over-emphasis on winning at the expense of fun involvement. This elitist reward system gives rise to an atmosphere wherein many youngsters eliminate themselves before they start. Organized sport appears to operate as an extremely efficient screening process for the elimination of children (p. 12).

In addition to studies concerned about the sport drop-out, a number of investigations have examined the detrimental effects on those who continue to participate. Berkowitz (1962) contended that competition is a highly stressful interaction for children and that all participants, winners and losers alike, experience frustration and anxiety that ultimately promotes interpersonal aggression and hostility. Several studies support this position. Nelson, Gelfand and Hartmann (1969) conducted a laboratory experiment with five- and six-year-old children to see if frustration-aggression or catharsis was the outcome of participation in competitive games. Their results clearly supported the view that competition promotes aggression (Nelson et al., 1969). In addition to studies carried out in laboratories, a number of field observational studies found that competitive games increased unfriendly behavior toward one's peers (Rausch, 1965; Rausch, Dittman and Taylor, 1959). Finally, in their classic study on intragroup and intergroup competition and cooperation, Sherif and his associates found that although competition tended to increase intragroup cohesion, it also excessively increased intergroup rivalries and hostilities, even among former friends (Sherif, Harvey, White, Hood and Sherif, 1961).

One major assumption in the early youth sport literature was the belief that cooperation is antithetical to competition. Critics therefore have tended to view cooperation in play and games as a panacea. Consistent with this viewpoint is the position put forth by Orlick, McNally and O'Hara (1978). These authors have argued for the creation and implementation of a cooperative games program. One primary goal of this program is to serve as a vehicle for "social change directed toward more humane games and lives" (p. 203). According to Orlick, et al. (1978), co-op games will attempt to increase cooperative behavior both in and out of games as well as try to provide for cooperative success experiences and individual feelings of acceptance. In short, cooperative games became the antithesis of competitive sports because there are no losers: all children will cooperate and help each other in experiencing goal attainment and control over their environment. Orlick, et al. (1978) argue that this approach is in sharp contrast to the competitive winner-take-all approach where there are only a few "winners" and many more "losers."

The most recent research examining the potential impact of competitive youth sort has begun to challenge the assumption that competition and cooperation are antithetical. In discussing the nature of youth sport as a den of iniquity or land of promise, Martens (1978) convincingly argues that asking whether youth sports creates sinners or saints is a moot question. According to Martens (1978), the answer is obvious: youth sport programs can facilitate moral and social development when conducted properly but can also increase antisocial behavior when carried out improperly:

> It is not the game, the play or the sport that automatically determines the worth of these activities for the child; it is the nature of the experiences within these activities. It is the interaction with parents, teammates and coaches that determine if sports help the child develop morally or immorally (p. 204).

This moral or immoral development depends in large part on how much emphasis is placed on winning at the expense of other values such as skill development and fair play. In fact, it is this overemphasis on winning which has led critics of youth sport to mistakenly believe that competition per se is the reason for the negative consequences of sport participation (Martens, 1978). A number of authors have argued precisely this point. Competition versus cooperation is *not* the key to balancing the detrimental effects of youth sport because competition and cooperation are not antithetical, they are complimentary and inextricably linked (Ellis, 1976; Martens, 1978; Sherif and Rattray, 1976). As Ellis (1976) points out, the competitors have to cooperate in order to compete. We see therefore that it is an overemphasis on winning, with an elitist reward system and not competition per se, which is at the heart of the youth sport dilemma.

This literature suggests that organized game play may well have a negative impact on the developing child. To resolve this, Orlick and his colleagues suggested that structured play forms be rethought and organized differently. Orlick, McNally and O'Hara (1978) argued for the creation and implementation of a cooperative games program. One primary goal of this program is to serve as a vehicle for "social change directed toward more humane games and lives" (p. 203). According to Orlick, et al., (1978), co-op games will attempt to increase cooperative behavior both in and out of games as well as try to provide for cooperative success experiences and individual feelings of acceptance. In short, cooperative games became the antithesis of competitive sports because there are no losers: all children will cooperate and help each other in experiencing goal attainment and control over their environment.

EDUCATIONAL SYSTEMS

The basic premise of this chapter is that young children learn through their play activities and that play is closely related to both social and cognitive development. Although there has been considerable research on the effects of play in a number of areas, the impact of educational programs on children's play behavior has been virtually ignored (Johnson and Ershler, 1982). One recent exception has been the examination of the relationship between classroom structure and differential play patterns. This relationship has been linked to the instruction versus enrichment debate in early childhood education (Elkind, 1973). In this controversy, educational systems are conceptualized along a continuum representing different degrees of classroom structure. On one end of the continuum is the more highly structured or "closed" programs which place heavy emphasis on the role of the teacher, didactic instruction and goal-directed, extrinsically motivated activities. In contrast, less structured or "open" classroom programs stress child-centered activities with particular emphasis on the emotional and social development of the child, learning by discovery and intrinsic motivation (Hein, 1976; Johnson and Ershler, 1982).

A number of studies have investigated the impact of the "open" vs. "closed" educational approach and found that classroom structure appears to be directly related to differential play patterns among children (Beller, Zimmie and Aiken, 1971; Huston-Stein, Freidrich-Cofer and Susman, 1977; Johnson and Ershler, 1982; Johnson, Ershler and Bell, 1980; Miller and Dyer, 1975; Rubin and Seibel, 1979; Tizard, Philps and Plewis, 1976). The results of these studies have suggested that highly structured programs tend to reduce or limit the range, diversity or maturity level of young children's play (Johnson and Ershler, 1982). For example, several authors have suggested that traditional or formalized instructional programs inhibit or constrain the development of imaginative play: young children enrolled in highly structured programs have consistently exhibited significantly less symbolic or imaginative play than have children attending open classrooms (Beller, et al., 1971; Huston-Stein, et al., 1977; Rubin, 1980; Tizard, et al., 1976). Examining structure in terms of teacher/child ratios and physical layout, Field (1980) discovered that the optimal environment for enhancing the development of imaginative play was severely restricted by high teacher/child ratios and large, open spaces with play areas in the corners. These findings have particular relevance in that imaginative play has been found to be directly related to creativity and divergent thinking (Dansky and Silverman, 1973, 1975; Rubin, Fein and Vandenberg, 1982; Sutton-Smith, 1967; Sylva, Bruner and Genova, 1976; Vandenberg, 1978, 1980a).

Perhaps an even more critical issue than classroom structure as it influences and channels specific play patterns, is the process by which educational systems may actually undermine or transform the very nature of play. We have just seen how traditional or structured classrooms have been associated with extrinsically motivated activities while less structured or open classrooms stress activities which enhance intrinsic motivation (Johnson and Ershler, 1982). This relationship has particular importance for play. Definitions and theoretical formulations of children's playful behavior have traditionally stressed an internal motivational state which instigates the child to initiate a play experience: play activities are engaged in for their own sake, for the enjoyment experienced by the participant (Barnett, 1980; Ellis, 1973; Kelly, 1972; Neulinger, 1974; Parker, 1971; Sapora and Mitchell, 1961). Thus we see that there is an intimate association between play and intrinsic motivation. Several authors have noted the distinction between intrinsic and extrinsic motivation and have argued that free range, exploratory activities are debilitated by specific extrinsic conditions or constraints (Berlyne, 1958, 1966; Hunt, 1965; Koch, 1956; White, 1959). More specifically, a number of studies have convincingly demonstrated that the offering of an external reward for engaging in an activity that was initially intrinsically interesting, lowered (or reduced altogether) subsequent interest in the task or activity (Bem and McConnell, 1970; Carlsmith, Collins and Helmreich, 1966; Deci, 1971, 1972; Greene and Lepper, 1974; Lepper, Greene and Nisbett 1973). It should be emphasized that several of these studies were carried out within a classroom setting. In addition to lowering subsequent interest in an activity, Kruglanski, Friedman and Zeevi (1971) demonstrated that offering a reward for undertaking an activity that was initially intrinsically motivating also lowered the quality of the performance within the activity itself.

What is of critical importance is how playful behavior, through the process of overjustification, becomes transformed into the antithesis of play. If play can be defined as an activity where participation is engaged in for its own sake or for some intrinsic goal, and if work can be defined as an activity which is undertaken to achieve some external goal or reward, then it is certainly possible to transform play-like behavior into a work-oriented task or activity. We would argue that this is precisely the effect that a highly structured classroom curriculum has on children's play behavior. In a highly formalized educational structure, opportunities for experimentation, exploratory discovery, and for risking new ideas are frequently absent (Johnson and Ershler, 1982; Maier, 1980). This situation is most apparent in structured classrooms where learning is oriented toward the passing of a course or "proving" one's self to the instructor. This is in sharp contrast to the more open or discovery-based classroom where the child plays for fun, for her/himself and learns for the sake of learning (Maier, 1980). It is within this atmosphere that "true" play (activity which is intrinsically motivated), fosters a creative environment and enhances instruction and learning.

CONCLUSION

Environmental factors such as the family, the peer group and the educational system play a major role in shaping children's play behavior. These external forces, by guiding or channeling natural playful expression, often minimize or substantially alter the child's playful experience. By placing restrictions on the range of play options available to the child, or by structuring play activities in such a way as to limit voluntary play involvement, the freedom to choose, to initiate playful, intrinsic activity for its own sake, becomes severely restricted by these environmental influences. We may therefore argue that there is an inverse relationship between playful behavior and environmental constraints. The greater the degree of external forces which impinge upon and restrict the child's play, the lesser the opportunity for social, emotional and cognitive development which is provided for the child within the play setting.

The home environment has a tremendous impact upon the child's play. Traditional parental expectations perceive the role of the family as one of nurturance, facilitating the child's healthy growth and development. Yet, as can be seen from the above, oftentimes parents direct their children into play with specific objects and in specific ways. These types of supervised play are not of the child's own volition and result in depressing the natural affective responses of glee and pleasure that accompany self-initiated play. As the cognitive, social, emotional and physical benefit of playful experiences become recognized by theoreticians and researchers, questions concerning the negative influences of parental supervision arise. Without the necessary prerequisite developmental maturity, accelerated play forms which are often imposed by parents may be more destructive to the child than facilitative.

The absence of a parent in the home and the separation anxiety that often results, takes its toll on natural playful expression. The fostering of sex-appropriate behaviors restricts the range of playful alternatives available to the child and thus constrains the child's perception of the freedom to choose, an underlying mechanism of any playful interaction.

Peer interaction during play is one of the primary mechanisms available to the young child for learning about his/her environment. Peer contact enables children to develop important social skills such as role taking, as well as the ability to achieve mastery over physical objects present in their immediate surroundings. What is of equal if not greater significance however, is how children who are lacking in specific social and physical skills are frequently excluded from positive peer interaction. Young children who possess negative or unfriendly styles of interacting, who are deficient in the "social knowledge" required for successful peer interactions, are excluded from play and games and are thus restricted in their ability to gain the valuable social and emotional lessons inherent in playful expression.

Contact with peers is also an important element of organized play, games and sports. Critics of these structured play activities have consistently argued that competitive (vs. cooperative) sports, by emphasizing a winning-at-all-costs approach, have a detrimental effect on a child's emotional and psychological development. Regardless of which side of the competition-cooperation debate one chooses, or whether one accepts the notion that it is a winning-at-all-cost attitude rather than competition which contributes to the negative aspects of youth participation, it appears that organized, structured youth activities may constrain childhood play with peers. And if it is true, as Devereux (1972) has argued, that adult organized and supervised play activities limit or restrict the development of spontaneous and informal play forms with one's peers, then an overemphasis on *structured* activities (as well as an overemphasis on winning) may ultimately have detrimental effects on children's play development.

The goal-directed nature of traditional educational programs also restrict children's play potential. Highly structured classrooms reduce or limit the range, diversity and maturity level of young children's playful behavior (Johnson and Ershler, 1982). In addition, traditional or structured educational approaches may actually transform the very nature of play. By emphasizing extrinsically motivating activities, the play experience (which is enhanced and sustained by an intrinsic motivational state) becomes irreparably altered within a goal-directed classroom environment. In a highly formalized educational structure, exploration and discovery are severely restricted if not entirely absent.

If we accept the definition of play as freedom from constraint, as the opportunity to experience all possible play options and alternatives, then any environmental constraint, whether in the family, among peers or within the classroom, which structures or emphasizes one play style over another, becomes, by definition, antithetical to play.

REFERENCES

Aberle, D. F., & Naegele, K. (1952). Middle-class fathers' occupational role and attitudes toward children. *American Journal of Orthopsychiatry, 22,* 366–378.

Asher, S. (1978). Children's peer relations. In M. E. Lamb (Ed.), *Social and personality development.* New York: Holt, Rinehart and Winston.

Ausbel, D. P., & Sullivan, E. V. (1970). *Theory and problems of child development.* New York: Grune and Stratton.

Bach, G. R. (1946). Father-fantasies and father-typing in father-separated families. *Child Development, 17,* 63–80.

Barnes, K. (1971). Preschool play norms: A replication. *Developmental Psychology, 5,* 99–103.

Barnett, L. A. (1980). The social psychology of children's play: Effects of extrinsic rewards on free play and intrinsic motivation. In S. Iso-Ahola (Ed.), *Social psychological perspectives on leisure and recreation.* Springfield, IL: Thomas.

Barry, H., Bacon, M. K., & Child, I. I. (1957). A cross-cultural survey of some sex differences in socialization. *Journal of Abnormal Social Psychology, 55,* 327–332.

Becker, J. M. T. (1977). A learning analysis of the development of peer-oriented behavior in nine-month-old infants. *Developmental Psychology, 13,* 481–491.

Beller, E. K., Zimmie, J., & Aiken, L. (1971). Levels of play in different nursery settings. *International congress of applied psychology.* Belgium: Liege.

Bem, D. J., & McConnell, H. K. (1970). Testing and self-perception explanation of dissonance phenomena: On the salience of premanipulation attitudes. *Journal of Personality and Social Psychology, 14,* 23–32.

Berkowitz, L. (1962). *Aggression: A social psychological analysis.* New York: McGraw-Hill.

Berlyne, D. E. (1958). The present status of research on exploratory and related behavior. *Journal of Individual Psychology, 14,* 121–126.

Berlyne, D. E. (1966). Curiosity and exploration. *Science, 153,* 25–33.

Biller, H. B. (1969). Father absence, maternal encouragement, and sex role development in kindergarten-age boys. *Child Development, 40,* 539–546.

Biller, H. B. (1970). Father absence and the personality development of the male child. *Developmental Psychology, 2,* 181–201.

Bishop, D., & Chase, C. (1971). Parental conceptual systems, home play environment and potential creativity in children. *Journal of Experimental Child Psychology, 12,* 318–338.

Blehar, R. H., Lieberman, A. F., & Ainsworth, M. D. (1977). Early face-to-face interaction and its relations to early infant-mother attachment. *Child Development, 48,* 182–194.

Brazelton, T. B., Koslowski, B., & Main, M. (1974). The origins of reciprocity: The early mother-infant interaction. In M. A. Lewis, & L. A. Rosenblum (Eds.), *The effect of the infant on its caregiver.* New York: Wiley.

Carew, J. (1980). Experience and the development of intelligence in young children at home and in day care. *Monographs of the Society for Research in Child Development, 45.*

Carlsmith, J. M., Collins, B. E., & Helmreich, R. G. (1966). Studies in forced compliance I: Pressure for compliance on attitude change produced by face-to-face role playing and anonymous essay writing. *Journal of Personality and Social Psychology, 4,* 1–13.

Castell, R. (1970). Effect of familiar and unfamiliar environments on proximity behavior of young children. *Journal of Experimental Child Psychology, 9,* 342–347.

Cheyne, J. A., Goyeche, J. R. M., & Walters, R. H. (1969). Attention, anxiety, and rules in resistance-to-deviation in children. *Journal of Experimental Child Psychology, 8,* 127–139.

Children's Bureau, Department of Labor. (1914). *Infant care.* Washington, DC: Government Printing Office.

Clarke-Stewart, K. A. (1973). Interactions between mothers and their young children: Characteristics and consequences. *Monographs of the Society for Research in Child Development, 38.*

Clarke-Stewart, K. A. (1977). *The father's impact on mother and child.* Paper presented at Society for Research in Child Development, New Orleans.

Clarke-Stewart, K. A. (1978). And daddy makes three: The father's impact on the mother and young child. *Child Development, 49,* 466–478.

Clarke-Stewart, K. A. (1980). The father's contribution to children's cognitive and social development in early childhood. In F. A. Pedersen (Ed.), *The father-infant relationship: Observational studies in the family setting.* New York: Praeger.

Cohen, N. L., & Tomlinson-Keasey, C. (1980). The effects of peers and mothers on toddlers' play. *Child Development, 51,* 921–924.

Corsaro, W. A. (1979). We're friends, right?: Children's use of access rituals in a nursery school. *Language in Society, 8,* 315–336.

Crawley, S. B., Rogers, P. P., Friedman, S., Iacobbo, M., Criticos, A., Richardson, L., & Thompson, M. A. (1978). Developmental changes in the structure of mother-infant play. *Developmental Psychology, 14,* 30–36.

Dansky, J. L., & Silverman, I. W. (1973). Effects of play on associative fluency in preschool children. *Developmental Psychology, 9,* 38–43.

Dansky, J. L., & Silverman, I. W. (1975). Play: A general facilitator of associative fluency. *Developmental Psychology, 11,* 104.

Deci, E. L. (1971). Effects of externally mediated rewards on intrinsic motivation. *Journal of Personality and Social Psychology, 18,* 105–115.

Deci, E. L. (1972). Intrinsic motivation, extrinsic reinforcement, and inequity. *Journal of Personality and Social Psychology, 22,* 113–120.

Deutsch, M. (1949). A theory of cooperation and competition. *Human Relations, 2,* 129–152.

Devereux, E. C. (1972). *Some observations on sports, play and games in childhood.* Paper presented at EAPEWC Conference on Physiology and Psychology of Sport, Denver.

Douvan, E., & Adelson, J. (1966). *The adolescent experience.* New York: Wiley.

Dunn, J., & Wooding, C. (1977). Play in the home and its implications for learning. In B. Tizard, & D. O. Harvey (Eds.), *Biology of play.* London: William Heinemann Medical Books.

Dweck, C. S., & Goetz, T. E. (1979). Attributions and learned helplessness. In J. H. Harvey, W. Ickes, & R. F. Kidd (Eds.), *New directions in attribution research.* Hillsdale, NJ: Lawrence Erlbaum.

Eifermann, R. R. (1971). Social play in childhood. In R. E. Herron, & B. Sutton-Smith (Eds.), *Child's play.* New York: Wiley.

Elder, J. L., & Pederson, D. R. (1978). Preschool children's use of objects in symbolic play. *Child Development, 49,* 500–504.

Elkind, D. (1973). Preschool education: Enrichment of instruction? In B. Spodek (Ed.), *Early childhood education.* Englewood Cliffs, NJ: Prentice-Hall.

El'Konin, D. B. (1966). Symbolics and its function in the play of children. *Soviet Education, 8,* 35–41.

El'Konin, D. B. (1969). Some results of the study of the psychological development of preschool-age children. In M. Cole, & I. Maltzman (Eds.), *A handbook of contemporary soviet psychology.* New York: Basic.

Ellis, M. J. (1973). *Why people play.* Englewood Cliffs, NJ: Prentice-Hall.

Ellis, M. J. (1976). Rewarding children at work and play. In J. G. Albinson, & G. M. Andrew (Eds.), *Child in sport and physical activity.* Baltimore: University Park Press.

Entwistle, D. R., & Doering, S. G. (1980). *The first birth.* Baltimore: Johns Hopkins University Press.

Fagot, B. I. (1973). Sex-related stereotyping of toddlers' behaviors. *Developmental Psychology, 9,* 429.

Fagot, B. I. (1974). Sex differences in toddlers' behavior and parental reaction. *Developmental Psychology, 10,* 554–558.

Fagot, B. I. (1978). The influence of sex of child on parental reactions to toddler children. *Child Development, 49,* 459–465.

Fein, G. G. (1975). A transformational analysis of pretending. *Developmental Psychology, 11,* 291–296.

Fein, G. G., Johnson, D., Kosson, N., Stork, L., & Wasserman, L. (1975). Stereotypes and preferences in the toy choices of 20-month-old boys and girls. *Developmental Psychology, 11,* 527–528.

Felner, R. D., Stolberg, A., & Cowan, E. L. (1975). Crisis events and school mental health referral patterns of young children. *Journal of Consulting and Clinical Psychology, 43,* 305–310.

Field, T. M. (1980). Preschool play: Effects of teacher/child ratios and organization of classroom space. *Child Study Journal, 10,* 191–205.

Fling, S., & Manosevitz, M. (1972). Sex typing in nursery school children's play interests. *Developmental Psychology, 7,* 146–152.

Frisch, H. (1977). Sex stereotypes in adult-infant play. *Child Development, 48,* 1671–1675.

Frodi, A. M., & Lamb, M. E. (1978). Sex differences in responsiveness to infants: A developmental study of psychophysiological and behavioral responses. *Child Development, 49,* 1182–1188.

Goldberg, S., & Lewis, M. (1969). Play behavior in the year-old infant: Early sex differences. *Child Development, 40,* 21–31.

Golumb, C. (1977). Symbolic play: The role of substitutions in pretense and puzzle games. *British Journal of Educational Psychology, 47,* 175–186.

Gottman, J., Gonso, J., & Rasmussen, B. (1975). Social interaction, social competence, and friendship in children. *Child Development, 46,* 709–718.

Gould, R. (1972). *Child studies through fantasy.* New York: Quadrangle.

Green, J. A., Gustafson, G. E., & West, M. J. (1980). Effects of infant development on mother-infant interaction. *Child Development, 51,* 199–207.

Greenberg, M., & Morris, N. (1974). Engrossment: The newborn's impact upon the father. *American Journal of Orthopsychiatry, 44,* 520–531.

Greene, D., & Lepper, M. R. (1974). Effects of extrinsic rewards on children's subsequent intrinsic interest. *Child Development, 45,* 1141–1145.

Gruber, J. J., & Kirkendall, D. R. (1974). Effectiveness of motor, intellectual and personality domains in predicting group status in disadvantaged pupils. *Research Quarterly, 44,* 423–433.

Gurin, G., Veroff, J., & Feld, S. (1960). *Americans view their mental health.* New York: Basic Books.

Gustafson, G. E., Green, J. A., & West, M. J. (1979). The infant's changing role in mother-infant games: The growth of social skills. *Infant Behavior and Development, 2,* 301–308.

Hale, C. J. (1959). What research says about athletics for pre-high school age children. *Journal of Health, Physical Education and Recreation, 30,* 19–21.

Hartley, R. (1959). Children's concepts of male and female roles. *Merrill-Palmer Quarterly, 6,* 83–91.

Hartup, W. W. (1976). Peer interaction and the behavioral development of the individual child. In E. Schopler, & R. L. Reichler (Eds.), *Psychopathology and child development.* New York: Plenum.

Hartup, W. W. (1977a). Peer relations and the processes of socialization. In M. J. Guralnick (Ed.), *Early intervention and the integration of handicapped and nonhandicapped children.* Baltimore: University Park Press.

Hartup, W. W. (1977b). Peers, play and pathology: A new look at the social behavior of children. *Society for Research in Child Development Newsletter,* pp. 1–3.

Hartup, W. W., Glazer, J. A., & Charlesworth, R. (1967). Peer reinforcement and sociometric status. *Child Development, 38,* 1017–1024.

Hay, D. F. (1979). Cooperative interaction and sharing between very young children and their parents. *Developmental Psychology, 15,* 647–653.

Hein, G. E. (1976). *Piaget, materials, and open education.* Paper presented at Play and Games Conference, Milwaukee.

Hetherington, E. M., Cox, M., & Cox, R. (1979a). The development of children in mother headed families. In H. Hoffman, & D. Reiss (Eds.), *The American family: Dying or developing.* New York: Plenum.

Hetherington, E. M., Cox, M., & Cox, R. (1979b). Stress and coping in divorce: A focus on women. In J. Gullahorn (Ed.), *Psychology and women in transition.* New York: Winston.

Hetherington, E. M., Cox, M., & Cox, R. (1979c). Family interactions and the social, emotional and cognitive development of children following divorce. In V. C. Vaughan, & T. B. Brazelton (Eds.), *The family: Setting priorities.* New York: Science and Medicine Publishers.

Hetherington, E. M., Cox, M., & Cox, R. (1979d). Play and social interaction in children following divorce. *Journal of Social Issues, 35,* 26–49.

Hoffman, M. L. (1971). Father absence and conscience development. *Child Development, 42,* 1071–1082.

Hunt, J. (1965). Intrinsic motivation and its role in psychological development. In D. Levine (Ed.), *Nebraska symposium on motivation.* Lincoln: University of Nebraska Press.

Huston-Stein, A., Freidrich-Cofer, L., & Susman, E. (1977). The relationship of classroom structure to social behavior, imaginative play, and self-regulation of economically disadvantaged children. *Child Development, 48,* 908–916.

Hyland, J., & Orlick, T. (1975). Children's sports: A revolution is coming. *Journal of the Canadian Association for Health, Physical Education and Recreation, 39,* 12–14.

Iwanaga, M. (1973). Development of interpersonal play structure in 3, 4 and 5 year-old children. *Journal of Research and Development in Education, 6,* 71–82.

Jacklin, C. N., Maccoby, E. E., & Dick, A. E. (1973). Barrier behavior and toy preference: Sex differences (and their absence) in the year-old child. *Child Development, 44,* 196–200.

Jeffers, V. W., & Lore, R. K. (1979). Let's play at my house: Effects of the home environment on the social behavior of children. *Child Development, 50,* 837–841.

Jeffree, D., & McConkey, R. (1976). An observation scheme for recording children's imaginative doll play. *Journal of Child Psychology and Psychiatry, 17,* 189–197.

Johnson, J. E. (1978). Mother-child interaction and imaginative behavior of pre-school children. *Journal of Psychology, 100,* 123–129.

Johnson, J. E., & Ershler, J. (1982). Curricular effects on the play of preschoolers. *Contributions to Human Development, 6,* 130–143.

Johnson, J. E., Ershler, J., & Bell, C. (1980). Play behavior in a discovery-based and a formal-education preschool program. *Child Development, 51,* 271–274.

Kagan, J., & Lewis, M. (1965). Studies of attention in the human infant. *Merrill-Palmer Quarterly, 11,* 95–127.

Kaye, K., & Fogel, A. (1980). The temporal structure of face-to-face communication between mothers and infants. *Developmental Psychology, 16,* 454–464.

Kelly, J. B., & Wallerstein, J. S. (1975). The effects of parental divorce. *American Journal of Orthopsychiatry, 45,* 253–254.

Kelly, J. B., & Wallerstein, J. S. (1976). The effects of parental divorce: Experiences of the child in early latency. *American Journal of Orthopsychiatry, 46,* 20–32.

Kelly, J. R. (1972). Work and leisure: A simplified paradigm. *Journal of Leisure Research, 4,* 50–62.

Koch, S. (1956). Behavior as "intrinsically" regulated: Work notes towards a pre-theory of phenomena called "motivational." In M. R. Jones (Ed.), *Nebraska symposium on motivation.* Lincoln: University of Nebraska Press.

Konner, M. (1975). Relations among infants and juveniles in comparative perspective. In M. Lewis, & L. Rosenblum (Eds.), *Friendship and peer relations.* New York: Wiley.

Kotelchuck, M. (1972). *The nature of the child's tie to his father.* Unpublished doctoral dissertation, Harvard University.

Kotelchuck, M. (1975). *Father caretaking characteristics and their influences on infant-father interaction.* Paper presented at American Psychological Association, Montreal.

Kotelchuck, M. (1976). The infant's relationship to the father: Experimental evidence. In M. E. Lamb (Ed.), *The role of the father in child development.* New York: Wiley.

Kruglanski, A. W., Friedman, I., & Zeevi, G. (1971). The effects of extrinsic incentives on some qualitative aspects of task performance. *Journal of Personality and Social Psychology, 39,* 606–617.

Lamb, M. E. (1976). The role of the father: An overview. In M. E. Lamb (Ed.), *The role of the father in child development.* New York: Wiley.

Lamb, M. E. (1977a). Father-infant and mother-infant interaction in the first year of life. *Child Development, 48,* 167–181.

Lamb, M. E. (1977b). The development of mother-infant and father-infant attachments in the second year of life. *Developmental Psychology, 13,* 639–649.

Langner, G. S., & Michael, S. T. (1963). *Life stresses and mental health.* New York: Free Press.

Lansky, L. M. (1967). The family structure also affects the model: Sex-role attitudes in parents of preschool children. *Merrill-Palmer Quarterly, 13,* 139–150.

Larsen, D. L., Spreitzer, E., & Snyder, E. (1976). An analysis of organized sports for children. *The Physical Educator, 33,* 59–62.

Lee, L. C. (1973). *Social encounters of infants: The beginnings of popularity.* Paper presented at International Society for the Study of Behavioral Development, Ann Arbor.

Lepper, M. R., & Greene, D. (1978). *The hidden costs of reward: New perspectives on the psychology of human motivation.* Hillsdale, NJ: Lawrence Erlbaum.

Lepper, M. R., Greene, D., & Nisbett, R. E. (1973). Undermining children's intrinsic interest with extrinsic rewards: A test of the overjustification hypothesis. *Journal of Personality and Social Psychology, 28,* 129–137.

Levin, H., & Turgeon, V. (1957). The influence of the mother's presence on children's doll-play aggression. *Journal of Abnormal Social Psychology, 55,* 304–308.

Lewis, M. (1972a). Culture and gender roles: There is no unisex in the nursery. *Psychology Today, 5,* 54–57.

Lewis, M. (1972b). State as an infant-environment interaction: An analysis of mother-infant behavior as a function of sex. *Merrill-Palmer Quarterly, 18,* 95–121.

Lewis, M., & Rosenblum, L. A. (Eds.). (1975). *Friendship and peer relations.* New York: Wiley.

Lewis, M., & Weinraub, M. (1974). Sex of parent x sex of child: Socioemotional development. In R. Richart, R. Friedman, & R. Vande Wiele (Eds.), *Sex differences in behavior.* New York: Wiley.

Lynn, D. B., & Sawrey, W. L. (1959). The effects of father-absence on Norwegian boys and girls. *Journal of Abnormal and Social Psychology, 59,* 258–262.

Maccoby, E. E., & Jacklin, C. (1974). *The psychology of sex differences.* Stanford: Stanford University Press.

Maier, H. W. (1980). Play in the university classroom. *Social Work With Groups, 3,* 7–16.

Manosevitz, M., Prentice, N. M., & Wilson, F. (1973). Individual and family correlates of imaginary companions in preschool children. *Developmental Psychology, 8,* 72–79.

Marcus, J. (1971). Early child development in Kibbutz group care. *Early Childhood Development and Care, 1,* 67–98.

Marlowe, M. (1980). Games analysis intervention: A procedure to increase peer acceptance of socially isolated children. *Research Quarterly, 51,* 422–426.

Marshall, H. R. (1961). Relations between home experiences and children's use of language in play interaction with peers. *Psychological Monographs, 75.*

Martens, R. (1978). Kids sports: A den of iniquity or land of promise. In R. Magill, M. Ash, & F. Smoll (Eds.), *Children in sport: Contemporary anthology.* Champaign, IL: Human Kinetics Publishers.

Matas, L., Arend, R. A., & Sroufe, A. (1978). Continuity of adaptation in the second year: The relationship between quality of attachment and later competence. *Child Development, 49,* 547–556.

McDermott, J. F. (1968). Parental divorce in early childhood. *American Journal of Psychiatry, 124,* 1424–1432.

McDermott, J. F. (1970). Divorce and its psychiatric sequelae in children. *Archives of General Psychiatry, 23,* 421–427.

Mead, G. H. (1934). *Mind, self and society.* Chicago: University of Chicago Press.

Messer, D. J. (1978). The integration of mothers' referential speech with joint play. *Child Development, 49,* 781–787.

Miller, L. B., & Dyer, J. L. (1975). Four preschool programs: Their dimensions and effects. *Monographs of Social Research and Child Development, 40.*

Mischel, W. (1961). Father-absence and delay of gratification. *Journal of Abnormal and Social Psychology, 62,* 116–124.

Mondell, S., & Tyler, F. B. (1981). Parental competence and styles of problem-solving/play behavior with children. *Developmental Psychology, 17,* 73–78.

Mueller, E., & De Stefano, C. (1973). Sources of toddlers peer interaction in a playgroup setting. *Early Child Development and Care, 6,* 1–19.

Mueller, E., & Lucas, J. (1975). A developmental analysis of peer interaction among toddlers. In M. Lewis, & L. Rosenblum (Eds.), *Friendship and peer relations.* New York: Wiley.

Mussen, P. H., & Rutherford, C. (1963). Parent-child relations and parental personality in relation to young children's sex-role preferences. *Child Development, 34,* 589–607.

Nelson, J. D., Gelfand, D. M., & Hartmann, D. P. (1969). Children's aggression following competition and exposure to aggressive models. *Child Development, 40,* 1085–1097.

Neulinger, J. (1974). *The psychology of leisure.* Springfield: Thomas.

Nye, F. I. (1957). Child adjustment in broken and in unhappy unbroken homes. *Marriage and Family Living, 19,* 356–360.

Orlick, T. D. (1974). The athletic drop-out: A high price to pay for inefficiency. *Journal of the Canadian Association for Health, Physical Education and Recreation, 40,* 12–14.

Orlick, T. D., & Botterill, C. (1975). *Every kid can win.* New York: Nelson Hall Publishers.

Orlick, T. D., McNally, J., & O'Hara, T. (1978). Cooperative games: Systematic analysis and cooperative impact. In F. Smoll, & R. Smith (Eds.), *Psychological perspectives in youth sports.* New York: Wiley.

Parke, R. D. (1979). Perspectives on father-infant interaction. In J. Osofsky (Ed.), *The handbook of infant development.* New York: Wiley.

Parke, R. D., & Sawin, D. B. (1980). The family in early infancy: Social interactional and attitudinal analyses. In F. A. Pedersen (Ed.), *The father-infant relationship: Observational studies in the family setting.* New York: Praeger.

Parke, R. D., & Tinsley, B. R. (1982). The father's role in infancy: Determinants of involvement in caregiving and play. In M. E. Lamb (Ed.), *The role of the father in child development.* New York: Wiley.

Parker, S. (1971). *The future of work and leisure.* New York: Praeger.

Parten, M. B. (1932). Social participation among preschool children. *Journal of Abnormal Social Psychology, 27,* 243–269.

Pawlby, S. J. (1977). Imitative interaction. In H. R. Schaffer (Ed.), *Studies in mother-infant interaction.* London: Academic Press.

Pedersen, F. A., Cain, R., Zaslow, M., & Anderson, B. (1980). *Variation in infant experience associated with alternative family role organization.* Paper presented at International Conference on Infant Studies, New Haven, CT.

Pedersen, F. A., & Robson, K. S. (1969). Father participation in infancy. *American Journal of Orthopsychiatry, 39,* 466–472.

Pemberton, D. A., & Benady, D. R. (1973). Consciously rejected children. *British Journal of Psychiatry, 123,* 575–578.

Piaget, J. (1926). *The language and thought of the child.* New York: Harcourt, Brace.

Piaget, J. (1932). *The moral judgment of the child.* New York: Free Press.

Piaget, J. (1951). *Play, dreams and imitation in childhood.* New York: Norton.

Pintler, M. H. (1945). Doll-play as a function of experimenter-child interaction and initial organization of the materials. *Child Development, 16,* 146–166.

Power, T. G., & Parke, R. D. (1981). Play as a context for early learning: Lab and home analyses. In I. E. Sigel, & L. M. Laosa (Eds.), *The family as a learning environment.* New York: Plenum.

Radin, N. (1976). The role of the father in cognitive academic, and intellectual development. In M. E. Lamb (Ed.), *The role of the father in child development.* New York: Wiley.

Rausch, H. L. (1965). Interaction sequences. *Journal of Personality and Social Psychology, 2,* 487–499.

Rausch, H. L., Dittman, A. T., & Taylor, T. J. (1959). Person, setting and change in social interaction. *Human Relations, 12,* 361–379.

Rebelsky, F., & Hanks, C. (1971). Fathers' verbal interaction with infants in the first three months of life. *Child Development, 42,* 63–68.

Rendina, I., & Dickerscheid, J. D. (1976). Father involvement with first-born infants. *Family Co-ordinator, 25,* 373–379.

Rheingold, H. L., & Cook, K. V. (1975). The contents of boys' and girls' rooms as an index of parents' behavior. *Child Development, 46,* 459–463.

Richards, M. P. M., Dunn, J. F., & Antonis, B. (1978). *Caretaking in the first year of life: The role of fathers' and mothers' social isolation.* Unpublished manuscript, University of Cambridge.

Robinson, E. F. (1946). Doll play as a function of the doll family constellation. *Child Development, 17,* 97–118.

Roff, M., Sells, S. B., & Golden, M. M. (1972). *Social adjustment and personality development in children.* Minneapolis: University of Minnesota Press.

Rosen, C. E. (1974). The effects of sociodramatic play on problem-solving behavior among culturally disadvantaged preschool children. *Child Development, 45,* 920–927.

Rosenberg, M. (1965). *Society and the adolescent self-image.* New Jersey: Princeton University Press.

Ross, H. S., & Kay, D. A. (1980). The origins of social games. In K. H. Rubin (Ed.), *Children's play.* San Francisco: Jossey-Bass.

Rothbart, M., & Maccoby, E. E. (1966). Parent's differential reactions to sons and daughters. *Journal of Personality and Social Psychology, 4,* 237–243.

Rubenstein, J., & Howes, C. (1976). The effects of peers on toddler interaction with mothers and toys. *Child Development, 47,* 597–605.

Rubin, Z. (1980). *Children's friendships.* Cambridge: Harvard University Press.

Rubin, K. H., & Pepler, D. J. (1980). The relationship of child's play to social-cognitive development. In H. Foot, T. Chapman, & J. Smith (Eds.), *Friendship and childhood relationships.* London: Wiley.

Rubin, K. H., & Seibel, C. G. (1979). *The effects of ecological setting on the cognitive and social play behaviors of preschoolers.* Paper presented at American Educational Research Association, San Francisco.

Rubin, K. H., Fein, G. G., & Vandenberg, B. (1982). Play. In E. M. Hetherington (Ed.), *Carmichael's manual of child psychology.* New York: Wiley.

Rutter, M. (1971). Parent-child separation: Psychological effects on the children. *Journal of Child Psychology and Psychiatry, 12,* 233–260.

Sachs, J. (1980). The role of adult-child play in language development. In K. H. Rubin (Ed.), *Children's play.* San Francisco: Jossey-Bass.

Santrock, J. W. (1970). Parental absence, sex-typing and identification. *Developmental Psychology, 2,* 265–272.

Santrock, J. W. (1975). Father absence, perceived maternal behavior, and moral development in boys. *Child Development, 46,* 753–757.

Santrock, J. W., & Wohlford, P. (1970). Effects of father absence: Influences of, reason for, and onset of absence. *Proceedings of the 78th Annual Convention of the American Psychological Association, 5,* 265–266.

Sapora, A. V., & Mitchell, E. D. (1961). *The theory of play and recreation.* New York: Ronald Press.

Scanlan, T. K., & Passer, M. W. (1978). Anxiety-inducing factors in competitive youth sports. In F. Smoll, & R. Smith (Eds.), *Psychological perspectives in youth sports.* New York: Wiley.

Schaffer, H. R. (1977). *Mothering.* Cambridge: Harvard University Press.

Schaffer, H. R., & Crook, C. K. (1978). The role of the mother in early social development. In H. McGurk (Ed.), *Childhood social development.* London: Methuen.

Seagoe, M. V. (1962). Children's play as an indicator of cross-cultural and intro-cultural differences. *Journal of Educational Psychology, 35,* 278–283.

Sears, R. R., Maccoby, E. E., & Levin, H. (1957). *Patterns of child rearing.* Evanston, IL: Row, Peterson.

Sears, R. R., Rau, L., & Alpert, R. (1965). *Identification and child rearing.* Stanford:

Stanford University Press.

Seefeldt, V. D., Gilliam, T., Blievernicht, D., & Bruce, R. (1978). Scope of youth sports programs in the state of Michigan. In F. Smoll, & R. Smith (Eds.), *Psychological perspectives in youth sports.* New York: Wiley.

Shaffer, H. R. (1978). Acquiring the concept of the dialogue. In M. H. Bornstein, & W. Kesson (Eds.), *Psychological development from infancy.* New York: Lawrence Erlbaum.

Sherif, C. W., & Rattray, G. D. (1976). Psychological development and activity in middle childhood (5–12 years). In J. G. Albinson, & G. M. Andrew (Eds.), *Child in sport and physical activity.* Baltimore: University Park Press.

Sherif, M., Harvey, O. J., White, B. J., Hood, W. R., & Sherif, C. W. (1961). *Intergroup conflict and cooperation: The robbers cave experiment.* Oklahoma City: University of Oklahoma Book Exchange.

Sherrod, L., & Singer, J. L. (1977). The development of make-believe. In J. Goldstein (Ed.), *Sports, games and play.* Hillsdale, N.J.: Erlbaum.

Shmukler, D. (1981). Mother-child interaction and its relationship to the predisposition of imaginative play. *Genetic Psychology Monographs, 104,* 215–235.

Siegman, A. W. (1966). Father-absence during childhood and antisocial behavior. *Journal of Abnormal Psychology, 71,* 71–74.

Singer, D. G., & Singer, J. L. (1977). *Partners in play.* New York: Harper and Row.

Singer, J. L. (1973). *The child's world of make-believe.* New York: Academic Press.

Singer, J. L. (1977). *Television, imaginative play and cognitive development: Some problems and possibilities.* Paper presented at American Psychological Association, San Francisco.

Singer, J. L., & Singer, D. G. (1976). Imaginative play and pretending in early childhood: Some experimental approaches. In A. David (Ed.), *Child personality and psychopathology: Current topics.* New York: Wiley.

Smoll, F. L. (1974). Motor impairment and social development. *Exceptional Children, 36,* 257–267.

Stern, D. (1977). *The first relationship: Infant and mother.* Cambridge: Harvard University Press.

Suedfield, P. (1967). Paternal absence and overseas success of Peace Corps volunteers. *Journal of Consulting Psychology, 31,* 424–425.

Sutton-Smith, B. (1967). The role of play in cognitive development. *Young Children, 22,* 361–370.

Sutton-Smith, B. (1971). A syntax for play and games. In R. E. Herron, & B. Sutton-Smith (Eds.), *Child's play.* New York: Wiley.

Sutton-Smith, B. (1979). A sociolinguistic approach to ludic action. In H. Lenk (Ed.), *Handlagen theorien interdisziplinar.* West Germany: Karlsbad University.

Sutton-Smith, B., & Sutton-Smith, S. (1974). *How to play with your children.* New York: Hawthorn.

Sylva, K., Bruner, J., & Genova, P. (1976). The role of play in the problem-solving of children 3–5 years old. In J. Bruner, A. Jolly, & K. Sylva (Eds.), *Play—its role in development and evolution.* New York: Penguin.

Tizard, B., Philps, J., & Plewis, I. (1976). Play in preschool centers: Effects on play of the child's social class and of the educational orientation of the center. *Journal of Child Psychology and Psychiatry, 17,* 265–274.

Tuckman, J., & Regan, R. A. (1966). Intactness of the home and behavioral problems in children. *Journal of Child Psychology and Psychiatry, 7,* 225–233.

Udwin, O. & Shmukler, D. (1981). The influence of sociocultural, economic and home background factors on children's ability to engage in imaginative play. *Developmental Psychology, 17,* 66–72.

Vandenberg, B. (1978). Play and development from an ethological perspective. *American Psychologist, 33,* 724–738.

Vandenberg, B. (1980a). Play, problem-solving and creativity. In K. H. Rubin (Ed.), *Children's play: New directions for child development.* San Francisco: Jossey-Bass.

Vlietstra, A. G. (1980). Effects of adult-directed activity, number of toys, and sex of child on sociological exploratory behavior in young children. *Merrill-Palmer Quarterly, 26,* 231–238.

Wallerstein, J. S., & Kelly, J. B. (1974). The effects of parental divorce: The adolescent experience. In J. Anthony, & C. Koupernik (Eds.), *The child in his family: Children at psychiatric risk.* New York: Wiley.

Wallerstein, J. S., & Kelly, J. B. (1975). The effects of parental divorce: Experiences of the preschool child. *Journal of the American Academy of Child Psychiatry, 14,* 600–616.

Watson, M. W., & Fischer, K. W. (1977). A developmental sequence of agent use in late infancy. *Child Development, 48,* 828–836.

Weininger, D. (1979). *Play and education.* Springfield, IL: Thomas.

Weinraub, M., & Frankel, J. (1977). Sex differences in parent-infant interaction during free play, departure and separation. *Child Development, 48,* 1240–1249.

White, B. L., & Carew-Watts, J. (1973). *Experiences and environment: Major influences on the development of the young child.* Englewood Cliffs, NJ: Prentice-Hall.

White, R. W. (1959). Motivation reconsidered: The concept of competence. *Psychological Review, 66,* 297–330.

Whiting, B. B. (1963). *Six cultures: Studies of child-rearing.* New York: Wiley.

Yogman, M. (1977). *The goals and structure of face-to-face interaction between infants and fathers.* Paper presented at Society for Research in Child Development, New Orleans.

Yogman, M. W. (1981). Development of the father-infant relationship. In H. Fitzgerald, B. Lester, & M. W. Yogman (Eds.), *Theory and research in behavioral pediatrics.* New York: Plenum.

Yogman, M. J., Dixon, E., Tronick, H., & Brazelton, T. (1977). *The goals and structure of face-to-face interaction between infants and their fathers.* Paper presented at Society for Research in Child Development, New Orleans.

Chapter VIII

BARRIERS TO LEISURE ACROSS FAMILY STAGES

Peter A. Witt and Thomas L. Goodale

There is a near infinite variety of family types and circumstances. The leisure experiences of members of large or small families, poor or affluent families, single parent or two parent families, rural or urban residing families are surely quite different. Consequently, it is impossible to compile a definitive list of constraints on family members' leisure that will apply to all.

It is possible, however, to identify potential constraints and mediating variables that will make the impact of constraints more or less critical to the achievement of satisfaction via leisure experiences. The ability of family members to engage in satisfying leisure is important as a means of communication and interaction and as a contributor to individual growth and overall family stability. Thus, leisure is both an end in itself, providing a basis for fun, enjoyment, pleasure and satisfaction and also a means for achieving the necessary ingredients for successful family life.

One concept that seems particularly important for understanding the role and value of leisure in the family context is the concept of lifecycle stages or family career. As Sessoms (1980) notes:

> Each life stage is characterized by a unique configuration of roles and dominant activities which seem to be related to biological and/or psychological (developmental) changes.... Each stage of life is characterized by certain "expected" behaviors. Consequently, as one moves from one life stage to the next, role modifications occur; new role sets emerge as we respond to both our own and society's perception of what is proper at any given stage. (p. 187)

Much recent discussion has been aimed at understanding differences in family satisfaction and interaction as a function of the stage within which a family is operating. Family stages have been broadly divided into four major segments with several possible sub-stages within each. The first segment usually considered is the childless stage. This stage is, in most cases, followed by the appearance of young children (youngest child less than 5), progressing to a stage where the youngest child is between 6 and 18, and culminating in a stage where all the children have left the "nest."

Numerous recent studies have indicated the value of considering lifecycle stages as a basis for understanding the dynamics of leisure involvement and enjoyment. Kelly (1974), for example, looked at changes in the form and orientation of leisure over the family lifecycle. His research points to the family as the seed bed for beginning new activities.

> A major shift was noted from unconditional activities engaged in primarily for their own sake in the preparental period to complementary activities related to family roles in parental years. In the post-parental period, a small shift on the part of men of higher education and occupation levels to work-related activities was indicated (pp. 191–192).

Kelly (1977) argues strongly for the concept of a "career of leisure, in which persons begin and develop, add and subtract, change and reorient their leisure participation patterns throughout the lifecycle. . . . " (p. 131)

Orthner (1976) investigated the relationship between patterns of leisure and marital interaction over different stages of the marital career. While inconclusive, the study did reveal different patterns of interaction at various lifecycle stages as demands on time, energy, obligations, and the efficiency of coping mechanisms change.

Rapoport and Rapoport (1975) provided a useful model for understanding the specific impact of lifecycle stages raised by Kelly and Orthner. The Rapoports sought to identify the preoccupations and potential problems associated with each stage of the family lifecycle (See Table 1). These preoccupations and problems are the basis of constraints on, among other things, how family members function during leisure, and the potential benefits they can derive from leisure experiences. These preoccupations and problems could serve as a basis for understanding the influence of the family as a socializing agent or the degree of marital interaction and its relationship to leisure at a given lifecycle stage.

Table VIII-1
Preoccupations and Potential Problems Associated with Various Lifecycle Stages*

Stage	Preoccupation	Potential Problems
Pre-Child Couples	Concern with *establishing* relationship, career, identity	Conflicts in breaking out of teenage, college patterns, independence, priorities
Presence of Pre-School Children	Concern with *productivity*: choice and plans	Conflicts in the allocation of one's energies
Children at School	Concern with *performance*:	Conflicts of loyalties and obligations; dissatisfaction
Children out of School	Concern with *evaluation*: the meaningfulness of commitments	Depression, boredom, feelings of entrapment, isolation, whether to change

*Adapted and modified from Rapoport and Rapoport (1975) (Table 2, p. 191).

In addition to identifying particular stages within the family lifecycle and the preoccupations and problems associated with each, several authors have referred to critical "seasons" (Levinson, 1978) "passages" (Sheehy, 1976) or socializing periods (Kelly, 1975) over the lifetime, such as marriage, birth of a child, death of a spouse or children leaving home. These passages are stressful to marital adjustment and personal satisfaction. There has been interest in the important shock absorber role that leisure activities may play in countering the impact of stress during periods of change or as a stabilizing influence over the entire marital career (Orthner, 1975).

It has been proposed that individuals can be designated at risk or at benefit as a function of their ability to deal with particular passages or stages. Rapoport and Rapoport (1975) note that for planning purposes it would seem profitable "to isolate categories of individuals 'at risk,' who feel disadvantaged as to their chances for enjoyment of life," and "to isolate categories of individuals 'at benefit,' who are 'happy' and feel that they enjoy life as a whole" (p. 264). The case for trying to understand those at risk is more obvious but it is equally important to know how those at benefit organize their lives, derive enjoyment, and adapt to new situations. Information concerning those at benefit may be useful in helping those at risk.

Whether individuals will meet the challenges posed within and between lifecycle stages depends, as noted by Rapoport and Rapoport (1975), upon resourcefulness.

> Resourcefulness means knowing and being able to make a meaningful life for oneself within the realities of one's existence as well as how to change these realities. So it requires being in touch with one's feelings on the one side, and one's environment on the other, and being able to manage the two in relation to each other.... a resourceful person can take the intelligence he has, the competence he is able to develop, and within the framework of his material means and social values, apply them to weave a life that is satisfying (p. 26).

Factors that could serve as indicators of or contributors to resourcefulness are an individual's locus of control and his adaptation and coping abilities.

Locus of control refers to the extent individuals believe that events in their lives are a consequence of their own actions or are a result of luck, fate or powerful others. Individuals who tend toward internal locus of control perceive positive or negative events as a consequence of their own actions and thereby perceive personal control. (Rotter, 1966) Korman (1970) noted the importance of a perception of internal control for marital satisfaction.

High adaptation and coping abilities are two other potential elements that seem to be significant attributes of resourcefulness. Adaptation involves the ability to change roles and structures to make a more satisfying life for oneself as well as one's family. Coping refers to a "response to external lifestrains that seem to prevent, avoid, or control emotional stress" (Rapoport and Rapoport, 1975, p. 3).

For leisure, resourcefulness would seem to include the ability to identify barriers to leisure enjoyment and develop strategies for overcoming those barriers. Exploring constraints to leisure enjoyment as a function of lifecycle stages may also provide additional data concerning the reciprocal influence of husband-wife-children relationships, communication patterns, task differentiation, and marital satisfaction on leisure fulfillment (Orthner, 1976).

Given the above context, what are some of the specific constraints to leisure enjoyment that are encountered at various stages of the family career? A recent study by Witt and Goodale (1981) supplied some pertinent data that helped to identify barriers that were more or less problematic at particular family stages. The findings are reviewed here in detail.

Witt and Goodale sought to identify key passages and stages for which particular barriers are critical. In addition, by using a list of barriers that went beyond the typical list of time, money, opportunity and skills, the authors hoped to broaden the understanding of the importance of motivation and attitudinal barriers to the leisure enjoyment process.

Witt and Goodale (1981) collected data from random samples of eligible voters in two communities in Ontario, Canada. Each respondent was asked the following: "According to your experience, what do you feel are the major barriers that prevent or hinder your enjoyment of leisure?" Eighteen barriers (See Table II) were rated on a five point scale from 1 = strongly disagree to 5 = strongly agree. Respondents were free to offer their own interpretation of "enjoyment of leisure." Interviews conducted during a pretest phase suggested that people interpreted "enjoyment of leisure" to mean satisfaction, happiness, or fun.

Barriers Showing a U-Shaped Relationship to Family Stage

Results from the analysis of each barrier can best be interpreted by grouping them according to the pattern of perceived influence over the family stages. The first seven barriers (See Table 2) showed an approximately U-shaped pattern with the barriers generally rated less problematic during the stages in which the youngest child was between 6 and 18 years of age. The seven items making up this group relate to difficulties in making and carrying out decisions about what activities to participate in and with whom

(See Figure 1).* Items included "not being sure what activities to get involved in," "not knowing what's going on or what's available," "not being sure how to use available resources," and "difficulty in planning and making decisions." In addition, "having nobody to do things with" and "not being at ease in social situations" also follow this same general pattern. For males (only) "difficulty in carrying out plans" also follows the same pattern.

Though children may be "critical to marital happiness" (Kelly, 1975, p. 559), sometimes the addition of children does not bring satisfaction. Indeed, this stage may even be the cause of a decrease in marital satisfaction (Spendle and Olsen, 1978). Although parenthood results in a shift to activities that complement the family role, this shift may not complement the individual's preferred roles. Parents change their activities in conjunction with their new perceived roles, even if these roles are not easily adapted to by the couple.

The first child creates stress on the parents unequalled at any other stage, although the subsequent leaving of the children from the home also requires adjustment in the couple's relationship (Orthner, 1976). Prior to the birth of children a married couple's life changes very little from before marriage.

In the "first child stage," parents must begin to consider someone else in their lives in addition to themselves (Korman, 1970). This someone is, from the first day, a very important part of the couples lives. "As parental roles and responsibilities increase, for many couples children become as significant as the marital partners" (Orthner, 1976, p. 109). The significance of this cannot be overstated. Due to the child, the parents must now face additional and different demands on their time, income and leisure. It would seem, then, that satisfaction is based on the couple's ability to adapt to their new situation, with its new demands. The couple must go from choosing activities for intrinsic satisfaction to those that are "perceived as having major components of role expectations" (Korman, 1970).

---

*A single graph, one for each of the three patterns of barriers' influence, is presented as indicative of each pattern.

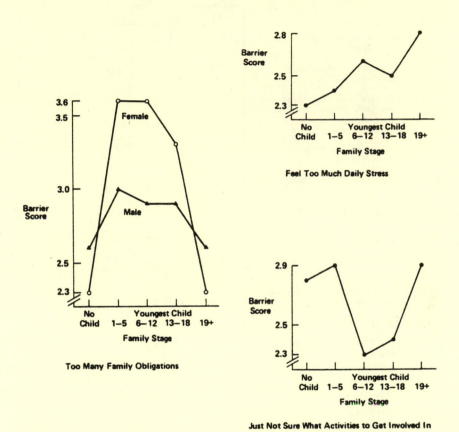

Figure VIII-1. Selected Graphs for Barriers by Family Stage.

Angrist (1967) noted that the role requirement of mothers with pre-school children, in particular, restricted the locale of leisure, but that leisure outside the home increased as children entered school. Once children are of school age, parents are less tied down than when the children were pre-school age; school-age children are capable of doing more on their own; and the community recreation system may be offering more opportunities for school age children. The family itself becomes an important source of

Constraints on Leisure

Table VIII-2. Means for Barriers to Leisure Enjoyment by Family Stage and Sex*

Barrier		No Child	1-5	6-12	13-18	19+	Grand Mean
				Family Stage			
1. Not sure how to use available resources		2.7	2.7	2.2	2.3	2.6	2.5
2. Don't know what's going on or what's available		2.7	2.9	2.2	2.3	2.5	2.5
3. Just not sure what activities to get involved in		2.8	2.9	2.3	2.4	2.9	2.6
4. Nobody to do things with		2.8	2.6	2.2	2.1	2.7	2.5
5. Planning and making decisions is difficult		2.1	2.3	1.9	2.0	2.4	2.1
6. Not at ease in social situations	M	2.5	2.2	1.9	2.2	2.5	2.3
	F	2.2	2.5	2.3	1.9	2.2	
7. Carrying out plans is often difficult							2.7
8. Don't have enough free time		3.1	3.3	3.4	3.3	2.7	3.2
9. Too many family obligations	M	2.6	3.0	2.9	2.9	2.6	2.9
	F	2.3	3.6	3.6	3.6	2.3	
10. Family and friends' expectations limit me	M	2.6	2.4	2.3	2.3	2.4	2.6
	F	2.2	2.5	2.9	2.6	3.3	
11. Feel too much daily stress		2.3	2.4	2.6	2.5	2.8	2.5
12. Often don't feel like doing anything		2.9	2.8	2.8	2.8	3.4	2.9
13. Not fit enough to get involved							2.1
14. Don't have the physical skills							2.3
15. Work is the main priority now							3.0
16. Programs, courses, facilities not available							2.3
17. Not enough money for leisure							2.6
18. Commitments are hard to maintain							2.7

*Adapted from Witt and Goodale(1981). $p < .05$ for all data presented. Where data for both males and females is presented, there was a sex by life cycle stage interaction.

social experiences as children become capable of doing more activities that adults can enjoy or that adults feel that they should do to promote the development and learning experiences of their children. In addition, school age children may serve as ambassadors or initiators of contact between families and as sources of information about community events. From the data it would appear that once children reach school age there is a lessening of uncertainty for parents as to what to do, what opportunities are available, and how to utilize opportunities that do exist. This is consistent with the Rapoports' (1975) finding of an increase in contact with the community and lessening of the burdens of establishing family and career as the family moves from an early establishment (preschool children) to mid establishment (children at school) stage.

The U-shaped pattern for these items also reveals the impact of the youngest child leaving the home on the parental planning and decision-making process. In each case the barriers in this group increase when children have left the parental home. Establishing an adult pattern of involvement free from the influence of children appears as a critical passage. Rapoport and Rapoport (1975) label this the stage of "revision," the time when adults have an opportunity to reflect on what they've accomplished and begin to establish a pattern of life without children. Again, resourcefulness is critical to counter the potential feelings of anti-climax, physical decline and loss of role.

Barriers Showing an Inverted U Relationship to Family Stage

For a second group of barriers (#8–9), the pattern is the reverse of those just discussed. The problem of "not having enough free time" seems to increase during the entire child rearing period and falls off sharply as a barrier once children have left the home. Kelly (1975) has discussed the reduced flexibility of time usage during the parenthood stage. The barrier thus may be interpreted as a problem of discretionary decision making as well as an actual reduction in available free time. Problems of time may also be a function of lack of synchronization of the diverse schedules of family members (Kelly, 1976).

In a like manner, family obligations (See Figure I) significantly increase for women and to a much lesser degree for men over this period. This highlights the primary responsibility of women for child-rearing. Staines (1980) reports that family roles tend to conflict with leisure roles for women but tend to overlap with leisure roles for men. Thus for men, child care and leisure may take place simultaneously via "playtime" or a game of catch in the backyard. Men may see time with family as more enjoyable because it is primarily recreational.

Together, these barriers illustrate the need for resourcefulness in meeting leisure needs that each parent experiences over the child-rearing stage. To further illustrate this point, Kelly (1974, p. 190) found that having children at home raised the proportion of role related activities by 23% and decreased activities engaged in primarily for intrinsic satisfaction by 18%. There is also some potential conflict between parental roles and marital roles which may be a significant factor in declining marital satisfaction through the child rearing years.

Barriers Having an Increasing Influence Over Family Stages

Barrier items 10–12 form a third group. The limitation of "family and friends expectations" increase over the lifecycle stages for women while for men these expectations are of a much lower order and more constant. On the other hand "feelings of daily stress" (See Figure I) increase over the stages for both sexes. "Often feel like not doing anything" stays relatively constant over the child rearing stage but increases dramatically once the children have left home. The first two items suggest the increased pressure that women feel in general and as a particular result of family expectations and the fact that if women go back to work or develop outside interests they do so only by adding responsibilities (and potentially conflicts) to their already defined family obligations (Hall, 1975). Although men also experience feelings of increased stress over time, it seems to have less to do with family expectations. Men appear to have greater latitude to pursue a career, interests outside the home, or personal interest within the home than do women.

Both males and females seem to experience a diminishing amount of motivation (#12) after the child-rearing stages. As discussed earlier, this may be due to a loss of the parenting role and the failure to have developed personally meaningful alternative interests (Rapoport and Rapoport, 1975, p. 248). It may also be indicative of the lack of norms or expectations that would sanction developing new interests or having a meaningful life once children have left the nest. Hall (1975) found that women during this period felt less potency, more conflict, less satisfaction and less happiness. Together with a potential decline in feelings of fulfillment via work, for the male in particular, these effects may be the result of the dominant work and child-centered ethic of the society that may cause a significant let down and confusion for individuals once they've fulfilled their essential parenting and support functions.

No significant differences were found for the final two barriers: "not enough money for leisure" and "commitments are hard to maintain." Both barriers rank in the middle of items based on overall means. These results support the relative importance placed on money as a significant general barrier to leisure over varying family stages for both sexes and for individuals in widely different social circumstances. It is interesting to note that almost all of us, regardless of our financial status or circumstance, report that we don't have enough money at our disposal at any given time. Higher levels of income seem to increase wants; thus more money is desired. Although there is some pressure to live within our means, the effect of advertising on creating wants and the conspicuous consumption habits of many North Americans lead to lack of money being perceived as a constraint at all family stages. The financial needs of first child couples (starting a home and family with one paycheck and beginning level salary) may be no less burdensome than the financial needs of a family of three teenagers (buying a larger house, putting in a swimming pool, allowances, clothing and saving to send children to college). Having enough money is not just a problem of amount, but how to deal with competing demands and desires.

"Ability to maintain commitments" is a problem but one which does not vary significantly over the stages studied. Failure to maintain commitments can be a function of several different factors. Some individuals may commit themselves to too many different tasks or obligations. Failure to keep some (or perhaps even all) commitments may be the result. Failure to keep commitments

could be part of a general depersonalization that puts little premium on carrying through on obligations or commitments. Perhaps the chief explanation for this finding may be that commitments
regarding leisure are often pre-empted by commitments to job,
family, community, and the like.

Discussion

The preceeding analysis indicates both the changing nature of
barriers over varying family stages and the relative importance of
barriers at a given family stage. This kind of information may lead
to a better understanding of the passages and stages that an individual goes through across the family cycle. This can facilitate identifying individuals at risk and at benefit at a point or during a
period of time.

Identifying whether a given stage or passage is problematic is of
course only the beginning. The fact that some individuals report
fewer or greater constraints at a particular stage leads to the
question "why." The mediating variable of resourcefulness seems
to be critical in differentiating individuals who successfully cope
with the constraints imposed by a given family stage. How to
improve resourcefulness is the next question.

There is a strong need for resourcefulness education for individual family members and families as a whole. Hopefully, attempts
at improving resourcefulness would not only be remedial, i.e.,
dealing with problems when they occur, but also developmental,
i.e., creating through the educational system a better awareness
and preparedness to deal with the leisure problems posed by
family life at various family stages. Within the education system
greater attention needs to be paid to what has been called leisure
education. This would include developing values, attitudes, skills
and knowledge (Mundy and Odum, 1979) consistent with achieving a feeling of fulfillment via leisure experiences.

For example, the domination of the work ethic influences people's
perceptions of their right to participate in leisure and even the
extent to which leisure ought to be enjoyed. The work ethic leads
many of us to believe that we work to live and have leisure to
prepare us to go back to work. Leisure thus becomes in and of

itself unimportant except as a means to re-create ourselves. The negative consequences of this attitude are reflected most dramatically when children grow up and leave the home and parents are left with free time but no purpose in living. Free time was justified if spent in child care or family obligations but is more difficult to justify if devoted to personally meaningful and satisfying interests.

During the child-rearing stages of the family, parents may feel so obligated to serve the needs of their children that they ignore their own leisure needs or those of the husband-wife dyad. In addition, parents with few leisure skills or interests can often avoid leisure via obligations and commitments to others. In a sense, because leisure has no meaning beyond the satisfaction derived by the individual, it is difficult for people to derive satisfaction through leisure.

Parents also transmit to their children a variety of attitudes toward leisure via the socialization process. Emphasizing playing by the rules over creativity or winning over participation may be good for acculturation but may destroy the spontaneity, joy, humor, and sense of freedom so necessary for meaningful leisure participation. Leisure seen as preparation for the realities of adulthood may remove the very essence of the experience that makes it critical for growth, development, personal satisfaction, and ultimately fun. Not having enough time or money or being over-committed are as much problems of perceptions, attitudes, and values as they are reflections of true need.

Besides working with attitudes, leisure education for families would need to include attention to: 1) decision making (identifying goals, identifying options for meeting goals and means of selecting among alternatives); 2) clarifying values (choosing what kind of life one wants to live and the role of leisure in achieving it); 3) motivating (making and keeping commitments); 4) developing physical and social skills necessary for leisure participation; and 5) learning of and being exposed to a wide range of leisure alternatives. The school system and the leisure services delivery system have important roles to play in all of these areas.

Sex-related roles and expectations and how these affect leisure participation and fulfillment also requires better understanding. The Witt and Goodale (1981) data and accompanying discussion make it clear that women and men are faced with differing leisure constraints as a function of role expectations at differing stages of the family cycle. Despite the feminist movement, women still bear the primary burden of child rearing. These responsibilities may limit personal leisure fulfillment or being able to fully enjoy family leisure. For the woman who establishes a career outside the home, this is usually done in addition to child-rearing and other responsibilities within the home. Leisure is bound to suffer. Though money may become less of a burden (unless wants also escalate), time for leisure certainly shrinks. Unless husbands are willing to share certain responsibilities with the woman, the situation may resemble a balancing act more than an integrated, fulfilling lifestyle.

For men, the work ethic may impose considerable demands on time and energy and the ability or willingness to get involved with family leisure experiences. This is especially true when trying to establish a career which, for many, coincides with the presence of young children in the home. Priorities may begin with work, closely followed by "male" chores at home, with time for children running a poor third.

Identification of barrier differences as a function of particular family stages also has implications for leisure service providers. For example, taking account of the special circumstances of newly married couples, mothers with young children, or couples whose children have just recently left home, may pose particular challenges for those providing leisure services. The differing functions of leisure and recreation experiences as preoccupations change, needs to be more fully recognized. Particular attention needs to be paid to identifying and serving those at risk who, because of personal or family circumstances, may not be able to benefit from involvement in leisure opportunities.

In addition, leisure service providers aware of different types of barriers and different amounts of constraint can devise new and better responses. More programs or more information, different schedules or fee structures may help overcome some barriers, but not others. Where resourcefulness is minimal, locus of control external, and purpose lost, the indirect services and facilitating functions must come to the forefront.

One final note should be made. No account has been made of

racial, ethnic and class differences in determining the quantity and quality of family leisure. A full understanding of the constraints to family leisure would have to take place in the context of the background characteristics of a given family and the associated values and attitudes toward family, work, leisure and sex-role related responsibilities. In addition, no mention has been made of problems caused by living location (rural-urban, or suburb-city), family size or composition, or the special situation of the increasing number of single parent families.

Being cognizant of the special circumstances and problems of each family within its own context may not be possible. However, the multitude of variables does suggest a more indepth approach to planning for and facilitating family leisure. If we want the family to play together, community and individual supports will have to be developed to help overcome the substantial constraints to leisure that individuals and families encounter.

REFERENCES

Angrist, S. S. (1967). Role constellation as a variable in women's leisure activities. *Social Forces, 45,* 423–431.

Hall, D. T. (1975). Pressures from work, self and home in the life stages of married women. *Journal of Vocational Behavior, 6*(1), 121–132.

Kelly, J. R. (1974). Socialization toward leisure: A developmental approach. *Journal of Leisure Research, 6*(3), 181–183.

Kelly, J. R. (1975). Lifestyles and leisure choices. *Family Coordinator, 24,* 185–190.

Kelly, J. R. (1976). *Synchronization of leisure conflicts in the family schedule.* Paper presented at the Midwest Sociological Society, St. Louis.

Kelly, J. R. (1977). Leisure socialization: Replication and extension. *Journal of Leisure Research, 9,* 121–132.

Korman, A. (1970, December). Environmental ambiguity and locus of control as interactive influences on satisfaction. *Experimental Republication System, 9,* manuscript No. 334-16.

Levinson, D. J. (1978). *The season's of a man's life.* New York: Random House.

Mundy, J., & Odum, L. (1979). *Leisure education: Theory and Practice.* New York: John Wiley and Sons.

Orthner, D. (1975). Leisure activity patterns and marital satisfaction over the marital career. *Journal of Marriage and Family, 32,* 91–103.

Orthner, D. (1976). Patterns of leisure and marital interaction. *Journal of Leisure Research, 8*(2), 98–111.

Rapoport, R., & Rapoport, R. N. (1975). *Leisure and the family lifecycle.* London: Routledge and Kegan Paul.

Rotter, J. B. (1966). Generalized expectancies for internal vs. external locus of control of reinforcement. *Psychology,* monograph 80.

Sessoms, H. D. (1980). Lifestyles and lifecycles: A recreation programming approach. In T. L. Goodale, & P. A. Witt (Eds.), *Recreation and leisure: Issues in an era of change* (pp. 178–196). State College, PA: Venture Publishing.

Sheehy, G. (1976). *Passages: Predictable crises of adult life.* New York: E. P. Dutton and Co., Inc.

Spendle, D., & Olsen, D. (1978, April 4). Circumplex model of mental systems: An empirical study of clinic and non-clinic couples. *Journal of Marriage and Family Counseling,* 59–74.

Staines, G. C. (1980, September). *Sex differences in the experience of family roles.* Paper presented at the American Psychological Association, 88th Congress, Quebec, Canada.

Witt, P. A., & Goodale, T. L. (1981). The relationships between barriers to leisure enjoyment and family stages. *Leisure Sciences, 4*(1), 24–49.

Chapter IX

ECONOMIC CONSTRAINTS ON LEISURE

Benjamin K. Hunnicutt

The relationship between leisure and economic matters can be viewed from at least two perspectives. Economists might explore this relationship by asking a question such as, "What are leisure's constraints on the economy?" An alternate question can be posed: "What are the economic constraints on leisure?" In either case, some value judgment—some "normative" stance, is conveyed through the use of the word "constraint," which usually implies placing a positive value on that which is being constrained and a negative value on the constrainer. It therefore makes considerable difference what is understood as being constrained and what is doing the constraining. In the question as it might be considered by economists, there is a hint that leisure has a negative value vis-a-vis the economy, whereas the economy itself takes on that negative aspect in the alternate question. To imply the contrary in either question, value-added modifiers must be employed to shift the weight of meaning. Consider the modified phrasing "an over-materialistic economy" in the first question, or "excessive leisure" in the second.

Since value judgments are clearly a part of a discussion of "constraints," the effort must be made to separate "normative" matters from objective considerations. In the field of economics, there is precedence for this exercise. Milton Friedman points out that economics is often divided into two distinct parts: "positive economics" and "normative economics" (Friedman, 1962, p. 8). Positive economics concerns itself with "what is" and strives to be as value free and objective as possible. It tends to be descriptive, moving toward a set of "substantive empirical propositions." Normative economics deals with values, with "what ought to be." Its

243

focus is how economizing *should* be accomplished. The trend in 20th century academic economics has been toward making the discipline scientific and value free, pursuing the elusive dream of logical positivism. Social goals or normative ends such as the elimination of poverty may be part of a scientific investigation, but only if exogeneously given. Values and goals are not understood as scientific products even though the *means* to a normative end may well be part of positive economics' prerogative (Ekelund & Hebert, 1975, p. 5).

In the following exploration of how leisure and economic matters relate, excursions are made into both the realms of positive and then normative economics. First the "positive" economic functions of leisure (where leisure is understood as a value free term — i.e., hours free from work) are described in historical, theoretical, and empirical terms. Once this firm base is established, the "normative" value assumptions present in the economics of leisure are examined. While normative economics has added much to the understanding of leisure as an economic act, it is the author's belief that normative matters have invaded the positive study of the economics of leisure and that a more rigorous sifting of normative and positive factors should be undertaken.

I. POSITIVE ECONOMICS AND LEISURE

A. A Short History of Theory

Economists have talked about leisure since there have been economists. Leisure, and its companion, recreation, relate to economic matters in a very obvious way: cost. Both cost relative to other things, are limited, and may be said to be economized — i.e., to be as carefully used and taken as any scarce thing. Leisure costs in terms of lost wages when one chooses to take time from work. Recreation costs in terms of direct spending on building, equipment, clothing, travel, etc. A common sense assumption is that as people earn more, they are able to afford more time off and to spend an ever larger part of their incomes on nonessentials such as savings and recreation. Poorer people, by contrast, must work long hours, forego leisure, and seek out free activities and public facilities.

1. Mercantilism. In the middle part of the 18th century, the Mercantilists (the first modern economists) developed a theory utilizing common sense reasoning similar to that described above. Their economic model, one of the oldest, most familiar, and most controversial of economic models, is known as the "backward bending supply curve of labor." It represents graphically the Mercantilists' understanding of what happened as workers offered their labor up for sale under a variety of wage conditions. The theorists reasoned that when wages were low—i.e., when people were poor, workers tended to supply more of their time and effort to productive labor in order to gain increased wages. The higher the wage the greater the supply of labor "for sale."

The labor supply curve so constructed initially appeared no different than the supply curves of other goods and services (shoes, for example): the higher the price the greater the supply for sale. However, argued the Mercantilists, at a certain point the labor supply curve contrasted sharply with other supply curves. At a certain wage level, the labor supply began *decreasing* as wages increased (Eklund & Hebert, 1975, p. 38). Pictorially (see Figure 1) this was represented by a negative slope on the graph and the labor supply curve appeared to be bending backwards on itself, hence the theory's name. (In Figure 1, the measure of labor supply = OX; OY = the measure of real wages. An increase in real wages from W1 to W2, for example, could result in a decrease in labor supply from L1 to L2.)

The Mercantilists, quite in keeping with the pessimistic Protestant/Calvinist world view then current, reasoned that this phenomenon was due to human nature. Human beings, due to original sin and the fall of man, etc., were naturally lazy and corrupt, and would prefer leisure (or idleness) to wages and work once they reached a comfortable, secure level of existence. The implication of the labor supply curve, to the Mercantilists' way of thinking, was that if national wealth came in the form of per capita wages, then the total amount of labor available would be reduced. They spoke therefore about the "utility of poverty," regarding poverty as the only effective prod to work. Clearly, too much wealth, widely distributed, would have a corrupting influ-

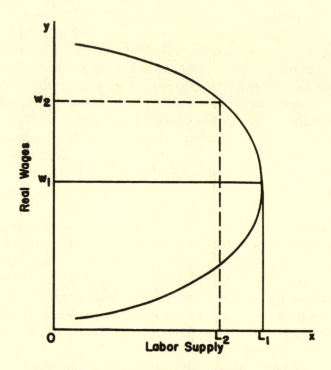

Figure IX-1. The Backward Bending Supply Curve of Labor.

ence on the people of a nation and interfere with the nation's wealth and well-being because, given the chance, people would choose leisure rather than work.

2. Classical Economic Theory. The classical economists who followed the Mercantilists doubted that too much wealth or too much leisure taking would ever be a problem for labor supply, arguing that other economic factors would prevent this. Men like Adam Smith, David Ricardo, and Thomas Malthus believed that human nature conspired with the harsh physical realities of life. Because people tended to reproduce themselves more rapidly than they produced the necessities of life, the press of population would keep poverty fairly constant among workers. Any one individual's share of the "wage fund" (the national economic wealth) would average out to a "bare minimum" as populations grew and more individuals added to the labor supply, thereby laying claim to a share of that wealth. The "natural wage" was just enough to keep workers at work, raising the next generation of workers.

Following this line of reasoning, the classical theorists pictured the supply curve of labor as horizontal at any wage level: increased wages meant increased population; increased population meant more people sharing the wage fund, which in turn meant a natural wage at subsistence levels. Increases in the labor supply were not the product of people freely giving up more time to work, but the result of population increase—a population all of whose workers were fully involved at work for the natural wage (Ekelund & Hebert, 1975, p. 69). Leisure taking under such circumstances was viewed as simply not possible, and so was no threat to the economy.

The dark predictions of the classical economists began giving way to brighter visions as the industrial process continued in the mid and latter parts of the 19th century. The workers' lot improved, wages increased, population grew more slowly than expected, and the mass starvation predicted by Malthus was left ever far behind. The optimism about economic progress, observed and predicted, afforded the new wave of theorists a new perspective on the labor supply and leisure. (In their writings, they offered a variety of recommendations about what *ought* to be done with increased wealth; leisure for the masses was a topic that was prominently supported. Because most of these works associated leisure with value judgments or a vision of progress, discussion of them will be postponed to the normative economics sections of this chapter.)

3. Neoclassical Marginalism. In terms of the theoretical function of leisure in the economy, the neoclassical marginalists are the most important and their influence is still strong. The marginalists assumed that human nature was neither good nor bad, but that the majority of people naturally tried to maximize pleasure and minimize pain—to seek their greatest happiness—in the market place (Ekelund & Hebert, 1975, p. 111). The very essence of economizing, therefore, was to provide or acquire "the greatest amount of what is desirable at the expense of the least that is undesirable." But goods and services available in the market place had no intrinsic utility or value. Rather, the acts of valuing, of working for and buying, of giving up one thing for another, were the basis of any given commodity's utility. As W. Stanley Jevons put it, "Anything which an individual is found to desire and to labor for must be assumed to possess for him utility" (Jevons, 1957 (1871), pp. 11–39). The "utility function" was the name for the relationships between commodities and the product of the individuals' aggregate acts of valuing.

Since all goods and services had utility relative to other possible consumption, each commodity could be thought of as having a utility that declined marginally. For example, the first loaf of bread that a worker purchased with his wages had a high marginal utility — it had a greater usefulness and hence more value for the worker than other things, such as a trip to the zoo. It also had a utility relative to but *above* the "cost incurred" by work. What worker would not stay on his job long hours if it was necessary for the daily bread for himself and his family? But each additional loaf had less and less utility and the utility of the *nth* loaf approached zero. Long before that final loaf was bought though, the worker would begin to spend a higher income on relatively more useful things — the trip to the zoo, for example. Thus the more one could get of any good or service, the less marginal utility it would have.

Applying the notion of declining marginal utility to the labor supply, the marginalists again raised the prospect of the backward bending supply curve of labor. Jevons speculated that most work was a combination of pleasure and pain, but that overall it had a "net pain sum." Work, in the final analysis, was a "cost incurred," which had to be balanced against the "utility gained" by work. Yet this utility gained tended to be less and less the more income was received. Workers would thus stop working earlier and earlier when things bought by wages had less positive utility, relative to the negative disutility of staying on the job (Jevons, 1957 (1871), pp. 11–19).

Other neoclassical writers added leisure to these ideas, assuming that leisure itself was a "normal good" or a "utility gained." The tendency for workers to desire shorter hours in the condition of increasing wages then seemed to be the result of both the carrot of leisure and the stick of work's disutility. For example, in his famous *Principles of Economics,* Alfred Marshall pointed out that history was full of "stories of people who in a sudden burst of prosperity, had contented themselves with wages to be earned with very little work." Increased wages and prosperity, after all, could "soon satiate" individuals' needs for "those enjoyments that can be gained only by work." As wages increased, bringing the worker nearer to the "stage at which his most urgent needs are satisfied," he could begin to "crave more rest and more opportunities for activities which are themselves pleasurable." (Marshall, 1907, pp. 528–529, 681, 719). While he made no grand statement about this tendency, Marshall hinted that it was prosperity which created the opportunity for work's reduction, leisure's increase, and production/consumption's stabilization.

Another neoclassical economist, Frank Knight (a founder of the Chicago School), expounded on Marshall's views:

> Suppose that at a higher rate per hour...a man...worked as before and earns a proportionately larger income. When, now, he goes to spend the extra money, he will naturally want to increase his expenditures for commodities consumed and to take some new ones. To divide his resources in such a way as to preserve equal expenditures in all fields he must evidently lay out part of his new funds for increased leisure: i.e., buy back some of his working time or spend some of his money by the process of earning it (Knight, 1964 (1921), p. 117).

Since the writings of Knight and other neoclassicists, observations of this nature have been somewhat simplified by the use of the two terms "substitution effect" and "income effect." The former refers to the tendency of workers to give up (substitute) their free time to work in a condition of wage increase. The latter refers to the tendency to buy back more free time with higher wages because of the affordability of all normal goods, leisure among them. Knight's prediction, in these new terms, was that the income effect would begin to swamp the substitution effect—that the elasticity of demand for income in terms of effort was or would in fact become less than proportional unity. Hence the backward bending supply curve of labor was again predicted.

Knight gave as empirical examples of this phenomenon the behavior of "native workers in backward countries" and certain highly paid occupations during the first World War. In very simplest terms, Knight believed that as prosperity increased in the

United States, hours would get shorter and wages would get higher, just as they had done for a century when he wrote (1921).

4. *Indeterminancy and the Modern View.* The marginalists' position was rigorously challenged during the 1920's and their ideas about declining utility and theories based on *a priori* speculation were replaced by more empirically based studies (Bye, 1924, pp. 275–277). For example, in his seminal article "The Elasticity of Income in Terms of Effort," Lionel Robbins questioned Knight's assumption about the dominance of the income effect. Since, as Knight had assumed, leisure was purchased by sacrificing income, Robbins pointed out that there was a "real income price of leisure." Making this assumption, he continued:

> Now when the money rate of wages rises . . . the real income price of leisure (the cost of leisure in terms of real income sacrificed) rises. And when the price of leisure (or anything else) rises it is not at all clear that more will be bought even out of an increased income. Again it is all a matter of elasticity (Robbins, 1930).

For example, if a worker's wages increased, the taking of an additional hour of leisure would be more expensive; he would have to give up more of the other goods and services that he could purchase with his potentially larger income. Hence the price of additional leisure had to be measured like any other commodity: against the universe of potential consumption. Robbins therefore concluded that "the attempt to narrow the limit of possible elasticity by *a priori* reasoning must be held to have broken down."

Put another way, Robbins pointed out that a wage increase would strengthen both the substitution effect and the income effect. On the one hand, workers would be drawn to increased income; on the other, and at the same time, they would be drawn to "spend more on everything, including leisure." According to Robbins, there was no way to predict what would happen under these circumstances. The substitution effect would be as liable to dominate the income effect as the other way around, or they might just offset each other. Thus the effect of wage increases on leisure taking was held to be indeterminant, *a priori.*

This theory has changed very little since it was formulated by Robbins fifty years ago. It remains a cornerstone for modern analysis of the economics of leisure. Since the theory's formulation, the relationship between leisure and wages has been tested by several empirical researchers. Both cross sectional studies and time series analyses have been conducted as researchers have tried to determine what other economic and social forces influence the income/leisure choice.

B. Empirical Studies

1. Cross Sectional Analyses. The first cross sectional study (Douglas, 1934) found strong evidence to support Knight's contentions about the strength of the income effect. Based on the reports of the Bureau of Census, the study covered 15 industries over the years 1890 to 1926. In it, Douglas concluded that:

> Knight therefore seems to have been correct in his general interpretation of what would happen if incomes were increased... Workers in the United States tend to divide an increase in hourly wages into two parts. The first is a higher material standard of living while the second is increased leisure... Approximately two-thirds of the gain is devoted to the first and approximately one-third to one-quarter to the second... The supply of hours of work is negatively inclined (Douglas, 1934, p. 313).

Douglas found that in 1890 a $-.78$ coefficient of correlation existed between average hourly earnings and the length of the full-time average work week. In 1914 it was $-.80$ and in 1926 $-.84$.

However, the next cross sectional study (Finegan, 1962) of 96 census industries for the same years found the coefficients of correlation, although still significant, to average only $-.27$. Updating and broadening Douglas' analysis by using 1940 and 1950 census data for 323 occupations, Finegan also found general support "for the orthodox construct of a negatively inclined supply curve of labor." But he cautioned that several other determinants of the work week had to be controlled in order for "a substantive inverse correlation between hours and earnings to appear." For example, the 1950 census data showed that for 353 occupations, the mean hours of work were negatively associated with hourly wages in a significant way for blacks and women, but *positively* associated for married men during the ages of 20 to 62 and for the number of years in school. No significant correlation showed up when age was controlled. The 1940 data, though, showed a negative association for the additional factor of unemployment, a positive association for age and no significance for blacks.

Cross sectional studies after Douglas' original attempt have tended to show that the relationship between wages and hours is much more complex than is shown by a simple regression—that mediating variables are a necessary part of the analysis. For instance, Koster (1969) studied "The Effect of an Income Tax on Labor Supply." Gordon C. Winston (1966), meanwhile, compared the distribution of the total "social time" between work and leisure internationally, and found that a ten percent differential increase in per capita income (taxes held constant) resulted in a .08 percent reduction in the time used for income acquisition. Musgrave and Musgrave (1973) supported Koster's finding (see also Hanoch & Honig, 1978).

Multiple factors were studied by Hall (1970), who found that the wage/hour relationship varied with the introduction of the variables age, sex, marital status, and race. Using the Survey of Economic Opportunity for 1967, Hall, like Finegan, found that married males ages 20 to 50 worked full-time regardless of wages. Single people (male and female teenagers as well as males ages 20 to 50) also were insensitive to wage rates in terms of hours worked. Hall did find, however, that married women in all age groups and married males over 60 showed a strong income effect: a substantial preference to work shorter hours at higher income levels. In comparison by groups, the data showed black married males demonstrating a stronger income effect than white married males and black married females a stronger substitution effect than white married females. Hence a negative coefficient relationship between earnings and hours worked was observable only if race, age, sex, and marital status were considered.

Unearned income (from things like inheritance, state welfare payment, or existing wealth and assets) were also observed to influence the leisure/wage choice somewhat. Theoretically, income received apart from wages paid would strengthen the income effect, more so than higher wages, and predispose workers to take more leisure at higher levels of such unearned income (Rees, 1973). Gallaway's (1961) study of males over 65 showed that old age pensions as a source of unearned income is inversely related to labor force participation rates. Barzel and McDonald (1973) have shown that at least nine alternative labor supply curves are generated, theoretically, with the introduction of the variables "wealth" and "subsistence wage."

The price of certain types of consumer goods was also suggested as a being a variable which influenced the income/leisure choice. Becker (1965) theorized that spending on goods and services for recreation was a *complementary* phenomenon associated with leisure taking (just as automobiles, for example, require complementary spending on gas, tires, repairs, etc.). He suggested that if the price of these complementary goods and services decreased, the price of leisure could also be said to decrease and thus increase the demand (the income effect would be strengthened). Alternately, if the cost of complementary goods and services increased, either there would be a shift toward "time intensive" activities in leisure or a strengthening of the substitution effect, whereby workers chose to offer more hours to work. (Becker's theory has not yet been empirically tested by cross sectional analysis; however, the time series analysis done by Owen (1970) suggests that Becker's theory has some validity. Owen's study is included below.)

Other types of cross sectional studies have made the basic assumption that since most people are not free to adjust their work hours as they wish because of inflexible work schedules and state and federal hours laws requiring time and a half overtime pay for work over 40 hours a week, then those studies (discussed above) that compare existing wages and hours do not accurately reflect worker preference. The research into subjective attitude preference includes the work of Thurstone (1931), Rousseau and Hart (1951), Becker, DeGroot, and Marschak (1964), and MacCrimmon and Toda (1969).

Katona, Strumpel, and Zahn's (1971, pp. 124–133) random sample of 1,322 respondents showed 56 percent satisfied with existing hours and wages, 34 percent exhibiting a desire for more work at the existing wage level and 10 percent a preference for more leisure. Nagley and Goodale (1967) questioned a small, non-random sample of predominantly male factory workers to determine preferences between a two percent pay raise and various leisure options. These leisure options included:

1. one week's paid vacation per year
2. five paid Fridays off per year
3. five weeks off every five years with pay
4. a four day week of 9 hours 45 minutes per day
5. early retirement by five days per year, accumulating
6. a five day week of 7 hours 50 minutes per day

Nagley and Goodale found that most workers they questioned ranked their preferences in the order listed above, placing their relative preference for the two percent pay raise between numbers four and five of the leisure options. The same sort of income/leisure preference order was shown by Chapman and Ottemann's (1975) study of 149 clerical and operative workers in a public utility and Best and Wright's (1976) study of municipal employees in California. These three studies also suggested that there existed a higher marginal rate of substitution, a greater willingness to substitute leisure for income at the existing wage for women, those under 20, older workers, white collar workers, and married people with few or no people living at home.

Best's (1980) work contains the most ambitious of the attitude studies. Among the studies he used was the August 1978 Lew Harris and Associates poll reporting a national random sample survey of 1,566 people (over 17 years of age). The purpose of this and other polls was to determine the income/leisure *preference* not showing up in actual hours/wage statistics. Of the 949 people used in the subsample (respondents at work), 60.7 percent of them were satisfied with their hours/wage balance, 28 percent reported that they would like to work longer at existing wage levels, and 11.3 percent said they would like to have more leisure and work less. Factors found to influence this choice included in order of importance: (1) family income—at higher family income levels respondents preferred more time off, supporting the traditional idea of the importance of the income effect; (2) age—the older the respondent the higher was the leisure preference; (3) education—the more education the higher the leisure preference. Surprisingly enough, occupation, sex, age of youngest child, and union affiliation influenced the subjective income/leisure choice very little.

2. *Historical Time Series Studies.* The strongest case for the claim that there is a strong direct, positive relationship between higher wages and increased leisure has been made by economic historians. Even though cross sectional studies have indicated that many "non-pecuniary determinants of the work week" need study in conjunction with the hours/wage correlation, many economists still accept and promote the backward bending supply curve of labor as a hard fact of the 20th century economy.

In basic texts, the backward bending supply curve of labor is faithfully reproduced together with an essentially marginalist explanation of its workings (Barzel & McDonald, 1973, p. 621). Heilbroner, for example, in his text (1970) explained the traditional labor curve by reference to the "rising marginal disutility of labor" added to "the falling marginal utility of income," i.e., if the latter was high enough and the former low enough a wage increase would result in "additional leisure." If a worker's pay went up 10 percent, for instance, he might reduce his work week by five percent. Heilbroner concluded:

> Backward bending supply curves help explain the long secular trend toward reducing the work week. Over the last century, weekly hours have decreased by about 40%. Although many factors have converged to bring about this result, one of them has certainly been the desire of individual men and women to exchange the marginal utility of potential income for that of increased leisure (Heilbroner, 1970, p. 459).

Similarly, Albert Rees in his influential book, *Economics of Work and Pay* (1973, p. 24), points out that even though "nothing in the utility theory requires" the *a priori* assumption that the income effect of wage increase is larger than the substitution effect, still "both the historical reduction in average hours of work and evidence from cross sectional analysis (*sic.* Rees quotes only Finegan's study) suggests that it has in fact been satisfied in most cases."

John Kenneth Galbraith makes perhaps the strongest marginalist case. Reviewing the "drastic decline" of the work week since 1850 from about 70 hours to the current 40 hours, he concludes that this reflects the "unmistakable acceptance of the declining urgency of goods. There is no other explanation" (Galbraith, 1958, p. 259). Hence the old neo-classical idea in its basic form is still around and still influential. Economists still accept to some extent the idea that leisure is a normal good, that work is a disutility, that the marginal utility of money falls as income increases and that given these facts higher wages mean increased leisure.

The longitudinal claims made by the economic historians were supported by specific time series studies. Verdoon (1947) showed that over the years 1850 to 1949 in the United States, with each one percent real income increase a corresponding .3% reduction in work hours was observable (see Zuzanek, 1974). Similarly, G. Kerr (1955) demonstrated that between 1920 and 1950, increased productivity was expressed as both increased income and more leisure in the United States at the ratio of 60 percent for the former and 40 percent for the latter. (This finding is similar to Douglas' study but in contrast to Finegan's.)

The most extensive time series study was done by Owen (1970). Using historical data from 1901 to 1961, Owen was able to show (based on hours worked per week, wage data, "and the price of market recreation") that over these years: "The simple regression of the demand for leisure time on the real wage rate yielded the expected positive relationship. Thus support was given to the hypothesis that there was a backward bending supply curve of labor." Owens viewed the price of recreation as a significant explanatory variable in the demand for leisure time and hypothesized that, as the commercial recreation industry developed and the relative price of recreation decreased, the demand for leisure time would increase, just as it did when wages were increased. As Owens observed, the price of recreation did not decline significantly from 1929 to 1956, and this "leveling off of the relative price of recreation since 1929 offers a partial explanation for the observed retardation in the rate of decline over time of the hours of work." Indeed, he estimated that 25 percent of the long term increase in the demand for leisure could be explained by the reduction of the market price of recreation (Owen, 1971).

Owen's conclusions, however, were not confined to a simple regression. He also considered other historical factors such as fatigue, education, commuting, working conditions, productive consumption, and unemployment, all of which he observed as having some influence on the basic income/leisure choice.

C. Findings, Implications, and Explanations

1. The Age of the Constant Work Week. One interesting finding has been uncovered by the time series, a fact supported as well by various cross sectional analyses done over several decades. As Douglas and Finegan showed, the coefficients of correlation between hours and wages were quite significant around the first decades of this century (1890 to 1930). Douglas showed them to be about $-.80$ and Finegan a $-.27$. But according to Finegan, as well as many other recent studies—Wilensky (1964), Zuzanek (1974), Linder (1970), and Barzel and McDonald (1973), the tendency of Americans to take more leisure at higher income levels has just about vanished since after the second world war (except for certain population groups, such as subgroupings of women, aged, etc.).

One way to illustrate this phenomenon is by plotting the Average Annual Earning of full time employees as a function of the Average Hours Worked per week by private, non-agricultural workers in two or five year intervals. In Figure 2, OH is the week's hours worked and OW is the annual wage paid. Figure 3 represents by Y and Y1 an approximate curve that shows the general tendency for the wage/hours function to become vertical.

The question comes to mind immediately: "Why has this happened?" Why did Americans (in general as distinguished from certain groups) have a much stronger preference for leisure at the first part of this century (indeed, for the hundred years before 1930) than the latter part? Why did we use increased productivity for more leisure during a time when this country was relatively poor and turn away from leisure over the years when the country was becoming the richest nation in history?

To date, only a handful of studies have raised this question and so far only tentative explanations have been offered. Again, economists and others have had recourse to "mediating variables." For example, Owen (1976) explained that after the second world war, the cost of raising families increased, the baby boom occurred, and the "pent-up" consumer demand left over from the Depression

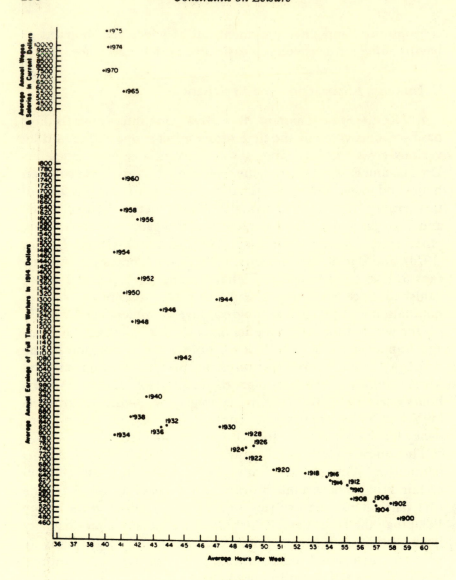

Figure IX-2.

was expressed. It has also been argued that this observed shift in leisure preferences has had something to do with the politics of the New Deal, the public policy established then (and still ongoing) about unemployment and the government's role in the economy

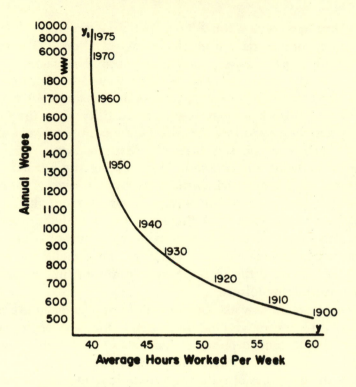

Figure IX-3. Hours/Wages Function in Historical Perspective.

as a "permanent stabilizing" force to assure "full employment," and the fact that as a political cause and a public issue, shorter hours stopped being important with the onset of the Great Depression (Hunnicutt, 1980). Owen (1970) envisioned a role played by the price of complementary recreation spending (see above).

Advertising and the "imperatives of consumer demand" have also been related to this phenomenon. Galbraith (1958) supposed that insofar as capital growth depended more on production and consumption than on leisure taking, capitalism has had a stake in convincing people to continue to work to buy more and new things with their higher wages rather than to abandon the market-place for leisure. Herbert Marcuse (1955) went so far as to see some sort of capitalist conspiracy operating to convince people to buy things they didn't need rather than to take leisure in order to satisfy "real human needs."

The historical alteration of occupational structures has also been understood as related to this change (Dalton, 1975) insofar as jobs, shifting from the primary and secondary sectors of the economy to the tertiary sectors, were viewed as being more "desirable" or "attractive," or at least less burdensome. In marginalists' terms, if work became less of a disutility, then the "stick" driving people toward free time became less important. Related to the changes in job structure, the "fatigue factor" has been suggested as being important in determining the attractiveness of leisure. For example, when the work day was over eight hours the fatigue factor would encourage leisure taking; during the age of the 40 hour work week this factor has been less important. Owen also suggested that "the great proliferation of educational opportunities — has tended to discourage the demand for leisure time." He also cited the increase in commuting time as another factor discouraging leisure.

Unemployment may also be understood as a factor in the age of the constant work week. It has been seen to increase leisure taking when labor demand declined in periods of recession (Winston, 1965; J. Fenlon, 1971). Alternately, work hours have seemed to increase during times of reducing unemployment and increasing labor demand (K. Kreps, 1968; Owen, 1970).

Dalton (1975) opined that the rise in consumer debt, allowing many middle class people access to things like single family housing and consumer durables, has functioned to "induce workers to give greater weight to increases in income . . . , as opposed to more leisure time." He also talked about a "psychological propensity to work," a concept amorphous at best — a simple renaming of the hours' reduction stabilization phenomenon.

The basic empirical finding that leisure preferences have changed in the United States over the course of this century has therefore been only tentatively explained. Some of those explanations have been challenged, and other possibilities have yet to be explored. But in light of the fact that the reduction of work time has ceased for over 50 years, economists have been forced to reexamine the basic theoretical foundations for the economics of leisure as formulated by Robbins.

2. *The Harried Leisure Class.* Steffan B. Linder in his influential

book, *The Harried Leisure Class* (1970), attempted to reassess the theoretical relationships between hours and wages. Linder claimed that a wage increase, far from making more leisure a greater possibility as was previously assumed, has had the opposite effect of making leisure more scarce and has changed the very type of activity done in free time. Linder reasoned that utility could be thought of as a function of commodities consumed and consumption time, i.e., $U = f(Q, Tc)$. For example, if I choose now to take a break from my writing tasks and go for coffee, I will need two things to enjoy the experience. I will need the money to buy it but I will also need sufficient time to drink it. As Linder points out, "whole sacks full of coffee" will do me no good, would not have utility for me, if I didn't have time to consume it.

Thus consumption takes time. But time is the one, perhaps uniquely, limited resource: we all have just so much. Making these minimal assumptions—that consumption takes time, that utility is a function of time in consumption, and that time is limited, Linder argued that as wages increased, pressures would be brought to bear on consumption time. With higher wages, more goods, services, and activities would have to be consumed in the limited time span. And those commodities whose consumption would be time intensive (taking more rather than less time), and inexpensive would be given up in favor of consumption of goods and activities inexpensive in time and expensive in money. With more wealth at their disposal, people would have to be more efficient in their use of time spent on consumption. And efficiency in production of commodities would have to be matched by efficiency in consumption. The key in both cases is more goods in less time.

In Linder's view, the dreams about progress throughout the ages, dreams about a democratic culture where every person would be able to enrich life through music, literature, art, history, and travel, improve the soul through prayer, contemplation, and good works, enjoy nature—such dreams would give way to the harsh realities of the modern consumer imperatives. Even the "pleasures of the table and the bed" tend to be time intensive; and good, inexpensive activities would prove inadequate.

So, Linder concluded that "economic growth entails a general

increase in the scarcity of time." Higher wages equaled less leisure
and leisure time was altered by higher wages. This did indeed
seem to be a reversal of the old logics about the workings of the
substitution effect and the income effect. Linder also suggested
that Western industrial civilization would eventually reach a
"consumption maximum." The day would come when people
would not have the time to use one extra thing—the time added
component of utility would diminish so much that the pleasure of
additional consumption would not be worthwhile. According to
Linder, "total affluence is a logical fallacy." If the consumption
maximum is therefore the compelling result of time use, then the
spector of secular (long-term) stagnation is again raised: a mature
economy without growth or direction.

3. *Kreps' Choice.* Even though the trend for Americans over the
last few decades has been to express their increased productivity in
terms of wages and consumption rather than more leisure, there is
still no *a priori* economic logic compelling the future to behave as
Linder imagined. Linder simply noted the trend in income/leisure
preference and projected it. His argument's power is more in the
treatment of American values and ideals than in his economic
theory. The fact that as a people and as a nation, we are infected
with, as Linder claimed, a "growth mania," that material values
have dominated other values such as culture and religion, love
and leisurely enjoyment, that "people want higher and higher
consumption, faster and faster increases in standards," and finally
that "economic growth has become an overriding end—not a
means" are all historical observations. Certainly a change toward
more leisure and a re-emergence of the dominance of the income
effect would mean a drastic change in American values and beliefs.
But this is not unthinkable—not logically contradictory, however
much unlikely. Leisure preferences have changed before, and they
could, conceivably, change again.

In this vein, Juanita Kreps (formerly President Carter's Secre-
tary of Commerce) has provided a healthy antidote to Linder's
musings. She, Joseph Spengler (1966, 1971) and Fred Best (1978),
have formulated models that describe the alternative, future use of
economic growth as either increased gross national product per
capita or decreased hours worked for the period 1960 to 2000. They

suggest that an inverse proportional relationship exists in the economy between the growth of GNP per capita and the increase of free time. These models demonstrate that economists as well as prominent political figures still feel, as they did when Robbins wrote in the 1920's, that increased industrial efficiency could be expressed in either of two ways: increased production or shorter hours. Today the choice between luxury or leisure remains a theoretical possibility.

For example, Fred Best (1978) suggested that, given current productivity trends and future projections made by the Bureau of Labor Statistics based on those trends, if GNP per capita would remain constant from 1976 until the year 2000, then the length of the work year would reduce to under 2,000 hours (20 hours a week). On the other hand, if the work week would remain constant, then, with current trends in GNP growth remaining the same, GNP per capita would nearly double (from $5,581 in 1976 to $10,494 in 2000). These predictive models make the luxury or leisure choice clear. Either Americans can use their increased wealth and productive ability as they have since the Depression, creating new goods and services and more of existing products, thereby increasing their material abundance and supporting their consumer society, thus becoming more "harried," as Linder predicted. Or else they can use their wealth for more free time, being satisfied with the existing standard of living.

Hence the future is still open. Robbin's ideas about indeterminancy and possible elasticity are not overturned by Linder's forecasts. The future, as always, will be shaped by future choice: by judgments of values, by hopes and ideals. Forecasts and predictions have a place, to be sure, but they do not foreclose the future.

It is about just such an open future that normative economics has had a lot to say. The forecaster's question, "What *might* happen?" is supplemented by the normative economists' question, "What *should* happen?" It is in the normative dimension of the economics of leisure that "constraint" becomes a permissible and useful word.

II. NORMATIVE ECONOMICS

A. Leisure's Constraint on the Economy

The possibility of maintaining a pure and clean separation between assumed values and objective, empirical observation is a topic that has been discussed endlessly in many circles, with little progress being made. Even the realm of positive economics has not been entirely free from normative value judgments. The line between what is objective and therefore scientific and what is given as an unscientific object or goal is still difficult to draw (Ekelund & Hebert, 1975, p. 5). More often than not, certain values are assumed to exist and empirical discussion revolves around how best to achieve some exogenous purpose—poverty elimination, for example.

1. Normative Economic Assumptions. Two strong and primitive assumptions have influenced the topic of the economics of leisure: 1) economic growth is desirable, and 2) work is very important. These two values seem almost self-evident; one runs the risk of economic heresy to gainsay them. Yet these are values after all, and it seems fair to point out that other normative positions have been taken.

John Kenneth Galbraith stressed the fact that modern economists have made value judgments about economic growth. He argued that "economic science" had a "vested interest" in economic growth, valuing anything that promoted increased production as good and "implicitedly important" and anything that retarded "output as *pro tanto* wrong." He portrayed economists as acting threatened whenever the "importance of production" was questioned or given anything less than full allegiance. According to Galbraith this primary allegiance led economists into a morass of muddy thinking, such as the denial of diminished utility.

He saw that holding production for its own sake to be the ultimate good led to "elaborate and ingenious defenses":

> ... economic theory has managed to transfer the sense of urgency in meeting consumer needs that once was felt in a world where more production meant more food for the hungry, more clothing

for the cold, and more houses for the homeless to a world where increased output satisfies the craving for more elegant automobiles, more exotic food, more exotic clothing, more elaborate entertainment — indeed for the entire range of sensual, edifying, and lethal desires.

Although the economic theory which defends these desires and hence the production which supplies them has an impeccable (and to an astonishing degree even unchallenged) position in the conventional wisdom, it is illogical and meretricious and in degree even dangerous (Galbraith, 1958, p. 114).

Certainly, "positive economics" would counter that it is *Americans* who really want these things; their behavior indicates that they do in fact want to earn and to spend more and demand a right to "full time work." Hence, it makes sense to investigate how growth is facilitated and how more jobs and more work might be provided.

One might argue whether the source of these values is internal when economists make value assumptions, or external when economists respond to social and cultural values. In either case, in the context of the two values of growth and work, leisure is at best a subservient good (valuable insofar as it provides jobs and generates spending) and at worse a destructive constraint of economic growth. Leisure, especially if it is time intensive and goods inexpensive, does take away time from work and production. If the trend in leisure taking that was exhibited in the early decades of this century had continued, the work week would have been less than 20 hours today, and as such, considerable portions of America's wealth would have been expressed in ways alternative to work and economic growth. People would have earned less and consumed less.

Kreps' choice is either/or, in the sense that the more leisure is taken the less goods and wages are possible. Economists, then, have often seen leisure as a constraint — a negative force working against economic growth. As Dalton (1975, p. 103) pointed out, "academic economists usually view shorter hours as detrimental to the interests of workers and the economy as a whole...". Beckerman (1956) concurred that in the U.S. economy, "leisure is barely moral" and "the problem of creating sufficient wants to absorb productive capacity may become chronic in the not too distant future."

Orthodox economists have tended to reject American labor's traditional argument that by reducing work hours, the supply of labor would be made more scarce and hence drive up wages and have the additional benefit of creating more jobs—or at least spread the available "lump of labor" equally. Economists such as Northrup (1965, p. 4) saw shorter hours resulting directly in "diminished total aggregate of real output" and, as such, inflationary if wages remained constant in the condition of hours reduction. Hicks (1932, p. 219) and others also saw increased leisure as reducing total employment since, as "labor costs are unchanged and gross receipts reduced, profits must be diminished. There will thus set in withdrawal of capital and contracting of employment."

Shorter hours have also been seen as being in direct competition with things such as profits and savings. Relative propensities to consume and to save would have been profoundly altered if the propensity to take leisure had continued to be as great as it was in the early 20th century. Hence, in theory, leisure is in direct opposition to two of the basic normative assumptions of economics: it seems to constrain both work and economic growth. No wonder few economists are entirely neutral and objective about the topic.

It also bears mentioning that economists pay a good deal less attention to leisure, and even to the economics of time use, than they do to questions about how best to achieve robust economic growth and how to assure "full time" jobs for those who need them. The focus of attention itself, or lack of it, is a good indication of value assumptions.

2. *John Maynard Keynes and Full Employment.* The argument that economic science is riddled with and warped by value assumptions may be countered by the argument that economists have simply described the theoretical relationship between wages and leisure, as objectively as humanly possible, showing how that relationship has worked itself out in the economy. Still the normative aspects of the economics of leisure cannot be abandoned. While not all economists make *categorical* judgments (such as more production should happen always), many economists employ normative terms, but do so carefully. In contrast to categorical terms such as always, ultimately, good, or ought to in all cases,

economists usually employ *hypothetical* language (Lane, 1978). The abstract form used is: if A is desired (is good or ought to happen), then B should occur. For instance, if you want only economic growth, more income, and a higher level of production, then you should take less time from the economy for leisure.

This type of hypothetical logic was used by John Maynard Keynes, one of the most influential of the 20th century economists, when he formulated his seminal theories about employment. In contrast to orthodox economists, Keynes supposed that the supply of labor was not determined by wage rates. Rather, it was aggregate demand that determined the amount of work available in the short run: "The propensity to consume and the rate of new investment determine between them the volume of employment . . . " (Keynes, 1936, p. 260).

Furthermore, Keynes did not assume that full employment was a more or less natural state, as the orthodox writers had. Since it was the result of effective demand which was in turn determined by consumption and investment, employment could stabilize at any level. Investment and consumption could impose "excessive" demands on the economy which even "full employment" could not meet, in which case inflation would result. They could also, and more likely, be low enough to require the efforts of only a fraction of the work force, in which case unemployment would result. Hence "full employment" was only one possibility among many; nothing in the marketplace assured that it would exist.

Keynes thereby reasoned, in good ethical fashion, that if "full employment" was *desired,* then governments *should* act. They must stimulate the economy in order to move toward full employment. Keynes laid the foundations for showing how governments could work toward full employment if they wanted to. The goal was to be reached primarily through the stimulation of effective demand (investments and consumption). In fact, the various ways the United States government has tried to do this throughout this century — with budget policies, tax cuts, enlarged government payrolls, public works projects, guaranteed loans, etc., are prefaced to some extent on that normative economic logic outlined by Keynes.

Of course, Keynes was dealing with unemployment and not with shorter work hours for leisure. But in contrast to orthodox writers he thought that the supply of labor was perfectly elastic in the short run—perfectly responsive to the wage inelastic demand for labor. Being the result of consumption and investment, the supply of labor could be manipulated by government policy; wages paid had no effect. Letiche (1958, p. 88) presented Keynes' theory of labor supply thus:

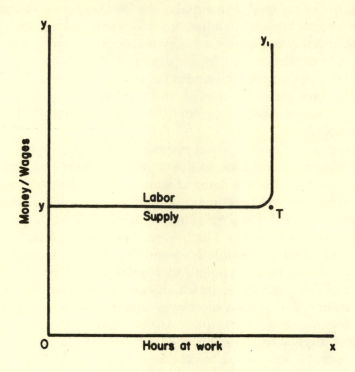

Figure IX-4. Keynes' Labor Market.

Labor supply would be wage inelastic only at point T, where an infinite wage could not call forth additional work, because full employment would have been reached (inflation would result).

Keynes evidently ignored shorter work hours in all forms except unemployment, disregarding the influence of wages on the level of employment (Dalton, 1975). He defined "full employment" without regard to the fact that workers had tended to reduce labor supply in the condition of increased wages (see Douglas' coefficients of correlation for the three decades prior to Keynes' writing).

For him full employment involved no involuntary unemployment at a certain given and stable work week. The idea that voluntary decreases in the hours of work could also determine what "full employment" was did not show up in his reasoning about labor supply elasticity.

Nowhere is Keynes' normative reasoning more in evidence than in his short discussion of leisure in his revolutionary book, *General Theory of Employment.* In response to the many proposals being made during the Great Depression to shorten the hours of work (share-the-work) as an unemployment remedy, he replied:

> Another school of thought finds a solution of the trade cycle, not in increasing either consumption or investment, but in diminishing the supply of labor seeking employment; i.e., by redistributing the existing volume of employment without increasing employment or output.
>
> This seems to be a premature policy—much more clearly so than the plan of increasing consumption. A point comes when every individual weighs the advantages of increased leisure against increased income. But at present the evidence is, I think, strong that the great majority of individuals prefer increased income to increased leisure; and I see no sufficient reason for compelling those who would prefer more income to enjoy more leisure (Keynes, 1936, p. 326).

3. Modern Public Policy. As a consequence of Keyne's influence, of the Great Depression, and of the public and political adoption of the ideal of "full employment at 40 hours a week," American public policy concerning employment has been redirected. Since the Depression, the United States government has consistently employed measures such as government deficit spending, liberal treasury policy, increased government payrolls, and expanded public work projects, whenever the private sector has shown indication of stagnation (reduced consumer and capital spending). In practical terms then, public policy has been, and continues to be, to remedy unemployment by acting as a "permanent stabilizing force in the economy," spending whenever and as much as necessary to stimulate the economy to "full employment" and "full production."

The shorter hour or leisure cure for unemployment has been

eclipsed for over 35 years by the public policy described above. Increased leisure simply has not had a political constituency since the Depression; it has not been an economic or political issue. The decisions made about the increase of free time during the Depression have become articles of modern economic faith and political dogma, which are demonstrated by modern public policy and economic assumptions. But they are manifest in the fact that the work week has remained almost unchanged since the Depression. Public policy, by assuming the intrinsic value of "full employment" and "full production," has eliminated the increase of free time as a desirable or even legitimate part of industrial structure.

Thus in the context of these two values—economic growth and full employment, leisure makes a poor showing, especially when unemployment has come to mean anything short of "full time work"—a standard work day, week, and year. Leisure is clearly not high on the list of governmental priorities. The dominant trend over the years has been for both government and public leaders to promote increased production and consumption and thus to seek after "full employment." Gross national product and unemployment figures are the bottom line today, the measures of the nation's health and well being. In this normative climate, leisure is hardly a blessing to be increased for all Americans. It is at best a second order value serving growth and full time work; at worst it is understood as being in opposition to economic growth and hence a constraint on the economy.

B. The Economic Constraints on Leisure

1. Leisure as a Medium. Leisure may be thought of as free time for other things, other purposes. It is a medium, valuable when it is used; it is a means to an end. In discussions of the economy, one way in which leisure has been seen is as a special way to promote extra-economic values such as culture, learning, spiritual development, physical excellence, individualism, community, creativity, self-fulfillment, peaceful enjoyment, interpersonal relationships, health, etc. In this view, these extra-economic values are somehow at odds with the economic values of growth and work in the industrial setting, and leisure is constrained by excessive work and concentration of growth for its own sake. Writers who have thought in these terms exhibit normative thinking in the form of categorical judgments: "Extra economic activities are more important than excessive consumption and *should* be developed through increased leisure."

In other cases, though, leisure has been understood as a means to more practical purposes. It has been seen as a legitimate way to deal with unemployment, raise the wages of workers, redistribute wealth, and channel production in necessary directions, thereby avoiding superfluous production and husbanding the earth's resources against the day when economic growth will have reached a limit. In these cases, leisure is seen not so much as being constrained by the economy or economic values, but as a way to make the economy function in a desired manner. Here the normative reasoning is of the hypothetical variety: "If you want to deal with unemployment you should reduce work hours."

These two types of normative judgments about leisure can be traced historically. Categorical thinking was typical of the late 19th and early 20th century, whereas current economic judgments tend to be more hypothetical in their explicit form.

2. *Leisure and Humanism: The Categorical Case.* Many writers of the 19th century objected to the materialism and obsession with economic matters that they observed around them. William Wordsworth's famous observation that "getting and spending we lay waste our powers" was often quoted and the thought behind the phrase elaborated by such writers as Sidney Lanier and John Ruskin. Coupled with the criticism of "philistine" materialism was a dream of a better world where people would at last be freed from the preoccupation with economic matters and be able to grow morally, spiritually, and aesthetically. Utopian novelists, almost without exception, looked forward to that bright future when only four hours a day was required for work, and where people would spend the remainder of their energies not on consumption or worrying about money, but on more important things.

Apart from literature and poetry, these sorts of ideas began to show up in the writings of late 19th century economists who, observing the real economic progress around them, were optimistic about the future. John Stuart Mill, for example, proposed that a "stationary state" of the economy was inevitable since the "increase of wealth is not boundless." At the end of economic growth lay a "stagnant sea" toward which the "stream of human industry" irresistibly flowed. But this ultimate point, this final goal, was not such a bad thing according to Mill, since human progress was more than economic progress. In fact, Mill was more than a little disillusioned with the prevailing idea that "the mere increase of production and accumulation" constituted progress:

> I know not why it should be a matter of congratulations that persons who are already richer than anyone needs to be, should have doubled their means of consuming things which give little or no pleasure except as representative of wealth; or that numbers of individuals should pass over, every year, from the middle classes into a richer class, or from the class of the occupied rich to that of the unoccupied. It is only in the backward countries of the world that increased production is still an important object . . .

In fact the best economic state for human nature would be stationary, one in which "no one is poor, no one desires to be richer." In this condition, laborers would be paid enough to meet their needs and no enormous fortunes would exist to excite the envy of others. People would then have "sufficient leisure, both physical and mental . . . to cultivate freely the graces of life." In such a stationary state, people would also be able to enjoy nature and its solitude, which too much economic development would destroy. They could "contemplate the world," and in doing so constitute a "happier population" (Mill, 1923 (1848), p. 749).

Mill concluded with the hope that "for the sake of posterity," people would be content with a stationary state long before they were forced to by necessity. This hope was based on Mill's belief that progress would not cease with the stationary state of the economy.

> It is scarcely necessary to remark that a stationary condition of capital and population implies no stationary state of human improvement. There would be as much scope as ever for all kinds of mental culture, and moral and social progress; as much room for improving the Art of Living, and much more likelihood of its being improved, when minds cease to be engrossed with the art of getting on. Even the industrial arts might be as earnestly and

successfully cultivated, with this sole difference, that instead of serving no purpose but the increase of wealth, industrial improvements would produce their legitimate effect, *that of abridging labor* [my italics] (Mill, 1923 (1848), p. 751).

John Stuart Mill's moral argument may thus be abstracted as follows: excessive attention to economic growth for its own sake gets in the way of real human needs and potential and corrupts life; human material needs are finite and can be met; once these needs are taken care of, other human needs—the extra-economic "graces of life" such as culture and learning—should be cultivated; leisure represents the way to reduce unnecessary production and unnecessary work and to make progress possible in other valuable human areas; hence leisure ("abridging of labor") *ought* to increase as productivity improves and as human material needs are met.

This sort of reasoning has appeared regularly in Europe and America among economists and others since Mill wrote. The actual trace of these ideas is complex and is beyond the scope of this chapter. A few representative samples will show that Mill's train of moral logic was not an aberration but was in fact the beginning of an important "current of thought" that has continued to question the assumptions of the modern industrial states about economic growth and to offer an alternative vision of human progress.

Bits and pieces of Mill's kind of moral reasoning may be found, of all places, in some of the speculative writings of John Maynard Keynes. Like Mill, Keynes believed that human material needs "fall into two classes." Some needs are always present (absolute) in all people—things like enough food. Others are present in a contingent manner, such as "those which are relative only in that their satisfaction lifts us above, makes us feel superior to, our fellows." Keynes supposed that "the economic problem" might well be solved within the century but that a larger problem would remain. "The permanent problem of the human race" would be what to do after having solved the "economic problem" (Keynes, 1963 (1931), pp. 365–373).

In his 1930 essay, "Economic Possibilities of our Grandchildren," Keynes saw a process beginning after the war that would result inevitably in the condition of plenty. But he feared that the habits and values acquired by centuries of scarcity would make the transition to abundance difficult. Keynes reasoned that "we have been expressly evolved by nature with all our impulses and deepest instincts for the purpose of solving our economic problems. If the economic problem is solved, mankind will be deprived of its traditional purpose." Whereas the common man fantasized that nothing could be sweeter than to "do nothing for ever and ever" and dreamed of heaven as a place and time to sing "eternal psalms," Keynes pointed out that the reality of abundant leisure would be troublesome. The condition would only be tolerable for those who did the singing, but, as Keynes added sadly, "How few of us can sing." So the new challenges of leisure would rival and even surpass those of the "traditional economic problems."

> Thus for the first time since his creation man will be faced with his real, his permanent problem—how to use his freedom from pressing economic cares, how to occupy the leisure, which science and compound interest have won for him, to live wisely and agreeably and well (Keynes, 1968 (1931), p. 767).

Keynes agreed with Mill on several points—the possibilities of a stationary state of the economy, the finiteness of real human needs, and the potential of leisure to open up man's "nobler faculties." But he stopped short of suggesting that leisure ought to happen or would automatically lead to a better life. He also did not condemn an excessive amount of attention to economic growth or see this as necessarily at odds with leisure.

Certain threads of Mill's logic also ran through the writing of America's prophet of abundance, Simon Patten (Fox 1967). Patten suggested as early as the 1880's that industrial productivity and technological advance were ushering in a new economic age, radically altering the demands previously made on individuals by the "age of scarcity." Since the beginning of human history, men had developed values and habits that were appropriate for economic survival in the constant condition of want and deprivation. But the advent of abundance made these values and habits lose their usefulness. The overriding problem in the "age of abundance" was to readapt old customs and concepts and find more appropriate economic values (Patten, 1893). The chief danger of abundance was that behavior, conditioned by the ages of scarcity, would survive unchanged. This sort of economic maladaptation could result in a generation of "gluttons" who worked more and harder to buy products in the accustomed ways when they were already satiated with too many things (Patten, 1889, pp. 30–60).

Patten suggested that proper guidance was needed to direct the masses into more appropriate and human activities. He thought that "non-economic pleasures" had to be sought in the condition of plenty, otherwise the sensual debauch in material goods would destroy the more human desires for aesthetic, cultural, and religious pursuits. These sorts of more worthwhile things had to replace the fascination with economic growth for its own sake in order to avoid economic chaos (Patten, 1968 (1897), p. 121).

Several of Patten's students, people such as Rexford Tugwell, Walter F. Weyl, and Frances Perkins, and some of his associates such as Stuart Chase, Edward Ross, and Edward R. A. Seligman, were deeply influenced by Patten's ideas about economic abundance. Each had strong views of leisure's role in the context of abundance, and tended to see free time as the opportunity to use increased wealth in human ways. For example, Walter Weyl (as editor of the *New Republic*) wrote in his influential book, *Tired Radicals* (1921), "Above all, pleasure is limited by the time to enjoy it. In enjoyment, time is more than money." He suggested that wealth should be wisely used, not for the constant "squirrel-cage existence" of making and spending, but for a better quality of life, "improved recreation and larger pleasures" (p. 73). In *The New Democracy* (1912), Weyl proposed that "the article of consumption most often neglected is leisure. Leisure is an indispensable element to all enjoyment. It is the thing is which the American, despite his overflowing wealth, is poorest" (p. 333).

Other examples of modern restatements of Mill's position may be found in the works of Monsignor John A. Ryan, Stephen Leacock, and Graham Lang. John Ryan reasoned that the "rational elemental wants of the majority were the only basis for real progress. He looked forward to a new type of progress, not in the production of luxuries and glittering promises but in the "expansion of human life in areas other than economic." Essential to the new "human progress" was free time. The shorter work week would accomplish such things as alleviation of unemployment and the "promotion of the social order" by itself. But once leisure was acquired, then the masses could be "taught to use it wisely" through educational institutions and the church for the human ends of religion and culture (Ryan, 1929).

As a professor of political economy at McGill University, Stephen Leacock commented at length on the impact of industrial growth on social values. Like Ryan, Leacock thought that industry's needs to grow, to promote more consumption, and to create new markets for luxuries were socially destructive. He believed that the concept of progress was changing: it had become a chasing after the "phantom of insatiable desires" and as such had little to do with the old progressive dreams of the good life. Industry and business were not interested in "producing plenty." They were attempting to "produce values" which had little relation to human needs. These values only served the cause of more unnecessary industrial growth and frayed "the nerves of our industrial civilization."

The creation of "luxuries and superfluities" was a perversion of progress, because "real human needs" were being ignored. Leacock suggested that "the shortening of the hours of work with the corresponding changes in the direction of production (was) really the central problem of social reform." In leisure time human needs could be satisfied as attention was directed from the artificial desires that were created by industry. Leacock thought that Edward Bellamy's utopian dream for a four hour workday was a perfectly reasonable objective for modern reform. He urged that society recognize the fact that "a working day of eight hours is too long for the full and proper development of human capacities and for the rationale enjoyment of life." If they could achieve the goal of a shorter work week, the American workers could begin to satisfy their real needs and begin to enjoy life "rationally." In this way workers could guide their own lives, appreciating spiritual and moral values of their own, deciding what was important for their own lives and demanding those things from industry, thereby directing production and the machine rather than having the values of "economic growth for its own sake" forced on them. The final end of industrial progress, therefore, could very well be enough time to watch a sunset (Leacock, 1920).

Graham Laing (professor of economics at the California Institute of Technology) also opposed the growth for growth's sake direction taken by the modern American economy. He proposed instead that a firmer foundation for progress was more leisure. He predicted that in 20 years, two or three hours of work would be all that was required to meet basic economic needs. The rest of the time, the worker could be his own master. Laing supposed that "our preoccupation with work led us into the confirmed habit of thinking there's nothing else worth doing, the obsession with work has almost killed the understanding of the purpose of life." The shortening of the work time would provide Americans with the opportunity to "pursue the sciences, cultivate spiritual values, and realize individual potential." He concluded with a strange statement for an economist: "After all, there's no need for human beings to be obsessed by economics" (Laing, 1933).

Thus, since John Stuart Mill wrote, a few economists have taken exception to the idea that economic growth is the only road to progress. Weyl's phrase, "squirrel cage existence," sums up their feelings about excessive attention to economic growth. They have assumed that human material needs are finite and that other areas of life should be developed as the primary economic needs are met. Economic growth is acceptable insofar as it is the instrument used to meet the finite material needs. But once what John Ryan called a life of "reasonable and frugal comfort" has been achieved, production should open up time necessary for more important things. Excessive attention to economic growth constrains leisure, and it is leisure, according to these economists, that is the medium: an industrial product as it were, that facilitates human potentials in ways that money or increased production and consumption cannot. Leisure, therefore ought to increase as basic needs are met, and increasing, will open up a richer human life wherein the full range of "non-pecuniary" or "extra-economic" needs—everything from playing a Bach Partita to walking in the woods to religious ritual—can be enjoyed.

3. Shorter Hours for the Economy. Apart from the larger concern for culture and learning, etc., increased leisure has also been seen as a practical way to achieve certain economic goals and as a method to deal with some very real economic problems. One of the oldest of these kinds of hypothetical proposals is the "shorter hour cure for unemployment." Since the 1820's American labor has pressed for shorter hours, and employed the argument that shorter hours were necessary in order to deal with "the employment displacing effect of technology." They believed that shorter hours would distribute the amount of work to be done more equally. For example, instead of ten percent of workers being unemployed, a ten percent reduction of the work week would absorb that "free time" and the worker would benefit by more leisure instead of being threatened by unemployment. Samuel Gompers' famous quip, which became a labor slogan in the latter part of the 19th century and early 20th century, summed up labor's position on shorter hours: "As long as one worker is unemployed, the hours of labor are too long."

This sort of reasoning found its fullest and most influential expression during the Great Depression when William Green, President of the AF of L, threatened on more than six occasions to call a "national strike" in support of the Black and Connery Bills in Congress during 1932 through 1936. These bills would have established a 30 hour work week in the United States as an unemployment measure.

During the age of the constant work week, labor has for the most part downplayed the shorter hours issue, concentrating instead on wages and other fringe benefits. Occasionally, however, union leaders have hung out the old shorter hour banner, making the same points about unemployment recently that they have for the last 130 years. For example, in 1961 Walter Reuther argued:

> We are prepared to work 40 hours a week if you can give every American who wants a job the 40 hours, and if they cannot, then we ought to fight to reduce the level of the workweek until every American who is willing and able to work has a job in the American economy (AF of L–CIO, 1961).

Several economists and a few elected government officials have revived labor's old cause recently in both theory and in direct legislative action (Levitan, 1964). Economists such as Fred Best, Joseph Spengler, and Juanita Kreps have seen value in the work-sharing idea especially when, as now, labor force participation rates are increasing. Best (1980, p. 97) spoke of the desirability of "transferring unemployment to leisure" by removing the "underlying constraints . . . which prevent temporary or permanent work time reduction." Since the 1978 Harris polls indicated that a significant number of Americans would voluntarily trade time for income, a flexible hours policy in the government and by industry could allow work sharing to happen naturally as more women, for example, give expression to their desires to work less than 40 hours a week.

In 1977 the California State Legislature held a series of hearings on "leisure sharing" as a modern unemployment solution. Pointing out that one job for every three presently existing will have to be created in the next 20 years in order for unemployment to remain at present levels (a feat never accomplished by the American economy before), witnesses at the hearing raised again the possibility that shorter hours would help create new jobs. During the hearing, the idea that free time was important for citizenship, learning, culture, and other extra-economic activities was again explored (California Senate, 1977).

The work sharing concept has also made an appearance in the United States Congress in 1979 in the form of House Bill, HR 1784, which would have modified the Fair Labor Standards Act of 1938 by setting the standard work week at 35 hours. The following quote is from a letter circulated in Congress by Representative John Conyers of Michigan, the Bill's sponsor. Conyers made many of the points about work sharing that have been made for over a century in America:

> One of the chief methods of keeping unemployment in check during the Depression was the adoption of the 40 hour work week. During the past 30 years, however, the work week has remained substantially unchanged, despite the frequency of massive unemployment, large-scale technological displacement of human labor, and considerable gains in productivity. We ought to look at reducing the working week and spreading employment among a greater number of workers, once again, as a means to reducing joblessness without sacrificing productivity (Conyers, personal letter, 1979).

The shorter hour solution to unemployment has been the single most important way that leisure has been seen as dealing with specific economic problems. However, a few others bear mentioning. In contradiction to the majority of academic economists' analyses, labor has traditionally reasoned that hours ought to get shorter because this would increase wages. The idea has been that by decreasing labor supply relative to demand, the price paid for labor would be driven up. The famous old doggeral repeated by generations of American workers contained this idea:

Whether you work by the piece
  or by the day
Decreasing the hours
  increases the pay.

Labor contended that instead of being inflationary, shorter hours would allow workers to achieve an advantage in the market place, commanding a larger share of the economic pie. But only a few economists have endorsed this idea. John Ryan, for example, thought that shorter hours would act to increase the workers' share of the national income because this reform would, in effect, redistribute wealth (Ryan, 1929). The idea that shorter hours would force owners, managers, and capitalists to pay workers a greater percentage, "their fair share," of the national wealth may also be found in the works of Karl Marx.

Aside from wage increases for workers and wealth redistribution, shorter hours have also been linked to the "rationalization" of industry. For example, Ryan supported shorter hours because he thought they would force industry to produce more "necessities" and avoid the production of "superfluous" things. Since the rich were the ones that made industry produce luxuries, wealth redistribution through shorter hours would put money into the hands of the poor worker who would then, by spending on basic needs, force industry to concentrate on providing those things necessary for life. Ryan and many other "welfare economists" made a basic, moral economic judgment, i.e., that an economy ought not to produce luxuries when people were going without necessities. Shorter hours, then, was seen as a method to ensure that this sort of immoral situation was less likely.

Lastly, shorter hours have been seen as a way to control unnecessary and excessive economic growth that exhausts the earth's resources and overburdens the human and natural environment. In the 1970's, some economists and others speculated that since the earth is a limited place—it has just so much land, mineral resources, water, energy, and capacity to absorb pollution—unlimited industrial growth was impossible. The most famous example of these new predictors of doom was the Club of Rome. This organization published two books in the 1970's which made the basic points about "the limits to economic growth." The Club pointed out that economic growth had to level off very soon in order to avoid exhausting the world's resources and irreparably poisoning the sea, the sky, and the land by the great outflow of pollutants, chemicals, and nuclear wastes. Several suggestions were made about how this necessary leveling off of growth (the equilibrium state) could be accomplished by governments. Among these suggestions was shorter hours of work.

> In any equilibrium state relative levels of capital and population could be adjusted to ensure that human material needs are fulfilled at any desired level. Since the amount of materials or production would be essentially fixed, every improvement in production methods could result in increased leisure for the population—leisure that could be devoted to any activity that is relatively nonconsuming and nonpolluting (Club of Rome, 1972, p. 175).

Like others, the Club of Rome coupled these practical economic purposes with idealist dreams of progress and a more humane existence. In fact, the Club of Rome referred specifically to Mills' 19th century vision of progress through leisure, using Mills' suggestions as an antidote to modern, mindless attention to economic growth for its own sake.

This demonstrates an important point: the two types of normative economic reasoning about leisure—as being categorically valuable or as being hypothetically valuable—are certainly not mutually exclusive. In fact, it is generally the case that those people who stress the intrinsic importance of leisure for non-pecuniary "human" purposes also stress the practical benefits of shorter hours, such as work-sharing. Conversely, those who are primarily interested in shorter hours as a tool to deal with practical economic problems also point to the "human byproduct" of increased leisure.

III. CONCLUSIONS

This analysis of the "positive" economic functions of leisure—how leisure has functioned in the *past* in the economy—has led to the consideration of categorical and hypothetical "normative" judgments about economic matters. Any speculation about *future* income/leisure choices necessitates an awareness of the assumptions underlying these positions. Simply put, if economic growth and "full employment at 40 hours a week" are assumed to be of the first order of importance, then leisure must be seen as a constraint on the economy in a serious and hard working world. If, on the other hand, value is placed on other types of "extra-economic" progress, then leisure may be viewed in a more positive light insofar as it makes things like learning, culture, and religion more possible for more people. To the extent that economic growth is excessive or in directions that are dangerous or not in line with physical and human needs, the economy may be understood as constraining leisure. Clearly, then, any discussions of the future of leisure must take into account the necessity of choice and the values that determine choice.

REFERENCES

AFL–CIO. (1961, December). *Proceedings of the fourth constitutional convention.* Miami Beach, FL.

Barnett, W. A. (1979). The joint allocation of leisure and goods expenditure. *Econometrica, 47,* 579–563.

Barzel, Y., & McDonald, R. (1973). Assets, subsistence, and the supply curve of labor. *American Economic Review, 63,* 621–633.

Baumol, W. (1973). Income and substitution effects in the Linder theorem. *Quarterly Journal of Economics, 87,* 629–634.

Becker, G. (1965). A theory of the allocation of time. *Economic Journal, 75,* 493–517.

Becker, G., DeGroot, M., & Marschak, J. (1964). Measurement utility by single-response sequential method. *Behavioral Science, 9,* 226–232.

Beckerman, W. (1956). The economist as a modern missionary. *Economic Journal, 66,* 108–115.

Best, F. (1980). *Flexible life scheduling.* New York: Praeger.

Best, F. (1978). The time of our lives. *Society and Leisure, 1,* 95–124.

Best, F., & Wright, J. (1978). The effect of scheduling on time-income tradeoff. *Social Forces, 57,* 136–153.

Bye, R. T. (1924). Some recent developments of economic theory. In R. C. Tugwell (Ed.), *The trend in economics.* New York.

California Senate Select Committee on Investment Priorities and Objectives in Leisure Sharing. (1977, November).

Chase, S. (1931). Leisure in a machine age. *Library Journal, 56,* 629–632.

Chapman, B., & Ottemann, R. (1975). Employee preferences for various compensation and fringe benefit options. *The Personnel Administrator, 35,* 30–36.

Conyers, J. (1979). Unpublished letter dated February 15. (Photocopy).

Dalton, D. H. (1975). *The age of the constant workweek: Hours of work in the United States since World War II.* Unpublished Ph.D. dissertation, Berkeley.

Dorfman, J. (1959). *The economic mind in American civilization: 1918-1933* (Volumes III & IV). New York: Viking Press.

Douglas, P. H. (1934). *Theory of wages.* New York: MacMillan.

Dunn, L. F. (1979). Measurement of internal income-leisure tradeoffs. *Quarterly Journal of Economics, 93,* 373–393.

Ekelund, R. B., & Hebert, R. F. (1975). *A history of economic theory and method.* New York: McGraw-Hill.

Fenlon, J. (1971). Recent trends in overtime hours and premium pay. *Monthly Labor Review.*

Finegan, T. A. (1962). Hours of work in the United States: A cross sectional analysis. *Journal of Political Economy, 70,* 452–470.

Fox, D. (1967). *The discovery of abundance.* Ithaca: Cornell University Press.

Friedman, M. (1962). *Price theory.* Chicago: Aldine.

Galbraith, J. K. (1958). *The affluent society.* New York: Mentor.

Gallaway, L. (1966). Negative income tax rates and the elimination of poverty. *National Tax Journal, 9,* 19–47.

Galloway, L. E. (1961). Real balances and the permanent income hypothesis. *Quarterly Journal of Economics, 75*(2), 302–312.

Gayer, D. (1977). The effects of wages, unearned income, and taxes on the supply of labor. *International Economic Review, 18,* 101–116.

Hall, R. E. (1975). *Wages, income and hours of work in the U.S. labor force.* Unpublished doctoral dissertation, Berkeley.

Hanoch, G. (1965). The "backward-bending" supply of labor. *Journal of Political Economy, 73,* 636–642.

Hanoch, G., & Honig, M. (1978). The labor supply curve under income maintenance programs. *Journal of Political Economy, 9,* 1–6.

Heilbroner, R. L. (1970). *The economic problem.* Englewood Cliffs, NJ: Prentice-Hall.

Henle, P. (1962, March). Recent growth of paid leisure for United States worker. *Monthly Labor Review*.

Hicks, J. R. (1932). *The theory of wages*. New York: MacMillan.

Hunnicutt, B. K. (1980). Historical attitudes toward the increase in free time. *Society and Leisure, 3*, 195–218.

Jevons, W. S. (1957) (1870). *Theory of political economy*. New York: Kelley & Millman.

Kalacheck, E. D., Raines, F. Q., & Larson, D. (1979). The determination of labor supply: A dynamic model. *International Labor Relations Review, 32*, 367–377.

Kajel, J. H., Battalio, R. C., Winkler, R. C., & Fisher, E. B. (1977). Job choice and total labor supply. *Southern Economic Journal, 44*, 15–24.

Katona, G., Strumpel, B., & Zahn, E. (1971). *Aspirations and affluence*. New York: McGraw-Hill.

Kerr, G. (1955). The shortening work week as a component of economic growth. *American Economic Review, Papers and Processings, 46*.

Keynes, J. M. (1920). *The economic consequences of peace*. New York: Harcourt.

Keynes, J. M. (1963) (1931). *Essays in persuasion*. New York: Norton.

Keynes, J. M. (1936). *The general theory of employment, interest and money*. New York: Harcourt, Brace.

Kniesner, T. J. (1976). The full-time workweek in the United States. *Industrial and Labor Relations Review, 20*, 3–15.

Knight, F. H. (1964) (1921). *Risk, uncertainty and profit*. New York: Kelley.

Kosters, M. (1969). Effects of an income tax on labor supply. In A. C. Harberger (Ed.), *The taxation of income from capital*. Washington, D.C.: Brookings.

Kreps, J. M. (1968). *Lifetime allocation of work and leisure*. Washington, D.C.: U.S. Department of HEW, Research Report No. 22.

Kreps, J. M. (1971). *Lifetime allocation of work and income: Essay in the economics of aging*. Durham: Duke University Press.

Kreps, J., & Spengler, J. (1966). The leisure component of economic growth. In *Report of the U.S. national commission on technology, automation and economic growth, appendix III*.

Laing, G. A. (1933). *Toward technocracy*. Los Angeles: Angelus Press.

Lane, R. (1978). Markets and the satisfaction of human wants. *Journal of Economic Issues, 12*, 799–823.

Leacock, S. (1920). *The unsolved riddle of social justice*. New York: Lane.

Letiche, J. M. (1958). *Balance of payments and economic growth*. New York: MacMillan.

Levitan, S. (1964). *Reducing worktime as a means to combat unemployment*. Kalamazoo: W. E. Upjohn Institute.

Linder, S. B. (1970). *The harried leisure class*. New York & London: Columbia University.

MacCrimmon, K. R., & Toda, M. (1969). The experimental determination of indifference curves. *Review of Economic Studies, 4*, 433–451.

Marcuse, H. (1955). *Eros and civilization*. New York: Vintage.

Marshall, A. (1907). *Principles of economics*. London: Fifth Edition.

Meadows, D. H., Meadows, D. L., Randers, J., & Behrens, W. (1972). *The limits to growth.* New York: Universe.

Mill, J. S. (1923) (1889). *Principles of political economics.* London: Longmans, Green & Company.

Musgrave, R. A., & Musgrave, P. B. (1972). *Public finance in theory and practice.* New York: McGraw-Hill.

Nagley, S. M., & Goodale, J. G. (1967). Worker preferences among time-off benefits and pay. *Journal of Applied Psychology, 51,* 357–361.

Northrup, H. R. (1965). The reduction in hours. In C. Dankert, F. Mann, & H. Northrup (Eds.), *Hours of work.* New York: Harper & Row.

Owen, J. D. (1971). The demand for leisure. *Journal of Political Economy, 79,* 56–76.

Owen, J. D. (1970). *The price of leisure.* Montreal: McGill-Queen's.

Owen, J. D. (1976). Workweeks and leisure: An analysis of trends, 1948–75. *Monthly Labor Review, 48,* 3–8.

Patten, S. N. (1889). *The consumption of wealth.* Philadelphia: Dorrance Press.

Patten, S. N. (1893). The economic causes of moral progress. *Annals, 3,* 129–147.

Patten, S. N. (1886). The effects of the consumption of wealth on the economic welfare of society. In R. T. Ely (Ed.), *Scientific economic discussions.* New York: Knopf.

Patten, S. N. (1968). The new basis of civilization. In D. Fox (Ed.), *The discovery of abundance.* Cambridge, MA: Delknap Press.

Phillips, L. (1978). The demand for leisure and money. *Econometrica, 46,* 1025–1043.

Pigou, A. C. (1920). *The economics of welfare.* London: MacMillan.

Pound, A. (1922). *The iron man in industry.* Boston: Atlantic Monthly Press.

Rees, A. (1973). *The economics of work and pay.* New York: Harper & Row.

Robbins, L. (1930). On the elasticity of income in terms of effort. *Economia, 10,* 123–129.

Rothschild, K. W. (1965). *The theory of wages.* New York.

Rousseau, S. W., & Hart, A. G. (1951). Experimental verification of a composite indifference map. *Journal of Political Economy, 59,* 288–318.

Ryan, J. A. (1929). The experts look at unemployment: A shorter work period. *Commonweal, 10,* 626–648.

Terkel, S. (1972). *Working.* New York.

Thurstone, L. L. (1931). The indifference function. *Journal of Social Psychology, 2,* 139–167.

Wales, T. J., & Woodland, A. D. (1977). Estimation of the allocation of time for work, leisure, and housework. *Econometrica, 45,* 115–132.

Walker, D. A. (1975). Marshall on the short run supply of labor. *Southern Economics Journal, 41,* 429–441.

Weyl, W. (1912). *The new democracy.* New York: MacMillan.

Weyl, W. (1921). *Tired radicals.* New York: Huebsch.

Wilensky, H. (1964). The uneven distribution of leisure: The impact of economic growth on free time. In E. O. Smigel (Ed.), *Work and leisure.* New Haven: Press.

Williams, C. G. (1970). *Labor economics.* New York: Wiley.

Winston, G. C. (1966). An international comparison of income and hours of work. *Review of Economics and Statistics, 48,* 28–39.

Winston, G. C. (1965). Income and the aggregate allocation of effort. *American Economic Review, 60.*

Zuzanek, J. (1974). Society of leisure or the harried leisure class? Leisure trends in industrial society. *Journal of Leisure Research, 6,* 294–304.

PART III
LEISURE CONSTRAINTS
ACROSS THE LIFE CYCLE

Chapter X

LEISURE AND RECREATION IN ADOLESCENCE: LIMITATION AND POTENTIAL

Douglas A. Kleiber and William H. Rickards

We don't need no education
We don't need no thought control
No dark sarcasm in the classroom
Teachers—leave the kids alone
Hey teacher leave us kids alone
All in all its just another brick in the wall

Pink Floyd

If these lyrics seem to represent the views of an extreme sector of contemporary adolescence, it may be worth noting that they are the words to the most popular song broadcast from the most widely-listened-to radio station in the United States during a period in the spring of 1980. While we should consider the attractiveness of the accompanying music, it is probably true that the words themselves touched a nerve in the collective consciousness of the adolescent subculture in this country at that particular point in time. It certainly sets a tone of resistance and defiance in response to the forces of authority in the lives of adolescents, especially within the public school.

Nevertheless, it is important to point out the difference between this symbolic expression of feeling and actual overt rebelliousness. The power of such lyrics may derive, in fact, from the extensive accommodation and conciliation which guides an individual's inter-personal relations—with adults *and* peers—over the course of adolescence. For the primary agenda of adolescents is to establish themselves as individuals, with a sense of self and with some legitimacy, by exercising their expanding abilities in ways which

289

make them effective in the larger society. In Erik Erikson's words, adolescents are "primarily concerned with what they appear to be in the eyes of others as compared with what they feel they are, and with the question of how to connect the roles and skills cultivated earlier with the occupational prototypes of the day" (1963, p. 261). Perhaps it is for this reason that, contrary to popular opinion, most adolescents report that they actually like school (Manaster, 1977, p. 176). After all, that is where they find their friends; and it is the companionship with peers which serves to mediate the transition to adulthood. Thus, while increasing independence from parents and growing intellectual and social skills provide a sense of equal access to the adult world and a growing resistance to the directiveness which marked authority in the years preceding, the adolescent is struggling plaintively to "fit" and to find direction in that bigger world and looks to friends and compassionate adults (even parents!) for help.

It is within this dialectic of individual self-expression and social accommodation that we consider the role and significance of leisure in adolescent development. Leisure is, essentially, doing what one wants; but deciding just what that is may be more difficult during adolescence than at any other time. As figure 1 implies, the adolescent must weigh more immediate satisfaction against the implications of choices for approaching the "real" world that exists outside of and beyond childhood. And indeed, the adolescent may come to see leisure choices as significant in his or her plans for the future (Noe & Elifson, 1976), a point to which we will return. Nevertheless, it may be that in experiencing this conflict and finding some compromise and resolution, however fleeting and imperfect, one holds at least the promise of happiness later on. It is perhaps in adolescence then that the tenuousness of leisure is first experienced.

In the following sections, some of the basic themes of adolescence will be reviewed, especially those with implications for leisure behavior. Leisure will then itself be the focus of inquiry: 1) what does it mean during adolescence? 2) how is it affected by this stage in the life course? 3) how does it contribute to adolescent development? Following this analysis, the factors which constrain leisure participation and reduce its adjustive functions in adoles-

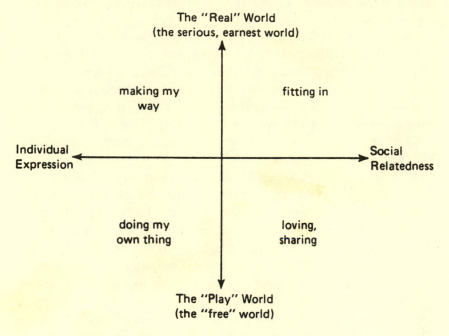

Figure X-1. Dimensions of Conflict in Adolescent Experience.

cence will be examined in relation to specific leisure activities; and then implications will be drawn for further research and for direct intervention in the lives of adolescents.

ADOLESCENCE

Adolescence as a stage has a clear beginning; puberty brings about physiological changes that are recognizable to every boy and girl. The emergent biological potential for full genital sexuality is experienced both personally and socially. Cognitive changes usually take place concurrently, in most cases allowing, among other things, for an individual to project him or herself into the adult culture.

The end of adolescence is not as clear. While spouse, parent and worker roles may serve to provide adult status for some, adolescence is mostly prolonged (or renewed) in college students and in

terms of the issues and tasks of adolescence, it may be continued
well into adult life.

As was noted earlier, the formation of a sense of self, an identity,
is a primary challenge for adolescents, but this is an achievement
that may allude a person throughout life. There is some argument
about how intentional the search is, if, in fact, there is any search
(see Manaster, 1977); but a clearer idea of self is to some extent
inevitable as one addresses the other major tasks of the period
such as separating from parents and selecting among vocational
alternatives (cf. Havighurst, 1972).

Identity formation requires both individuation (separating from
others) and gaining autonomy by moving toward other relationships,
roles, and activities (Josselson, 1980). While the "storms" of adolescence are often exaggerated, the tension and confusion created in
the process of identity formation do keep the period unsettled.
And, those who "foreclose" the issue—by pat acceptance of the
standards, norms and values of parents or peers in some preliminary attempt to reduce dissonance—seem not to develop
psychologically in other respects. Marcia (1980) differentiates those
showing a pattern of "foreclosure" from "the diffuse" who have no
direction, from those in "moratorium" who show some autonomy
and moral maturity while struggling with issues and alternatives,
and from those who have obtained a degree of "identity achievement," albeit temporarily, after establishing some psychological
independence from parents and resolving at least some of the
issues confronting them. These four patterns have been studied
extensively (see Marcia, 1980 for a review), but their effective
place in the process of adjusting to adolescence may be simplified
in relation to the dimensions of anxiety and confusion and ego
development or individuation as in Figure 2.

The existing measures of identity formation rarely take into
account anything other than occupational orientation or political
or religious ideology (cf. Marcia, 1980). While those most clearly
represent adult concerns, the potential of leisure-related experience for clarifying both distance from others and autonomous
direction seems worth examining more closely—a matter to which
we will return. But it is interesting to note that the patterns of
identity formation and its consequences for adjustment are different for males and females (Marcia, 1980). Apparently social rela-

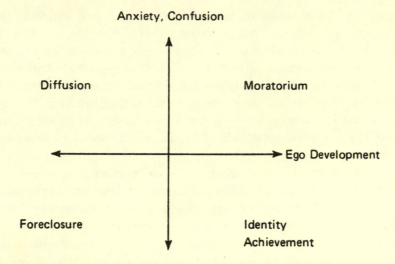

Figure X-2. Typology of Identity Formation Status in Relation to Ego Development and Adjustment.

tions are more significant in ego development during a girl's adolescence than occupational directions. While this may be changing, we may regard it as an indication that identity may be formed around other roles and activities than simply those of the work culture of adults.

There is also a dramatic change in cognitive (intellectual) potential which comes with transition from puberty. Piaget and Inhelder (1958) referred to it as the development of formal operations, but it includes such things as impression formation, differentiation, abstraction, and inference (Hill & Palmquist, 1978). It allows for movement to higher levels of moral reasoning and social awareness. However, since this change also brings the ability to analyze one's own thinking and behavior, it is also the source of the intense self-consciousness that can be so terribly constraining and frustrating to many young adolescents (cf. Elkind, 1978). And the more that alternative possibilities are consciously considered the more it is that ambiguity and ambivalence may lead to a nearly paralyzing self-doubt.

While this self-consciousness may be ultimately useful in the process of identity formation — by allowing for the consideration of alternatives (as with those in "moratorium") — it is rarely clarifying. An antidote to such confusion and one which at the same time contributes to a sense of self is to become involved in activities which are both unself-consciously absorbing and reflective of growing competence (cf. Csikszentmihalyi, 1982). And while such intense involvement is not uncommon in the conventional activities associated with entry into adult culture (e.g., school and work) it is more likely to be found in activities which are relatively more self-appropriated—and thereby more individually defining.

Of course, the angst of self-consciousness may also be avoided by becoming committed rather exclusively to one way of thinking or one group of thinkers. Erikson refers to this as "overidentification" (1963, p. 262); and he sees it as both a defense against "identity confusion" and the source of ideological intolerance. As such, the orientation of a given "in-group" makes it a powerful force in dictating the behavior of its members and those who want to belong. And this most certainly includes leisure behavior.

The intense interest in and reliance on peers as reference points dictates a wide assortment of shared activities and experiences but the relationships themselves are generally superficial. Theoretically, the potential for intimacy in adolescence is limited until issues of identity are largely resolved (Erikson, 1963). Nevertheless, if there is a potential for the development of an internalized feeling of community, it may lie in leisure experience. In contrast to the imposition of school and the dependence on family, one chooses association freely in the context of leisure, the leanings of the in-group notwithstanding. "Best friends" or first loves represent prototypes of the intimates of later life, however limited and superficial those relationships may be in actuality. Even so-called "vertical" relationships with adults, if freely elected, may provide a bonding which projects to an idealized adulthood rather than from a dependent childhood.

Leisure experiences, especially those shared with peers, may thus provide a kind of "shelter" within which to experiment with alternative ways of being and relating. At the same time, however, a leisure activity often serves as a medium of acculturation where social norms are clarified and wherein one may find a bridge to the world beyond the family. Of course, leisure activities may vary in providing for such experiences, and thus, activities such as sports, dancing, drug use, and others need to be examined separately. Before doing so however, the concepts of leisure and recreation in this study must be more adequately clarified.

LEISURE AND RECREATION

To see leisure as "normative" or socially instrumental rather than as individually expressive suggests the problems of understanding leisure in general and leisure in adolescence more specifically. Leisure is commonly regarded as free time, but the emptiness of that "residual" definition has led contemporary theorists to emphasize perceived freedom, intrinsic motivation and enjoyment (e.g., Neulinger, 1974). All things considered, it is generally regarded as activity which is more expressive than instrumental (Gordon, Gaitz & Scott, 1976).

However, for the reasons implied above, Noe (1969) argued that in adolescence leisure was more instrumental than expressive. Where one boy goes to a basketball game because he has had an abiding interest in the game for many years (expressive), two others go because friends will be there and opportunities exist to meet others, preferably female (instrumental). "Hustling" has few age limitations (Erikson [1963] has characterized 5 year-olds as being "on the make"), but in many respects it is a uniquely adolescent style, having both instrumental and expressive elements. While there are certainly elements of freedom and enjoyment in such social activities, they often serve simply as a context for social advance (see also Noe and Elifson, 1976).

For the purpose of discussion we choose here to consider leisure in two specific ways and to further distinguish it from three types, or "functions," of recreation. Leisure in the first sense is *perceived opportunity*. It is *free* time without necessarily dictating a purely expressive or personal behavioral orientation. But it does seem reasonable to contrast it with the "work" of school attendance, largely because it is compulsory and is generally regarded as a means of social control. Personal discretion about time use and alternative activity possibilities thus characterize the leisure of after-school, after-work hours.

A narrower and yet more substantial definition of leisure is that which regards it as a condition of being, within which people elect to become what they are capable of becoming. This notion of leisure—as self-development, self-expansion and self-actualization—is traceable to the ideals of Plato and Aristotle (cf. deGrazia, 1962). While this idea is far less commonly used than the first, it is nevertheless worth examining in relationship to the adolescent processes of individuation and identity formation.

Recreation in a general sense is the *action* of leisure, especially if leisure is regarded more as a context of freedom and opportunity. It is whatever a given culture regards as recreation—such as play, games and sport, entertainment, picnics, festivals, etc.—whether or not participants experience any great degree of enjoyment or self-expansion. But on the other hand, it is an *effect*, "re-creation," where some positive changes have taken place (Gray, 1972). Dumazedier's (1974) "functions" of leisure are useful for characterizing three different effects or uses of recreation. First is *relaxation,* where an activity, or the lack of activity, is used to reduce the tension that exists. Secondly, an activity may be used to *stimulate,* to create some excitement in response to conditions which are otherwise boring and dulling. These first two are primarily *adjustive* or compensatory functions of recreation, but Dumazedier (1974) also allowed that recreation could be a matter of *self-development.* If there is a distinction to be drawn between this and the second concept of leisure described above, let it be that recreation in this sense is more purposive or instrumental, where one uses an activity to "get ahead" or where the goal of the activity itself (e.g., being "number one") constitutes a level of achievement (cf. Noe & Elifson, 1976).

In this sense recreation may be "enculturating" in the way that games have been regarded as a kind of anticipatory socialization (e.g., Roberts & Sutton-Smith, 1962). But unlike other forms of instrumental behavior, those done in the name of recreation or in the context of leisure are done without a willingness to delay gratification. Enjoyment must be intrinsic to the process of the activity. It is usually effected when there is a match between the demands of the activity and the skills of the participant, such that—whatever the ultimate goal—a person may become fully immersed in the action (see Csikszentmihalyi, 1975, for a more complete discussion of the experience of enjoyment).

Recreation is in that sense, however, a matter of engagement. If we return to Dumazedier's first function, relaxation, we may also see freedom and recreation as the products of disengagement. As will be made clearer shortly, such disengagement becomes somewhat critical in the process of individuation or separation from others. And yet a given activity may be used in both ways: playing a guitar alone in one's room may serve to engage a person's attention while disengaging that person from the expectations of friends or family members.

These variations in the meaning of leisure and recreation imply different relationships to development. The more expressive aspects, representing the uses and expressions of freedom, would be expected to reflect the predictable preoccupations of any age while being vulnerable to the same constraints to freedom and participation which characterize a given developmental period. In adolescence, the unique contribution of leisure to development should be related to the adolescent's exploration of identity, potency, and autonomy. As an expression of freedom it should involve relief from particular pressures as well as an expression of personal direction. A given leisure involvement may indeed be the basis for an expanding sense of self (cf. Csikszentmihalyi, 1982).

As it serves a balancing role, it may also mediate extremes, reducing the potential for overidentification with normative roles and expectations or for complete absorption in personal desires. To the extent that leisure serves as a format for social relations or as an opportunity for social achievement as Noe and Elifson (1976) suggest, it serves a "normative" function, facilitating the fit between individuals and their social environment. This is an important developmental function, involving the learning of appropriate social skills and the shaping of certain social aspects of identity.

While the choice of a particular definition of leisure will thus determine just how much emphasis is given to the enculturation potential or how much to the self-expressive and self-expansive potentials of leisure, it is true more generally that the freedom a person exercises and the constraint he or she feels are experienced dialectically. Such conflict is, of course, not limited to the leisure of adolescence, but it may be more vivid and dynamic at that point in the life span than at any others. What must also be granted, however, especially with regard to the influence of external forces, is the fact that leisure activities themselves, by their accepted structures, exert a determining influence in their own right and it is to such influences that we now turn.

ADOLESCENT LEISURE ACTIVITIES

As was stated earlier, the presence of significant peers is often a primary condition of satisfaction for nearly all activities in adolescence. Most have a relational, even a socially instrumental, quality which often overshadows any expressive or intrinsic quality in a given activity (See also Kelly, 1981). Some very common activities seem almost devoid of structural distinctiveness. "Hanging out" is the pastime of those who use shopping centers, parks, street corners and schoolyards merely as contexts within which to see and be seen and to share time with friends. Touring a given locale in a car with friends, or "cruising," while adding the car to that which is exhibited, serves mostly to extend the domain of the hangout and provide a sense of territorial possession (Kroeger, 1980). In addition to cars, clothing styles, radio music and assorted paraphenalia are among the other symbols used by adolescents for identification. The context or the action may be largely irrelevant.

Nevertheless, other activities are themselves worthy of closer scrutiny, especially those which have proven to be controversial in the evaluation of adolescent experience. Following from the previous discussion, we can examine each activity as it affords or constrains the possibilities for self-definition and social relatedness and as it promotes a degree of acculturation or serves as a rejection of mainstream social values.

Music and Dance

While the most celebrated value of music is that it allows for self-expression and self-transcendence, the experience of most adolescents is to be caught up in the lyrics and the styles of contemporary music which are shared with their peers. Appreciating the same music is probably the most common of all adolescent recreational experiences. Such is the character of "pop" music (e.g., Pop Rock, New Wave, etc.).

Dance also has this character, offering new styles for new ages, the learning of which is virtually mandated for those who want to dance publicly with their peers. And it may thus serve as a significant means of status for those deprived of recognition in other conventional settings such as the classroom or athletics (Kelly, 1969). It may be more *individually* significant to the extent that it becomes a means of deep involvement. Csikszentmihalyi (1975) described rock dancing as one of several "flow"-producing activities where one enters into a pattern of activity which is absorbing and unself-conscious. The challenge of such activities usually requires full attention to the exclusion of a focus on self which, paradoxically, may enhance the sense of self through the growing competence which is subsequently realized (Csikszentmihalyi, 1982).

Making music may have such an impact on individuation; more so than simply listening to it with others. One with enough talent and skill to play a musical instrument may establish a degree of identity with growing competence and the reflected appraisal of others. The musician may even feel the freedom and potential for experimentation with the art form. But even this kind of "playing" may be subject to the constraints of peer approval. For example, being a "good guitarist" may lead to social approval within the "in-group" while being a "good cellist" might serve in another case to alienate one from peers.

Of all the art forms, music—and its attendant phenomena (e.g., dancing, buying records, going to concerts)—has become perhaps the most emblematic for adolescents. It is useful to consider why this may be. Any of the expressive forms might serve as an appropriate medium for adolescent-relevant ideas; but music offers a variety of roles for participation and unique possibilities for personal identification. This particular identification is one which draws clear lines, distinct from parental tastes, allied with peers, and containing enough symbols and alternatives to permit individual expression. On the performing side, there are the musicians, composers, technical assistants, costumers, dancers and choreographers. Marketing offers other roles, from the disc jockey to record store clerk. And the consumer collects records, selects radio and television stations, and attends concerts. These alternatives thus provide options for self-expression and for age-related group identification as well.

Sports

It is probably safe to say that music and dance are more common in the experience of most adolescents than sports, but we go now to sport because it is enormously significant throughout our culture and has an influence on adolescents regardless of whether or not they participate. We will argue, and with some supporting evidence, that sport has some different effects on those actively participating than on those who watch or ignore; but it seems clear, at least in this era, that sport sits favorably with modern society at large. This may or may not be exactly why athletes are so popular with their adolescent peers (see for example, Coleman, 1961; Eitzen; 1976) but the fact that athletes are found to reflect more favorable patterns of social mobility (e.g., Schafer & Rehberg, 1970), does suggest that there is strong social support for what the athlete is doing, especially if that person is a male.

Gender is one of the first factors to appear as significant in an analysis of sport in adolescence. Mores are changing very rapidly and it may be far less problematic for girls to participate in—and even enjoy—sport than it used to be, but it is still largely identified as a male domain. This factor alone limits participation and there are only a few who have questioned efforts to change it (e.g., Michener, 1976; Novak, 1976); but the forces of socialization begin early enough to preempt attempts at intervention. By adolescence boys have had, in general, much more encouragement from parents and other significant adults than girls have (Greendorfer & Lewko, 1978; Lewko and Greendorfer, 1979) and peer and media influences also contribute substantially.

Nevertheless, the institutional constraints which restrict sport participation for girls have been aggressively attacked in recent years, and increasingly girls arrive at adolescence with experience in organized sports and encouragement to continue. Unfortunately, it is also at this point that social influence reaches its zenith. Girls who are very able, and well prepared physically and encouraged by family, other adults, and friends may still eschew the sport role as one inconsistent with feminine popularity.

As noted previously, involvement in sport is associated with social status in high school. James Coleman (1961) and other researchers (e.g., Eitzen, 1976) have established that students are more attracted socially to athletic classmates than those with high intellectual aptitude or academic success. But female athletes in high school enjoy much less positive regard and may even be rejected for their involvement in sport (Kane, 1982). This may be changing, however, as more and more women find sport a suitable domain for achievement and serve as models for others.

For boys then, and perhaps increasingly for girls, sport is a vehicle for entry into mainstream culture. Sports are highly valued in this culture and youth involvement in sport generally meets with approval in adult society. Accordingly, the argument is often made that sport is a good means of social mobility for disadvantaged children and even deters delinquency. While there is some evidence supportive of a positive association between sport involvement and occupational aspiration and a negative relationship between delinquency and sport involvement, it is probably masking the influence of other factors such as socioeconomic status (See, for example, Landers and Landers, 1978 and Otto and Alwin, 1977). Those who are advantaged have the best of *all* cultural opportunities.

In the case of social mobility and sport, it appears that extracurricular involvement more generally and the significant personal associations made within such activities often lead to higher aspirations for youth and pave the way to subsequent success (Otto & Alwin, 1977). And with respect exclusively to sport, whatever effect there is is likely to be shortlived, lasting only while association with a sport is maintained (Spady, 1970).

As to the question of delinquency and sport, the embeddedness of sport in mainstream culture makes it often off limits to those who are alienated and disenfranchised. While it may be the case that some delinquent adolescents are ill-equipped psychologically to endure the rigors of sports training (Smith, 1981), it is probably more commonly true that the social context of participation and the lack of compatible peers are seen as obstacles to the troubled adolescents (see Donnelly, 1981; Rickards, 1982). Continuing with simple correlational studies of each will do little to sort this out, but suffice it to say that despite its popularity, sport is much more readily available to some segments of the adolescent population than to others.

And the general point made earlier bears repeating. Leisure activities in adolescence are frequently used more instrumentally than expressively (Noe, 1969); that is, they are the means to desired social ends (e.g., heterosexual contacts; social opportunities) rather than ends in themselves (see also Noe & Elifson, 1976). Sport is certainly no exception and may even be the prototype. While some adolescent athletes are committed to their sports and see them as personally meaningful, others are using them for social advance; and those who are the spectators of sporting events are as likely to be concerned with seeing and being seen by other spectators as with viewing the action before them in the sport context. The presence of the "right" people on the field or in the stands is an attraction to some, while their absence is a sufficient deterrent to others.

Beyond the potential impact of sport on social inclusion and social mobility, its value may lie more subtly for some in the experience itself. While the contribution of sport to the development of character is often overstated, the context is a deliberately structured test of strength, courage, endurance and self-control. One learns to be aggressive without being hostile, to persist and be resourceful. Even losing has its virtue in teaching one to manage failure and disappointment (Winer, 1979). The impact of such experiences on a sense of self are probably considerable, subject additionally, as they are, to the reactions of coaches, teammates, parents and peers.

The *social* values of sport however, may be more gravely overstated. The lack of autonomy in organized sports often works to limit social interaction. Cooperation is a matter of compliance and coordination rather than self-initiated negotiation and compromise. Nevertheless, it is likely that committing oneself to a coach and a team has both personal and social benefits. Porter (1967) has pointed out that a coach may be the first adult to be *chosen* by a child. This may serve as an important experience in the transition from the family to adult society. Perhaps more importantly, the identity structured through sport is a social one. One becomes a valued member of a valued social group. To function effectively in such a role affords an integration of both personal and social needs and may provide a bridge to more serious commitments and associations in adulthood (see also Kleiber, 1983).

But such a resolution is likely to be only temporarily useful. Equally possible are two disabling turns in the individual-social dialectic. By becoming so thoroughly committed to sport, identity may become "foreclosed" in the manner described by Marcia (1980); one becomes a "jock" and is thus responsive only to the conditions and people supporting that self-definition. Alternatively, one becomes thoroughly a part of the sport culture of adolescence, a joiner whose identity is diffused into all (and only) those action possibilities that peer culture offers.

Ironically, while girls find it hard to get into sports, they may be less vulnerable to these particular constraining possibilities. Because they may be involved in sport in spite of rather than because of social influence, they are probably better able to separate their experience in sports from the rest of their social existence. That it is personality rather than social support which permits entry and maintains involvement for female athletes is suggested in a number of studies (See Kleiber & Hemmer, 1980).

Currently underway is research which will examine the after-effects of sport involvement for male and female athletes. Often, the ending of eligibility—either at the end of high school or college—is a kind of mandatory, hence unwanted, retirement. And since the intensity of the commitment may be even greater than that of a person for his/her work at age 65, we are curious about the consequences of such a transition. For example, a foreclosed identity must inevitably be reopened with such a change. How will this be felt? Should we expect, following Erikson, that renewed identity confusion will preclude the ability to establish intimacy? Viewed in this manner we have moved from sport as constrained to sport as the constraint.

On balance however, we must put sport back where it typically sits—as a central part of school experience and inextricably woven into the fabric of our society. In that sense it is neither good nor bad; it is just there. But beside continuing to understand the factors which prevent some from being as involved in sport as they might like to be, we should persist with efforts to understand how sport works to facilitate or hinder self-expression and self-actualization.

Drug Use and Delinquency

If sport is consistent with mainstream culture then drug use and delinquency may be considered the opposite; they are behaviors which meet with strong disapproval within adult society. And yet they share with sport the quality of being instrumental means of social approval within adolescent peer groups in many cases. Drinking alcohol, smoking marijuana and using other drugs is often influenced strongly by reference groups and may serve as rites of passage to fuller participation in these groups (e.g., Ginsberg & Greenley, 1978). Similarly, though not always recreational in nature, delinquent acts often prove a degree of commitment to groups which exist by virtue of shared antipathy toward normative societal patterns.

But the recreational nature of these behaviors needs to be further established. If drug use is a response to social pressure, should it be regarded as a recreational activity? It is only recreation to the point that it is freely chosen. But not commonly considered with respect to drug use is the extent to which it is intrinsically enjoyable and provides an opportunity for experimentation. And rather than an isolated behavior, drinking or smoking is often used in conjunction with other recreational activities or even more "serious" endeavors. (It is not uncommon for students to be "stoned" in school.) Whether or not it is traditionally defined as recreation, the possibility that drug use is a quick route to excitement or pleasure and may be chosen when other recreational possibilities are restricted is worthy of further study.

Much the same picture exists with many forms of delinquency. Whether or not the deviant behaviors are supported by gangs or other peer groups, there is evidence that some forms of delinquency—such as breaking and entering and vandalism—may be intrinsically enjoyable (Anson, 1977; Csikszentmihalyi & Larson, 1976; Langston, 1981) and even aesthetically pleasing (Allen & Greenberger, 1976). Even if the challenge comes in "getting away with it," the fact that skills are tested and control is asserted to a degree that may be missing for an individual in more legitimate contexts makes such activities very comparable to the most enjoyable sport activities and outdoor adventures. Even allowing for the likelihood that such motives play a relatively minor role in the etiology of delinquency, we must ask whether they are manifestations of restricted recreational alternatives (Rickards, 1982).

"Recreational deviance" (Anson, 1977) is certainly inconsistent with accommodation to and acculturation within mainstream society; but it may be instrumental to social relatedness for those who find themselves otherwise disenfranchised. Furthermore, where such activities are demanding of certain physical and psychological competencies, they may be reinforced to the extent that a sense of self is built around them.

Television Watching

One thing that does not change appreciably from later childhood to adolescence is the predominance of television watching. It remains the most preoccupying activity for the average individual, absorbing 4–5 hours of free time per day. While the type of programming, the impact of commercials and the context within which it is watched may well be examined as factors limiting the value of television, it is equally as important to consider how television watching is actually experienced and how it may limit other experiences in adolescence.

While the effects of television viewing have been the subject of a great deal of research, only a few studies have dealt with its significance in adolescence. Using a behavioral sampling technique to study the "ecology" of adolescence, Csikszentmihalyi, Larson and Prescott (1977) found that for adolescents, as is evident with younger children, television watching was among the most prevalent leisure activities, second only to conversation. More importantly, their procedures allowed them to assess a subject's mood, feelings of challenge and control and desire to be doing something else while watching television. Television watching was found to be associated with low levels of involvement and satisfaction, i.e., with what the investigators regarded as a rather "mindless" attentional pattern. And with respect to its broader social significance, it was also associated with deviant and antisocial activities. More research is required to establish how and when, if at all, television is used in a self-expansive and developmentally enhancing pattern. Generally it appears to be devoid of such effects and, by preoccupying an adolescent's time, to preclude them from happening in other activities as well.

Television watching is physically passive, but unlike reading and conversation it is also noninteractive. It may be argued that one can choose the programs to be watched—and this is a more active practice to be encouraged, perhaps—but once the program begins, the viewer is merely a recipient. Of course, television becomes interactive when combined with the emerging technology of video games, and these have become dramatically popular in recent years. To the extent that such activities demand skilled and effective responses, they may contribute to a sense of competence; but the exclusive relationship one has with the available technology makes it similar to normal television watching in rendering it a rather asocial experience. In any case the rapid growth of this phenomenon has attracted the critical attention of researchers and clinicians alike and we will learn much more about its value and significance in years to come.

Sexual Activities

Sexuality provides a major theme in adolescence with a wide range of behavioral characteristics and personal and interpersonal meanings (See Blos, 1962). In early adolescence, a variety of more or less appropriate heterosexual behaviors including dating and mild forms of physical intimacy serve to affirm gender identity and adequacy (Miller & Simon, 1980). Survey research suggests that while sexual intercourse is becoming more frequent during this period—i.e., before the 15th birthday—it is still the exception rather than the rule (Vener & Stewart, 1974; Zelnick & Kantner, 1972). In high school, the frequency of incidents of full sexual relations have increased greatly with few differences in prevalence between the genders (Jessor & Jessor, 1975; Miller & Simon, 1980; Vener & Stewart, 1974). In college, frequency figures continue to increase during the first two years, then level off in the last two (Hopkins, 1977).

In reviewing a series of studies from the last decade, Miller and Simon (1980) found support for the concept that sexual behavior continues to hold traditional meanings—that is, that it plays a critical role in long term, dyadic relations and is essentially tied to the family. Accordingly, sexual promiscuity was found to be related to other behaviors conventionally labeled as deviant (e.g., drug use) and to estrangement from social institutions associated with conventional values. But Miller & Simon (1980) also noted that the significance of actual sexual activities to the actors is inadequately understood, and that "coital activity per se neither generates nor certifies developmental difficulties" (p. 393).

Sexual activities offer valuable illustrations of the kinds of conflict which characterize adolescent development and which are expressed in leisure. On the one hand, physiological changes will have had a major influence on motivation and on the responses to various experiences while, on the other hand, social expectations will assign meanings to the feelings, behaviors and responses. And even differences in social expectations—as between the parent ideal and the peer ideal, for example—may result in very different meanings. The adolescent experiences the influence of physical desire, preoccupations with fantasy, the stigma of social labels, parental concern and restriction, doubts about sexual adequacy or some combination of these. And such will inevitably be a gross oversimplification of the real conflicts which the adolescent actually feels. Nevertheless, the positive attitude most adolescents have toward sexuality is based on a recognition of its potential for producing pleasure and intimacy. These are not insignificant effects, and they readily predispose one to accept the discomfort that seems necessary for the "promise of joy," whether or not it is achieved.

For the purpose of the current discussion then, and in accord with the previously mentioned views of leisure and recreation, we must regard sexuality as a free time activity with social expectations and as a source of interpersonal play and personal gratification. Like drug use and delinquency, it may also be socially deviant; but an argument can also be made for its potential as a developmentally enhancing leisure experience.

For the adolescent, the experience of sexuality offers an occasion for exploring identity. The symbolic rewards and social implications associated with sexuality — particularly for adolescents — gives it the character of theatre, for playing out issues of autonomy and potency. As Miller and Simon (1980) put it, "actual or anticipated sexual encounters provide the adolescent with one of the few instances where ordinary people doing relatively ordinary things experience themselves as extraordinary actors in the moral universe" (p. 392).

Free time experiences provide opportunities for exploring sexual feelings. In the best of circumstances, over the course of adolescence, these explorations will lead to a valuing of individual sexuality and sensuality, a sense of competence in the appropriate sharing of pleasure and a personal foundation for continuing intimacy. In the worst, they may lead to an overidentification with societal labels (e.g., a "bad girl") and an inability to learn beyond these. While current norms generally endorse the importance of sexuality in healthy adult relationships, the process by which the adolescent develops personal sexual aspects is not so well understood. Without adequate insight into personal sexual functioning a young adult could enter a relationship with high expectations for the role of sexuality but inadequately prepared to participate in the mutual learning which is critical to intimacy.

Solitude

As noted earlier, leisure and recreation may be reflected in patterns of retreat from action or disengagement. Spending time alone appears to have its own problems and potentials as an interesting series of studies by Csikszentmihalyi and his colleagues have shown. Using an experiential time sampling technique (Csikszentmihalyi, Larson and Prescott, 1977) adolescents carried electronic paging devices and, when they were paged at various times during the day, they would record their activities and feelings.

Various personality measures were also gathered. Larson and Csikszentmihalyi (1978) raised the question of how time alone functioned in the overall experience of this sample. They found, in general, that time alone was associated with negative feelings, but that variations in amount of time alone reflected personal preference more than the dictates of circumstance (see also Larson, Csikszentmihalyi and Graef, 1982). By comparing the quantities of time alone with the scores on the personality measures they also found a curvilinear relationship between being alone and adjustment. Up to a certain point, for more mature individuals, increased time alone was associated with better adjustment; beyond this point, increased time alone was associated with increasing maladjustment. Although the experience of time alone was not particularly pleasant, it appeared that those adolescents who spent at least a moderate amount of time alone were better adjusted, and that being alone might serve a developmental function.

Time alone, from this perspective, can be assessed as a kind of leisure activity using the dimensions discussed earlier. Ecologically, time alone serves a freedom-defining function by removing factors which might heavily determine behavior. Alone, certain activities are not available, but, given the alternatives perceived as available, the individual has complete freedom of choice and the opportunity to become what he or she can. However, without peers and companions to contribute to the activities available, a different aspect of the self may emerge; that is, one not conditioned by feedback from companions.

According to Erikson, the adolescent's perception of self at this time might well be a confused one. The lack of companions might mean freedom from the pressure of group identity and at the same time a lack of the resource of group identity, an opportunity to be oneself but the absence of others to affirm one's differences. The feelings might predictably be negative ones. It is within the nonenjoyment realm of leisure that such behavior may then be placed, but it is still leisure to the extent that it is chosen and brings with it a degree of freedom and the opportunity for self-directed growth.

LEISURE AND DEVELOPMENT IN ADOLESCENCE

The preceding discussion of specific activities reflects several ways of looking at the limitations to leisure in adolescence and the role and potential of leisure in adolescent development. We have looked at the social and developmental factors which lead to or restrict certain leisure activities in adolescence and the manner in which some leisure activities contribute to the transition through adolescence while others may in some ways restrict development. When leisure experience does contribute, it may be a means of partial participation in the broader culture or a source of identity formation by serving as a more personal mode of self-expression. A given activity may do both or it may do neither. While circumstances will inevitably dictate specific effects, our analysis would suggest that popular music and dance may serve individual self-expression and self-definition in some important ways while accommodating the individual primarily within the culture of peers. Sport experience is usually accommodating to mainstream society while being individually restrictive in some respects, especially for males. Cultural restrictions are likely to be strong with respect to drug use, delinquency and sexual activities though such activities may be both individually expressive and subculturally responsive. Though television watching is culturally conditioned, its passivity makes it largely unsupportive of social relatedness or individual self-definition. And solitude both reflects and creates a degree of cultural alienation but may be an important resource for self-development. These are necessarily oversimplifications and there are certainly many more activities which could be examined; but perhaps we can even risk some broader generalizations.

The leisure activities which are most popular with adolescents are those which allow them to share an experience which makes them independent from the family but affords them the support of significant others at the same time. Nevertheless, leisure in the purest sense, as freedom, is inevitably restricted. Adolescents do not yet have the full freedom of movement and opportunity that adults do. Since they reside with parents and are required to attend school their behavior is to a great extent proscribed. And yet the protected status of younger children is also beginning to be withdrawn as increasing responsibility is expected. Thus adolescents use a good deal of energy preparing for their adult futures, however unrealistically, however tentatively. Such goal-directedness determines a great deal of behavior.

It is in leisure activity — such as talking, listening to music or attending a sporting event — that a pause is effected in this transition to the assumption of new responsibilities. The reference group is a means for checking ones progress. But it is because the social context of leisure activities (i.e., who is there) is so important in adolescence that the "opportunity to participate" must be considered as a *subjective* matter (see also Rickards, 1982). Thus a 13-year-old girl rejects the "opportunity" to play basketball and a troubled and disadvantaged 14-year-old boy regards his teacher's invitation to join the drama club with great ambivalence.

And yet it may be those experiences in those situations that illustrate the best that leisure has to offer in adolescence. For if identity formation is important in adolescence, the exercise of choice in responding to possibilities other than those created by the structure of the peer group may be of special importance. And even the choice to be alone, to be separate, even if conflicted, may move the growing child toward greater independence and autonomy.

Some leisure activities, the socially-endowed "recreation" of adolescence, may serve more generally to constrain such movement. Peer groups may determine what will be done and who will do it. And while participation may provide the makings of a preliminary support structure for social mobility; it may, in the end, be constraining to the individuation which is necessary for movement into adulthood.

IMPLICATIONS

Implications For Further Research

To begin to take the concepts advanced above — the varied meanings of leisure and the individual-society dialectic — and offer concrete suggestions for utilizing the information, more investigation is required. In so doing, we fully expect that our oversimplification of the various phenomena of leisure and recreation in adolescence will be more and more apparent. It is clear already from other evidence (e.g., Freeberg and Rock, 1973) that it is a mistake to assume continuity of experience in adolescence. And more than other developmental periods, adolescence may be characterized by enormous changes of mood (Csikszentmihalyi & Larson, 1984; Larson, Csikszentmihalyi and Graef, 1980). Some of this may actually be the result of leisure experience; but it is safe to say that a given experience may work radically differently for a given individual on two consecutive days in the years between twelve and twenty. More needs to be known about the role of leisure activity (e.g., television watching, social involvement, drug use) in ongoing emotional experience. And leisure behavior itself—its actuality and its absence—may serve as the evidence of the various dynamics of adolescent existence.

We have also suggested that leisure experience may assist in identity formation and this assertion would seem readily testable. And even more speculative is the idea that leisure may offer a unique domain for *intimacy* in adolescence, a social emotion thought to be largely missing until a level of adult maturity is achieved. Perhaps in research on adolescent leisure we will find cause for revising our general theories of adolescence.

Implications For Practice

With the assumption that leisure experience may contribute to both personal and social development, to individuation and socialization, implications may be drawn for intervening in the lives of adolescents who are having developmental difficulties and who are at odds with society. Public schools, municipal recreation programs, family and social service agencies are among those who constitute the intermediaries between the troubled adolescent and a society perceived as hostile and alien.

Such a backdrop has been the basis for establishing recreation programs for the treatment and prevention of delinquency. But such efforts have been largely ineffective (Beck and Beck, 1970). They have been mostly diversionary in character, providing recreation opportunities as alternatives to inappropriate antisocial or illegal pursuits. They have largely consisted of traditional sports, crafts and social activities. In light of the concepts presented above, certain aspects of these programs seem appropriate while others seem considerably inadequate. To the extent that they engage the youth over time in successful social experiences, the programs may improve social skills and positive associations with legitimate activities; but they generally fail to substitute for the pleasure and satisfaction which can be found in some illegitimate activities, especially as they fail to be responsive to individual differences in interests and abilities. Furthermore, having the endorsement of mainstream society, "legitimate" activities are not often appealing to an adolescent who has established a sense of self in some opposition to mainstream values.

As mentioned earlier, an adolescent subculture can provide an alternative to mainstream society which to some extent may facilitate identity exploration; but it too, can assert a rigid structure of norms which reduces the individual's potential for exploration. In this sense it serves as a constraint to certain fundamental aspects of leisure and reduces its adjustive potential. To the extent that youth service practitioners can use alternative activities different from those of both mainstream society and subcultural reference groups, leisure may be optimally useful to a troubled or delinquent adolescent. Finally, the free exploration of individual alternatives may provide a measure of autonomy—in itself, leading to the thought that, "I have the right and responsibility as an individual to examine my life." More concretely, it can encourage the skill development needed to actualize these possibilities. Such are the purposes of leisure education and leisure counseling.

At the same time, it must be recognized that changes in the individual are ultimately meaningful only in the context of a real social setting. To conceptualize treatment solely as building social skills and expressive behaviors is to assume that these are necessarily faulty or inadequate. "Constructing a bridge to the real world" involves an assumption of the basic correctness of that world. In all cases, practitioners must be concerned with the relationships between adolescent clients and their surrounding world and they must allow for the possibility that it is the environment which must be changed. This specifically involves a familiarity with the structure of opportunities—which circumstances permit participation and which are constraining (cf. Rickards, 1982). Services must be designed to increase opportunities for participation not only by expanding the number and variety of activities offered but by improving the access of individuals to them.

Of course, in many cases, encouraging participation in mainstream recreation may be the most appropriate goal of the counselor or agency. Such activities have the potential to compensate for an individual's sense of alienation. The power of recreation to engage the youth in team activities—say, social service projects or sports— provides a basis for building normative relations. It also offers the opportunity to realize personal competence in a group; that is, it provides a concrete opportunity for self-expression in a way that is socially accommodative. Recreation can thus serve as a normative context and, through the expression of personal competence in socially appropriate ways, as a bridge back to society. But for such activities to work, they must be freely chosen and personally meaningful.

The practitioner working with adolescents must develop the ability to recognize identity and relatedness strivings in clients and to provide appropriate opportunities for further development. These strivings must be evaluated in relationship to social norms and individual potential. The counselor must help the individual express and negotiate the dialectic between self-expression and social accommodation.

Conclusion

Troubled and delinquent adolescents stand out as a population for which the notions advanced about leisure and recreation in adolescence may be particularly relevant. Certainly the challenges of a "normal" adolescence suggest that we further our understanding of the relevance of leisure and its potential as a resource during this often difficult period. And perhaps we have in the leisure of adolescence—that stretch between childhood and adulthood—some number of secrets about how best to negotiate the rest of life's many transitions.

REFERENCES

Allen, V., & Greenberger, D. (1978). An aesthetic theory of vandalism. *Crime and Delinquency, 24,* 309–321.

Anson, R. (1977). Recreation deviance: Some mainline hypotheses. *Journal of Leisure Research, 8,* 177–180.

Beck, B., & Beck, D. (1970). Recreation and delinquency. In J. Nesbitt, P. Brown, & J. Murphy (Eds.), *Recreation and leisure services for the disadvantaged.* Philadelphia: Lea and Febiger.

Blos, P. (1962). *On adolescence: A psychoanalytic interpretation.* Glencoe, IL: Free Press.

Bruner, J. (1972). The nature and uses of immaturity. *American Psychologist, 27,* 687–708.

Coleman, J. (1961). *The adolescent society.* New York: Free Press.

Csikszentmihalyi, M. (1975). *Beyond boredom and anxiety.* San Francisco: Jossey-Bass.

Csikszentmihalyi, M. (1982). Toward a psychology of optimal experience. In L. Wheeler (Ed.), *Review of personality and social psychology* (Volume 3). Beverly Hills, CA: Sage.

Csikszentmihalyi, M., & Larson, R. (1984). *Being adolescent.* NY: Basic Books.

Csikszentmihalyi, M., & Larson, R. (1978). Intrinsic rewards in school crime. *Crime and Delinquency, 24,* 322–330.

Csikszentmihalyi, M., Larson, R., & Prescott, S. (1977). The ecology of adolescent activity and experience. *Journal of Youth and Adolescence, 6,* 281–294.

deGrazia, S. (1962). *Of time, work and leisure.* Garden City, NY: Doubleday.

Donnelly, P. (1981). Athletes and juvenile delinquents. *Adolescence, 16,* 415–432.

Dumazedier, J. (1974). *Society of leisure.* Amsterdam: Elsevier.

Eitzen, S. (1976). Sport and social status in american public secondary education. *Review of Sport and Leisure, 1,* 139–155.

Erikson, E. (1963). *Childhood and society.* New York: Norton.

Elkind, D. (1978). Understanding the young adolescent. *Adolescence, 13,* 127–134.

Freeberg, N., & Rock, D. (1973). Dimensional continuity of interests and activities during adolescence. *Human Development, 16,* 304–316.

Ginsberg, I., & Greenley, J. (1978). Competing theories of marijuana use: A longitudinal study. *Journal of Health and Social Behavior, 19,* 22–34.

Gordon, C., Gaitz, C., & Scott, J. (1976). Leisure and lives: Personal expressivity across the life span. In V. Bengston, and E. Shanas (Eds.), *Handbook of aging in the social sciences.* New York: Van Nostrand and Rhinehold.

Gray, D. (1972, December). Exploring inner space. *Parks and Recreation,* 18–20.

Greendorfer, S., & Lewko, J. (1978). The role of family members in the sport socialization of children. *Research Quarterly, 49,* 146–152.

Havighurst, R. (1972). *Developmental tasks and education.* New York: Longmans-Green.

Hill, J., & Palmquist, W. (1978). Social cognition and social relations. *International Journal of Behavioral Development, 1,* 1–36.

Hopkins, J. (1977). Sexual behavior in adolescence. *Journal of Social Issues, 33,* 67–85.

Jessor, S., & Jessor, R. (1975). Transitions from virginity to nonvirginity among youth. *Developmental Psychology, 11,* 473–485.

Jossleson, R. (1980). Ego development in adolescence. In J. Adelson (Ed.), *Handbook of adolescent psychology.* New York: Wiley.

Kane, M. J. (1982). *Female athletic participation and status rankings.* Unpublished manuscript, University of Illinois, Urbana-Champaign.

Kelly, J. (1981). *Leisure.* Englewood Cliffs, NJ: Prentice-Hall.

Kelly, H. (1969). The meaning of current dance forms of adolescent girls. *Nursing Research, 17,* 513–519.

Kleiber, D. (1983). Sport and human development: A dialectical interpretation. *Journal of Humanistic Psychology, 23*(4), 76–95.

Kleiber, D., & Hemmer, J. (1981). Sex differences in the relationships of locus of control and recreational sport participation. *Sex Roles, 7,* 801–809.

Kroeger, L. (1980). *"Cruising": The use of automobiles by teenagers as a social/recreation experience.* Unpublished manuscript, University of Illinois, Champaign.

Landers, D., & Landers, D. (1978). Socialization via interscholastic athletics: Its effects on delinquency. *Sociology of Education, 51,* 299–303.

Langston, D. (1981). *The perception of enjoyment in selected activities among delinquent and non-delinquent adolescents.* Unpublished manuscript, University of Illinois, Champaign.

Larson, R., & Csikszentmihalyi, M. (1978). Experiential correlates of time alone in adolescence. *Journal of Personality, 46,* 677–693.

Larson, R., Csikszentmihalyi, M., & Graef, R. (1980). Mood variability and the psychosocial adjustment of adolescents. *Journal of Youth and Adolescence, 9*(6), 469–490.

Larson, R., Csikszentmihalyi, M., & Graef, R. (1982). Time alone in daily experience: Loneliness or renewal. In L. Peplau, & D. Perlman (Eds.), *Loneliness: A source book of current theory, research and therapy.* New York: Wiley.

Lewko, J., & Greendorfer, S. (1979). Family influence and sex differences in children's socialization into sport. In G. Roberts, & K. Newell (Eds.), *Psychology of sport and motor behavior.* Champaign, IL: Human Kinetics.

Manaster, G. (1977). *Adolescent development and the life tasks.* Boston: Allyn and Bacon.

Marcia, J. (1980). Identity in adolescence. In J. Adelson (Ed.), *The handbook of adolescent psychology.* New York: Wiley.

Miller, P., & Simon, W. (1980). The development of sexuality in adolescence. In J. Adelson (Ed.), *The handbook of adolescent psychology.* New York: Wiley.

Michener, J. (1976). *Sports in America.* Greenwich, CT: Random House.

Neulinger, J. (1974). *The psychology of leisure.* Springfield, IL: Thomas.

Noe, F. (1969). An instrumental conception of leisure for the adolescent. *Adolescence, 4,* 385–400.

Noe, F., & Elifson, K. (1976). The pleasures of youth: Parent and peer compliance toward discretionary time. *Journal of Youth and Adolescence, 5*(1), 37–58.

Novak, M. (1976). *The joy of sports.* New York: Basic Books.

Otto, L., & Alwin, D. (1977). Athletics, aspirations and attainments. *Sociology of Education, 42,* 102–113.

Piaget, J., & Inhelder, B. (1958). *The growth of logical thinking from childhood to adolescence.* New York: Basic Books.

Porter, R. (1967). Sports and adolescence. In G. Slovenko, & J. Knight (Eds.), *Motivation in play, games and sport.* Springfield, IL: Thomas.

Rickards, W. (1982). *A comparison of the perception of leisure opportunity between behavior disordered and general education adolescents.* Unpublished doctoral dissertation, University of Illinois, Champaign.

Roberts, J., & Sutton-Smith, B. (1962). Child training and game involvement. *Ethnology, 1,* 166–185.

Schafer, W., & Rehberg, R. (1970). Athletic participation, college aspirations and college encouragement. *Pacific Sociological Review, 13,* 182–186.

Smith, R. (1981). Sports and delinquency. In L. Gross (Ed.), *The parent's guide to teenagers.* New York: MacMillan.

Spady, W. (1970). Lament for the letterman: Effects of peer status and extracurricular activities on goals and achievement. *American Journal of Sociology, 75,* 680–702.

Vener, A., & Stewart, C. (1974). Adolescent sexual behavior in middle America revisited: 1970–1973. *Journal of Marriage and Family, 36,* 728–735.

Winer, F. (1979). The elderly jock and how he got that way. In J. Goldstein (Ed.), *Sports, games and play: Social psychological viewpoints.* New York: Wiley.

Zelnick, M., & Kantner, J. (1972). The probability of premarital intercourse. *Social Science Research, 1,* 335–341.

Chapter XI

CONSTRAINTS ON LEISURE IN MIDDLE AGE

M. Jeanine Bennett

Middle age can be objectively defined simply as a period of time comprising those middle years of life bounded roughly by ages 40 and 65. But here the simplicity ends, for entry into this period of life is heralded by a complex array of new experiences and changing conditions. At this time, events arising from both personal and environmental forces interact in intricate ways to awaken the individual to the arrival of middle age.

So this chapter begins in the middle. The individual is not yet ready to leave the magical years of early adulthood, yet the advertising media and educational agencies no longer lavish devotion. In fact, economic and social forces begin to abandon the life traveler in the later period of this age and long-term physiological changes become noticeable. The beginning of losses and social insecurity that discriminate with age may plot a crisis of identity and disruption to the once youthful personality.

Events of middle age do not always conspire to heap unwelcome constraints or tumultuous disorganization on a person's life. Indeed, middle age can be and often is filled with positive, gratifying experiences and optimistic challenge. Undeniably, though, there is also a variety of both potential and real changes and disturbances which may alter youthful identity and the very pace of time. For example, disrupted career goals or anticipated retirement tends to produce a disordered time and perhaps a disordered life that may unravel one's social fabric and even contribute to the divestment of personal competency and autonomy. Attendant concern about material losses can compound insecurity by yielding increased vulnerability and feelings of impotence.

Such constraints of external origin may compel an unfamiliar

319

internal reorientation to time. With age, time seems to pass more rapidly and a growing sense of urgency may develop to achieve unrealized goals. This paradox of perception of time-compression coupled with a need for more time to complete unfinished hopes and plans can exert a unique and forceful influence on leisure behavior. The accumulation of signals of obsolescence from the social environment combines with a sense of goal-urgency and shortness of time. Thus, constraints are created that compel a reformulation of meanings for time and life itself.

The cumulative impact of interacting factors which may produce constraints on leisure during the middle years of life provides the central theme for this chapter. Discussion will focus initially on the etiology of these constraints on leisure behavior. They will be explored in the context of the disquieting arrival of middle age and the attendant dissonance induced by perceptions of premature disenfranchisement from the mainstream. In addition, time required for adjustment to role changes, internal time constraints, and cultural-societal expectations regarding the meaning of both middle age and leisure will be addressed.

The discussion is based on the premise that the middle age experience can and should be a time of creative growth in response to the challenge of change. However, to the extent that life events, societal expectations, and personal perceptions introduce turmoil, conflict, or disenchantment, these forces create constraints on the individual's pattern of leisure behavior.

Thus, whether leisure becomes a thwarted fantasy or a positive opportunity hinges on new ways of thinking about the latter half of life and a fresh conceptualization of the education-work-leisure triumvirate. The concluding sections will develop a futuristic orientation formulating needed alternative conceptualizations which can reduce constraints on time and leisure during midlife.

THE UNEXPECTED ARRIVAL OF MIDDLE AGE

At the onset of chronological middle age, most midlife individuals are not yet disposed to be "over the hill." But caught at middle age, there is no retreat as the prospect of old age looms even though the feeling of youth remains tantalizingly fresh. As youthful identity gradually but incessantly disappears, the external and internal forces which increasingly affect the aging individual begin to shape the horizon. Cultural signals of obsolescence begin to be transmitted all too clearly. So, although the individual still "feels the same," a new sense of urgency to reach goals and leave one's mark pervades. Time seems to pass more quickly than during the earlier years of life.

Midpoint of life is poignantly evident when the individual recognizes that time has begun to stretch farther behind than forward and one's mortality like that of all others is keenly apparent. Probably, if birth anniversaries and alterations in physical appearance did not incessantly intrude, the inevitable passage into middle age might scarcely be noticed. However, inventory and assessment of expectations, hopes, and obligations must now be balanced with time. Gradually, introspective reflections begin to infringe on leisure time.

The individual seldom fully reckons for the unique episodes that may shift the delicate balance of midcourse time. The most imposing signal of middlescence is the dramatic change in physical features. Biophysiological changes occur throughout the entire body—the bone, muscle, and connective tissue, and cardiorespiratory, sensory, and motor functions alter slightly. Women are reminded of transformations as functions demonstrably slow in the hormonal and reproductive systems and menstruation ceases. Calories that once were parlayed into vivacious energy tend to cling and redistribute their end products so that more body fat is carried in the middle years than at any other age. In contrast, the subcutaneous tissue slowly changes so that the face becomes wrinkled and appears thinner, the limbs seem longer, and the skin and external organs noticeably lose elasticity. Although these changes are subtly progressive since peak growth in the second decade of life, obvious and more rapid alterations now are apparent and effect an increase in time spent monitoring the appearance. For some, minor health problems may quietly portend the increased vulnerability of the physical system to the ravages of time. However, from a physiological perspective, aging is not deleterious to the extent that preferential use of leisure hours will be influenced unless exceptional chronic disease impinges. It is likely that any restrictive reduction in normal physical capabilities during middle age will be the result of sedentary or abusive behaviors.

RETIREMENT—READY OR NOT

For many, midlife brings recognition that one must soon retire to the culturally meaningless role as a consumer of leisure time (Havighurst, 1961). The negative impression of leisure, derived from our heritage of Judeo-Christian notions of "idleness is the devil's handiwork," stigmatizes leisure as a violation of national values, for only through hard work can brief respite in playful leisure be justified. Thus, for middle-aged persons who are uncomfortable with the odious prospect of several decades of enforced leisure, employment may soothe the guilt induced by visions of future idleness.

Work may become an overriding gratification that represses contemplation of playful avocations, so that after years of work some individuals are uncomfortable with the thought of substantial leisure time even though a brief annual vacation can be enjoyed. In a survey of a large sample of Americans aged 46 to 71, 90% of the men and 82% of the women indicated that they would prefer to work even if it were not necessary (Pfeiffer and Davis, 1974). In the same study, 52% of the men and 56% of the women indicated that they derived more pleasure from work than from leisure. Only 13% of the men and 16% of the women reported greater satisfaction in leisure. The remainder found work and leisure to be equally fulfilling.

Time has a tendency to become disordered for work-centered individuals who are not employed. It is not surprising, then, that chief among the anxieties of many middle aged persons is concern for employment security. Indeed, threatened or real loss of employment is viewed as one of the most critical life crises by the work-centered and self-supporting midlife individual.

Locating employment in late middle age is decidedly more hazardous than during the younger years. Not only are financial security and retirement benefits for the remainder of life perceived as threatened, but equally at risk are self- and social authenticity. Maintaining the self-efficacy and authenticity of the individual must become increasingly significant as a social issue, as advancements in technology punitively discard middle aged persons when their work experience and knowledge become obsolete.

The traditional education-work pattern, in which there is a concentration of education in early years followed by work until retirement and without further formal learning, has become anachronistic in our rapidly changing world. Such a pattern is not supportive of authenticity and will remain inadequate until a model is implemented which allows workers time to re-create technical expertise or prepare for career change with the option to continue employment throughout the remainder of life. Flexible work schedules, dual sharing of one job, and teams of semi-retired job sharers suggest adaptive work patterns that can interchange cyclically with leisure and structured learning experiences throughout the entire adult life cycle. Such models can reduce the insidious alienation from a marketplace that progressively discriminates with age and vitiates life during its second half.

In the United States, where adequate employment becomes increasingly scarce for those past 50, the implications for work throughout life are profound. The anxiety that accompanies real or perceived threat of job loss in late middle age can powerfully suppress functional use of time. Loss of employment is almost always accompanied by divestment of those social contacts, roles, identities, and authenticity that work has provided. As mandatory retirement symbolically announces to the world the passage from middle to old age, loss of income, contacts, and role opportunities confound the choices of how the ensuing enforced leisure will be expressed. Urgently needed is a reformulation of the system which compelled Alex Comfort (1976) to describe retirement as "hell" and leisure as a "con." Transition without involuntary disengagement from employment, the opportunity to maintain or regain self-support, and a balance of elected activities offer an enticing alternative to the mandate of enforced retirement and its constraints.

TIME TO ADJUST

Work and nonwork roles and identities acquire complex meanings over time in terms of their usefulness within society. It is understandable that enforced and unexpected role changes require time for sorting out and seeking new meanings. This process of developmental sorting and seeking parallels the function of play in childhood serving as rehearsal and preparation for living successfully. Unfortunately, however, the sociodramatic process enacted by adults in transitional rehearsal is accorded neither the support nor tolerance which society bestows upon the process in childhood. Such cultural intolerance can be a powerful deterrent to effective rehearsal that is needed for a successful transition which maintains a person's self-actualization, competency, and authenticity.

An effective rehearsal can be judged by the extent to which the individual is able to either maintain or find meaning and authenticity in the face of imposed role changes. Thus, the outcome of the transitional rehearsal can be one of either constructive renewal and challenge or, conversely, frustration, resignation, and possibly depression. Unfortunately, depression is a common symptom in midlife that can dissipate time and resources and fog one's clarity of perspective.

How people use time to rehearse and then to accommodate to disruptions in their usual style of living will ultimately determine the nature of the aging experience. Ideally, release from some of life's obligatory activities and working through transitional losses will lead to new experimentation, self-expression, personal growth, and eventually regeneration of a sense of playfulness. As an example, grandparents who remain active and who are playful with their children and grandchildren may remain less susceptible to depression and less likely to perceive themselves as old. On the other hand, for the individual who has succumbed to intense seriousness and introversion, playful leisure may be lost forever from the vocabulary of living.

INTERNAL TIME CONSTRAINTS

Though external time and its duration are measurably the same, internal time seems to differ both during the life span of an individual and among individuals. Youth time can be expansively abundant and only slowly unravels to the first year of the teens; then there seems to be a long interim until age 21 followed by social and emotional crescendos of independent income, marriage, and family. Time use and leisure activities through adolescence and early adulthood are significantly influenced by peer relationships until nesting tensions stimulate a redistribution of time. Then, investment of time is typically redirected to establishing a home, active parenting, and family-type relationships.

It has been the custom in the United States for the husband to develop socioeconomic stability and identity outside the home while the wife has assumed identity as homemaker and mother. Today, adults may be caught up in many roles, but to different degrees each tends to become most centered and find greatest authenticity in the family, partner, work, or social organization. This centeredness will account significantly for the amount of leisure time that is available and affect its use until normative and idiosyncratic experiences ripple the pattern of life choices. Then, changes of gains or of losses over which the individual may wield little or no control perturb stability, role, position, identity, or authenticity and disruptively intrude into the cognitive and physical spheres of activity.

Adaptive transition and the stress responses to life events appear to be relative both to the degree of centeredness and to the adapting mechanisms at the disposal of the individual. Thus, stress from anticipated loss of employment for the work-centered person, or anxiety felt by the family-centered individual when the children leave home (the "empty nest" syndrome) may be expressed by an Adaptive Response Index (Bennett, 1981): the ratio between a perceived loss or change and successful activation of adaptive responses that can be generated from the strength of attachments to other support systems. For example, these might include the spouse, work, or social groups for the family-centered person when the children are gone. Distress will be less during critical midlife events when the woman or man has well-developed adapting capabilities and more than one support system that is as strong or stronger than that attachment which is being bombarded.

Leisure will be constrained during any critical midlife event that requires time to grieve and adapt, and it may be modified markedly for the remainder of life to the extent that the individual does not have the appropriate resources to become reconciled adequately to the new conditions. Lieberman's (1975) data indicated that the strongest predictor of adaptation-maladaptation is the similarity-dissimilarity between a person's Time 1 and Time 2 environments, in which Time 1 is designated as past time and Time 2 is that time currently or yet to be experienced. This notion underscores the radical change in Time 2 from that of Time 1 for those in midlife who must endure drastic or multiple changes. These changes often mean losses of the social, emotional, and intellectual gratifications that have been derived from employment, social activities, active parenting, or significant cohorts and family members. It follows that the closer the person's Time 2 activity resembles the Time 1 preferred style, the more likely any increase in leisure time will be met with continued or heightened satisfaction and happiness.

CULTURAL-SOCIETAL EXPECTATIONS

The dis-ease of both the individual and society toward the physical features of aging affects the entire psychosocioeconomic fabric of life and time during midlife, and it becomes more intense until there is almost total alienation of the very old. Societal discomfort regarding the aging process operates progressively to invalidate individuals of both sexes, but often it is manifested earlier and more intensely against women. The cultural tendency is to label older men as dignified and distinguished, whereas the aging woman more typically is viewed as less effectual and decreasingly attractive. Men will most likely first sense and experience this alienation in the socioeconomic arena.

Contrary to cultural assumptions, the alleged intellectual and biophysiological incompetence associated with chronological aging is a myth. Nevertheless, the stigmas of aging and change in physical appearance persist and consort with the political and economic exigencies of the culture to reduce communication and socioeconomic engagement as the individual ages. The proposition that societal attitudes and behaviors toward age initiate and are accountable for disengagement of the society from the aging person is far more realistic and convincing than the disengagement theory which proposes that the individual willfully arranges to disengage from a familiar social pattern and time-use style. Accordingly, gradual withdrawal from the mainstream might more accurately be viewed as an enforced response of aging individuals to the increasing sense of social and economic powerlessness.

Age-linked pressures that dictate to "act one's age" present another category of cultural constraints on middle-aged demeanor. For example, those who prefer to continue in roles which endorse conventional accoutrements of youth must choose either to endure subtle or overt displeasure of the society or forego their desires. Similarly, age-related codes unique within family, social, and religious organizations will circumscribe the leisure behavior of the adult participant.

Other age-oriented responses that can influence leisure modes are those that are self-imposed as a result of real or perceived physical or mental underperformance: "After all, I'm not as young as I used to be," and "I'm not getting any younger, you know." These insistent reminders to monitor cognitive and affective conditions in terms of age may be further reinforced through incidental interpretation of the actions of others toward aging adults: the inattentiveness of a young clerk toward an older person in a waiting group of young people, or the remark of one's physician or peer "to consider your age." Collectively, behaviors that are outside of the age-graded assumptions of propriety held by society are viewed as violations of age norms.

Election of the oldest President in the history of the United States is a striking example of such a violation which created national concern about the influence of age on mental and physical competence. Another example is the physical prowess of the participants in the Senior Olympics and Master's competitions which has amazed the public because it seems to be unconventional.

In agro-cultures where chronological age does not discriminate so distinctly against involvement throughout the life space, the level of physical strength and stamina seen among the middle aged and very old are inordinate by our standards. The admirable motor capabilities and physical capacities of the healthy aging person in countries such as China suggest that Western society has critically underestimated and misused human potential and has failed to check effectively the cultural and biophysiological variables that precipitate premature agedness.

Seventy-two percent of the population aged 45 to 65 in the United States is reported to have minor to serious chronic physically debilitating restrictions (National Council on Aging, 1978). These debilities cover a broad spectrum of problems such as obesity, arthritis, diabetes, cardiovascular disease, and terminal diseases. For this substantial portion of the middle-aged population, it is likely that socialization into inappropriate and inaccurate age-coded behaviors which generate stress, misuse, and sedentary habits for organisms designed to be active may be responsible for early deterioration of physiological and cognitive capacity far beyond the minor transmutations due to natural aging.

Significantly, men and women who are healthy and engaged in physical activity have been identified as more likely to age successfully (Palmore, 1979). However, understanding is far from complete concerning the interaction between the psychosocial, pathophysiological, and environmental stressors which begin to accumulate during middle age. These stressors may be implicated in the broad spectrum of midlife pathologies, such as obesity, heart disease, and cancer, that contribute to early aging and midlife death. The vulnerability to heart disease in some middle-aged personalities (Friedman and Rosenman, 1975) strongly suggests a connection between stressors and abnormal or possibly accelerated physiological deterioration during the midstage of life.

THE MEANING OF LEISURE IN MIDLIFE

The many definitions for leisure and work operate within their own constraints. The movement to "leisure educate" sets leisure apart as learned, rather than a spontaneous and intrinsic part of life's style and passages. For some, leisure and play are cloaked in the rigor and schedules characteristic of work. For others, work that has been chosen and honed is consummate leisure and is treasured for its potential to keep one in the mainstream.

For those who recall The Depression of the 1930's, residual insecurity may have influenced obsessions about work and leisure, resulting in attitudes and beliefs which are significantly different from those of their descendents. Hopefully the society can rectify its constraining dichotomy of values about work-as-worthy and leisure-as-suspect in order to become emancipated from guilt of "doing nothing" or "having nothing to do." Even so, the orientation remains pervasive in our culture to work hard and psychologically save or earn play time for the middle and later years.

LEISURE—A THWARTED FANTASY?

Playful leisure can become an unfulfilled fantasy when the rhythm of time is disrupted by stressful problems that spill into life's hours. Life events such as those prioritized by Holmes and Rahe (1967) may create crises at any age, but many are predictably ominous and unavoidable during the second half of life. These stressors can include real or threatened loss of spouse, midlife marital maladaptation, unexpected responsibility to care for dependent family members, death of parents, children, or siblings, personal illness, being fired or retired from a job, job change, financial and security diminishment, enforced change in residence and lifestyle, and change in sleep and biological patterns. Although the full effect is not known, insults from these stressors may be accentuated by the normal modest loss of resiliency in various biological systems.

Clearly, these potential stressors may profoundly and unexpectedly rearrange leisure plans which have been scheduled or put off for the middle and late years. Thus, the major developmental task of midlife is to adapt to these and other stressors that cumulatively impact mental and physical time. A midlife that seems to approach standstill or encounters losses and disruptions must be mutated by futuristic resolve.

Butler's (1975) life review is a technique that uses reminiscence in order to integrate the past with the realities of the present for aging persons. It is profitable to the extent that it develops an equilibrium that will then lead to the attitude that "you are your future." A realistic futurism in middle and late life can activate imaginative self-directedness and willingness to continue to risk. Such self-determined intention retains a sense of control over one's lifetime which often diminishes with aging but is fundamental for hope and continued fulfillment.

Concomitant with realistic futurism is the need for creative support and acceptance from society. Unfortunately, in a culture which weighs worth based on productivity, the socialization process for aging adults can be harsh. The late middle-aged person must anticipate the possibility of spending decades of remaining time without productive employment, often in sculpted sensory experiences at segregated centers. The result is wasteful and inhumane; figuratively, in the apt words of one adult, "How much bingo can you play?"

It is noteworthy that both life satisfaction and happiness are low during middle age. In contrast, youth have a high level of happiness and high life satisfaction (George, 1980). Highest incidence of psychoneurosis, suicide, depression, disillusionment with marriage, self-doubt, and desperation that time is running out to complete life as planned, creates a "crisis pile" in the middle years (Stevens-Long, 1979).

As Levinson (1977) reports, 80% of men beyond age 40 have experienced tumultuous struggles both within themselves and with the external world during their middle years. Unexpected and novel life events precipitate asynchrony and introspective uncertainty in the changing relationship between self and environment. Cumulative collection and interaction of stress-inducing events in close time-space intensify the stress level and complicate the selection and use of effective adaptive strategies.

Because these disruptions to baseline lifestyle characteristically begin to accumulate in midlife, the stress quotient and drain on internal time can accelerate rapidly. Assumptions that hard work and striving throughout life guarantee stability and security later on often prove to be naive and faulty. Instead, shattered illusions may complicate and compress time that must be spent adjusting to

changes and rebuilding in midlife. Development of skills to anticipate midlife events and to cope with changes and availability of
external support systems may be important hedges against a
tarnished middle age and the cultural false promises of leisurely
golden years.

A NEW CONCEPT FOR LEISURE

A cultural revision of the life plan in which the three major
elements of education, work, and leisure interchange in adaptable
and cyclical patterns throughout adult life would provide for
more behavioral flexibility in the event one component becomes
diminished. Interwoven with work, extended periods of leisure
would more likely receive societal and individual approbation. In
such a model, work need no longer be the dominant theme, but
would be shared in continuing exploration with education and
leisure. The breaks in life's pattern would be less severe than those
experienced by the contemporary individual at the crossroads of
graduation from school and again at mandatory retirement. There
would be less need to spend time, rehearsing the impending
passages into middle and old age with their accompanying crises
in identity and security. Late life might at least transcend the
status of a wrinkled childhood filled with enforced leisure.

Obviously, if there were no changes, life would become stagnant.
However, an integrated lifetime of work, education, and leisure
could become its own source of continual growth and development until death. As it is now, activities center around youth with
only incidental concern for elders.

The masses of children from the "baby boom" era are encountering their middle years as demonstrated by the remark that
members of the "Hair" generation are losing theirs. This segment
of the population, the youth culture of the 1960 and 1970 era, will
become the middle majority in the next decades and will comprise
the majority of the "gray culture" in the years which follow. They
have been identified as more vigorous and better educated with an
expectancy of more middle and late years than their elders. Perhaps the impact of their massive population and the active conduct of their early years will assure a lasting influence in political

and social activism. But will the culture and media that have courted them during youth and fashioned their trends and fads follow them through the years to complement and flatter their aging minds and bodies? Parents and grandparents of this generation have received a message of cultural obsolescence and disenfranchisement from the canons of this massive youth network. They have been compelled to an assessment of an impotent self-image. Their developmental task has been to recognize the conditions and attempt to make sense of the distance created between themselves and younger adults. How will the same passage of their children into an older age differ? What will be the passage that will chart their children's sense of time in midlife and beyond?

The philosophy of lifelong learning that is evolving is one important and promising concept that can deal with leisure and provide counsel for those traversing midlife with its accompanying anticipation of increased non-assigned time. The school campus provides a milieu in which the society can cross the barriers of age to begin to realign its attitudes and valuations toward the life-time of its citizens, and toward the work and leisure fulfillment of its population throughout the post-youth life span. Adults need this accepting climate in which it is "okay" to be older, to be wrinkled, to change, to risk new goals, to work through transient conflicts and life transitions, and to become better masters of their time as they age.

CHALLENGE AS OPPORTUNITY

The chapter of middle life is founded upon time. A life is time. Leisure is time. As the years pass, time can become inordinately overcommitted to responding to the pleasures and prescriptions of the culture and of others at the expense of self-care. But the same circumstances that demand adaptation can afford opportunity for self-directed change and a chance to explore the art of self-concern. The transitions of middle age are a third quarter chance to develop a midlife morality of commitment to the self—to identify and not neglect those attitudes and experiences that will enrich the remainder of Life's Time.

REFERENCES

Bennett, M. J. (1981). *Adaptive Response Index (ARI)—A hypothetical index for the measurement and prediction of adaptive response potential to critical life events in the adult.* Unpublished paper, University of Oregon, Eugene.

Butler, R. N. (1975). *Why survive? Being old in America.* New York: Harper and Row.

Comfort, A. (1976). *A good age.* New York: Crown.

Friedman, M., & Rosenman, R. H. (1975). *Type A behavior and your heart.* Greenwich, CT: Fawcett.

George, L. K. (1980). *Role transitions in later life.* Monterey: Brooks/Cole.

Havighurst, R. J. (1961). The nature and values of meaningful free-time activity. In R. J. Kleemeier (Ed.), *Aging and leisure.* New York: Oxford University Press.

Holmes, T. H., & Rahe, R. H. (1967). The Social Readjustment Rating Scale. *Journal of Psychosomatic Research, 11,* 213–218.

Levinson, D. J. (1977). The male mid-life crises. In N. K. Scholossberg, & A. D. Entine (Eds.), *Counseling adults.* Monterey: Brooks/Cole.

Lieberman, M. A. (1975). Adaptive processes in late life. In N. Datan, & L. H. Ginsberg (Eds.), *Life-span developmental psychology: Normative Life Crises.* New York: Academic Press.

National Council on Aging. (1978). *Fact book on aging: A profile of America's older population.* Washington, D.C.: Author.

Palmore, E. (1979). Predictors of successful aging. *Gerontologist, 19*(5), 427–431.

Pfeiffer, E., & Davis, G. C. (1974). The use of leisure time in middle life. In E. Palmore (Ed.), *Normal aging II.* Durham, NC: Duke University Press.

Stevens-Long, J. (1984 2nd edition). *Adult life developmental processes.* Palo Alto: Mayfield.

Chapter XII

CONSTRAINTS IN LATER LIFE

By Francis A. McGuire

The American society is growing older. Approximately 5,000 persons reach their 65th birthday daily. At the same time, about 3,600 persons aged 65 or over die. Therefore, there is a net increase of 1,400 individuals every day, or approximately 511,000 per year, who enter into the arbitrarily designated category of old age (Harris, 1978). Today one out of every ten Americans, or 22.4 million people, are 65 years of age or over. By the year 2000 it is expected that one out of every eight individuals in this country will be at least 65 years of age. This means that 30.6 million people will be in this age group. Simply put, more people are living longer than ever before and this trend can be expected to continue. It is evident that we are experiencing the "graying of America." Demographic data attest to the fact that the quantity of life has increased for Americans.

But what of the quality of life? As early as 1961 Robert Havighurst expressed concern about the need to not merely add years to life, but also to add life to those years. He recognized the importance of enjoying life and deriving satisfaction from it at any age. Many of today's older individuals are desirous of an active, involved lifestyle (Cowgill, 1977). It is through this active involvement that quality can be added to the later years. Atchley (1977) suggested that this active involvement can be attained by either finding work substitutes to fill the unobligated time experienced by many older individuals, or by using this time to pursue leisure activities. Neugarten (1975) predicted that older individuals will seek out a wide range of options and opportunities and will seek environments which maximize the use of their increased leisure. In addition, they will want an "age-irrelevant" society in which constraints to leisure based on chronological age are removed. One of the key elements in adding life to the later years appears to lie in the provision of leisure opportunities to meet existing needs and desires. As an individual enters into what has been labeled as old age he or she experiences many role changes. Along with retirement comes a loss of the work role. Reduced income may result in a perceived reduction of the "family head" role. The parent role will be lost as children grow and leave the household. A widow or widower no longer has a spouse role to play. What can be done about this role loss? Kutner, Fanshel, Togo and Langner (1956) stated that leisure activities may be a functional substitute for employment, family rearing and homemaking. Havighurst (1970) suggested that one way to eliminate adjustment problems in old age is to adopt the role of "leisure time user." However, this may not be easily accomplished.

It has been suggested by Goldman (1971) that it is appropriate to "use loss of choice as a measure of aging" (p. 158). He presented a hypothetical curve which illustrated the changes in choice opportunities with age. It indicated that beginning at approximately age 60 there is a steady decline in opportunities to make choices. He listed several reasons for this constriction. They included the following:

1. Cultural and environmental factors
    a. Cultural pressures to accept a particular role in a particular age range.
    b. Social and economic age discrimination
    c. Aging of friends and associates
2. Internal factors
    a. Physiological limitations in energy, speed and endurance
    b. Psychological limitations in attention span, memory, etc.
    c. Decline in drive and initiative
    d. Emotional factors such as loss of self-confidence, fear of health disaster, exaggeration of limitations imposed by society
    e. Prejudices and related reasons
    f. Disuse atrophy of social skills and connections

If these factors exist, as they do for some older individuals, then leisure choices will be constricted as well as choices in all spheres of behavior.

Schwartz and Proppe (1970) echoed this apparent constriction of choice with age. They postulated that old age is marked by a loss of control and effectiveness within the environment. Since leisure is built on a sense of control and freedom, this postulated loss would result in a decreased ability to adopt a leisure time user role in the later years.

Although the authors cited above were concerned with loss of choice in all spheres of behavior, it can be assumed that leisure choices are also constricted since leisure is part of the whole of social behaviors. If life is marked by loss of choice, then leisure will also be a victim of choice constriction.

Atchley (1977) addressed the question of whether older individuals face increasing difficulty in using leisure time. He wrote:

> Leisure participation in later years is individualized in the sense that each person is free to choose from a wide variety of possibilities. Yet this variety is limited by physical, financial, and transportation factors. A few older people are hamstrung by an ethic that does not allow play without work. Personality, family, and social class values narrow the field of choice still more. Lack of facilities can also limit options. If the older person is to be able to enjoy creative, self-enhancing leisure in retirement, options must be as wide as possible (pp. 176–177).

Crandall (1980) supported the belief that leisure opportunities may decline in the later years. He stated that "most of the activities in which the aged would like to engage are not available in their community" (p. 361). It appears that one of the paradoxes of old age is that just when free time increases (Kaplan, 1979, estimated that the average retiree has 20,000 hours of unobligated time) and the need to use this time for leisure may be more important than ever, the options, access to those options, and resources necessary to take advantage of that time diminish.

It is necessary to be aware of the constraints which limit leisure and work toward the creation of a physical, social, and psychological environment which eliminates, or at least mitigates, them. Such an effort is needed to open leisure to individuals of any age. There is a need to remove those obstacles which limit choice and result in an incongruence between the activities people undertake during their free time and the activities in which they would prefer to participate during that time. The joining of these two spheres, actual and desired leisure involvement, by the identification and elimination of those factors which limit options, access to those options and resources needed to take advantage of them is important for age groups. The removal of those constraints is necessary to make the widest possible range of leisure opportunities available to the individual.

The need to increase opportunities for choice and control in leisure is important not only to leisure satisfaction but also to life satisfaction. Schwartz and Proppe (1970) stated that "loss of control seems highly correlated with both subjective and objective estimates of 'successful' or 'satisfactory' aging" (p. 230). Many older people are forced to relinquish control in many areas of life. Forced retirement, declining health, loss of leadership roles in organizations, the growing up of children, loss of a driver's license, and reduced income may all result in declining feelings of mastery and control. For many older people, leisure may be one of the few remaining areas where control can be exerted. There is a growing body of evidence that involvement in activities, including leisure, is significantly related to life satisfaction in the later years (Larson, 1978). The importance of identifying and eliminating constraints to leisure involvement is present for all age groups. However, because of the impact of loss of control in later life, the need to return as much choice and control in leisure behavior is magnified with older age groups. To do so has implications not only for leisure but also for life in general. It allows older people to move one step closer to adding life to their years.

LEISURE CONSTRAINTS AND THE AGING PROCESS

Aging itself, or the passage of years, is not a constraint to leisure involvement. However, the concommitants of aging, the things that happen during the years, may impede leisure involvement. The losses which accompany the aging process are variable. No two people age in the same way or at the same rate. It is important too, not to lose sight of the individual. However, many of the factors discussed below will become a factor in the lives of many individuals and directly effect their leisure.

According to Atchley (1980) biological and health changes in later life are important because "they represent the concrete physiological limits around which social arrangements would ideally be built" (p. 38). Health problems in later life are a major limiting factor in leisure behavior. The percentage of individuals reporting some degree of limitation in activity involvement as a result of poor health is large. Harris (1978) reported that over 45% of the individuals surveyed in a national sample had some limitation in activity. Chronic health conditions such as heart problems, diabetes, asthma and arthritis were the major causes of activity limitation.

Visual and auditory impairments are also potential constraints on leisure involvement. There is a gradual decline in visual acuity with increasing age. Approximately 7% of all individuals aged 65 to 74 and 16% of those 75 and over are blind or have severe visual impairment. Up to 60% of the aged show some signs of cataracts. The effect of visual impairments of everyday activity can be significant (Crandall, 1980). The effect of loss of sight, diminished visual acuity, difficulties in adjusting to changes in light intensity, and problems in coping with glare are obvious. Individuals who have such problems may not be able to drive to leisure locales, may be deprived of total participation unless adaptions are made, or may feel uncomfortable or embarrassed and therefore not engage in leisure activities. Hearing impairments may also result in reduced leisure involvement. Approximately 13% of all individuals aged 65–74 have hearing difficulties. Additionally, 26% of those 75 and over have serious hearing problems. As a result, activities requiring the ability to hear, such as dancing, attending concerts, or listening to the radio, may be closed to hearing impaired individuals unless adaptions are made.

Aging is marked by a general decline in all biologic functioning. These declines can have a major impact on leisure involvement and function as a constraint on participation. Lowered energy levels, losses in all five senses, difficulty in responding to and recovering from stress, and decreased functioning in all the systems and organs of the body can exact a toll on leisure participation.

Psychomotor performance declines with increasing age. Atchley wrote that "the most important difference from the point of view of social functions are in reaction time, speed and accuracy of response, and the ability to make complex responses" (p. 49). In addition to declines in reaction time there may be a decrease in learning and memory (Crandall, 1980). In spite of declines in this area, it appears that many individuals do not curtail everyday activities as a result. According to Crandall:

> Although the initial image of the psychology of aging is fairly depressing and bleak, a closer examination of the literature reveals some positive elements. For example, although the aged do not perform as well in laboratory studies as young adults, the differences in scores are often very small. Although the differences may be statistically significant, it is doubtful that the differences are significant in most cases in everyday life (p. 267).

If there is an impact on functioning as a result of losses in the psychomotor area it is primarily a shift from speed to accuracy. Activities which require an accurate response, such as puzzles, may take older individuals longer to complete. However, they are still capable of pursuing such activities.

It appears that the declines accompanying old age have been over emphasized. As a result of ageism, the existence of age related myths, and inaccurate research, the plight of older individuals has been seen as a negative experience. The assumption that many of the biological and psychological losses which accompany the aging process result in decreased functioning is not always true. Many older people are able to cope with and adapt to the losses of aging. Nonetheless, these declines do result in decreased opportunity for leisure involvement for many individuals.

Other factors which are not related to aging per se but which are social impositions may act to reduce leisure involvement. Forces such as reduced income, negative attitudes of aging and the aged, lack of transportation, and lack of accessible facilities may reduce involvement.

The elderly are a low income group. In 1975, families headed by a person 65 years of age or over had a median income of $8,057. Families with household heads under 65 had median incomes of

$14,698 (Harris, 1978). Income can play a major role in leisure involvement. In addition to the direct problem caused by inability to pay for leisure activities, low income is also related to poor health which can serve to reduce participation. Approximately 25% of those individuals aged 65 or over were classified as either poor or "near poor" in 1975 (Harris, 1978). It is unlikely that these individuals were able to pursue their leisure desires. Individuals 65 years of age and over spent the same proportion of their income (6.5%) on recreation as individuals aged 55 to 64. However, their income was less and therefore, their actual expenditure for leisure was less. This indicates a constriction with age in involvement in activities which cost money.

Transportation may also be a major factor in limiting leisure involvement. If individuals are unable to get to leisure opportunities, that is, if they lack access to resources, they will be severely limited in their leisure behavior. The percent of households not owning an automobile goes from a low of 12% in families where the head of the household is between the ages of 35 and forty to a high of 39% in those families where the head of the household is 65 or over.

Other factors which may constrict leisure involvement are related to an individual's attitudes. A strong belief in the work ethic may make it difficult for individuals to become leisure time users (Miller, 1965). If leisure has always been earned through work, the absence of work makes it impossible to justify leisure. There is uncertainty as to whether this is in fact a major problem (Atchley, 1971).

Fear of crime, lack of facilities, lack of time and lack of leisure companions may also restrict leisure behavior. The section which follows examines the research which has attempted to determine the role of these, and other forces, is constricting leisure behavior.

RESEARCH INTO LEISURE CONSTRAINTS

When examining the role of constraints in limiting leisure involvement in later life, it is important to establish whether there is an incongruence between actual and desired behavior as a result of these limiting factors. It may be that identifiable constraints do exist but that their effect on behavior is negligible. The first part of this section will examine research which looked at the incongruence between actual and desired leisure behavior in old age.

Once it has been established that leisure behavior is in fact disrupted by constraints, it then becomes necessary to identify them. In this way it is possible to assist individuals in overcoming the factors which result in the inability to engage in desired activities. The second part of this section will review research which has examined and identified the constraints to leisure experienced by older individuals.

Little research has been done which focuses specifically on whether older individuals are able to participate in leisure at desired levels. Chalfen (1956), and Cowgill and Baulch (1962), found that a discrepancy existed between actual and desired leisure involvement. Bultena and Wood (1970) and Oliver (1971) found that moving into a leisure rich environment, such as a retirement community, increased leisure participation. Their findings indicated that prior to moving to such settings, individuals were unable to be as involved in leisure as desired and that living in such communities eliminated barriers which reduced participation. Carp (1978–1979) sought to determine whether moving to a living environment rich in leisure opportunities would increase activity level. She assumed that a "latent demand" for leisure existed and that the rate of observed activity involvement of the study participants was lower than their rate of preference as a result of environmental limitations. Carp hypothesized that activity rate would rise in the presence of an environment which provided increased opportunity for activity. Data were collected over an eight year period from individuals moving into a senior citizen high rise and an equivalent group of non-movers. Those people moving into the high rise, or the opportunity rich environment, participated more in volunteer activities, participated in a significantly larger number of leisure activities, participated in more active activities, showed a smaller increase in the passive use of time, and felt they were more active than the non-movers. Carp included that:

> The data document the existence of 'latent demand' for activity within the community residential elderly population and indi-

cate that environmental intervention can increase activity rate among older people over what it would have been otherwise. Since better life satisfaction and life expectancy accompanied this higher level of activity, it seems safe to conclude also that for intact people who choose it—a living environment which provides for and expects an active life-style can be a beneficial setting in which to grow old (p. 88).

McGuire (1979) studied 125 individuals residing in their own homes in a large mid-western community. The individuals were asked to indicate whether they were satisfied with their leisure involvement or whether there were some activities in which they would have liked to either increase or initiate participation. It was found that the activities in which the respondents were actually involved were not related to those in which they would have preferred to be involved. The respondents were primarily engaged in passive activities, often done alone. Many of the activities in which they were actually engaged can be seen to be "traditional" senior citizen activities and in keeping with what is believed to be the activity preferences of older people. However, the activities in which the respondents indicated an interest in either increasing involvement or initiating involvement were primarily active and/or social activities. It appeared that a large discrepancy existed between actual and desired leisure behavior.

Lambing (1972) studied leisure preferences of retired black residents of Gainesville, Florida and found that many of the respondents were able to identify a wide range of activities in which they were not involved but would have liked to have been. Similarly, data gathered from a sample of individuals in their later years, as part of the 1975 Pennsylvania Outdoor Recreation Survey, indicated that individuals 65 years of age and over were not participating in many outdoor activities even though they wished to. These activities included bicycling, swimming, tennis, fishing, golf, camping, boating, and hunting.

A gap between actual and desired participation by the elderly in outdoor recreation activities was also found by Strain and Chappell (1982). They examined the participation patterns of older residents in two rural communities in Manitoba, Canada.

Finally, Seleen (1982) documented the deleterious impact constraints can have on life satisfaction. They surveyed 205 individuals, attending senior citizen centers in Rhode Island, and found respondents spending their time as they desired even more satisfied with their lives than those experiencing an incongruence between actual and desired time use.

These studies provide evidence that older individuals are not participating in those activities they prefer. It is clear that environmental intervention can reduce the difficulties experienced in attempting to participate in desired activities. It appears that the "latent demand" for leisure activities identified by Carp (1978–1979) can be eliminated by removing constraints to involvement in leisure activities.

The first step in removing constraints which limit leisure opportunities and result in a latent demand for leisure is the identification of those factors which block leisure fulfillment. Once these constraints have been identified, they can be eliminated and thereby create an environment conducive to freedom choice in leisure participation.

Anderson (1963) defined a constraint as "any factor which tends to limit the full range of behavior and possibilities of exploration" (p. 235). If leisure activities are defined as chosen primarily for their own sake, then it is imperative that factors which limit this choice be eliminated. Little information, however, is available about the specific constraints to leisure experienced by individuals. The factors previously discussed, including health, psychomotor decline, income and transportation, may be constraints to leisure. However, few studies have been conducted which systematically examine these and other possible constraints.

Trela and Simmons (1971) studied factors affecting participation in senior citizens centers. They interviewed joiners and non-joiners of a center in Cleveland, Ohio. When examining reasons for not joining the center, it was found that:

> The majority of S's were constrained by competing activities and interests; ambivalence toward organizational activity; poor health; or limited access to transportation (p. 47).

They also asked individuals who had terminated their memberships in the center their reasons for doing so. Competing activities and interests resulted in 31.1% of the terminations. This was followed by poor health (16.0%), moving from the community (14.2%), center not meeting expectations (12.3%), and death (15.1%).

Harris and Associates (1976) conducted a nationwide study of the myth and reality of aging in America. One of the areas examined was participation in senior centers. It was found that only 18% of the study respondents had attended a center in the year preceeding the study. The reasons given for not attending organized programs in senior citizen centers, in rank order from the most to least frequent response, were:

1. No facilities available; don't know where they are located
2. No time; too busy
3. Transportation problems
4. Poor health
5. Never got around to it
6. Have no one to go with; don't want to go alone
7. Not interested
8. Afraid to go out at night; fear of crime
9. Too young; they are just for old people

Goodrow (1975) interviewed 268 randomly selected residents of Knox County, Tennessee, to identify the factors which constrained their participation in continuing education programs. All the interviewees were at least 65 years of age. They were asked to select those reasons, from a list of 31 presented to them, which would keep them from participating in an adult learning program. They were also asked to identify and rank order the three most important serious constraints. Poor vision was reported to be the most serious constraint. It was followed by poor health, home responsibilities, and lack of transportation. It was found that there was a sex difference in the constraints to participation. Males were primarily constrained by the strict attendance requirements of such courses, failure to include courses of interest to them, job responsibilities, low grades in the past, not enjoying studying, the amount of time required, being tired of schools and classrooms, and feeling too old to learn. Females reported that a lack of desired courses, poor eyesight, home responsibilities, not liking to go out at night, lack of transportation, too much red tape in getting enrolled, not liking to take tests, and an ability to learn without going to classes were the primary reasons they did not participate in organized continuing education programs.

A study by McAvoy (1976) was designed to determine the recreation activities preferred by the elderly residents of Minnesota and the problems they encountered in attempting to participate in preferred activities. He interviewed 540 non-institutionalized residents of Minnesota who were randomly selected from nine target areas throughout the state. They were asked to identify the five activities in which they most preferred to participate and whether they were participating in them as often as they wished. If not, it was assumed that they were experiencing constraints to their leisure involvement. They were then asked to indicate which of nine constraints were preventing their participation in desired activities. Based on interviewee response, McAvoy added a tenth constraint, fear of crime, to his original nine. The constraints identified by the study participants, ranked from the most frequently identified to the least, were as follows:

1. Lack of physical ability
2. Lack of companionship
3. Lack of time
4. Lack of transportation
5. Finances
6. Fear of crime
7. Lack of facilities
8. Physical barriers
9. Lack of skill
10. Social pressures

In examining the change in constraints over time, McAvoy found that lack of physical ability and transportation were more important to the older respondents while lack of time was more important to the younger respondents.

DeGroot (1976) also examined constraints to leisure involvement and the differences in constraints experienced by older individuals and younger ones. He randomly selected the names of 1,000 individuals from the telephone directory of Tempe, Arizona. He used a mail questionnaire to measure the frequency of participation, attitudes toward participation, and whether individuals were able to participate as often as they would have liked in leisure activities. If an individual indicated that he was not participating in an activity as often as he would have liked, he was asked to state why not. DeGroot collected 625 useable questionnaires. The reasons for not participating in desired activities, in rank order, were:

1. Lack of time
2. Lack of facilities
3. Lack of money
4. Too old
5. Poor health
6. The weather

The percentage of respondents who listed health as a limiting factor was higher for the older respondents than for the younger one while the percentage listing money decreased with age.

Scott and Zoernick (1977) conducted in-depth interviews with 366 individuals over the age of 55 who were residing in Central Missouri. They also interviewed a matched sample of 357 people under 55 years of age. Each interviewee was asked to indicate whether each of seven factors constrained their leisure involvement. The younger respondents indicated that the most prohibitive factor to their leisure involvement was cost. This was followed by time, interest, availability, health, transportation, and skill. The older group reported that health was the primary factor constraining their leisure involvement. This was followed by interest, cost, availability, transportation, time, and skill.

The constraints to outdoor recreation participation identified by Strain and Chappell (1982) were similar to those found in previous studies. Thirty-six percent of the eighty individuals interviewed claimed lack of facilities prevented participation in desired activities. This was followed by lack of time (17%), lack of companionship (15%), health problems (14%) and transportation (4%). It was found that asking respondents specific questions about constraints resulted in different findings. For example, 14% of the respondents identified transportation as a problem when asked to name constraints for specific activities. The authors concluded that identified constraints may vary as a result of how the question is asked.

McGuire (1979) conducted a comprehensive study of leisure constraints in advanced adulthood. He interviewed 125 residents of a large mid-western city. They ranged in age from 45 to 93 and had a mean age of 63.7. A questionnaire was developed which incorporated the leisure constraints identified in previous studies. Respondents to telephone interviews were asked to indicate which of 30 potential constraints were responsible for any discrepancy between their actual and desired leisure involvement. The mean number of constraints identified by the respondents was 9.59. If a respondent indicated that a constraint did in fact limit his leisure involvement, he was asked to indicate whether it was a "somewhat important" or "very important" deterrent to leisure involvement. Nine constraints were either somewhat important or very important to at least 40% of the respondents. These were: lack of time (68% identified this as a constraint); the weather (68%); lack of money (58.4%); having more important things to do (53.6%); being too busy with work (44.8%); health reasons (44.8%); being too busy with other activities (49.6%); lack of energy (48%); and, not having anyone to do them with (40%). Eight constraints were identified by fewer than 20% of the respondents as limiting their leisure. Included were: a feeling that family or friends would not approve of participation; fear others would make fun of participation; feeling guilty about doing leisure activities; fear of making a mistake; having to make too many decisions; not getting a feeling of accomplishment from leisure; and a feeling of being no good at the activities. The most important constraints were primarily time related. The least important constraints were related to feelings and attitudes toward leisure involvement.

The question of whether constraints to leisure experienced by older individuals differed from those of younger individuals was also examined. Eleven of the thirty constraints were significantly related to age. Lack of friends doing preferred activities, fear of crime, feeling too old to learn activities, health reasons, lack of transportation, not getting a feeling of accomplishment from leisure involvement, and a feeling that family and friends would not approve, were more important to the older respondents. Younger individuals indicated that lack of time, being too busy with work, too many family responsibilities, and having more important things to do were constraints more often that of older individuals. Although the types of constraints varied by age, it was found that the total number of constraints to leisure was not age related.

Based on the studies reviewed above it is evident that identifiable constraints to leisure do exist. The effect of these constraints is the limitation of the freedom of choice required for leisure. Examination of the studies point toward the possible existence of three broad categories of constraints.

The first category of constraints are those which result from an abundance of choices and the need to eliminate some because of time limitations. Many individuals are unable to be involved in leisure at desired levels because they are too busy with work or family, have more important things to do, or were too busy with other activities. The discrepancy between actual and desired leisure results from a decision to sacrifice participation in some activities in order to have time to do others. Individuals constrained by this type of limitation are unable to find enough hours to do all the things they would either like to do or are obligated to do. Their problems with leisure do not arise from a lack of options, access, or resources. Rather, the restriction on their leisure behavior was caused by too many options, in all realms of behavior and too little time. The individual in this situation has some control over the extent to which such constraints will limit leisure. However, it appears from the above studies that these types of constraints become less important as age increases. The role loss which accompanies the aging process removes many time related constraints. Therefore, many older individuals are not compelled to limit leisure to meet other obligations.

The second category of constraints appear to arise from attitudes held by the individual which result in self-imposed limits on leisure choices. Constraints such as feeling too old to learn new activities, not knowing how to do activities, feeling guilty about leisure participation, fear that family or friends would not approve of involvement, and fear of making a mistake fall into this cluster. These constraints are related to the need for options for leisure to exist. They limit leisure by reducing options an individual perceives himself as having. The image an individual has of himself as a result of internal feelings limit participation. Even if resources required for leisure and access to those resources are present, they are inoperable. The opportunities they imply are closed to individuals whose attitudes and self-image do not allow them to take advantage of them.

The third cluster of constraints result from conditions beyond the control of the individual experiencing the constraints but within the control of others. Lack of transportation, lack of money, and lack of facilities fall into this category. Forces external to the individual impinge on his leisure by limiting resources and access to resources. Those activities in which an individual is interested and which he considers viable leisure options are unavailable if constraints of this type are present. Leisure options are eliminated by forces beyond his control and the direction his free time will take is externally controlled. The data indicate that constraints of this type become more salient with increasing age.

The above studies seem to support the belief of Goldman (1971) that increasing age is marked by decreasing control. The types of constraints to leisure experienced by individuals shift from self-imposed time related constraints to either external factors such as money or transportation or restrictions such as health and attitudes.

IMPLICATIONS FOR THE LEISURE SERVICE PROVIDER

If leisure is to be a path to fulfillment, growth and development in later life, it is necessary that individuals be able to participate in self-selected and self-directed leisure activities. However, constraints prohibit some older individuals from exerting control over their leisure. If leisure is to be used to its fullest, people must have options to pursue during their free time, access to those options, and resources to take advantage of them. However, constraints can block the options available to a person, limit access, and reduce resources. One way to reduce the constraints to leisure is by structuring the physical, social and psychological environment in such a way that constraints are eliminated, by-passed or compensated for. A function, therefore, of the leisure service provider is to act as a social environmentalist. This role entails identifying and reducing those factors limiting leisure involvement. The actual provision of activities, which is often seen as the major function of the leisure service provider, is only one step in this process of social planning. If external resources, such as facilities, equipment, transportation or money, are limiting participation, then the service provider must either provide the resources, assist in finding substitute activities, or assist the participant in finding required resources. If an individual is constrained from participating in activities because of self-image, then the building of an improved self-image becomes part of the service provider's function. If an individual is blocked from participation by a negative attitude toward leisure, then the provider may need to institute a leisure counseling program designed to assist in the development of a more positive outlook. If an individual is unaware of opportunities to meet leisure desires, then the service provider must provide leisure education to increase awareness. The focus shifts from activities to the creation of an environment which is as free of constraints as possible.

Most adults can provide for their own leisure and are able to make their own leisure decisions. However, they may need help in maximizing their leisure choices through the recognition and elimination of constraints. The traditional approach in providing leisure services has been a decision to offer particular activities to people, often based on tradition, the area of expertise of the leadership, or assumed knowledge of potential participants, and expect them to be flexible enough to participate. However, a more realistic approach would be to allow individuals to select their own activities and then for the service provider to be flexible and resourceful enough to help them meet their leisure desires. Such an approach demands a re-focusing on the part of the individual providing leisure services. The focus is not on activities and getting as many people as possible into an organized program but rather on identifying individual leisure needs and interests and helping individuals remove whatever obstacles exist which prevent them from realizing their leisure preferences. Control shifts from the service provider to the leisure participant. To do any less reduces the potential of leisure as a major force in an individual's life.

As roles are lost in later life, such as the worker role, spouse role, and parent role, opportunities to make choices and exert control narrow. As a result the urgency of eliminating constraints to leisure choices increases. All individuals experience constraints on their leisure behavior. However, the limited opportunities for choice and control in other spheres of behavior, in addition to the increase in externally imposed leisure constraints, increases the importance for the leisure service provider to adopt an environmentalist role. This helps assure control over a major sphere of behavior.

REFERENCES

Anderson, J. E. (1963). Environment and meaningful activity. In R. H. Williams, C. Tibbitts, & W. Donahue (Eds.), *Processes of aging: Social and psychological perspectives.* New York: Atherton Press.

Atchley, R. C. (1971). Retirement and leisure participation: continuity or crises. *The Gerontologist, 11,* 13–17.

Atchley, R. C. (1977). *The social forces in later life* (2nd ed.). Belmont: Wadsworth.

Atchley, R. C. (1980). *The social forces in later life* (3rd ed.). Belmont: Wadsworth.

Bultena, G., & Wood, V. (1970). Leisure orientation and recreational activities of retirement community residents. *Journal of Leisure Research, 2,* 3–15.

Carp, F. M. (1978–1979). Effects of the living environment on activity and the use of time. *International Journal of Aging and Human Development, 9,* 75–91.

Chalfen, L. (1956). Leisure-time adjustment of the aged: II. activities and interest and some factors influencing choice. *Journal of Genetic Psychology, 88,* 261–276.

Cowgill, D. O. (1977, September-October). The revolution of age. *The Humanist,* pp. 10–13.

Cowgill, D. O., & Baulch, N. (1962). The uses of leisure time by older people. *The Gerontologist, 2,* 47–50.

Crandall, R. C. (1980). *Gerontology: A behavioral science approach.* Reading, MA: Addison Wesley.

DeGroot, W. L. (1976). *Analysis of leisure time profiles of selected adult males.* Doctoral dissertation, Arizona State University.

Goldman, S. (1971). Social aging, disengagement and loss of choice. *The Gerontologist, 11,* 158–162.

Goodrow, B. A. (1975). Limiting factors in reducing participation in older adult learning opportunities. *The Gerontologist, 15,* 418–422.

Harris, C. S. (1978). *Fact book on aging.* Washington, D.C.: National Council on Aging.

Harris, L., et al. (1976). *The myth and reality of aging in America.* Washington: National Council on Aging.

Havighurst, R. J. (1961). Successful aging. *The Gerontologist, 1,* 8–13.

Havighurst, R. J. (1970). Leisure and aging. In A. M. Hoffman (Ed.), *The daily needs and interests of old people.* Springfield: C. C Thomas Publishing Company.

Kaplan, M. (1979). *Leisure: Lifestyle and lifespan.* Philadelphia: Saunders.

Kutner, B., Fanshel, D., Togo, A., & Langner, T. (1956). *Five hundred over sixty.* New York: Russell Sage.

Lambing, M. L. B. (1972). Leisure time pursuits among retired blacks by social status. *The Gerontologist, 12,* 363–367.

Larson, R. (1978). The well-being of older americans. *Journal of Gerontology, 33,* 109–125.

McAvoy, L. H. (1976). *Recreation preferences of the elderly persons in Minnesota.* Doctoral dissertation, University of Minnesota.

McGuire, F. A. (1979). *An exploratory study of leisure constraints in advanced adulthood.* Doctoral dissertation, University of Illinois.

Miller, S. S. (1965). The social dilemma of the aging leisure participant. In A. M. Rose, & W. A. Peterson (Eds.), *Older people and their social world.* Philadelphia: F. A. Davis.

Neugarten, B. L. (1975). The future and the young old. *Journal of Gerontology, 15,* 4–9.

Oliver, D. B. (1971). Career and leisure patterns of middle aged metropolitan out-migrants. *The Gerontologist, 11,* 13–20.

Pennsylvania State Office of Planning and Development. (1975). *The Pennsylvania recreation survey, principle findings-recommendations.* Commonwealth of Pennsylvania.

Seleen, D. R. (1982). The congruence between actual and desired use of time by older adults: A predictor of life satisfaction. *The Gerontologist, 22,* 95–99.

Scott, E. O., & Zoernick, D. A. (1977). Exploring leisure needs of the aged. *Leisurability, 4,* 25–31.

Schwartz, A. N., & Proppe, H. G. (1970). Toward person/environment transactional research in aging. *The Gerontologist, 10,* 228–232.

Strain, L. A., & Chappell, N. L. (1982). Outdoor recreation and the rural elderly: Participation, problems and needs. *Therapeutic Recreation Journal, 16,* 42–48.

Trela, J. E., & Simmons, R. W. (1971). Health and other factors affecting membership and attrition in a senior citizen center. *Journal of Gerontology, 26,* 46–51.

EPILOGUE

In his Foreword to this volume, Mike Ellis raised the concept of degrees of freedom as it relates to leisureliness. Leisure itself is not an inert concept, and whether the activity involved is motor or purely social, the degrees of freedom analogy serves well as a descriptor for both. For man to move in and interact with his environment, irrespective of the nature of that movement, the question of regulating the available degrees of freedom in the muscle/joint system sits at the very heart of making movement purposeful and intentful. There is, in a real sense, a behavioral analogy to this regulation problem that relates to leisure in a social context. Both the social and the motor component focus on regulating the constraints that are inherent in the activity. The preceeding chapters in this volume attempted, each in their own way, to present something of the nature and scope of these constraints. This volume has been divided into three parts and provides only a superficial organization around three areas of leisure focus. Each has an established literature, and research is currently ongoing on the problems in those areas, yet as distinct foci there is considerable overlap. Leisure as an experience is both multicontextual and multidimensional, and any attempt to draw boundaries between such foci is artificial.

Leisure occurs in many places, and often under the strangest of conditions. What may well begin as labor often evolves into a leisure experience. Delineating the constraints of the leisure enterprise enables us to seek ways of removing the costs of such constraints and rehabilitating the activity into an optimal leisure experience. How often do we as individuals embark on an activity because of some outside demand for us to do it, and find that over a period of time the external demand for our participation quickly recedes into the background, and we express the activity because of its own intrinsic enjoyment? I recall a live performance by the comedian Steve Martin: He was entertaining a live audience by playing trivial tunes on his banjo and making innocuous remarks, which all assembled found very amusing. At the end of this particular skit, he ruefully noted that he "gets paid for doing this!" This, to me, illustrates the arbitrary boundary between activity which is demanded of us and activity which is intrinsically motivating and enjoyable. For some time, leisure scientists sought to make meaningful distinctions between work and leisure by defining one as being necessary and the other as unnecessary. This static perspective of work and leisure is unacceptable, for depending upon the conditions and the attitude of mind of the individual, work and leisure become interchangeable; at least the distinguishing features blur at the interface.

This volume acquaints the reader with the constraints placed on leisure behavior and recognizes that the study of leisure behavior will be better advanced by understanding the constraints involved. The notion of constraints has its roots in physics (Pattee, 1972); constraints can both enrich or deplete an interaction. A better understanding of the constraints on leisure will permit further enrichment of the leisure experience.

—Michael G. Wade

REFERENCE

Pattee, H. D. (1972). Laws and constraints, symbols and language. In C. H. Waddington (Ed.), *Towards a theoretical biology*. Chicago: Aldine.

INDEX